Communications in Computer and Information Science 2698

Rationale

The CCIS series is devoted to the publication of proceedings of computer science conferences. Its aim is to efficiently disseminate original research results in informatics in printed and electronic form. While the focus is on publication of peer-reviewed full papers presenting mature work, inclusion of reviewed short papers reporting on work in progress is welcome, too. Besides globally relevant meetings with internationally representative program committees guaranteeing a strict peer-reviewing and paper selection process, conferences run by societies or of high regional or national relevance are also considered for publication.

Topics

The topical scope of CCIS spans the entire spectrum of informatics ranging from foundational topics in the theory of computing to information and communications science and technology and a broad variety of interdisciplinary application fields.

Information for Volume Editors and Authors

Publication in CCIS is free of charge. No royalties are paid, however, we offer registered conference participants temporary free access to the online version of the conference proceedings on SpringerLink (http://link.springer.com) by means of an http referrer from the conference website and/or a number of complimentary printed copies, as specified in the official acceptance email of the event.

CCIS proceedings can be published in time for distribution at conferences or as post-proceedings, and delivered in the form of printed books and/or electronically as USBs and/or e-content licenses for accessing proceedings at SpringerLink. Furthermore, CCIS proceedings are included in the CCIS electronic book series hosted in the SpringerLink digital library at http://link.springer.com/bookseries/7899. Conferences publishing in CCIS are allowed to use our online conference service (Meteor) for managing the whole proceedings lifecycle (from submission and reviewing to preparing for publication) free of charge.

Publication process

The language of publication is exclusively English. Authors publishing in CCIS have to sign the Springer CCIS copyright transfer form, however, they are free to use their material published in CCIS for substantially changed, more elaborate subsequent publications elsewhere. For the preparation of the camera-ready papers/files, authors have to strictly adhere to the Springer CCIS Authors' Instructions and are strongly encouraged to use the CCIS LaTeX style files or templates.

Abstracting/Indexing

CCIS is abstracted/indexed in DBLP, Google Scholar, EI-Compendex, Mathematical Reviews, SCImago, Scopus. CCIS volumes are also submitted for the inclusion in ISI Proceedings.

How to start

To start the evaluation of your proposal for inclusion in the CCIS series, please send an e-mail to ccis@springer.com

Jiye Liang · Guolong Chen · Kang Liu ·
Jing Zhang · Zhichun Wang · Hongyu Lin ·
Yongbin Liu
Editors

Knowledge Graphs and Semantic Computing

10th China Conference, CCKS 2025
Fuzhou, China, September 19–21, 2025
Proceedings

Springer

Editors
Jiye Liang
Shanxi University
Taiyuan, China

Kang Liu
Chinese Academy of Sciences
Institute of Automation
Beijing, China

Zhichun Wang
Beijing Normal University
Beijing, China

Yongbin Liu
University of South China
Hengyang, China

Guolong Chen
Fuzhou University
Fuzhou, China

Jing Zhang
Renmin University of China
Beijing, China

Hongyu Lin
Institute of Software, Chinese Academy of Sciences
Beijing, China

ISSN 1865-0929 ISSN 1865-0937 (electronic)
Communications in Computer and Information Science
ISBN 978-981-95-8524-3 ISBN 978-981-95-8525-0 (eBook)
https://doi.org/10.1007/978-981-95-8525-0

This Springer imprint is published by the registered company Springer Nature Singapore Pte Ltd.
The registered company address is: 152 Beach Road, #21-01/04 Gateway East, Singapore 189721, Singapore

Preface

This volume contains the papers presented at CCKS 2025: the China Conference on Knowledge Graph and Semantic Computing, held during September 19–21, 2025, in Fuzhou.

CCKS is organized by the Technical Committee on Language and Knowledge Computing of the Chinese Information Processing Society, and has previously been held in Beijing (2016), Chengdu (2017), Tianjin (2018), Hangzhou (2019), Nanchang (2020), Guangzhou (2021), Qinhuangdao (2022), Shenyang (2023), and Chongqing (2024). CCKS has become a core national academic conference in the fields of knowledge graph and semantic technology, bringing together researchers and developers in the fields of knowledge representation and reasoning, natural language understanding and knowledge acquisition, graph data management and graph computing, question answering, etc. It aims to become the top forum on knowledge graph and semantic technologies for Chinese researchers and practitioners from academia, industry, and government.

The 19th China Conference on Knowledge Graph (CCKS 2025) was organized by Fuzhou University and held in Fuzhou from September 19th to 21st, 2025.

The theme of this year's conference was "Large Model Agents and Knowledge Computing". It aimed to explore how large model agents can improve their accuracy and reliability in knowledge computing with the support of knowledge graphs. The conference focused on key technologies such as knowledge representation, storage, mining, fusion, reasoning, explainability, ethics, knowledge graph-enhanced large models, and agent architectures. The goal was to guide paradigm shifts in knowledge computing and promote the development of knowledge-enhanced large model agents. The program featured tutorials, keynote talks, frontier forums, industry forums, young scholar forums, evaluations and competitions, paper presentations, posters, and system demonstrations. Distinguished scholars and industry leaders were invited to share the latest developments and foster academic-industry collaboration.

As for peer-reviewed papers, 112 submissions were received in the following six areas,

- Knowledge Representation and Reasoning over Knowledge Graphs
- Knowledge Graph Construction and Integration
- Graph Database and Knowledge Management
- Large Models Enhanced by Knowledge Graphs
- Applications of Knowledge Graphs and Large Models/Agents
- Open Resources for Knowledge Graphs and Large Models

During the double-blind reviewing process, each submission was assigned to at least three Program Committee members. The committee decided to accept 14 full papers.

Additionally, the evaluation track of this year set up 8 tasks, which attracted more than 2946 teams to participate, forming a highly influential event. Besides the bonuses and issued certificates for the top three teams in each task, the committee also encouraged them to submit evaluation papers. After peer review by experienced researchers and task organizers, 8 papers were accepted (after revision) for inclusion in this volume of proceedings.

The hard work and close collaboration of a number of people have contributed to the success of this conference. We would like to thank the Organizing Committee and Program Committee members for their support, and the authors and participants who were the primary reason for the success of this conference. We also thank Springer for their trust and for publishing the proceedings of CCKS 2025.

Finally, we appreciate the sponsorships from Ant Group, Meituan, and Zhipu AI as platinum sponsors, Baidu, Global Tone Communication Technology, and Lanyun as gold sponsors and, U2Talent, and Hangzhou Bywin Technology, and BaYou as silver sponsors.

September 2025

Jiye Liang
Guolong Chen
Kang Liu
Jing Zhang
Zhichun Wang
Hongyu Lin
Yongbin Liu

Organization

General Chairs

Ji-ye Liang	Shanxi University, China
Guo-long Chen	Fuzhou University, China
Kang Liu	Institute of Automation, Chinese Academy of Sciences, China

Program Committee Chairs

Jing Zhang	Renmin University of China, China
Zhichun Wang	Beijing Normal University, China

Local Chair

Xiangwen Liao	Fuzhou University, China

Registration Chair

Xiaoyan Yu	Fuzhou University, China

Publicity Chairs

Yi Cai	South China University of Technology, China
Lei Hou	Tsinghua University, China

Publication Chairs

Hongyu Lin	Institute of Software, Chinese Academy of Sciences, China
Yongbin Liu	University of South China, China

Tutorial Chairs

Tieyun Qian	Wuhan University, China
Yang Yang	Zhejiang University, China

Evaluation Chairs

Feiliang Ren	Northeastern University, China
Sheng Bi	Southeast University, China

Frontiers and Trends Forum Chairs

Xiaoling Wang	East China Normal University, China
Hu Zhang	Shanxi University, China

Young Scholar Forum Chairs

Xiang Zhao	National University of Defense Technology, China
Yixin Cao	Fudan University, China

Poster / Demo Chairs

Tingwen Liu	Institute of Information Engineering, CAS, China
Wen Zhang	Zhejiang University, China

Sponsorship Chairs

Zhixu Li	Renmin University of China, China
Changliang Xu	UCAS Institute for Advanced Study, Hangzhou, China

Industry Chairs

Lei Liang	Ant Group, China
Quan Wang	Beijing University of Posts and Telecommunications, China

Website Chairs

Chao Chen	Harbin Institute of Technology, Shenzhen, China
Pengfei Cao	Institute of Automation, CAS, China

Area Chairs

Knowledge Representation and Reasoning over Knowledge Graphs

Yifan Zhu	Beijing University of Posts and Telecommunications, China
Qiannan Zhu	Beijing Normal University, China

Knowledge Graph Construction and Integration

Ge Shi	Beijing University of Technology, China
Yuting Wu	Beijing Jiaotong University, China

Graph Database and Knowledge Management

Jie Ma	Xi'an Jiaotong University, China
Yakun Li	Beijing Forestry University, China

Large Models Enhanced by Knowledge Graphs

Liner Yang	Beijing Language and Culture University, China
Lingyun Song	Northwestern Polytechnical University, China

Applications of Knowledge Graphs and Large Models/Agents

Shumin Deng	National University of Singapore, Singapore
Daifeng Li	Sun Yat-sen University, China

Open Resources for Knowledge Graphs and Large Models

Xin Xin	Beijing Institute of Technology, China
Kaiyu Huang	Beijing Jiaotong University, China

Program Committee

Bing Wei	Hainan University, China
Bo Wang	Beijing Institute of Technology, China
Chengzhi Zhang	Nanjing University of Science and Technology, China
Chunxia Zhang	Beijing Institute of Technology, China
Cuiyun Gao	Harbin Institute of Technology, China
Daifeng Li	Sun Yat-sen University, China
Di Huang	Communication University of China, China
Gang Wu	Northeastern University, China
Gen Shi	Beijing University of Aeronautics and Astronautics, China
Gong Cheng	Nanjing University, China
Guoqiang Li	Shanghai Jiao Tong University, China
Guoxin Zhang	Beijing University of Posts and Telecommunications, China
Han Liu	Dalian University of Technology, China
Hanyang Chen	Beijing Jiaotong University, China
Hao Yu	Dalian University of Technology, China
Haoran Luo	Nanyang Technological University, Singapore
Heng-Da Xu	Beijing Institute of Technology, China
Huaiyu Wan	Beijing Jiaotong University, China
Huiying Li	Southeast University, China
Jia Li	Peking University, China
Jiahao Teng	Beijing University of Technology, China
Jiali Shi	Beijing Language and Culture University, China
Jiaxin Yuan	Beijing Language and Culture University, China
Jinyu Guo	University of Electronic Science and Technology of China, China
Jiyuan An	Beijing Language and Culture University, China

Juan Li	Zhejiang University, China
Jun Hu	National University of Singapore, Singapore
Jun Pang	Wuhan University of Science and Technology, China
Junpeng Liu	Hong Kong University of Science and Technology (Guangzhou), China
Kang Xu	Nanjing University of Posts and Telecommunications, China
Kunli Zhang	Zhengzhou University, China
Lei Xu	Wuhan University, China
Long Bai	Chinese Academy of Sciences, China
Luming Lu	Beijing Language and Culture University, China
Mengyang Sun	Tsinghua University, China
Ning Qu	Xi'an Jiaotong University, China
Ningyu Zhang	Zhejiang University, China
Qi Huang	Jiangxi Normal University, China
Ruihan Hu	Beijing University of Posts and Telecommunications, China
Shaoru Guo	Shanxi University, China
Shichang Sun	Dalian Minzu University, China
Shuai Lyu	Beijing University of Posts and Telecommunications, China
Shuang Zeng	ByteDance Inc., China
Shufeng Hao	Taiyuan University of Technology, China
Shuo Li	Xidian University, China
Sihao He	Beijing University of Posts and Telecommunications, China
Tianxing Wu	Southeast University, China
Wangchun Sun	Xi'an Jiaotong University, China
Wei Hu	Nanjing University, China
Wei Huang	Beijing University of Posts and Telecommunications, Chinad
Wei Shen	Nankai University, China
Weibin Liao	Peking University, China
Weixin Zeng	National University of Defense Technology, China
Wen Zhang	Zhejiang University, China
Wenbin Jiang	Beijing Normal University, China
Wenliang Chen	Soochow University, China
Wenpeng Lu	Qilu University of Technology, China
Wenqiang Liu	Tencent America, USA
Wenqing Du	Northwest Polytechnical University Xi'an
Xiaodong Feng	Sun Yat-sen University, China

Xiaolin Han	Northwestern Polytechnical University, China
Xiaowang Zhang	Tianjin University, China
Xu Wang	Suzhou University of Science and Technology, China
Xuefeng Xi	suzhou universtiy of science and technology, China
Yaojie Lu	Chinese Academy of Sciences, China
Yinglong Ma	North China Electric Power University, China
Yizheng Zhao	Nanjing University, China
Yongbin Liu	University of South China, China
Yongpan Sheng	Southwest University, China
Yu Feng	China Mobile Research Institute, China
Yu Mao	Minnan Normal University, China
Yudai Pan	Northwestern Polytechnical University, China
Yuhang Tian	Beijing Institute of Technology, China
Yuntao Hua	Northwestern Polytechnical University, China
Yurong Cheng	Beijing Institute of Technology, China
Yuxiang Wang	Hangzhou Dianzi University, China
Yuxuan Lai	Open University of China, China
Zechang Xiong	Beijing Jiaotong University, China
Zequn Sun	Nanjing University, China
Zhichun Wang	Beijing Normal University, China
Zhipeng Luo	Southwest Jiaotong University, China
Zhitao Gao	Xi'an Jiaotong University, China
Zhixu Li	Renmin University of China, China
Ziyang Chen	National University of Defense Technology, China

Sponsors

Platinum Sponsors

Gold Sponsors

Silver Sponsors

Contents

Applications of Knowledge Graphs and Large Models/Agents

Open Resources for Knowledge Graphs and Large Models

Evaluations

Knowledge Graph Construction and Integration

A Cross-Subgraph Attention Fusion and Comparison Method for Contrastive Learning Based Knowledge Graph Completion

Yashen Wang[1], Xiaoling Zhu[2], Yanhui Li[3], Huan Chang[1], Xiaoye Ouyang[2(✉)], Tianzhu Chen[1], and Xiaowan Li[1]

[1] Artificial Intelligence Institute of CETC, Beijing 100049, China
[2] China Academy of Electronics and Information Technology, Beijing 100041, China
wysys@126.com
[3] National University of Defense Technology, Nanjing 210039, China

Abstract. Knowledge Graphs (KGs) furnish reliable and structured information that is vital for several downstream applications, including information retrieval and recommendation system. However, the pervasive incompleteness inherent in KGs frequently constrains the efficacy of these applications. To mitigate this limitation, researchers have introduced the Knowledge Graph Completion (KGC) task, which aims to supplement missing facts within incomplete triples. In recent times, contrastive learning has been incorporated into the domain of KGC, yielding substantial enhancements to the discriminative power of KGC models and establishing new performance benchmarks. Nevertheless, current contrastive methodologies usually face the problems of insufficient generalization ability of sparse relations, poor understanding of importance differences towards heterogeneous relations, as well as information redundancy in single-view comparison. To overcome these challenges, this work proposes a novel cross-subgraph attention fusion and comparison method, consisting of oriented noise injection, cross-subgraph attention fusion and cross-subgraph contrastive loss. Especially, it helps to enhance the neighboring aggregation procedure as well as the comparative loss function in existing models, by fully utilizing beneficial and complementary semantic signals from different views in the given KG. Furthermore, this contribution can be regarded as a flexible and easily adaptable plug-in component, engineered for seamless compatibility with extant contrastive learning based KGC architectures.

Keywords: Knowledge Graph · Knowledge Graph Completion · Contrastive Learning · Cross Subgraph · Graph Convolutional Networks

1 Introduction

Knowledge Graphs (KGs), exemplified by Freebase and Wikidata, serve as repositories of relational facts that have emerged as indispensable knowledge sources in knowledge-intensive applications. A typical KG consists of a set of triples, with each triple (e_i, r, e_j) representing the association between a head entity e_i, a tail entity e_j, and the pertinent relation r. Given the virtually boundless and dynamically changing

J. Liang et al. (Eds.): CCKS 2025, CCIS 2698, pp. 3–14, 2026.
https://doi.org/10.1007/978-981-95-8525-0_1

nature of factual knowledge, concerns arise regarding the *incompleteness* of KGs [3,19]. To address this challenge, researchers have concentrated on Knowledge Graph Completion (KGC) models designed to automatically infer *missing* triples. These models are broadly classified into two primary categories: embedding-based approaches and text-based approaches (or so called large language model (LLM) based approaches). Wherein, embedding-based methods involve learning low-dimensional vector representations for entities and relations through the minimization of a loss function [2,3,18]. Conversely, LLM-based methods [17,19,22] exploit accessible textual data to amass textual information pertaining to entities and relations.

Recently, Contrastive Learning (CL) [14] has been introduced to the domain of KGC, markedly enhancing the discriminative capabilities of KGC models and establishing new performance benchmarks [8,9,12]. The core workflow of this methodological paradigm proceeds as follows: To start, a mechanism for generating positive and negative sample pairs is devised, with these pairs subsequently fed into the encoder. Following this, a loss function, rooted in a predefined distance metric, is constructed to direct the learning trajectory. Among the commonly adopted loss functions are contrastive loss and InfoNCE loss, whose purpose is to *strengthen* the similarity between positive sample pairs while *weakening* that among negative ones. The gradients of the loss with respect to the encoder's parameters are derived via the back-propagation algorithm, and the encoder's weights are modified using an optimization technique such as stochastic gradient descent (SGD). By means of this sequence of operations, contrastive learning frameworks capture the intrinsic structure of data without reliance on explicit labels, thereby delivering robust feature representations suitable for a range of tasks [7,11,15].

Unfortunately, the existing KGC models based on contrastive learning framework, have the following shortcomings: (i) `Problem #1`. Insufficient generalization ability of sparse relationships: The embedding of *low*-frequency relationships (e.g., "number_of_awards") is susceptible to *noise* interference, leading to a decrease in predictive performance [9,12]. (ii) `Problem #2`. Poor understanding of importance differences with respect to heterogeneous relationships: Different relationships contribute *differently* to entity semantics (e.g., "nationality" being more discriminative than "place_of_birth"), however traditional contrastive learning based methods generally treat all relationships *equally* [11,20]. (iii) `Problem #3`. Information redundancy in single-view comparison: Current work *only* relies on a *single* global embedding for comparison, ignoring the *complementary* and verifiable information from different relationship subgraphs (e.g., the semantic differences between "profession" and "research_field" subgraphs) [7,17].

To address the aforementioned issues, we have intuitively observed the following phenomenon, which reveals corresponding motivations of this work: (i) `Motivation #1`. Noise robustness theory: In information theory, robust representations are *insensitive* to small perturbations [13]. Since the embedding variance of the *low*-frequency relationship subgraph is relatively *large*, and hence it is necessary to enhance *stability* through noise injection. (ii) `Motivation #2`. Cognitive Theory of attention allocation: There exist significant *differences* in the importance of different relationships in human cognition [6]. Hence, the neighborhood information of *high*-frequency relationships (e.g., "occupation") is *denser* and requires *dynamic* allocation of attention weights. (iii) `Motivation #3`. Multi-view semantic complementarity: Inspired by multimodal learning mechanism etc., different views provide *complementary* information [10,19]. Hence, embedding the same entity in different relationship views (respect to different *subgraphs*), is expected to eliminate semantic ambiguity (e.g., "apple" in the "fruit" and "company" subgraphs).

Hence, inspired by the motivations mentioned above, this work proposes a novel cross-subgraph attention fusion and comparison method for KGC task, to fully utilize beneficial complementary signals from different views. Especially: (i) The insufficient generalization of sparse relation has been alleviated and hence the embedding stability of sparse relationships has been improved, through oriented noise injection in this work (respect to `Problem #1`); (ii) This work proposes a cross-view (i.e., cross-subgraph) dynamic attention fusion mechanism, hence the difference of relationship importance is captured and the weight proportion of key relations has been increased (respect to `Problem #2`); and (iii) Information redundancy is eliminated here, with help of incorporating cross-subgraph comparison loss into the loss function, as well as forcing the embeddings to capture commonalities across multiple views (respect to `Problem #3`). Furthermore, the proposed work here could be utilized as a readily implementable plug-in module, that can be seamlessly integrated into any existing contrastive learning based KGC architectures [8,9,11,19]. To validate the rationale and effectiveness of the proposed methodology, we perform comparative experiments on real-world datasets. The experimental outcomes substantiate the performance enhancement *imparted* by the innovations of this study to existing contrastive learning based KGC models.

2 Methodology

The current comparative learning based KGC models, aim at enhancing the discriminability of entity and relationship embeddings, by comparing positive samples (real triples) with negative samples (constructed fake triples), which could reduce the dependence on annotated data through self-supervised signals [8,9] (Sect. 2.2). However, this line of methodology usually faces with the problems of insufficient generalization ability of sparse relations, insufficient understanding of importance differences with respect to heterogeneous relations, as well as information redundancy in single-view comparison [7,19], which hinder performance improvement. To overcome these challenges, this work proposes a novel cross-subgraph attention fusion and comparison method, which could be utilized as a flexible plug-in for current models, for enhancing the neighboring aggregation procedure (Sect. 2.4) as well as the comparative loss function (Sect. 2.5) from multi-view perspectives (Sect. 2.3). The schematic diagram of the proposed work, is sketched in Fig. 1, wherein symbols ①, ②, ③ in this figure respectively solve the above problems faced with existing methods.

2.1 Initialization

Given KG G, each entity $e_i \in E$ is initialized with a trainable representation $\mathbf{h}_{e_i}^{(0)} \in \mathbb{R}^d$, pre-trained through conventional KGE frameworks including TransE [3] and DistMult

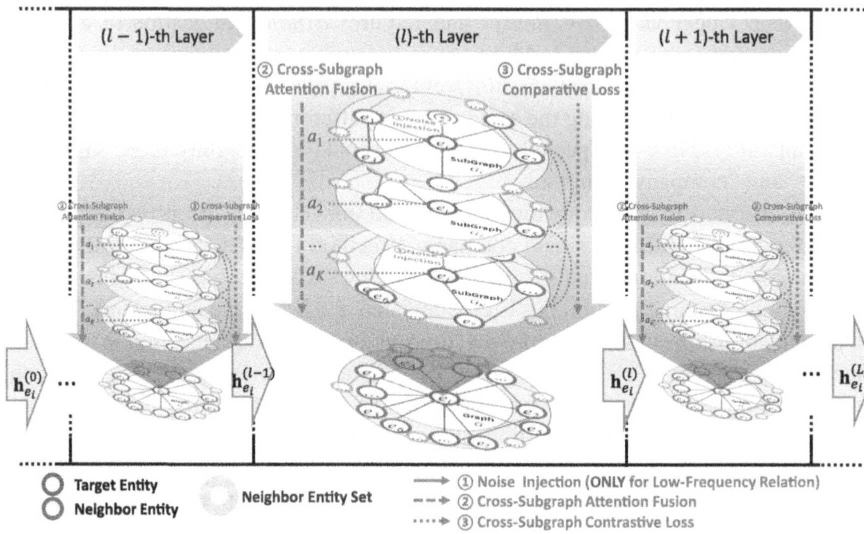

Fig. 1. The architecture of the proposed model.

[21]. Notably, this initial representation propagates directly to the Graph Convolution Network (GCN)'s initial convolutional layer without feature transformation, as GCN architecture is usually used for iterative optimization of entity's representation in existing comparative learning based KGC models. The relation embedding initialization process ($\mathbf{r}$ for relation $r \in R$) maintains structural symmetry through parameter sharing mechanisms, ensuring parametric equivalence across heterogeneous graph elements. E and R indicate the entity set and relation set in current KG, respectively.

2.2 General Comparative Learning Framework for KGC Task

Generally, comparative learning based KGC model, aggregates neighborhood information through graph convolution operations in l-th layer (total L layers), as follows:

$$\mathbf{h}_{e_i}^{(l+1)} = \sum_{e' \in \mathcal{N}(e_i)} \frac{1}{\sqrt{|\mathcal{N}(e_i)|}} \mathbf{h}_{e'}^{(l)} \tag{1}$$

Note that, the attention factor in the above equation, has been simplified and could actually be replaced with other forms of attention definition. Then, in the process of contrastive loss optimization, we aim at maximizing the similarity between *positive* sample pairs and minimizing the similarity between *negative* sample pairs, as follows (taking InfoNCE loss as example):

$$\mathcal{L}_{\mathrm{CL}}(e_i, r, e_j) = -\log \frac{\exp(\mathbf{h}_{e_i}^{(L)\top} \cdot \mathbf{h}_{e_j}^{(L)}/\tau)}{\sum_{(e_i', r, e_j') \in \Delta^-} \exp(\mathbf{h}_{e_i'}^{(L)\top} \cdot \mathbf{h}_{e_j'}^{(L)}/\tau)} \tag{2}$$

Wherein, parameter τ indicates temperature coefficient, and Δ^- represents the negative triple set. In the above formula, $\mathbf{h}_{e_i}^{(L)^\top} \cdot \mathbf{h}_{e_j}^{(L)}$ could be replaced by cosine similarity (or other similarity measurement forms), formed as function $\mathrm{sim}(\mathbf{h}_{e_i}^{(L)}, \mathbf{h}_{e_j}^{(L)})$.

Based on the above efforts, the existing comparative learning based KGC model usually performs the following task-loss synergistic optimization, which is combined with link prediction loss:

$$
\begin{aligned}
\mathcal{L} &= \mathcal{L}_{\mathrm{LP}} + \lambda_1 \cdot \mathcal{L}_{\mathrm{CL.}} \\
&= \sum_{(e_i,r,e_j)\in\Delta^+,(e_i^{'},r,e_j^{'})\in\Delta^-} -\log \phi(f(e_i,r,e_j) - f(e_i^{'},r,e_j^{'})) \\
&+ \lambda_1 \cdot \sum_{(e_i,r,e_j)\in\Delta^+} -\log \frac{\exp(\mathbf{h}_{e_i}^{(L)^\top} \cdot \mathbf{h}_{e_j}^{(L)}/\tau)}{\sum_{(e_i^{'},r,e_j^{'})\in\Delta^-} \exp(\mathbf{h}_{e_i^{'}}^{(L)^\top} \cdot \mathbf{h}_{e_j^{'}}^{(L)}/\tau)}
\end{aligned}
\tag{3}
$$

Wherein, Δ^+ and Δ^- indicate the positive triple set and negative triple set, respectively. $e_i^{'}$ or $e_j^{'}$ represents negative sampling entity, which is obtained by replaced native entity (e_i or e_j) in given triple. Function $\phi(\cdot)$ denotes the activation function. It should be noted that, the link prediction loss formula $\mathcal{L}_{\mathrm{LP}}$ in the aforementioned equation, uses a simplified approach (taking the loss formula of the TransE model [3] as an example here, and hence the scoring function $f(\cdot)$ is defined as $f(e_i,r,e_j) = \| \mathbf{h}_{e_i}^{(L)} + \mathbf{h}_r - \mathbf{h}_{e_j}^{(L)} \|_2$), which could be conveniently replaced with *other* definitions.

2.3 Subgraphs Construction

In order to form a multi-view knowledge comparison and complementarity capability, this work first segments a given KG into several subgraphs. Given KG G, several methods could be adopted here to form subgraphs with controllable quantity and quality. Without loss of generality, this study adopts the classic subgraph construction method (as well as the corresponding constraints) of previous work [1,8], which is called Biased Random Walk with Restart (BRWR), and could balance efficiency as well as performance.

Especially, for each central (or target) triple (e_i, r, e_j), we select the starting entity e_s (choose from e_i or e_j) with a probability proportional to its inverse-degree, meaning that entities with *lower* degrees are more likely to be selected. Then, in the next random walk process, each step returns to the starting entity e_s with a probability p, or with a probability $1-p$ moves to the neighbor of the current node. Note that, The selection of neighbors is also based on the inverse-degree distribution, where neighbors with *lower* degrees have a higher probability of being selected. Repeat the above process and continue walking until the number of triples in the sampling reaches the preset upper limit (discussed in experimental section). It is easy to observe that, this process aims to enhance the coverage of *low*-degree entities and alleviate the *long*-tail distribution problem of entity frequency in the given KG G. In addition, we strongly suggest adding a subgraph dynamic adjustment strategy into the forthcoming training process: we could record the number of times each triple is accessed, prioritize selecting the subgraph central triple with the *least* number of visits, and ensure that marginalized and *low*-frequency triples are fully trained.

In this work, the number of subgraphs (denoted as K) is *not* explicitly fixed by hyperparameters, but is dynamically determined by the number of positive triples ($|\Delta^+|$) in the training set of the given KG G, as follows: $K = \max(10, \lceil \ln(|\Delta^+| + 1)/\ln(C) \cdot 10 \rceil)$. Wherein, C is an adjustment constant, used to control the sensitivity of the number of subgraphs to data size (details in experimental section). Function $\lceil \cdot \rceil$ indicates an upward rounding function. Note that, the subgraph construction procedure could be truly completed *offline*, so this process has a relatively small impact on computational overhead. In addition to the above strategy, the method of combining unsupervised clustering (e.g., spectral clustering [5]) to automatically partition semantic subgraphs, is also highly recommended, as it can avoid subgraph partitioning relying too much on predefined rules. Similarly, if the scale of KG being processed is too *huge*, subgraph merging strategy could be leveraged here for reducing the number of subgraphs K. Specifically, merging semantically similar relationships (e.g., "father" and "mother" refer to "relative"), can drive subgraph merging and hence reduce the number of subgraphs.

2.4 Propagation Enhancement Based on Cross-Subgraph Attention

In order to effectively utilize the complementary information provided by different views (i.e., different subgraph derived from Sect. 2.3), this work performs neighborhood aggregation on each subgraph G_k:

$$\mathbf{h}_{e_i}^{(l+1)(k)} = \sum_{e' \in \mathcal{N}^{(k)}(e_i)} \frac{1}{\sqrt{|\mathcal{N}^{(k)}(e_i)|}} \mathbf{h}_{e'}^{(l)(k)} \tag{4}$$

Wherein, $\mathcal{N}^{(k)}(e_i)$ represents the neighboring entity set with respect to entity e_i in k-th subgraph. As discussed earlier in Sect. 2.2, the above equation about inner-subgraph attention could be replaced with other forms.

Besides, in order to solve the problem of unstable embedding of low-frequency relationship subgraphs and improve the model's generalization ability, we achieve data augmentation through oriented noise injection operations. Specifically, this work adds noise to *low*-frequency subgraphs (e.g., subgraphs respect to low-frequency relations with constraint of $\text{count}(r) < (\log(|\Delta^+|+1)/\log(|R|+1)))$, to enhance the robustness of embedding to data sparsity and noise, as follows. This is because we has observed that, the embedding variance of the low-frequency relationship is *large*, and noise injection could improve its *stability* (in line with the principle of robust representation in information theory).

$$\tilde{\mathbf{h}}_{e_i}^{(l+1)(k)} \leftarrow \mathbf{h}_{e_i}^{(l+1)(k)} + \overline{N}, \quad \| \overline{N} \|_2 = \gamma \tag{5}$$

Wherein, notation $\overline{N}$ represents random noise vector, which usually obeys the zero-mean Gaussian distribution (i.e., $\overline{N} \sim \mathcal{N}(0, \sigma^2 I)$) and its L_2 norm is normalized to γ. Herein, aforementioned $\gamma \propto 1/\sqrt{\text{count}(r)}$ indicates noise intensity hyper-parameter, which controls the amplitude of noise vector $\overline{N}$ (i.e., the intensity of noise), and is usually *adaptive* and determined through experimental optimization (within the range of [0.01,0.1]). Hence, $\overline{N}$ in Eq. (5) can simulate the noise disturbance in real data and prevent the model from over fitting the low-frequency relationship.

With efforts above, we ultimately achieve cross-subgraph attention fusion, by dynamically fusing multiple subgraph embeddings into a unified embedding, as follows:

$$\tilde{\mathbf{h}}_{e_i}^{(l+1)} = \sum_{k=1}^{K} \alpha_k \cdot \tilde{\mathbf{h}}_{e_i}^{(l+1)(k)} \tag{6}$$

Among them, notation α_k is the attention weight of subgraph G_k, dynamically calculated through learnable parameters:

$$\alpha_k = \frac{\exp(\mathbf{W}_1^\top \cdot \phi(\mathbf{W}_2[\mathbf{h}_{e_i}^{(0)} \parallel \tilde{\mathbf{h}}_{e_i}^{(l+1)(k)}]))}{\sum_{j=1}^{K} \exp(\mathbf{W}_1^\top \cdot \phi(\mathbf{W}_2[\mathbf{h}_{e_i}^{(0)} \parallel \tilde{\mathbf{h}}_{e_i}^{(l+1)(j)}]))} \tag{7}$$

Wherein, $\{\mathbf{W}_1 \in \mathbb{R}^{d\times 1}, \mathbf{W}_2 \in \mathbb{R}^{2d\times d}\}$ are learnable parameters. Finally through the above efforts, this work has updated the neighbor semantic aggregation procedure in the existing native comparative learning based KGC architecture, by replacing the original formula Eq. (1) in Sect. 2.2 with its cross-subgraph variant formula Eq. (6).

2.5 Loss Optimization Based on Crossing Subgraphs

Similarly, we also incorporate the strategy of crossing subgraphs into the loss function of contrastive learning mechanism (originally defined as Eq. (2) in Sect. 2.2). Specifically, this paper redefines the cross-subgraph comparative learning loss function, by enforcing the embedding consistency of the same entity in different subgraphs (taking k-th subgraph and m-th subgraph as example), as follows:

$$\begin{aligned}\mathcal{L}_{\mathrm{CL}}(e_i, r, e_j; k, m) = \frac{1}{2}[&- \log \frac{\exp({\mathbf{h}_{e_i}^{(L)(k)}}^\top \cdot \mathbf{h}_{e_i}^{(L)(m)}/\tau)}{\sum_{(e_i^{\prime}, r, e_j)\in\Delta^-} \exp({\mathbf{h}_{e_i^{\prime}}^{(L)(k)}}^\top \cdot \mathbf{h}_{e_i^{\prime}}^{(L)(m)}/\tau)} \\ &- \log \frac{\exp({\mathbf{h}_{e_j}^{(L)(k)}}^\top \cdot \mathbf{h}_{e_j}^{(L)(m)}/\tau)}{\sum_{(e_i, r, e_j^{\prime})\in\Delta^-} \exp({\mathbf{h}_{e_j^{\prime}}^{(L)(k)}}^\top \cdot \mathbf{h}_{e_j^{\prime}}^{(L)(m)}/\tau)}]\end{aligned} \tag{8}$$

Where k and m are different subgraph indexes, and $k \neq m$. Therefore, we could update the native overall contrastive learning loss function (shown in Eq. (2)) for KGC task:

$$\tilde{\mathcal{L}}_{\mathrm{CL}}(e_i, r, e_j) \leftarrow \mathcal{L}_{\mathrm{CL}}(e_i, r, e_j) + \lambda_2 \cdot \frac{1}{K\cdot(K-1)/2} \sum_{k\neq m} \mathcal{L}_{\mathrm{CL}}(e_i, r, e_j; k, m) \tag{9}$$

Similarly, by incorporating the cross-subgraph contrastive loss into the total loss function, the total loss (initially defined as Eq. (3)) is visually updated to the weighted sum of the link prediction loss $\mathcal{L}_{\mathrm{LP}}$ (such as cross entropy) and the contrastive loss $\tilde{\mathcal{L}}_{\mathrm{CL}}$ discussed above, as follows:

$$\mathcal{L} = \mathcal{L}_{\mathrm{LP}} + \lambda_1 \cdot \tilde{\mathcal{L}}_{\mathrm{CL}} \tag{10}$$

Finally through the above efforts, this work has updated the loss function in the existing native comparative learning based KGC architecture, by replacing the original formula Eq. (3) in Sect. 2.2 with its cross-subgraph variant as formulated in Eq. (10).

3 Experiments

3.1 Datasets and Baselines

For empirical validation, we employ two benchmark datasets widely recognized in the KGC domain: WN18RR [4] (derived from its parent corpus WN18) and FB15k-237 [16] (a refined version of FB15k), establishing a comprehensive experimental evaluation. To systematically assess the efficacy of our enhanced approach within the paradigm of comparative learning based KGC models, we conduct comparative analyses across a spectrum of state-of-the-art baseline architectures: (i) CLGAT [9]; (ii) ComplEx-CL [12]; (iii) SimKGC [17]; (iv) KRACL [15]; (v) InCL [7]; (vi) MEGA [19]; (vii) StructKGC [11]; and (viii) SATKGC [8]. With respect to each of these benchmark models, comparisons are drawn between the original contrastive learning-based KGC model and its modified variant. In this modified version, our proposed work is integrated as an auxiliary plug-in component, denoted by the suffix "+(Ours)". For evaluation, we predominantly employ a suite of widely-utilized automatic metrics: (i) Mean Reciprocal Rank (MRR), a metric that captures the average reciprocal rank across all test triples; (ii) HITS@N (where $N \in \{1, 3\}$), a measure that computes the proportion of correct entities ranked among the top N positions (Table 1).

Table 1. The statistical profiles of WN18RR and FB15k-237 employed in experiments.

Dataset	$\|E\|$	$\|R\|$	#Train	#Valid	#Test
WN18RR	40,943	11	86,835	3,034	3,134
FB15k-237	14,541	237	272,115	17,535	20,466

3.2 Experimental Settings

Barring the learning rate and training epochs, the bulk of hyperparameters are applied consistently across all datasets to preclude adjustments that are specific to individual datasets. As discussed in Sect. 2.3, the number of subgraphs (K) is dynamically determined by the number of positive triples in the training set of the given KG G, with a adjustment constant C as constraint. Based on the experimental results, we chose $C \sim 10^4$ because it provides the optimal *balance* between performance and computational cost among numerous experimental configurations like $\{\sim 10^2, \sim 10^3, \sim 10^4, \sim 10^5, \sim 10^6\}$. In fact, by adjusting constant C, it can adapt to different scene requirements: if K needs to be more strictly restricted, C can be increased; conversely, if slight fluctuations are allowed, C can be reduced. The definition of intensity hyper-parameter γ has been described in Sect. 2.4, which controls the amplitude of noise vector $\overline{N}$, and this work selects its optimal value on the validation set through grid search mechanism.

γ can balance the disturbance level of noise injection: (i) Small γ indicates insufficient noise disturbance, unable to effectively enhance robustness; (ii) Excessive γ leads that noise destroys the original semantic information, resulting in performance degradation. Regarding the selection of noise distribution, we have found through experiments that: (i) Gaussian distribution is suitable for *most* scenarios and conforms to the central limit theorem; (ii) Uniform distribution may be more stable when the embedding space is *limited*. λ_1 in Eq. (3) controls the weight between link prediction loss and comparative learning loss, and is set as 0.4 here, which is based on both previous work and our experimental conclusions. Besides, λ_2 in Eq. (9) is used to control the gain ratio caused by the proposed cross-subgraph contrastive loss (Eq. (8)), and in this experiment 0.6 is chosen because it has produced the optimal results among many experimental configurations $\{0.3, 0.4, 0.5, 0.6, 0.7, 0.8\}$.

Table 2. A comprehensive performance summary for the relation prediction task.

	WN18RR						FB15k-237					
Method	MRR↑	MRR%	H@1↑	H@1%	H@3↑	H@3%	MRR↑	MRR%	H@1↑	H@1%	H@3↑	H@3%
CLGAT [9]	0.484	100.00%	0.448	100.00%	0.550	100.00%	0.364	100.00%	0.274	100.00%	0.402	100.00%
CLGAT+(Ours)	0.509	105.17%	0.468	104.57%	0.571	103.74%	0.384	105.55%	0.294	107.35%	0.422	105.03%
ComplEx-CL [12]	0.505	100.00%	0.458	100.00%	0.601	100.00%	0.377	100.00%	0.285	100.00%	0.430	100.00%
ComplEx-CL+(Ours)	0.543	107.47%	0.495	107.99%	0.641	106.66%	0.412	109.19%	0.317	111.38%	0.466	108.35%
SimKGC [17]	0.666	100.00%	0.587	100.00%	0.717	100.00%	0.336	100.00%	0.249	100.00%	0.362	100.00%
SimKGC+(Ours)	0.693	104.03%	0.613	104.44%	0.744	103.82%	0.361	107.54%	0.273	109.65%	0.388	107.11%
KRACL [15]	0.527	100.00%	0.613	100.00%	0.547	100.00%	0.360	100.00%	0.548	100.00%	0.395	100.00%
KRACL+(Ours)	0.540	102.41%	0.626	102.14%	0.560	102.34%	0.372	103.29%	0.561	102.33%	0.407	103.04%
InCL [7]	0.678	100.00%	0.571	100.00%	0.749	100.00%	0.393	100.00%	0.287	100.00%	0.433	100.00%
InCL+(Ours)	0.714	105.32%	0.605	105.88%	0.787	105.03%	0.422	107.51%	0.313	109.11%	0.463	106.92%
MEGA [19]	0.700	100.00%	0.617	100.00%	0.735	100.00%	0.353	100.00%	0.267	100.00%	0.362	100.00%
MEGA+(Ours)	0.722	103.17%	0.639	103.55%	0.757	103.03%	0.374	105.98%	0.288	107.81%	0.383	105.84%
StructKGC [11]	0.696	100.00%	0.623	100.00%	0.741	100.00%	0.383	100.00%	0.289	100.00%	0.419	100.00%
StructKGC+(Ours)	0.730	104.83%	0.656	105.34%	0.775	104.57%	0.405	105.75%	0.311	107.46%	0.441	105.30%
SATKGC [8]	0.694	100.00%	0.626	100.00%	0.743	100.00%	0.370	100.00%	0.279	100.00%	0.403	100.00%
SATKGC+(Ours)	0.716	103.18%	0.647	103.42%	0.766	103.04%	0.389	105.09%	0.297	106.43%	0.422	104.76%

3.3 Performance Summary

Integrated findings regarding relation prediction in the KGC task, are consolidated in Table 2. Here, the symbols MRR%, H@1%, H@3% signify performance percentages relative to the original baseline, where values surpassing 100% indicate performance *enhancement*. These empirical results validate the effectiveness of the proposed modular component. On WN18RR and FB15K-237 datasets, *all* baseline models have achieved performance *improvement* after the proposed adding plug-in. E.g., with the help of this plug-in, the MRR index of the newly proposed contrastive learning based KGC model InCL [7], has been increased by 5.32% and 7.51%, respectively on WN18RR data set and FB15K-237 dataset.

It is amazing to find that, the performance gain brought by our plug-in is *greater* on the more *complex* FB15K-237 dataset. E.g., for MRR, the average improvement on FB15K-237 dataset is 6.31%, while the average improvement on WN18RR dataset is

4.39%. The different performance of other metrics in different datasets, is *consistent* with the above. Hence, we could draw the following conclusion: the plug-in improves *more* significantly (more than 5%) on the more *sparse* FB15k-237, which verifies its optimization motivation for data *sparsity*. This phenomenon is due to the more robust embedding of *low*-frequency relation subgraphs derived from our plug-in, which alleviates the data sparsity. Moreover, the experimental data also reflects another conclusion: our plug-in improves the challenging head prediction (e.g., H@1) *more* dramatically, indicating that it enhances the ability to capture key relationships. Taking the FB15k-237 dataset as an example, looking at the improvement of all models, the H@1 index brought by our plug-in is increased by 7.72%, and the H@3 index is increased by 5.86%, while the former metric is obviously a more challenging and *persuasive* indicator.

Besides, the experimental results show that, the effects of plug-ins on different kinds of models are *different*. In summary, this plug-in has *better* performance gain for the traditional and earlier models (e.g., ComplEx-CL [12] and CLGAT [9]), while that for the recently proposed models (especially LLM-based KGC models like KRACL [15] and StructKGC [11]) is relatively *limited*. E.g., the improvements of MRR for CLGAT [9] are 5.17% and 5.55% on aforementioned datasets, while the corresponding improvements are only 2.41% and 3.29% towards KRACL [15]. The reason for this phenomenon is quite intuitive, as follows: the introduction of LLM improves the ability of contrastive learning based KGC model to capture *long*-distance relationships, which to some extent coincides with the cross-view (i.e., cross-subgraph) semantic interaction component of our plug-in. However, from the other perspective, even under the above circumstances, our plug-in can still improve the current contrastive learning based KGC model driven by LLM, which shows that our cross-subgraph strategy and the existing LLM strategy have positive *complementary* prospects. In addition, we also observe that the performance gain of this plug-in for the recently proposed sub-graph -aware baselines (e.g., SATKGC [8]) or meta-path (as well as meta-graph) -aware baselines (e.g., MEGA [19]), is relatively *small*. E.g., the improvement of MRR are only 3.17% and 5.98% for MEGA [19] respectively, significantly *less* than the gains of other models.

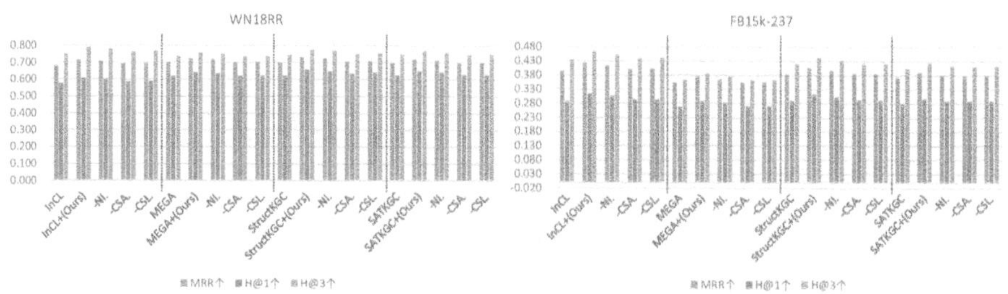

Fig. 2. Ablation study.

3.4 Fine-Grained Analysis

As discussed above, this work consists of Noise Injection module (Eq. (5) in Sect. 2.4, and abbreviated as "NI."), Cross-Subgraph Attention module (Eqs. (6) and (7) in

Sect. 2.4, and abbreviated as "CSA."), and Cross-Subgraph Loss module (Eqs. (8) and (9) in Sect. 2.5, and abbreviated as "CSL."). This section examines which module demonstrates the most substantial impact. Ablation study experimental outcomes are depicted in Fig. 2, corresponding to different datasets respectively. The findings from the ablation study exhibit consistency across both datasets: (i) The Noise Injection module is essential for enhancing the aggregation process, as it aids in strengthening the native KGC model's robustness to sparse data by introducing controlled random perturbations into the embeddings of low-frequency relationship subgraphs. However, compared to other modules (i.e., "CSA." and "CSL."), this module has a relatively smaller overall improvement in results (shown as "-NI."), but has a relatively *larger* gain for FB15k-237 dataset with uneven data distribution and frequent low-frequency relationships. (ii) Removing the Cross-Subgraph Attention module (shown as "-CSA."), results in the *greatest* performance loss, indicating that this module has the greatest impact in our work. (iii) The Cross-Subgraph Loss module functions as a valuable complement to the two aforementioned modules, considering that the original model's performance persists in improving upon the incorporation of this module (shown as "+(Ours)").

The computational complexity analysis of the proposed work is concluded as follows: (i) the increased computational costs for noise injection (Eq. (5)) is $O(K \cdot d)$ (linear with the number of subgraphs K and embedding dimension d); (ii) the computational costs of cross-subgraph attention fusion (Eqs. (6) and (7)) is $O(K \cdot d^2)$; and (iii) computational cost for cross-subgraph comparison loss (Eq. (8)) is $O(2 \cdot K^2 \cdot d)$. The above increase in computational overhead is acceptable, because K is usually *small* [8] (e.g., $K \sim 10$ in our experiment derived by the formula in Sect. 2.3). Overall, performance improvement boosted from our work, is significantly *higher* than the increase in complexity. Therefore, this work demonstrates a promising *balance* between performance improvement and computational overhead.

4 Conclusions

To enhance and optimize the information aggregation efficiency within the existing contrastive learning framework for KGC tasks, this research proposes a novel mechanism tailored to the aggregation procedure, which utilizes a cross-view (i.e., cross-subgraph) attention fusion and loss comparison mechanism.

Acknowledgements. We thank anonymous reviewers for valuable comments. This work is funded by: Technical Field Foundation (No. 2023-JCJQ-JJ-0747); National Natural Science Foundation of China (No. U22B2061).

References

1. Ahrabian, K., Feizi, A., Salehi, Y., Hamilton, W.L., Bose, A.J.: Structure aware negative sampling in knowledge graphs. arXiv preprint: arXiv:2009.11355 (2020)
2. Balazevic, I., Allen, C., Hospedales, T.M.: Tucker: tensor factorization for knowledge graph completion. ArXiv abs/1901.09590 (2019)

3. Bordes, A., Usunier, N., Garcia-Duran, A., Weston, J., Yakhnenko, O.: Translating embeddings for modeling multi-relational data. In: NIPS'13, pp. 2787–2795 (2013)
4. Dettmers, T., Minervini, P., Stenetorp, P., Riedel, S.: Convolutional 2D knowledge graph embeddings. In: AAAI (2018)
5. Ding, L., Li, C., Jin, D., Ding, S.: Survey of spectral clustering based on graph theory. Pattern Recogn., 110366 (2024)
6. Gabaix, X., Laibson, D.I., Moloche, G., Stephen, W.: The allocation of attention: theory and evidence (2003)
7. Hu, J., Yang, H., Teng, F., Du, S., Li, T.: A knowledge graph completion model based on triple level interaction and contrastive learning. Pattern Recogn. **156**, 110783 (2024)
8. Ko, Y., Yang, H., Kim, T., Kim, H.: Subgraph-aware training of language models for knowledge graph completion using structure-aware contrastive learning. In: Proceedings of the ACM on Web Conference 2025, pp. 72–85 (2025)
9. Li, L., et al.: A knowledge graph completion model based on contrastive learning and relation enhancement method. Knowl.-Based Syst. **256**, 109889 (2022)
10. Li, X., Wang, B., Shi, G., Feng, C., Teng, J.: Mitigating the discrepancy between video and text temporal sequences: a time-perception enhanced video grounding method for LLM. In: Proceedings of the 31st International Conference on Computational Linguistics, pp. 9804–9813 (2025)
11. Lin, J., Wang, L., Lu, X., Hu, Z., Zhang, W., Lu, W.: Improving knowledge graph completion with structure-aware supervised contrastive learning. In: Proceedings of the 2024 Conference on Empirical Methods in Natural Language Processing, pp. 13948–13959 (2024)
12. Luo, Z., Xu, W., Liu, W., Bian, J., Yin, J., Liu, T.Y.: KGE-CL: contrastive learning of tensor decomposition based knowledge graph embeddings. arXiv preprint: arXiv:2112.04871 (2021)
13. Steinhardt, J.: Robust Learning: Information Theory and Algorithms. Stanford University (2018)
14. Su, Q., Feng, C., Shi, G., Wang, B., Zhuang, Y.: Enhancing discriminative ability in multimodal LLMs: a contrastive learning approach for CT report generation. Inf. Fusion, 103240 (2025)
15. Tan, Z., et al.: KRACL: contrastive learning with graph context modeling for sparse knowledge graph completion. In: Proceedings of the ACM Web Conference 2023, pp. 2548–2559 (2023)
16. Toutanova, K., Chen, D.: Observed versus latent features for knowledge base and text inference. In: Proceedings of the 3rd Workshop on Continuous Vector Space Models and their Compositionality (2015)
17. Wang, L., Zhao, W., Wei, Z., Liu, J.: SimKGC: simple contrastive knowledge graph completion with pre-trained language models. arXiv preprint: arXiv:2203.02167 (2022)
18. Wang, Y., Liu, Y., Zhang, H., Xie, H.: Leveraging lexical semantic information for learning concept-based multiple embedding representations for knowledge graph completion. In: APWeb/WAIM (2019)
19. Wang, Y., Ouyang, X., Guo, D., Zhu, X.: Mega: meta-graph augmented pre-training model for knowledge graph completion. ACM Trans. Knowl. Discov. Data **18**(1), 1–24 (2023)
20. Wang, Y., Zhang, H.: HARP: a novel hierarchical attention model for relation prediction. ACM Trans. Knowl. Discov. Data **15**, 1–22 (2021)
21. Yang, B., tau Yih, W., He, X., Gao, J., Deng, L.: Embedding entities and relations for learning and inference in knowledge bases. CoRR abs/1412.6575 (2014)
22. Yao, L., Mao, C., Luo, Y.: KG-BERT: BERT for knowledge graph completion. ArXiv abs/1909.03193 (2019)

A Preliminary Attempt to Generate a Sichuan Dialect Handbook by LLMs

Xi Wang and Xin Xin(✉)

School of Computer Science and Technology, Beijing Institute of Technology, Beijing, China
{xiwangai,xxin}@bit.edu.cn

Abstract. Against the background that structured resources are rare and manually compiled dictionaries are inefficient, this paper puts forward an automatic construction framework for Sichuan dialect handbook based on the LLM. We propose an end-to-end pipeline consisting of corpus generation, vocabulary filtering, and entry explanation generation. Corpus generation is guided by scenario prompt templates, which instruct the DeepSeek language model to generate excellent dialect dialogues. And candidate vocabulary is filtered by word rule extraction. Finally, corresponding explanations are automatically generated. The experimental results show that the obtained handbook contains about 15,270 entries of dialects in total. And in evaluation we use three labels (Generally Accurate, Incorrect, Uncertain) to annotate all our words. The results showing 38.9% labeled as Generally Accurate, 48.1% as Uncertain, and 12.9% as Incorrect. This approach provides a practical technical solution for the digitization of dialects and the development of low-resource language corpora.

Keywords: Sichuan dialect · handbook construction · large language model · lexical resources · low-resource NLP

1 Introduction

Corpus in Sichuan dialect has many special words, grammar and meanings. The rich local characteristics and non-standardized characteristics of the corpus make it difficult to process the corpus simply by tools trained by standard Chinese. It brings about bad results in tasks such as speech recognition, QA, sentiment analysis, etc. There is a research showing that different data, models, and evaluation criteria should be adapted according to the specific task when using them for dialects [1]. Dialect-specific structured knowledge can also improve the generalization and coverage of models.

Currently, manual collection and annotation are still the widely-used method of language resource development [13]. However, traditional dialect dictionaries are based on manual compilation and investigation, which are labor-intensive and difficult to expand [14]. Recent researches have explored automatic approaches

J. Liang et al. (Eds.): CCKS 2025, CCIS 2698, pp. 15–25, 2026.
https://doi.org/10.1007/978-981-95-8525-0_2

like sentiment lexicons generated via classification models [10,12] and lexical association networks constructed through crowdsourcing [4]. However, pre-trained language models and tools trained on Mandarin are hard to effectively process the phonetic, lexical, and semantic variations present in dialects such as the Sichuan dialect.

This paper presents an automatic framework combining LLM and conventional methods. Firstly, scenario-based dialect corpus are generated by LLM. Then, dialect-specific candidates are extracted through word frequency filtering and cleaning. Finally, prompt-based generation produces handbook entries consisting of definitions, usage and phonetics. The obtained Sichuan Dialect Handbook contains about **15,270** entries, and we did evaluation on it at the end of this paper.

2 Related Work

2.1 Current Status of Dialect Language Resource Construction

Excellent construction of Chinese language resource is a core task in language engineering [15]. However, Although Chinese language resources have rapidly expanded over the past few years, dialect resource construction remains limited. The most work done by researchers is about dialect grammar, phonetics and region division; however, most dialect dictionaries have only been printed and do not even have a lexicon or corpus, leave alone an excellent digital handbook.

Corpus of Grammatical Features in Chinese Dialects [6] is another good resource, which collected data from 29 dialect sites via questionnaires. The corpus contains 711 grammatical sentences in 22 categories per site, plus natural conversation data, providing some valuable and useful data for dialect grammar studies. However, it cannot be used to wider range due to small scale and narrow regions. Such kind of language corpus materials can hardly be used for building dialect dictionaries as well.

2.2 Handbook Construction Based on Large Language Models

With the continuous improvement of LLMs in natural language, some researches have tried to use LLMs for automatically compiling a dictionary. Some systems combine LLMs with specific corpora and supplemented by human assistance mechanisms to automatically generate definitions for entries of loanwords, trace them back to their origins, and provide example sentences, making certain achievements [5]. This kind of methods provide us beneficial inspiration on building an automatic knowledge system of multiple language resources.

3 Construction Process of Sichuan Dialect Lexical Handbook

Usually, dialect experts use manual dialect dictionary compilation, which is authentic though, has lots of shortcomings like high costs, low coverage, and poor scalability. Especially for Sichuan dialect, which is both geographically and linguistically diverse.

Such limitations spur us to construct an automatic construction frame-work of LLMs. We use prompt templates to guide LLMs to generate dialect corpora, from which candidate word terms can be extracted, filtered, and deduplicated. Structured definitions including Mandarin equivalents, phonetics, usage, examples, regional variants, and cultural notes are then automatically generated for each extracted word.

In this section, we will detail our end-to-end pipeline, which is used to generate our dialect handbook with LLM (Fig. 1).

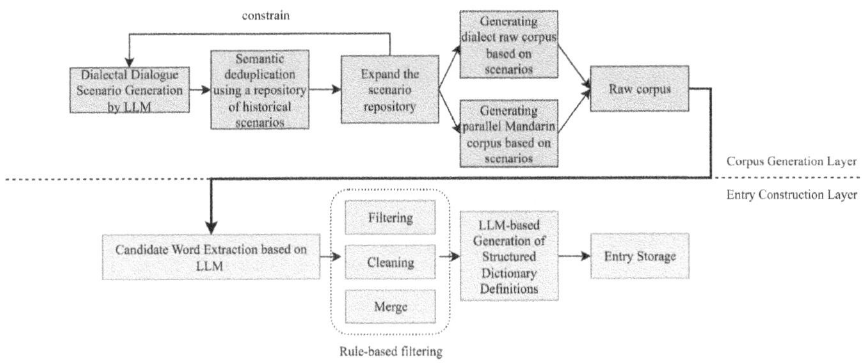

Fig. 1. Sichuan Dialect Lexicon Construction Process

3.1 Generation of Raw Dialect Corpus

Over the past few years, large language models (LLMs) have made great progress in text generation and can produce high-quality texts from input prompts [9]. In order to automatically construct a Sichuan dialect handbook, we put forward the corpus generating method of two stages according to the generative ability of the LLM.

Scenario-Based Generation: Firstly, We defined some initial prompts to instruct the LLM to generate lots of natural scenarios for dialect (e.g., teahouse chats, market bargaining, family talk), which should ensure that the output reflects authentic usage for dialect.

Dialectal Dialogue Generation: Based these generated scenarios, we use another prompt to generate dialogues that have lots of Sichuan dialect vocabulary and contextual usage.

However, there exists lots of redundancy in this scenario generation process. To overcome this, we propose a dynamic memory mechanism. Once a scenario is generated, we use another prompt to incorporate keywords from it. And add these keywords to the scenario generation prompt, which keeps the most recent m scenarios in its content. This strategy has promoted the diversity of our scenarios. All specific prompt designs used in this study are shown below (Fig. 2).

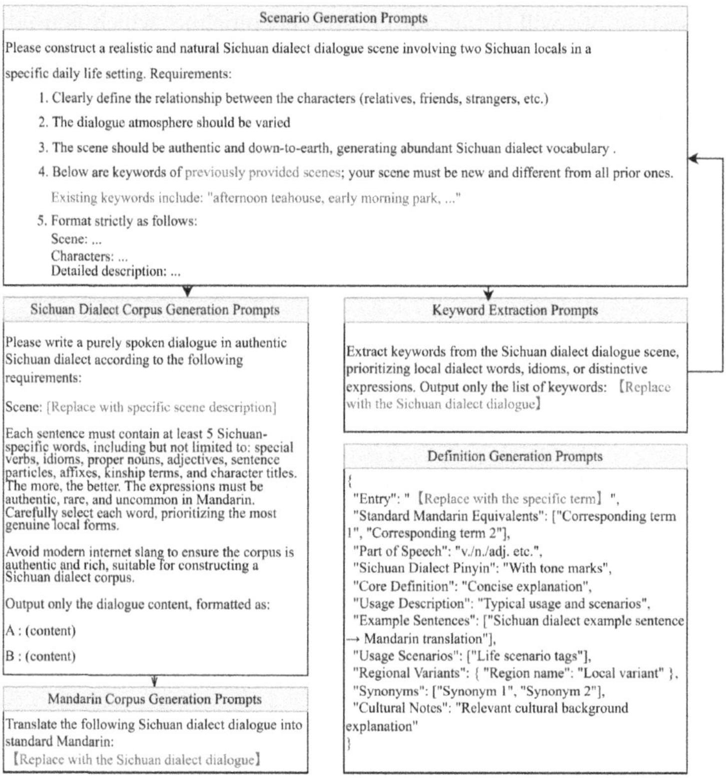

Fig. 2. Prompts Used in This Paper

To improve the diversity in corpus generation, we use similarity-based deduplication mechanism during the scenario generation phase. Specifically, we use the Zhipu AI's embedding-2 vector model to semantically encode each newly generated scenario string s_i, obtaining its corresponding vector representation $\mathbf{v}_i$.

Then, we compute the cosine similarity between the current vector and all the historical vectors $\{\mathbf{v}_j\}_{j=1}^{i-1}$. If the similarity exceeds a predefined threshold τ, where $\tau = 0.9$, we just consider it as a duplicate scenario, which will be regenerated. We present the effect of this strategy in the table below (Table 1).

Table 1. Comparison of generated scenario strings before and after applying deduplication

Scenario (No Deduplication)	Similarity	Scenario (With Deduplication)	Similarity
Buying vegetables at the market, bargaining	0.85	Buying vegetables at the market, discussing price	0.85
Buying vegetables at the market, talking about price	0.95	Discussing the freshness of ingredients at the market	0.83

3.2 Dialect Lexicon Filtering and Selection

After the corpus was generated, lots of candidate lexical items were extracted, including Sichuan dialect words, Mandarin words, internet slang, and artifacts due to noise and ambiguity. Due to the lack of dialect specialization in LLMs, some plausible items lacked dialect grounding. In order to ensure linguistic reliability, we filtered out entries that might be noise and with low-frequency, retaining representative and commonly used dialect forms via lexical extraction, statistical thresholds, contextual constraints, and contrastive analysis.

Dialect Candidate Extraction. Given that most pretrained segmenters trained on Mandarin perform not well on dialect data. We didn't use the word segmentation tools in this work, but rather relied on LLM to extract the words that have Sichuan dialect characteristics. The specific method is that we input a dialogue corpus into the LLM and ask it to mark Sichuan dialect words with special symbols (e.g. "[]"). Then, we extract the dialect-related vocabulary based on these markings. And these words are then taken as candidate words with Sichuan dialect characteristics.

Dialect Word Filtering and Cleaning Strategy. After the segmentation and frequency-based filtering stage, there are still many noises existing in the candidate set. Through analyzing, we have identified five major noise types in the initial candidate set as follows. To improve the quality of the Sichuan dialect lexicon, we performed a cleaning on the preliminary candidate set C_0, which contains 32,584 items, by removing redundancies and noise. The main cleaning steps include:

1. **Named Entity Removal**: The candidate set contains lots of local personal names, nicknames, and aliases (e.g., "陈二娃", "李幺妹") which lack generality and is not appropriate to add to the handbook. So we constructed a Chinese surname dictionary and defined a function is_name(w) using the "surname + given name" structure rules to identify the personal names.

2. **Compositional Redundancy Removal**: Some entries are redundant, because some shorter words are already included in it. For example, "挨边边站" contains the existing entry "挨边". So we detect whether a word w contains any other candidate $w' \in C_0$ with length $|w| \geq 3$, and mark it as redundant if true.
3. **Illegal Character Filtering**: Words containing non-Chinese characters (letters, digits, symbols), e.g., "吃9碗", "你&我", are all removed by regular expression matching has_illegal(w).
4. **Excessively Long Word Filtering**: Through obervation, we dicover that most of the Sichuan dialect word is not too long. Based on this, we define the longest string length $L_{\max} = 6$. Words exceeding this length limit are going to be considered as wrong word and we cut them off.
5. **Phonetic Variant Merging**: Sometimes, a dialect word has some variants which share the same pinyin but have different look (e.g., "爪子/抓子"). To solve this redundancy, we compute each word's pinyin $\pi(w)$ and gather all words with the same pinyin into sets $\mathcal{G}_\pi$, retaining the most frequent ones in each set.

Through the above strategies, we have removed 15,937 noisy entries, taking up approximately 50.2% of all words, which significantly promoted the lexicon's consistency and representativeness.

3.3 Generation of Lexical Entry Definitions

For the selected Sichuan dialect words, we use the LLM to generate corresponding lexical entries. Our goal is to build explanatory and vivid structural knowledge units. Our generation process mainly focuses on two core steps:

1. **Defining Structured Field Templates**: Firstly, we designed a standardized template about different lexical angle contents such as pronunciation, meaning, usage etc., including those specific fields: keyword entry, mandarin counterpart word, pos., ipa spelling (International Phonetic Alphabet), pinyin, tone marks, core words explanation, word collocation and usage, examples, situations, dialect words, synonyms, notes, and arranging it in json format for later parsing storage.
2. **Prompt Construction and Invocation**: To generate the final entries, we embedded each word into an explanation prompt, which is prepared in advance, to make the LLM to return an entry of the word following our given JSON format, which ensures the reflection of Sichuan regional language characteristics.

After receiving the output from the LLM, we parses the JSON content to extract each field of a word. Entries with blank fields or contain semantically incorrect information are marked invalid and will be excluded from the official lexicon to ensure our data quality. Finally, we constructed perfectly formatted and relatively complete explanatory entries for each dialect word, which provides data support for handbook publication, user queries, and academic analysis (Fig. 3).

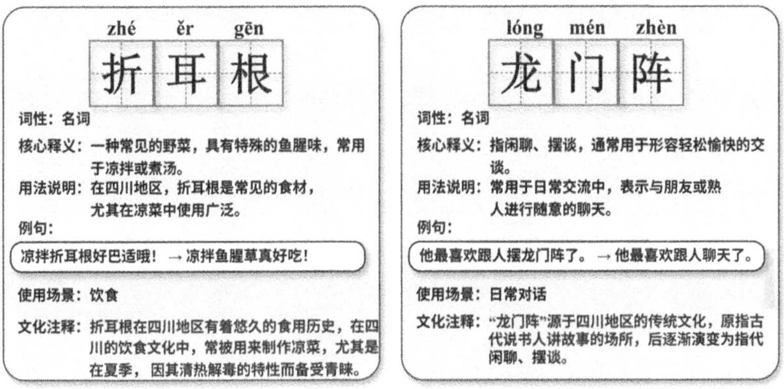

Fig. 3. Example of Generated Entry Explanation

4 Analysis of the Sichuan Dialect Handbook

4.1 Handbook Scale

In the experiment, our project has built about **15,270** entries of Sichuan dialect vocabulary and generated a parallel corpus of Sichuan dialect and Mandarin with about **2,746** dialogues and about **57000** comprehensive sentences, which cover multiple linguistic regions including Western Sichuan, Eastern Sichuan, Southern Sichuan, and Northern Sichuan. The core corpus was generated by a LLM under various everyday communicative scenarios and thematic prompts, covering various fields of daily life in Sichuan. And various strategies and methods were used to simulate everyday oral expression forms from local characters, plots, special event stories in prompts, etc., so as to enrich the content scope of the corpus and enhance its naturalness in everyday's life (Fig. 4).

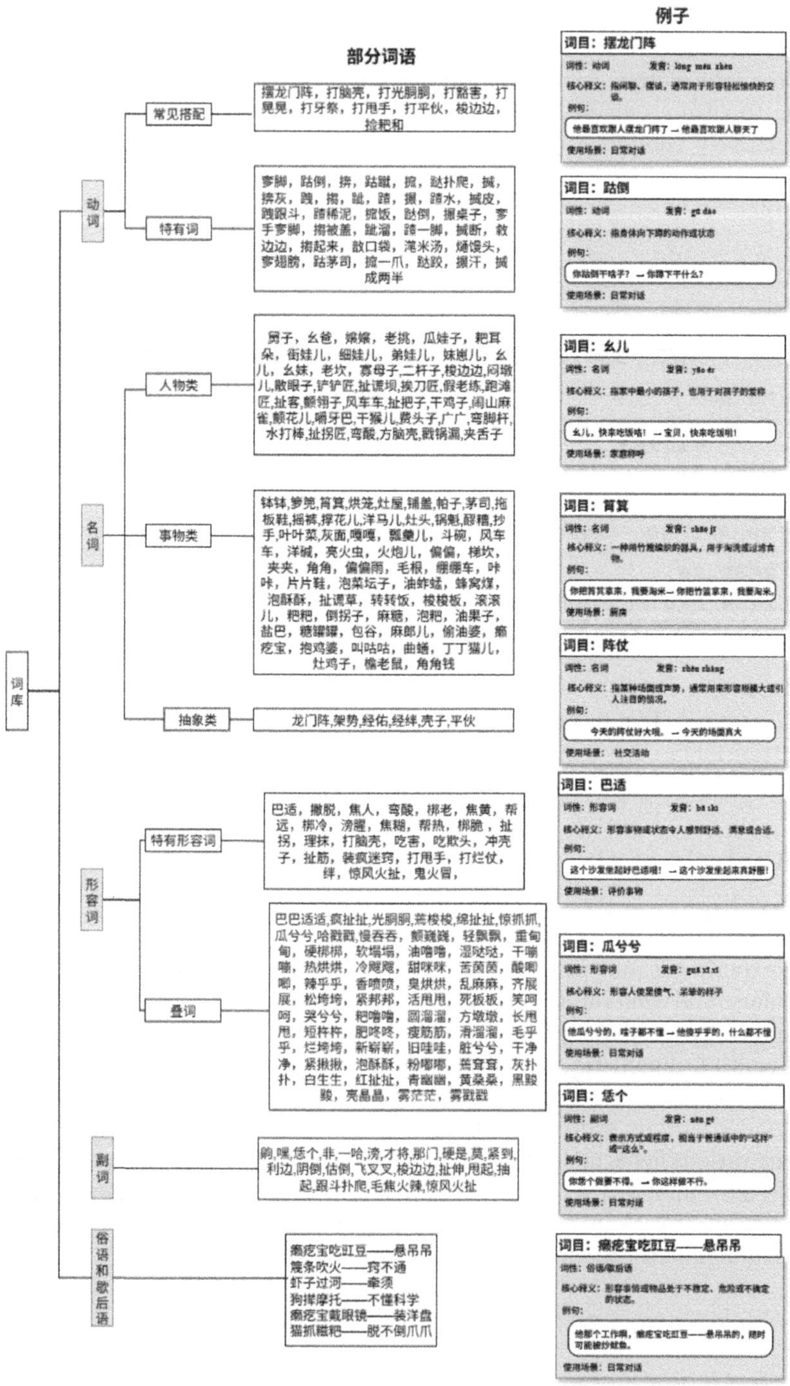

Fig. 4. Examples of entries categorized by type in the handbook

4.2 Vocabulary Categories

In order to better organize the lexical content of our Sichuan dialect handbook, we classified the words and arranged the entries by their various features like the parts of speech and the semantic categories mentioned in the studies of Sichuan dialect characteristic words by [7] and [2]. Table 2 shows the proportion of each lexical categories, typical word-formation features, and their representative words.

Table 2. Sichuan Dialect Vocabulary Classification and Representative Entries (Based on Cleaned Vocabulary). Since each word may have multiple parts of speech, we take the first listed part of speech of each word for classification.

Part of Speech	Proportion	Word Formation Method	Representative Entries and Semantic Explanation
Verb	42.2%	Monosyllabic + Complement/Reduplication	拱倒 (knock over), 打堆堆 (gather), 扯拢 (bring closer)
Noun	39.6%	Relatives/Position	幺儿 (child), 幺妹 (sister), 斗底 (corner)
Adjective/Adverb	17.6%	State Description	恼火 (angry), 惨兮兮 (pitiful), 头头是道 (organized)
Others	0.6%	Negation/Function Words	莫得 (none), 啥子 (what), 要得 (okay)

4.3 Coverage and Accuracy Analysis

Our handbook contains totally 15270 Sichuan dialect words, in contrast, the present "Sichuan Dialect Dictionary" compiled by [11] only contains about 7000 dialect words. Though there exists some mistakes and wrong word in our handbook, it still can be used as a valuable reference for dialect research.

To evaluate the accuracy of our handbook, we reviewed all our entries by a native Sichuan dialect speaker on whether the entries conform in basic meaning and usage habits in Sichuan. And we set up three evaluation labels: Generally Accurate, Uncertain, and Incorrect. In the review, our annotator labeled 48.1% of the entries with Uncertain, mainly because he didn't recognize these words. And among the other 51.9% words, he labeled 75.1% of them with Generally Accurate, the detailed results are presented in the table below (Table 3):

Table 3. Manual Annotation Results of the Recognized 51.9% of Entries

Label	Definition	Proportion (%)	Remarks
Generally Accurate	Entry conforms to Sichuan dialect usage	75.1	Mostly high-frequency and common expressions
Incorrect	Entry does not reflect correct meaning or usage	24.9	Often due to hallucination or lexical confusion

After evaluating, we conducted a further study on the entries labeled as Incorrect. We found that these entries mainly have two kinds of problems. The first is that some terms are likely to be produced by the hallucinations of the LLM, because they do not appear in either Sichuan dialect or Mandarin usage. The other is that some entries have entirely wrong or inaccurate definition, because LLM is likely to simply translate them into their meanings in standard Mandarin rather than dialect.

5 Conclusion

In this paper, we present an LLM driven handbook construction method, consisting of word mining, word filtering, definition generation, and structured storage. Experimental results showed that it had broader coverage and good quality and could scale up accordingly with performance. The next step is to perform regular updates, introduce audio materials, and complete dialectal knowledge transfer tasks.

Acknowledgements. This work is supported by the National Natural Science Foundation of China (Grant No. 62172044). We thank the anonymous reviewers for their constructive comments.

References

1. Joshi, A., et al.: Natural language processing for dialects of a language: a survey. ACM Comput. Surv. **57**(6), 149, 1–37 (2025)
2. Tang, H.: A review of "Sichuan Mandarin" in the studies of Eastern Sichuan dialects. Educ. Reform Dev. **6**(11), 106–111 (2024)
3. Zouhar, V., Tomášek, M., Bojar, O.: A formal perspective on byte-pair encoding. In: Findings of the Association for Computational Linguistics: EMNLP, pp. 5982–5997 (2023)
4. 丁宇, 车万翔, 刘挺, 张梅山. 基于众包的词汇联想网络的获取和分析. 中文信息学报, **27**(3):100–106 (2013). https://doi.org/10.3969/j.issn.1003-0077.2013.03.013
5. 柳长青. 基于大语言模型的词典自动化编纂实验及思考. 语言战略研究, **10**(02), 61–72 (2025). https://doi.org/10.19689/j.cnki.cn10-1361/h.20250206
6. 刘丹青, 夏俐萍 主编. 汉语方言语法特征语料库. (2023)

7. 沈益宇. 四川方言特征词研究. 东北师范大学 (2011)
8. 孙茂松, 左正平, 黄昌宁 . 汉语自动分词词典机制的实验研究. 中文信息学报, 2000(1):1–6
9. 王东清, 芦飞, 张炳会. 大语言模型中提示词工程综述. 计算机系统应用, **34**(01), 1–10 (2025)
10. 王科, 夏睿. . 情感词典自动构建方法综述. 自动化学报, **42**(04), 495–511 (2016). https://doi.org/10.16383/j.aas.2016.c150585.D
11. 王文虎, 张一舟, 周家筠. . 四川方言词典. 四川人民出版社 (2014)
12. 杨小平, 张中夏, 王良, 张永俊, 马奇凤, 吴佳楠, 张悦. . 基于Word2Vec的情感词典自动构建与优化. 计算机科学, **44**(1), 42–47 (2017)
13. 杨尔弘. 语言资源库的建设与共享. 语言教学与研究, (2):13–15. (2022). https://doi.org/10.3969/j.issn.0257-9448.2022.02.006
14. 张世方, 沈丹萍. 中国语言资源保护的理念与实践——以汉语方言为视角. 语言学研究, **1**(1), 6–16 (2017)
15. 詹卫东. 大数据时代的汉语语言学研究. 山西大学学报（哲学社会科学版, (5), 70–77 (2013)
16. 赵海, 蔡登, 黄昌宁, 揭春雨 . 中文分词十年又回顾 arXiv preprint: arXiv:1901.06079 (2018)

EDREL: Document-Level Relation Extraction with Evidence and Logical Rules

Han Xue[1], Huiying Li[2](✉), and Shuo Kou[2]

[1] College of Software Engineering, Southeast University, Nanjing, China
hanxue@seu.edu.cn

[2] School of Computer Science and Engineering, Southeast University, Nanjing, China
{huiyingli,213210928}@seu.edu.cn

Abstract. Document-level relation extraction (DocRE) is the task of extracting all relations between entities in a whole document. Previous research has demonstrated that sentence-level evidence information can enhance the accuracy of relation extraction. Existing joint relation and evidence extraction methods mostly rely on neural networks to learn the semantic information of local contexts, thereby capturing the interdependencies between entity pairs. However, these methods lack the ability to reason about the potential structural relations between entities, resulting in deficiencies in both relation and evidence prediction. To address this problem, we propose a Evidence-enhanced Document-level Relation Extraction with Logical rules method (EDREL), integrating semantic modeling with structural rule-based reasoning. By incorporating a logical rule mechanism as a supplement to semantic representation, this method simultaneously improves the structural modeling and reasoning capabilities for both relation and evidence extraction. We further design a simple yet effective structured evidence scoring method. Based on relation prediction, this method calculates the evidence confidence of sentences in a reverse manner through structural rules of co-occurrence and bridge entity paths. Experiments show that our method outperforms existing DocRE methods on both DocRED and Re-DocRED datasets.

Keywords: Relation extraction · Evidence extraction · Rule reasoning

1 Introduction

The task of Document-level relation extraction (DocRE) [7] aims to extract relations among multiple entities within a document. Compared to sentence-level relation extraction, DocRE requires the model to capture cross-sentence information in a longer context. Typically, only a few sentences rather than the entire document are sufficient to infer the relation of an entity pair. Therefore, DocRE models are expected to focus more on sentences relevant to the current decision of relation extraction (RE), thereby introducing less noise caused by

J. Liang et al. (Eds.): CCKS 2025, CCIS 2698, pp. 26–39, 2026.
https://doi.org/10.1007/978-981-95-8525-0_3

irrelevant sentences. Consequently, the accurate identification of key evidence sentences and their utilization for enhancing RE has emerged as a critical subtask in DocRE.

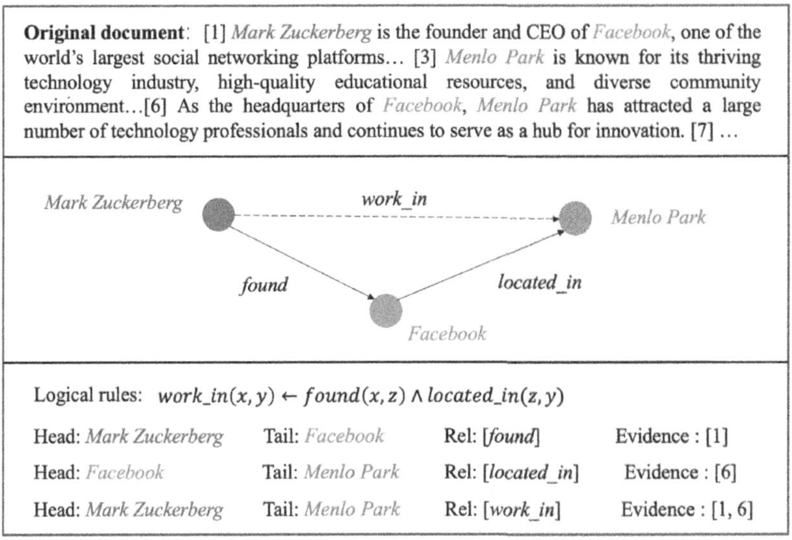

Fig. 1. An example of DocRE, where the ith sentence in the document is marked with [i] at the start.

Although an increasing number of studies [14,16] have achieved progress in the joint modeling of relation and evidence extraction, most current methods focus on neural networks to semantically model local contexts. These methods generally lack the capacity to explicitly construct and reason over latent structural relations between entities, especially in complex scenarios involving bridge entities, multi-hop relations, or inter-sentence evidence [11,20], which imposes constraints on the model's performance in both relation and evidence prediction.

As illustrated in Fig. 1, to predict the relation between "*Mark Zuckerberg* and "*Menlo Park*", the model needs to construct a multi-hop reasoning path: "*Mark Zuckerberg* → *Facebook* → *Menlo Park*". This relation is neither explicitly stated within a single sentence nor inferable through surface-level lexical cues. Moreover, the 1st and 6th sentence provide the first hop and the second hop information between entities respectively, which should be regarded as evidence sentences to support this relation. Although the sentence 3rd also mentions *Menlo Park* and is closer to the head entity *Mark Zuckerberg*, it has no connection with the target relation in structure and should be excluded. According to the example, it is likely to make inaccurate relation predictions and be prone to selecting irrelevant or redundant sentences as evidence without structural modeling mechanisms.

In this work, we propose Evidence-enhanced Document-level Relation Extraction with Logical rules (EDREL), a method designed to simultaneously enhance the structural modeling and reasoning capabilities of relation evidence extraction. For relation extraction, we introduce a rule reasoning mechanism to simulate the potential structural paths between entities by the combination of candidate relations through a set of learnable logical rules.

For evidence extraction, we further design a structured evidence scoring mechanism guided by the relation prediction results. Unlike conventional approaches, our method starts from the predicted relation and utilizes structural rules, such as co-occurrence and bridge-entity paths, to calculate the confidence scores of candidate evidence sentences. The design is based on the hypothesis that high-confidence relation predictions, enhanced by rule reasoning, indicate the existence of supporting structural patterns, so they can be used to calculate the scores of evidence sentences from the perspective of structured rules.

The main contributions of this work are as follows:

(1) We propose EDREL, a method where rule reasoning mechanism is introduced as a logical complement to neural representation learning to enhance the structural modeling of relations and evidences.

(2) We design an evidence scoring mechanism based on predicted relations, leveraging co-occurrence and bridge-entity patterns to assign confidence scores to sentences as potential supporting evidence.

(3) We perform the experiments on two public datasets DocRED [17] and Re-DocRED [12]. The results demonstrate the superiority of our method compared to baselines.

2 Related Work

The mainstream methods for DocRE can be broadly categorized into graph-based and transformer [13]-based approaches. Graph-based DocRE methods typically construct a graph with mentions, entities, sentences, or the document as nodes, and infer relations through reasoning on this graph [8]. Zhang et al. [18] proposed the Multi-granularity Graph (MGG), which connects entity pairs via short paths to address cross-sentence interactions. Ji et al. [4] introduced a module that integrates relation reasoning and heterogeneous graph neural networks, determining the relations between entity pairs through meta-paths and multi-hop reasoning.

Transformer-based methods capture long-range contextual information in the text by extracting related features between entities [19]. Zhou et al. [20] adopted local context pooling extracting useful context through an attention matrix and applied adaptive thresholds for each entity pair. Tan et al. [11] utilized axial attention to model the associations between entity pairs. Ma et al. [6] employed evidence information as a supervisory signal during training to guide the model in assigning higher weights to evidence sentences. Han et al. [2] introduced two co-occurrence prediction subtasks to model the relations between entity pairs from coarse to fine-grained perspectives.

Furthermore, logical rules have been applied to enhance DocRE models in recent years. Ru et al. [10] used logical rules to refine the output of a trained DocRE model. Fan et al. [1] extracted logical rules from the labeled data and subsequently incorporated these rules into the DocRE model through an auxiliary training objective. Qi et al. [9] developed a method that jointly learns the DocRE model and logical rules in an end-to-end fashion, explicitly modeling the reasoning process by parameterizing a rule reasoning module to simulate the inference of logical rules.

3 Method

The framework of the EDREL model is shown in Fig. 2. Overall, we first encodes the document and computes the prediction results for all potential relations and evidences. In the logical rules module, the relation prediction results are taken as input to calculate relation truth degrees though logical rule reasoning, which are then combined with the original relation predictions through residual connections to obtain enhanced relation logits. In the evidence extraction module, evidence confidence scores are derived based on the enhanced predicted logits and rules such as entity co-occurrence and bridge paths, and these scores are aggregated with the original evidence predictions. The entire model is trained by minimizing the weighted sum of the classification losses computed from the three modules.

3.1 Relation Extraction Module

Given a document $\mathcal{D}$ consisting of N sentences $\{s_n\}_{n=1}^{N}$ and E named entities $\{e_i\}_{i=1}^{E}$, and a pre-defined relation set $\mathcal{R} \cup \{NA\}$, the task of document-level relation extraction (DocRE) aims to predict all possible relations between every entity pair (e_h, e_t) in $\mathcal{D}$.

For a document $\mathcal{D} = \{h_i\}_{i=1}^{L}$, we insert a special token "*" at the beginning and end of each entity mention $\{m_j^i\}$ to mark its position and use the embedding of the start symbol * as the mention embedding $\boldsymbol{m}_j^i$ of the entity e_i. The embedding of entity e_i and sentence s_n are computed through LogSumExp pooling [5]. Then the context embedding $\boldsymbol{c}_{h,t}$ of entity pair (e_h, e_t) is obtained by local context pooling:

$$\boldsymbol{c}_{h,t} = \boldsymbol{H}^T \frac{\boldsymbol{A}_h \circ \boldsymbol{A}_t}{\boldsymbol{A}_h^T \boldsymbol{A}_t} \tag{1}$$

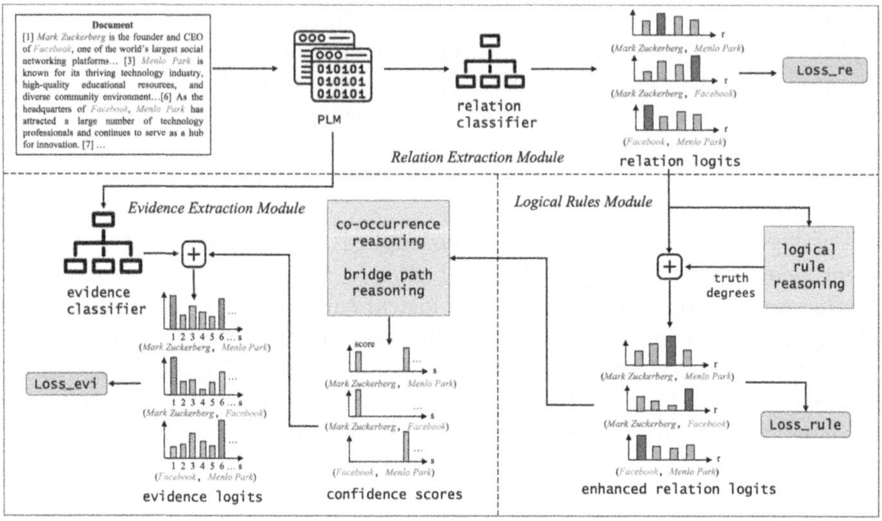

Fig. 2. Overall framework of EDREL.

where $\circ$ is the Hadamard product prioritizing tokens attended by both entities, $\boldsymbol{A}_i$ is the attention distribution of the entity e_i to all tokens in the document. The token embeddings $\boldsymbol{H}$ and the cross-token attention matrix $\boldsymbol{A}$ are obtained by encoder.

We compute the context-aware representations and apply a bilinear classifier to them to obtain the relation score $\boldsymbol{y}_r^{(h,t)}$ when predicting the relation between an entity pair (e_h, e_t). Subsequently, we use the Adaptive Thresholding Loss proposed by Zhou et al. [20], which learn a dummy threshold class *TH*. The form of loss is as follows:

$$L_{\mathrm{RE}} = -\sum_{h \neq t} \left[\sum_{r \in \mathcal{R}_P} \log \left(\frac{\exp(\boldsymbol{y}_r^{(h,t)})}{\sum_{r' \in \mathcal{R}_P \cup \{TH\}} \exp(\boldsymbol{y}_{r'}^{(h,t)})} \right) + \log \left(\frac{\exp(\boldsymbol{y}_{TH}^{(h,t)})}{\sum_{r' \in \mathcal{R}_N \cup \{TH\}} \exp(\boldsymbol{y}_{r'}^{(h,t)})} \right) \right] \tag{2}$$

3.2 Logical Rules Module

Logical rules module aims to enhance the predictive ability of relation extraction model by simulating the inference process of logical rules. Inspired by Qi et al. [9], the module represents the logical rules through a set of parameters that determine how to derive a new relation score from an existing relation score. The parameters of each rule are composed of relation selection weight $\boldsymbol{w}$ and rule confidence weight $\boldsymbol{\alpha}$.

We first define an extended logit $F^+(h,t)$:

$$F^+(h,t) = [\sigma(\boldsymbol{y}_r^{(h,t)}), \sigma(\boldsymbol{y}_r^{(t,h)}), I^{(h,t)}] \tag{3}$$

where $F^{+}(h,t) \in \mathbb{R}^{2|\mathcal{R}|+1}$, the first $|\mathcal{R}|$ dimensions for the original relations, the dimensions from $|\mathcal{R}|+1$ to $2|\mathcal{R}|$ for the inverse relations and the $(2|\mathcal{R}|+1)^{th}$ dimension for the identity relation I. $I^{(h,t)}=1$ if $h=t$ or 0 otherwise.

Suppose N is the maximum number of rules to be learned, and T is the maximum number of steps in each rule. Our goal is to estimate a truth degree $\boldsymbol{m}_{h,r,t}^{(N,T)}$ for each triple (e_h, r, e_t) in document $\mathcal{D}$, which indicates the probability that the relation r is established on the entity pair (e_h, e_t) through N chain rules with length T. For every normal relation $r \in \mathcal{R}$, the truth degree $\boldsymbol{m}_{h,r,t}^{(N,T)}$ is calculated as:

$$\boldsymbol{m}_{h,r,t}^{(n,st)} = \begin{cases} \sum_{k=1}^{2|\mathcal{R}|+1} w_k^{(r,n,st)} [F^{+}(h,t)]_k, & st=1 \\ \sum_{k=1}^{2|\mathcal{R}|+1} w_k^{(r,n,st)} \sum_{z\in\{e_i\}} \boldsymbol{m}_{h,r,z}^{(n,st-1)} [F^{+}(z,t)]_k, & 1 < st \leq T \end{cases}$$
$$\boldsymbol{m}_{h,r,t}^{(N,T)} = \sum_{n=1}^{N} \alpha_r^n \boldsymbol{m}_{h,r,t}^{(n,T)} \tag{4}$$

where the trainable weight $\boldsymbol{w}^{(r,n,st)} \in [0,1]^{2|\mathcal{R}|+1}$ denotes the probability distribution of the relation selection from the extended relation score $F^{+}(h,t)$ for the st^{th} step in the nth rule, $\alpha_r^n \in [-1,1]$ denotes the contribution of rule n to relation r.

In order to ensure that the enhancement of logical rules will not have a negative impact on the results of the original relation extraction, we incorporate the output logits from the original RE module and the estimated truth degrees through residual connection mechanism. The ultimately predicted logit is calculated by:

$$\boldsymbol{f}_r^{(h,t)} = \boldsymbol{y}_r^{(h,t)} + \boldsymbol{m}_{h,r,t}^{(N,T)} \tag{5}$$

Adaptive Thresholding Loss [20] is apply to $\boldsymbol{f}_r^{(h,t)}$ to calculate the loss of logical rules module, denoted as L_{Rule}.

3.3 Evidence Extraction Module

This module is designed to predict whether each sentence s_n is an evidence sentence of entity pair (e_h, e_t). If a sentence s_n serves as evidence for the entity pair (e_h, e_t), it is natural to assume that the tokens in s_n are pertinent to predicting the relation between the entities. To quantify the significance of s_n to the entity pair (e_h, e_t), we use a bilinear function that operates between the context embedding $\boldsymbol{c}_{h,t}$ and the sentence embedding $\boldsymbol{s}_n$:

$$a_{s_n}^{(h,t)} = \boldsymbol{s}_n \boldsymbol{W}_v \boldsymbol{c}_{h,t} + \boldsymbol{b}_v \tag{6}$$

where $\boldsymbol{W}_v$ and $\boldsymbol{b}_v$ are trainable parameters.

We calculate the score of each sentence $b_{s_n}^{(h,t)}$ by the result of relation extraction, so as to quantify the support degree of entity pair (e_h, e_t) on each sentence.

For each entity pair (e_h, e_t), we first filter the relation scores set composing of relation scores higher than their corresponding relation thresholds: $\mathcal{V}_{h,t} = \left\{\sigma(\boldsymbol{f}_r^{(h,t)}) \mid \sigma(\boldsymbol{f}_r^{(h,t)}) > T_r,\ r \in \mathcal{R}\right\}$ and the sentence set with co-occurrence of head and tail entities: $\mathcal{S}_{ht} = \{s_n \mid e_h \in s_n \ and \ e_t \in s_n, 1 \leq n \leq N\}$, where the trainable parameter T_r represents the threshold of the relation r.

For the sentences with direct co-occurrence of head and tail entities, we take the maximum value in $\mathcal{V}_{h,t}$ as the score of these sentences:

$$b_{h,t,s_n}^{co-occur} = \begin{cases} max(\mathcal{V}_{h,t}), & s_n \in \mathcal{S}_{ht} \\ 0, & s_n \notin \mathcal{S}_{ht} \end{cases} \tag{7}$$

In addition, we indirectly calculate the sentence score by finding the bridge entity z. The bridge entity needs to satisfy the following conditions: (1) The bridge entity z co-occurs with the head entity h and the tail entity t, respectively, but cannot co-occur with them in the same sentence, i.e. $\mathcal{S}_{hz} \cap \mathcal{S}_{zt} = \emptyset$. (2) For (h, z), there exists at least one relation whose score higher than the corresponding threshold, and similarly for (z, t), i.e. $\mathcal{V}_{h,z} \neq \emptyset$ and $\mathcal{V}_{z,t} \neq \emptyset$. Then we calculate the bridge path sentence score:

$$b_{h,t,s_n}^{bridge} = \begin{cases} max(\mathcal{V}_{h,z}), & s_n \in \mathcal{S}_{hz} \\ max(\mathcal{V}_{z,t}), & s_n \in \mathcal{S}_{zt} \\ 0, & s_n \notin \mathcal{S}_{hz} \ and \ s_n \notin \mathcal{S}_{zt} \end{cases} \tag{8}$$

The rule confidence score of each sentence for the entity pair (e_h, e_t) can be obtained by the weighted sum of the co-occurrence sentence score and the bridge path sentence score. Then we apply the inverse sigmoid (logit) function to recover the logit from the normalized rule confidence scores:

$$b_{s_n}^{(h,t)} = \text{logit}(\beta_1 b_{h,t,s_n}^{co-occur} + \beta_2 b_{h,t,s_n}^{bridge}) \tag{9}$$

where the hyper-parameters β_1 and β_2 are the weight coefficient of the direct co-occurrence sentence score and the bridge path sentence score respectively.

The ultimate sentence logit is calculated by:

$$x_{s_n}^{(h,t)} = \gamma a_{s_n}^{(h,t)} + (1 - \gamma) b_{s_n}^{(h,t)} \tag{10}$$

where γ is a hyper-parameter.

As an entity pair may have more than one evidence sentence, we use the binary cross-entropy as the objective to train the evidence extraction model:

$$L_{\text{Evi}} = -\sum_{h \neq t} \sum_{s_n \in \mathcal{D}} y_n^s \cdot \log \sigma(x_{s_n}^{(h,t)}) + (1 - y_n^s) \cdot \log(1 - \sigma(x_{s_n}^{(h,t)})) \tag{11}$$

where the evidence label y_n^s is 1 when s_n is golden evidence and otherwise 0.

Finally, we optimize our model by the combination of relation extraction loss L_{RE} logical rules loss L_{Rule} and evidence extraction loss L_{Evi}:

$$L = L_{\text{RE}} + \lambda_1 L_{\text{Rule}} + \lambda_2 L_{\text{Evi}} \tag{12}$$

where λ_1 and λ_2 are hyper-parameters to trade-off the three losses.

3.4 Inference

We also adopt the inference stage fusion strategy proposed by Xie et al. [15]. Specifically, for each predicted relation triple (e_h, r, e_t) that has evidence prediction $\Phi_{h,r,t}$, we construct a pseudo-document $\mathcal{D}'_{h,r,t}$ by collecting only evidence sentences $s_n \in \Phi_{h,r,t}$. These pseudo-documents are then input into the trained model to re-evaluate the scores of the relation triples. Then we use a blending layer to combine the predictions from the pseudo-documents and the entire document.

Table 1. Evaluation results on development and test sets of DocRED. Results with * are reported in their original papers. Others are based on our implementation. We divide the methods into two groups according to PLM. B-b refers to BERT$_{base}$ and R-l refers to RoBERTa$_{large}$.

Model	PLM	Dev				Test	
		Ign F1	F1	Intra F1	Inter F1	Ign F1	F1
E2GRE* [3]	B-b	55.22	58.72	–	–	55.40	57.80
ATLOP	B-b	59.08$_{\pm 0.21}$	60.97$_{\pm 0.15}$	67.22$_{\pm 0.16}$	53.17$_{\pm 0.21}$	59.26	61.25
EIDER	B-b	60.01$_{\pm 0.27}$	61.86$_{\pm 0.31}$	67.79$_{\pm 0.22}$	54.66$_{\pm 0.19}$	59.97	61.83
KD-DocRE	B-b	59.52$_{\pm 0.24}$	61.45$_{\pm 0.20}$	67.34$_{\pm 0.30}$	54.30$_{\pm 0.24}$	59.48	61.50
DREEAM	B-b	59.93$_{\pm 0.24}$	61.81$_{\pm 0.25}$	67.68$_{\pm 0.29}$	54.70$_{\pm 0.18}$	60.03	61.79
JMRL-ATLOP	B-b	59.53$_{\pm 0.15}$	61.36$_{\pm 0.19}$	67.69$_{\pm 0.30}$	53.56$_{\pm 0.24}$	59.60	61.58
EDREL(Ours)	B-b	**60.68**$_{\pm 0.12}$	**62.67**$_{\pm 0.18}$	**68.45**$_{\pm 0.26}$	**55.57**$_{\pm 0.23}$	**60.57**	**62.63**
E2GRE* [3]	R-l	59.55	62.91	–	–	60.29	62.51
ATLOP	R-l	61.28$_{\pm 0.13}$	63.12$_{\pm 0.20}$	69.58$_{\pm 0.31}$	54.99$_{\pm 0.25}$	61.36	63.37
EIDER	R-l	61.72$_{\pm 0.32}$	63.63$_{\pm 0.19}$	69.73$_{\pm 0.29}$	56.23$_{\pm 0.28}$	62.27	64.15
KD-DocRE	R-l	61.58$_{\pm 0.22}$	63.59$_{\pm 0.23}$	69.71$_{\pm 0.30}$	56.19$_{\pm 0.19}$	61.97	63.68
DREEAM	R-l	61.74$_{\pm 0.24}$	63.61$_{\pm 0.27}$	69.65$_{\pm 0.34}$	56.29$_{\pm 0.25}$	61.54	63.68
JMRL-ATLOP	R-l	61.65$_{\pm 0.23}$	63.51$_{\pm 0.27}$	70.09$_{\pm 0.34}$	55.47$_{\pm 0.28}$	61.85	63.72
EDREL(Ours)	R-l	**62.54**$_{\pm 0.19}$	**64.51**$_{\pm 0.28}$	**70.63**$_{\pm 0.26}$	**56.95**$_{\pm 0.23}$	**62.89**	**64.87**

4 Experiments

4.1 Experiment Setup

Datasets. We conduct experiments on two public datasets: (1) DocRED [17], the largest dataset for DocRE with human annotations, comprises 96 distinct relations and consists of 3053, 1000, and 1000 documents for training, development, and test, respectively. (2) Re-DocRED [12] is a high-quality revision of DocRED. It contains 3053 documents for training, 500 for development, and 500 for the test set.

Baselines. We adopt several competitive baselines for comparison, including E2GRE [3], ATLOP [20], EIDER [15], KD-DocRE [11], DREEAM [6], and JMRL-ATLOP [9]. E2GRE, EIDER, and DREEAM are methods widely recognized for their effectiveness in evidence extraction in addition to relation extraction. To ensure rigorous evaluation, we restrict KD-DocRE and DREEAM to the fully-supervised setting for comparison.

Evaluation Metrics. We use F1 and Ign F1 as the primary evaluation metrics for relation extraction, where Ign F1 measures the F1 score excluding relations shared between the training and development/test sets. Additionally, we report precision(P), recall(R), Intra F1 and Inter F1. We also calculate the F1 score of evidence extraction results, denoted as Evi F1.

Table 2. Results on development and test sets of Re-DocRED. Results are based on our implementation. All the methods here adopt RoBERTa$_{large}$ as PLM.

	Dev				Test	
Model	Ign F1	F1	P	R	Ign F1	F1
ATLOP	75.88$\pm$0.33	76.15$\pm$0.27	78.54$\pm$0.45	74.26$\pm$0.35	76.83$\pm$0.30	77.47$\pm$0.31
KD-DocRE	77.12$\pm$0.24	77.88$\pm$0.32	**85.16**$\pm$0.31	71.30$\pm$0.39	77.60$\pm$0.28	78.28$\pm$0.22
EIDER	77.17$\pm$0.24	77.78$\pm$0.27	80.77$\pm$0.39	76.48$\pm$0.26	77.43$\pm$0.28	78.04$\pm$0.37
DREEAM	77.31$\pm$0.25	78.23$\pm$0.26	75.53$\pm$0.30	**81.14**$\pm$0.19	77.38$\pm$0.22	78.33$\pm$0.23
JMRL-ATLOP	76.84$\pm$0.33	77.60$\pm$0.20	83.83$\pm$0.30	72.24$\pm$0.29	77.00$\pm$0.35	77.75$\pm$0.27
EDREL(Ours)	**77.79**$\pm$0.27	**78.75**$\pm$0.26	84.02$\pm$0.33	74.11$\pm$0.24	**78.01**$\pm$0.23	**78.91**$\pm$0.26

Implementation Details. We use BERT$_{base}$ and RoBERTa$_{large}$ as the base encoders trained with NVIDIA GeForce RTX 3090 GPU and optimize the model using AdamW with learning rate 5e-5 for the encoder and 1e-4 for other parameters. The ratio between relation extraction, logical rules and evidence extraction losses is set to 1:1:0.2. In the evidence extraction module, the weight coefficient of two rules is set to 1 and 0.7 and the ratio between evidence scores based on semantic representations and rule confidence is set to 0.7:0.3.

4.2 Main Results

Relation Extraction Results. Tables 1 and 2 report the comparison results on the DocRED [17] and Re-DocRED [12] datasets, respectively. The results demonstrate that our proposed EDREL model outperforms all baseline methods in both F1-scores and Ign F1-scores. As shown in Table 1, our improvement of Inter F1 is larger (e.g., 0.54/1.48 Intra/Inter F1 compared to JMRL-ATLOP), which can be attributed to the explicit modeling of structural paths between entities—such as multi-hop relational chains—enabled by the logical rule reasoning mechanism, thereby effectively alleviating the challenge of inter-sentence dependencies.

As shown in Table 2, EDREL generally achieves greater improvement in precision than in recall. The logical rule reasoning mechanism of the model can verify the structural validity of predicted relations rigorously and filter out false positive relations effectively, thereby enhancing precision. However, such a reasoning approach, which relies heavily on the completeness of structural paths, may introduce limitations in recall. In cases where the document contains ambiguous co-reference or complex relation patterns not fully covered by the rules, potential positive instances may go undetected due to broken reasoning paths. Moreover, ATLoss encourages the model to assign scores above the threshold to positive instances and below the threshold to negatives, thereby making the model may underperform in identifying marginal positives, such as weakly expressed relations.

Table 3. Evidence extraction results on DocRED. Results with * are borrowed from corresponding papers.

Model	PLM	Dev Evi F1	Test Evi F1
E2GRE* [3]	BERT$_{base}$	47.14	48.35
EIDER	BERT$_{base}$	50.51	50.94
DREEAM	BERT$_{base}$	**51.46**	51.13
EDREL(Ours)	BERT$_{base}$	51.12	**51.64**
E2GRE* [3]	RoBERTa$_{large}$	51.11	50.51
EIDER	RoBERTa$_{large}$	52.54	53.01
DREEAM	RoBERTa$_{large}$	**53.65**	53.51
EDREL(Ours)	RoBERTa$_{large}$	52.99	**53.57**

Evidence Extraction Results. As shown in Table 3, EDREL outperforms both E2GRE and EIDER in evidence extraction performance, but does not completely surpass DREEAM. On one hand, DREEAM directly supervises attention weights using KL-divergence and treat evidence as a sentence-level probability distribution rather than binary labels, which better reflects the gradient of each sentence's contribution during reasoning. In contrast, EDREL relies on a binary cross-entropy loss for hard classification, forcing the model to make absolute decisions for each sentence (evidence or not).

On the other hand, EDREL generates evidence scores based on the predicted relation. Errors in relation prediction propagate to evidence scores, causing biased sentence selection. While DREEAM avoids this problem by directly aligning with the gold evidence distribution via KL-divergence, eliminating the dependency on relation prediction. Although Evi F1 is limited by reliance on relation predictions, the F1 gain in relation extraction demonstrates that our method effectively propagates structural constraints between tasks.

4.3 Detailed Analysis

Table 4. Ablation results on the Re-DocRED dataset.

Model	Ign F1	F1	Intra F1	Inter F1
EDREL	78.01	78.91	81.38	76.69
w/o LR module	77.17	78.05	80.67	75.66
w/o residual connection	77.51	78.35	80.96	75.99
w/o EE module	76.88	77.63	80.18	75.12
w/o evi-scoring	77.37	78.28	80.85	75.87

Ablation Study. Table 4 presents the results of ablation study analyzing the utility of each module in EDREL. For *w/o LR module*, we use the results of RE module to calculate the scores of sentences in evidence extraction. For *w/o residual connection*, truth degrees are directly taken as the results of LR module without incorporating the original logits. For *w/o evi-scoring*, we directly use $a_{s_n}^{(h,t)}$ as the ultimate sentence logit.

The results indicate that the Evidence Extraction module is the most critical contributor to the performance improvement of EDREL, which not only provides semantic information but also incorporates structured information based on co-occurrence and bridge entity path rules. The independent removal of the Logical Rules module or the evidence scoring mechanism makes Inter F1 decrease significantly, demonstrating the crucial role of logical rule reasoning in enhancing the structural information expression. When residual connection is removed, there also remains a degradation in model performance.

Overall, the removal of any component results in performance degradation, fully indicating the indispensable synergistic effect of logical rules, residual connection mechanism, evidence extraction and their scoring mechanism on the performance of the model.

Analysis on Sentence Intervals. To verify whether the model is capable of capturing long-distance dependencies between entities, we separate the set of entity pairs into five groups according to the distances between entity pairs, which was measured by the minimum number of sentence intervals between the two entities in the document.

As shown in Fig. 3, our model outperforms all baselines regardless of whether head entity and tail entity are in the same sentence. The performance of all baselines gradually decreases with the increase of sentence intervals, whereas the performance of EDREL improves. This is because long-range cross-sentence relations are often strong signals, and only those with explicit reasoning chains are labeled as positive instances, making it easier for the model to learn these strong signals. Since there are fewer samples with large sentence intervals, the

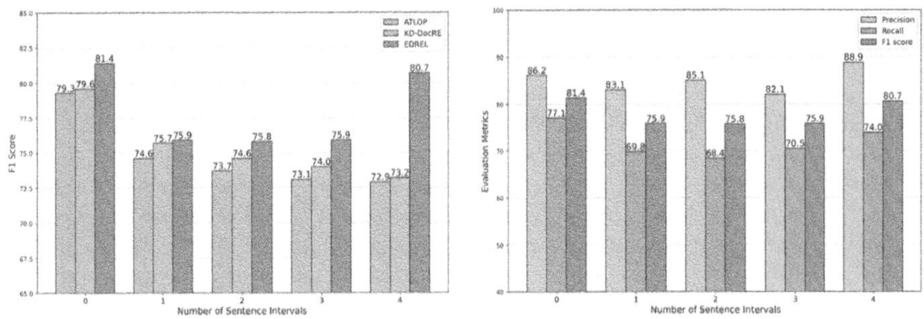

Fig. 3. Model performance for DocRE changing with the length of sentence intervals on dataset Re-DocRED. Left: The performance of different DocRE models. Right: The performance of EDREL on different evaluation metrics.

rule reasoning mechanism of the model is more adept at capturing long-distance dependencies, leading to more accurate relation predictions and a reduction in false positives, thereby resulting in a more pronounced increase in precision.

5 Conclusion

In this work, we propose a logical rule-based relation extraction method, EDREL, which enhances relation and evidence extraction by incorporating a rule-based reasoning mechanism on the basis of neural model semantic representations. In relation extraction, it simulates the potential structural paths between entities by combining candidate relations between entity pairs through a set of learnable logical rules. In evidence extraction, it calculates the structured evidence confidence of sentences based on structural rules of entity pair co-occurrence and bridge entity paths. Experimental results show that EDREL outperforms existing methods on two public datasets, especially in long-distance relations.

6 Limitations

A primary limitation of this work is that our evidence scoring mechanism is unable to compute evidence sentences for each individual relation. When an entity pair is associated with multiple relations, the same sentence scores are calculated regardless of the relation types. Even though these evidences may be valid for some relations, they might not be applicable to others. Moreover, EDREL relies on binary cross-entropy loss to make absolute judgments about each sentence. This rigid classification renders the model incapable of accurately expressing uncertainty. As a result, when confronted with ambiguous evidence, the model's judgments are not sufficiently precise, leading to the omission of some potentially valuable evidence.

References

1. Fan, S., Mo, S., Niu, J.: Boosting document-level relation extraction by mining and injecting logical rules. In: Proceedings of the 2022 Conference on Empirical Methods in Natural Language Processing, pp. 10311–10323 (2022)
2. Han, R., Peng, T., Wang, B., Liu, L., Tiwari, P., Wan, X.: Document-level relation extraction with relation correlations. Neural Netw. **171**, 14–24 (2024)
3. Huang, K., Qi, P., Wang, G., Ma, T., Huang, J.: Entity and evidence guided document-level relation extraction. In: Proceedings of the 6th Workshop on Representation Learning for NLP (RepL4NLP-2021), pp. 307–315 (2021)
4. Ji, W., Dong, Y., Chen, T.: Document-level relation extraction with relational reasoning and heterogeneous graph neural networks. In: International Conference on Advanced Data Mining and Applications, pp. 182–195. Springer (2023)
5. Jia, R., Wong, C., Poon, H.: Document-level N-ary relation extraction with multiscale representation learning. arXiv preprint: arXiv:1904.02347 (2019)
6. Ma, Y., Wang, A., Okazaki, N.: DREEAM: guiding attention with evidence for improving document-level relation extraction. arXiv preprint: arXiv:2302.08675 (2023)
7. Peng, N., Poon, H., Quirk, C., Toutanova, K., Yih, W.T.: Cross-sentence N-ary relation extraction with graph LSTMs. Trans. Assoc. Comput. Linguist. **5**, 101–115 (2017)
8. Peng, X., Zhang, C., Xu, K.: Document-level relation extraction via subgraph reasoning. IJCAI, 4331–4337 (2022)
9. Qi, K., Du, J., Wan, H.: End-to-end learning of logical rules for enhancing document-level relation extraction. In: Proceedings of the 62nd Annual Meeting of the Association for Computational Linguistics (Volume 1: Long Papers), pp. 7247–7263 (2024)
10. Ru, D., et al.: Learning logic rules for document-level relation extraction. arXiv preprint: arXiv:2111.05407 (2021)
11. Tan, Q., He, R., Bing, L., Ng, H.T.: Document-level relation extraction with adaptive focal loss and knowledge distillation. arXiv preprint: arXiv:2203.10900 (2022)
12. Tan, Q., Xu, L., Bing, L., Ng, H.T., Aljunied, S.M.: Revisiting DocRED-addressing the false negative problem in relation extraction. arXiv preprint: arXiv:2205.12696 (2022)
13. Vaswani, A., et al.: Attention is all you need. In: Advances in Neural Information Processing Systems, vol. 30 (2017)
14. Xiao, Y., Zhang, Z., Mao, Y., Yang, C., Han, J.: SAIS: supervising and augmenting intermediate steps for document-level relation extraction. arXiv preprint: arXiv:2109.12093 (2021)
15. Xie, Y., Shen, J., Li, S., Mao, Y., Han, J.: EIDER: empowering document-level relation extraction with efficient evidence extraction and inference-stage fusion. arXiv preprint: arXiv:2106.08657 (2021)
16. Xu, W., Chen, K., Mou, L., Zhao, T.: Document-level relation extraction with sentences importance estimation and focusing. arXiv preprint: arXiv:2204.12679 (2022)
17. Yao, Y., et al.: DocRED: a large-scale document-level relation extraction dataset. arXiv preprint: arXiv:1906.06127 (2019)
18. Zhang, J., Liu, M., Xu, L.: Multiple-granularity graph for document-level relation extraction. In: International Conference on Web Information Systems and Applications, pp. 126–134. Springer (2022)

19. Zhang, N., et al.: Document-level relation extraction as semantic segmentation. arXiv preprint: arXiv:2106.03618 (2021)
20. Zhou, W., Huang, K., Ma, T., Huang, J.: Document-level relation extraction with adaptive thresholding and localized context pooling. In: Proceedings of the AAAI Conference on Artificial Intelligence, vol. 35, pp. 14612–14620 (2021)

Knowledge Retrieval-Augmented Interest Learning for Recommendation

Guangyun Yao[1], Meng Jian[1(✉)], Wei Zhou[2], and Yashen Wang[3]

[1] School of Information Science and Technology, Beijing University of Technology, Beijing, China
mjian@bjut.edu.cn

[2] Naval Aviation University, Yantai 264001, China

[3] Artificial Intelligence Institute of CETC, Beijing 100049, China

Abstract. Existing recommendation methods rely on user-item interactions for interest modeling but struggling to the data sparsity issue. Knowledge graphs (KGs) provide rich semantic signals for mitigating this issue, yet existing KG-based methods often introduce redundant/irrelevant signals causing semantic noise that degrades recommendation performance. A possible solution is to filter task-relevant knowledge from KG to aid learning in the task domain. In this work, we propose a knowledge retrieval-augmented interest learning for recommendation (KRAR) to transfer semantic knowledge from KG to enhance interest learning on behavioral interaction graph. KRAR elaborates a dual retrieval from both users and items to filter interest-relevant items for augmenting the neighborhood in interest learning. The retrieved items participate in encoding users' interests implementing a cross-graph knowledge transfer, which enhances interest learning for recommendation. Experiments show that KRAR outperforms the baselines, demonstrating the superiority of knowledge retrieval and embedding augmentation in handling data sparsity for promoting recommendation performance.

Keywords: Collaborative Filtering · Knowledge Graphs · Recommendation Systems · Bidirectional Retrieval

1 Introduction

In today's era of information explosion, users are overwhelmed by the massive amount of online content, making it increasingly challenging to locate information aligned with their interests [3,15,16]. As a result, how to effectively filter and recommend relevant content has become a core problem for intelligent recommender systems.

(CF) [6,7,11], as one of the most widely adopted recommendation methods, relies on users' historical behavioral data to mine latent associations between users and items, achieving promising results in many scenarios. However, traditional CF methods model user interests solely based on user-item interaction

J. Liang et al. (Eds.): CCKS 2025, CCIS 2698, pp. 40–52, 2026.
https://doi.org/10.1007/978-981-95-8525-0_4

data, which often suffers from the data sparsity problem. This limitation significantly restricts the performance of CF, particularly in scenarios where user-item interactions are sparse. To address this challenge, researchers have introduced Knowledge Graphs (KGs) as a means of incorporating rich semantic information to supplement collaborative signals [1,2]. KGs provide multi-faceted attributes of items and semantic relationships among entities, enabling recommender systems to inject external domain knowledge from the item side. By jointly modeling user-item interaction graphs and knowledge graphs, recommendation models can enrich user representations with semantic knowledge while preserving behavioral patterns. Although such joint modeling frameworks offer potential improvements, they also bring new difficulties in practical applications. Since KGs often contain a large number of task-irrelevant entities and relations, naively incorporating them may introduce semantic noise, thereby degrading recommendation performance. Hence, a critical challenge is how to effectively retrieve knowledge that is highly relevant to a user's interest from such large and complex graph structures.

In this paper, we propose a novel framework named Knowledge Retrieval-augmented Interest Learning for Recommendation (KRAR). KRAR aims to enhance user representation by jointly modeling the user-item interaction graph and the knowledge graph, and selectively retrieving relevant semantic information through a decoupled retrieval strategy. Specifically, KRAR performs fine-grained semantic retrieval from both the user and item sides, constructing interest-relevant semantic paths from the item-side knowledge to filter out noise introduced by task-irrelevant information. This dual-perspective retrieval mechanism significantly improves the accuracy of user interest learning and enhances recommendation quality. The major contributions of this paper are summarized as follows:

- We propose a novel mechanism to retrieve interest-relevant semantic information from item-side knowledge graphs, which effectively alleviates the impact of task-irrelevant knowledge on user representation.
- We design a recommendation-aware dual-perspective cross-graph retrieval strategy and construct the KRAR framework, enabling semantic retrieval guided from both user and item sides to enhance user modeling and recommendation performance.
- We conduct extensive experiments on two public datasets to demonstrate the effectiveness of the proposed KRAR framework in extracting meaningful semantic signals, improving interest modeling, and boosting recommendation accuracy.

2 Related Work

2.1 Collaborative Filtering-Based Recommendation

Traditional collaborative filtering methods primarily rely on modeling user-item historical interaction behaviors. Matrix Factorization (MF) [10] is one of the most classic approaches, where the core idea is to decompose the user-item interaction matrix into low-dimensional latent factor matrices, capturing the match between user preferences and item attributes. While effective in early-stage recommender systems, these methods are heavily dependent on static interaction data and lack the ability to model complex semantic relationships.

In recent years, Graph Neural Networks (GNNs) [4] have been introduced to recommender systems to better capture high-order relationships between users and items. A representative method is LightGCN [5], which improves recommendation performance by propagating information through multi-hop neighbors. LightGCN treats the user-item bipartite graph as an unweighted graph, simplifying the traditional graph convolution propagation process by removing learnable weight matrices and non-linear activation functions, and retaining only the mean aggregation of neighboring features. This design significantly reduces the model's parameter complexity and computation while efficiently aggregating high-order neighborhood information.

In addition, several new methods have been proposed in recent years to further improve the performance of graph-based collaborative filtering models. For instance, HIID [12] hierarchically models users' interests, addressing the problem of capturing diverse user interests that traditional methods cannot handle. The method disentangles short-term and long-term user interests, enabling the recommender system to more accurately capture users' complex behavioral patterns. Another method, GASD [8], combines geometric augmentation with self-distillation techniques to further improve the performance of graph neural networks in recommendations. Through this self-supervised learning mechanism, the model enhances user representations on top of the graph structure, further improving recommendation accuracy. These methods introduce various technical innovations that enhance recommender systems' ability to model user interests, improve recommendation performance, and address data sparsity issues. Despite the significant achievements of these graph-based collaborative filtering methods, they still face some key limitations: (1) they are heavily dependent on interaction data, leading to unstable performance in sparse scenarios; (2) they lack external semantic information, which hinders their ability to deeply understand user intent, thereby limiting their capacity to model user interests.

2.2 Knowledge Graph-Based Recommendation

To address the semantic limitations of traditional collaborative filtering, researchers have integrated Knowledge Graphs (KGs) into recommendation systems to enhance user interest modeling. KGs, consisting of entities and semantic relations, provide structured item descriptions, improving recommendation interpretability and accuracy.

KGCN (Knowledge Graph Convolutional Network) [9], an early representative, combines GCNs with KGs: it treats KGs as heterogeneous structures, using local neighbor sampling and graph convolution to extract entity semantics for enhancing item representations. While effective in fusing structured knowledge with collaborative filtering, it is limited in multi-hop semantic propagation and user-interest guidance.

KGAT (Knowledge Graph Attention Network) [13] further introduces attention mechanisms to KGs, enabling weighted aggregation of neighbor information. It integrates user-item interaction graphs and KGs into a multi-hop relation graph, using graph attention for selective neighborhood aggregation to achieve personalized semantic enhancement.

KGIN (Knowledge Graph-Induced Network) [14] extends this by introducing an interest transition mechanism, dynamically mining semantically relevant paths from KGs based on user interests. It models latent user interest drift in graph structures to improve representation personalization. However, such methods focus primarily on entity semantic modeling and lack full consideration of bidirectional guidance/filtering from both user and item sides, limiting their ability to filter task-irrelevant information.

3 Problem Formulation

User-Item Interaction Graph. Historical user-item interactions are modeled as a bipartite graph $G_R = (\mathcal{U} \cup \mathcal{I}, \mathcal{E}_R)$, where $\mathcal{U}$ and $\mathcal{I}$ denote users and items, respectively, and $\mathcal{E}_R$ contains interaction edges (u, i) indicating that user u has interacted with item i. This structure is represented by a binary matrix $\mathbf{R} \in \{0, 1\}^{M \times N}$ where $\mathbf{R}_{ui} = 1$ for observed interactions. G_R encodes core behavioral patterns, forming the basis for collaborative recommendation.

Knowledge Graph. To enhance semantics and mitigate sparsity, we introduce a knowledge graph (KG) $KG = (\mathcal{V}, \mathcal{R}, \mathcal{T})$, where $\mathcal{V}$ includes items and auxiliary entities, $\mathcal{R}$ denotes semantic relations, and $\mathcal{T} = \{(h, r, t)\}$ represents triples (head entity h, relation r, tail entity t). KG provides structured multi-hop semantic information to enrich item representations and reveal latent user interests, improving model expressiveness and interpretability.

Recommendation Objective. Given $\mathbf{R}$, KG, and parameters Θ, the task is to predict user u's preference score y_{ui} for item i as:

$$y_{ui} = P(\mathbf{e}_u, \mathbf{e}_i \mid \mathbf{R}, KG, \Theta), \tag{1}$$

where $\mathbf{e}_u$ and $\mathbf{e}_i$ are embeddings of user u and item i. The goal is to estimate the user-item matching probability by jointly modeling collaborative interaction signals and knowledge-aware semantics.

4 Method

This chapter elaborates on the cross-graph joint optimization recommendation method proposed in this study. The overall architecture is shown in Fig. 1, and the model mainly consists of three modules: the graph convolution module including LightGCN encoding for user-item interaction graph and knowledge -

aware graph convolution module for collaborative knowledge graph (CKG)), the cross-graph interest augmentation module including bilateral interest retrieval for users and items, cross-graph mapping, and user interest enhancement, and recommendation and optimization. This method aims to enhance user interest representation by introducing a bilateral interest retrieval and fusion mechanism for structured knowledge, thereby improving recommendation accuracy.

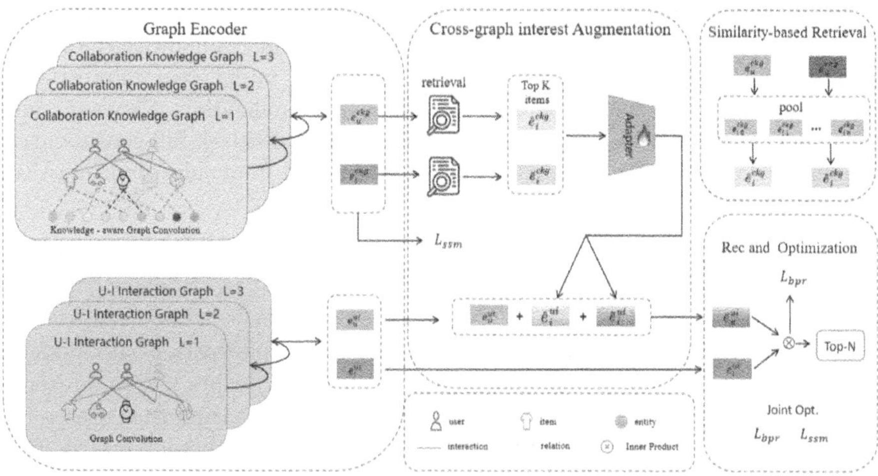

Fig. 1. Overall Framework of the KRAR

4.1 Graph Representation Learning and Encoding

We first perform representation learning and encoding for the user-item interaction graph $\mathcal{G}_{ui}$ and the collaborative knowledge graph (CKG) $\mathcal{G}_{ckg}$. For the user-item interaction graph, we employ LightGCN to encode and learn the graph. LightGCN aggregates multi-hop neighbor information to learn node embeddings, omitting non-linear activation and feature transformation operations, so as to capture the structural information of the interaction graph more effectively.

The initial user and item embeddings are denoted as $\mathbf{e}_u^{(0)}$ and $\mathbf{e}_i^{(0)}$, respectively, and L represents the propagation depth. At each layer, the user and item embeddings are influenced by the neighbor nodes' information. The final user and item embeddings are computed as follows:

$$\mathbf{e}_u^{ui} = \sum_{l=0}^{L} \alpha_l \cdot \mathbf{e}_u^{(l)}, \quad \mathbf{e}_i^{ui} = \sum_{l=0}^{L} \alpha_l \cdot \mathbf{e}_i^{(l)}, \tag{2}$$

where α_l represents the aggregation weight for each layer (which can be set as the mean or learned), and $\mathbf{e}_u^{(l)}$ and $\mathbf{e}_i^{(l)}$ are the embeddings after propagation at the l-th layer. With this encoding process, we obtain the user and item representations in the UI graph, denoted as $\mathbf{e}_u^{ui}$ and $\mathbf{e}_i^{ui}$.

For the collaborative knowledge graph $\mathcal{G}_{ckg}$, we use a multi-head attention mechanism to aggregate information for the entity nodes. Each edge (h, r, t) in the graph represents a triplet where h and t are the head and tail entities, and r denotes the relation. For each edge (h, r, t), the attention weight is computed as follows:

$$\alpha_{(h,r,t)} = softmax\left(\frac{(\mathbf{W}\mathbf{e}_h)^\top(\mathbf{W}\mathbf{e}_t \odot \mathbf{r}_r)}{\sqrt{d_k}}\right), \tag{3}$$

where $\mathbf{e}_h$ and $\mathbf{e}_t$ are the embeddings of the head and tail entities, $\mathbf{r}_r$ is the relation embedding, $\mathbf{W}$ is a trainable projection matrix, $\odot$ denotes element-wise multiplication, and d_k is the dimension of the attention head. The final entity representation is obtained by aggregating the attention-weighted information:

$$\mathbf{e}'_h = \sum_{(h,r,t)\in\mathcal{G}_{ckg}} \alpha_{(h,r,t)} \cdot (\mathbf{e}_t \odot \mathbf{r}_r) \tag{4}$$

The user's representation $\mathbf{e}_u^{ckg}$ in the CKG is obtained by aggregating the entity representations of the items they have interacted with in the CKG, while the item embedding $\mathbf{e}_i^{ckg}$ corresponds directly to its entity representation in the CKG.

4.2 Cross-Graph Interest Enhancement

To achieve semantic complementarity between the UI graph and CKG, we design a cross-graph interest enhancement mechanism. This mechanism mainly includes bilateral interest retrieval for users and items, cross-graph mapping, and user interest enhancement. By utilizing the complementary information from both graphs, the method effectively improves the quality of user interest representation.

First, we perform bilateral interest retrieval for users and items. For the user's representation $\mathbf{e}_u^{ckg}$ in the CKG space, we retrieve the K most relevant item embeddings in the CKG, denoted as $\hat{\mathbf{e}}_i^{ckg}$:

$$\hat{\mathbf{e}}_i^{ckg} = \left\{\mathbf{e}_j^{ckg} \mid j \in TopK\left(sim\left(\mathbf{e}_u^{ckg}, \mathbf{e}_j^{ckg}\right)\right)\right\} \tag{5}$$

Additionally, based on the user's interaction in the UI graph, we retrieve the N most relevant item representations in the CKG, resulting in $\tilde{\mathbf{e}}_i^{ui}$:

$$\tilde{\mathbf{e}}_i^{ui} = \left\{\mathbf{e}_j^{ckg} \mid j \in TopN\left(sim\left(\mathbf{e}_i^{ui}, \mathbf{e}_j^{ckg}\right)\right)\right\}, \tag{6}$$

where $sim(\cdot, \cdot)$ denotes the cosine similarity function.

Next, we introduce a cross-graph mapping function $f_{map}(\cdot)$, which maps the retrieved CKG representations $\hat{\mathbf{e}}_i^{ckg}$ and $\tilde{\mathbf{e}}_i^{ui}$ into the UI graph space for further fusion. This mapping function is typically implemented as a two-layer MLP to align the semantics:

$$\hat{\mathbf{e}}_i^{ckg} = f_{map}\left(\hat{\mathbf{e}}_i^{ckg}\right), \quad \tilde{\mathbf{e}}_i^{ui} = f_{map}\left(\tilde{\mathbf{e}}_i^{ui}\right) \tag{7}$$

Finally, the user's final representation is obtained by fusing the UI-encoded user embedding with the cross-graph retrieved items. The fusion is done via a weighted sum:

$$\bar{\mathbf{e}}_u^{ui} = \gamma \cdot \mathbf{e}_u^{ui} + (1-\gamma) \cdot \sum_j \omega_j \cdot \mathbf{e}_j, \tag{8}$$

where $\mathbf{e}_j \in \hat{\mathbf{e}}_i^{ckg} \cup \tilde{\mathbf{e}}_i^{ui}$, γ is a gating factor, and ω_j is the attention weight for each retrieved item. This process combines information from both graphs to enhance the user interest representation.

4.3 Recommendation Prediction and Model Optimization

After the cross-graph interest enhancement, the model performs recommendation prediction by calculating the interaction score between user representations and item representations. Specifically, the preference score of user u for item i is computed as the inner product between the enhanced user representation and the item embedding in the UI graph:

$$\hat{y}_{ui} = \langle \bar{\mathbf{e}}_u^{ui}, \mathbf{e}_i^{ui} \rangle, \tag{9}$$

where $\bar{\mathbf{e}}_u^{ui}$ is the user representation after cross-graph enhancement, and $\mathbf{e}_i^{ui}$ is the item embedding in the UI graph. This inner product effectively captures the matching degree between the user and item in the joint semantic space, facilitating accurate recommendations.

To comprehensively optimize model performance, we design a joint loss function that balances recommendation accuracy and cross-graph semantic consistency. To preserve the relative order information of user interactions, we adopt the Bayesian Personalized Ranking (BPR) loss as the primary training objective:

$$\mathcal{L}_{BPR} = -\sum_{(u,i,j)\in\mathcal{D}} \log \sigma\left(\hat{y}_{ui} - \hat{y}_{uj}\right), \tag{10}$$

where $\mathcal{D} = \{(u,i,j) \mid upprefersioverj\}$ represents the set of training triples, and σ is the sigmoid function. This loss function encourages the model to predict higher scores for user-preferred items over non-preferred items, thus optimizing the ranking performance.

To enhance the semantic consistency between the UI graph and CKG, we design a structural contrastive learning loss (SSM). This loss is based on a contrastive learning framework, maximizing the similarity of user representations across different graph spaces while minimizing the similarity with negative samples:

$$\mathcal{L}_{SSM} = -\sum_{u\in\mathcal{U}} \log \frac{\exp(sim(e_u^{ui}, e_u^{ckg})/\tau)}{\sum_{u'\in\mathcal{N}(u)} \exp(sim(e_u^{ui}, e_{u'}^{ckg})/\tau)}, \tag{11}$$

where $\mathcal{N}(u)$ denotes the set of negative samples for user u, $sim(\cdot, \cdot)$ is the cosine similarity function, and τ is the temperature parameter. This loss encourages the model to learn cross-graph consistent user representations, thus enhancing the knowledge transfer capability.

The final optimization objective is a weighted combination of the above loss functions and a parameter regularization term:

$$\mathcal{L} = \mathcal{L}_{BPR} + \alpha\mathcal{L}_{SSM} + \beta\|\Theta\|_2, \tag{12}$$

where α and β are hyperparameters that balance the importance of each loss term, and Θ represents the set of all trainable parameters in the model. The regularization term helps prevent overfitting and control the model complexity.

5 Experiments

To verify the effectiveness and generality of the proposed method, this paper conducts systematic experimental evaluations on two public recommendation system datasets and compares it with various representative recommendation methods. The experiments mainly focus on the following questions: 1) Can the proposed cross-graph interest enhancement mechanism significantly improve recommendation performance? 2) What is the generalization ability of the model on different types of data? 3) What is the effectiveness of different cross-graph retrieval configurations, so as to analyze the role and contribution of the bidirectional interest transfer mechanism in enhancing user representation and modeling potential preferences.

5.1 Experimental Settings

Datasets. We adopt two widely-used datasets for evaluation: Last-FM and MovieLens-1M. Last-FM is a music recommendation dataset that contains user-artist interaction logs (e.g., play counts, frequencies), along with rich auxiliary entity information such as artist genres, countries, and tags. MovieLens-1M is a classic movie recommendation dataset where each movie is associated with various metadata including genres, actors, and directors. The statistics of both datasets are summarized in Table 1.

Evaluation Metrics. To comprehensively assess recommendation performance, we adopt two commonly-used top-K ranking metrics: Normalized Discounted Cumulative Gain (NDCG@K) and Recall@K, where $K \in \{10, 20\}$. NDCG@K(N@K) reflects the ranking quality of relevant items in the recommendation list, assigning higher scores to relevant items appearing at higher positions. Recall@K(R@K) measures the proportion of ground-truth items successfully retrieved within the top K recommendations, indicating the model's ability to cover user interests. Higher NDCG and Recall values indicate better recommendation performance.

Table 1. Statistics of the datasets.

	Last-FM	MovieLens-1M
User-Item Interaction		
#Users	1,872	6,036
#Items	3,846	2,254
#Interactions	21,173	376,886
Knowledge Graph		
#Entities	9,364	6,729
#Relations	56	7
#Triplets	15,462	20,195

Implementation Details. To ensure fair comparisons and reproducibility, all models are implemented with the same configurations: embedding dimension is set to 64, batch size to 1024, and the number of GNN propagation layers L is set to 3 based on validation performance. We use the Adam optimizer with an initial learning rate of 0.001 and apply L2 regularization with weight $\beta = 1 \times 10^{-4}$. In the cross-graph interest retrieval module, the retrieval quantities Top-K and Top-N are tunable with respect to dataset characteristics; in our experiments, we set Top-K to 5 and Top-N to 3. The temperature parameter τ in the contrastive loss is set to 0.2.

Baselines. We compare the proposed model with the following representative baselines:

- **MF:** A classical matrix factorization model that captures user-item preferences via inner product.
- **LightGCN:** A lightweight GCN-based model that performs simplified neighborhood aggregation on user-item graphs.
- **KGAT:** A knowledge-aware attention network that integrates knowledge graph semantics into recommendation.
- **KGIN:** A KG-based recommendation model that incorporates interest propagation over multi-hop relational structures.
- **KGCL:** A contrastive learning approach that enhances recommendation robustness via cross-view consistency on knowledge graphs.

5.2 Overall Performance Comparison

Table 2 presents the overall recommendation performance of KRAR compared with several representative baseline models on the Last-FM and MovieLens-1M datasets. In the table, bolded values denote the best-performing results among the baseline methods, while values marked with an asterisk (*) indicate the performance of our proposed KRAR. It can be observed that KRAR consistently

Table 2. Overall Performance Comparison.

	Last-FM				MovieLens-1M			
	R@10	N@10	R@20	N@20	R@10	N@10	R@20	N@20
MF	0.2089	0.1503	0.2895	0.1763	0.1882	0.2495	0.2895	0.2661
LightGCN	**0.2716**	**0.1954**	**0.3785**	**0.2301**	**0.2187**	**0.2894**	**0.3253**	**0.3037**
KGAT	0.2355	0.1730	0.3341	0.2048	0.2058	0.2702	0.3091	0.2850
KGIN	0.2591	0.1869	0.3669	0.2221	0.2139	0.2810	0.3208	0.2967
KGCL	0.2049	0.1791	0.3241	0.2059	0.2130	0.2823	0.3190	0.2969
KRAR	**0.2991***	**0.2188***	**0.3949***	**0.2498***	**0.2307***	**0.3031***	**0.3379***	**0.3166***
%Improv.	10.12%	11.97%	4.33%	8.17%	5.49%	4.73%	3.87%	4.25%

achieves the best performance across all metrics on both datasets, demonstrating strong generalizability and robustness.

Compared with collaborative filtering methods (MF and LightGCN), KRAR achieves substantial performance improvements. For instance, on the Last-FM dataset, KRAR reaches a Recall@10 of 0.2991, representing an improvement of approximately 10.1% over the best collaborative filtering baseline LightGCN (0.2716); in terms of NDCG@20, KRAR improves from 0.2301 to 0.2498. These gains can be attributed to the cross-graph retrieval augmentation mechanism introduced in KRAR, which effectively incorporates semantic information from the knowledge graph to compensate for the lack of semantic understanding in collaborative filtering models. This dual enhancement of structure and semantics is particularly beneficial in scenarios with sparse user behavior or diverse interests.

Compared with knowledge graph-based methods (KGAT, KGIN, KGCL), KRAR also achieves consistent improvements. On MovieLens-1M, its Recall@20 (0.3379) surpasses KGIN (0.3208), and NDCG@10 rises from KGCL's 0.2823 to 0.3031. Existing KG methods alleviate sparsity but struggle to model cross-graph user interests; KRAR's dual-side retrieval enhances interest modeling and semantic context effectively.

5.3 Ablation Study

To further verify the effectiveness of each key component in the KRAR model, we design three ablation variants: (1) removing the user-side cross-graph retrieval while retaining item-side retrieval enhancement; (2) removing item-side retrieval while keeping user-side enhancement; and (3) removing both user-side and item-side retrieval mechanisms, which reduces the model to the standard LightGCN. These variants allow us to systematically analyze the contribution of different retrieval strategies to interest modeling and recommendation performance.

Figure 2 presents the performance comparison of all variants across both datasets. As shown, the complete KRAR model consistently outperforms all its ablated versions on all metrics, which confirms the necessity and effectiveness of the dual-sided retrieval mechanism in jointly modeling user interests.

Among the variants, user-side retrieval shows a more noticeable impact in capturing semantic user preferences, yielding slightly higher performance improvements than item-side retrieval. This is primarily because user-side retrieval leverages knowledge graph entities associated with users to recover their latent intent more accurately. This semantic augmentation is especially valuable in sparse interaction scenarios, where explicit behavioral data are limited. In contrast, item-side retrieval mainly enhances item representations from a structural perspective, contributing to target matching but offering less direct benefits for user modeling.

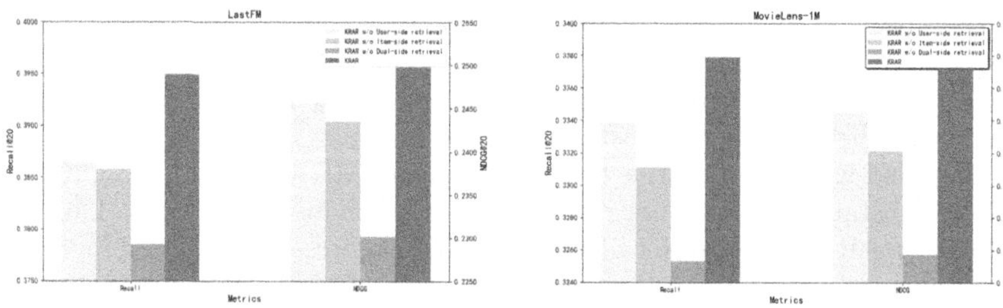

(a) Last-FM (b) MovieLens-1M

Fig. 2. Performance comparison of KRAR and its variants on two datasets.

When both retrieval components are removed, the model relies solely on structural signals from the user-item graph, leading to the most significant performance drop. This observation underscores the limitations of pure collaborative signals in capturing nuanced user interests. The proposed dual-sided retrieval design in KRAR effectively bridges this gap by introducing complementary semantic and structural information from heterogeneous graphs.

6 Conclusion

This paper presents KRAR (Knowledge Retrieval-augmented learning for Recommendation), a knowledge retrieval-enhanced framework for recommendation interest modeling. It integrates structural and semantic information from user-item interaction graphs and collaborative knowledge graphs (CKG) to improve user interest modeling accuracy and recommendation performance. KRAR uses unified graph representation learning to model interaction and knowledge graphs, and introduces bidirectional interest retrieval (from user and item sides) to explicitly bridge user behaviors and knowledge semantics. A cross-graph semantic mapping module aligns and fuses heterogeneous representations, generating richer, more semantically aware user representations. Experimental results show KRAR outperforms existing collaborative filtering and knowledge graph-based methods on multiple real-world datasets and standard metrics, with notable gains in recommendation accuracy and ranking quality. Ablation studies confirm the critical role of bidirectional retrieval and representation enhancement, demonstrating KRAR's effectiveness and robustness in modeling complex graphs. Future work will explore lightweight designs for efficiency, more effective retrieval path strategies (e.g., learnable interest guides), and integration of multimodal content, linguistic knowledge, or pretrained large model priors to enhance knowledge graph expressiveness.

Acknowledgement. This work was supported by the National Natural Science Foundation of China under Grant NO. 62176011, the Beijing Natural Science Foundation under Grant NO. L241053, and the Technical Field Foundation under Grant NO. 2023-JCJQ-JJ-0747.

References

1. Cao, Y., Hou, L., Li, J., Liu, Z.: Neural collective entity linking. arXiv preprint arXiv:1811.08603 (2018)
2. Cao, Y., et al.: Joint representation learning of cross-lingual words and entities via attentive distant supervision. arXiv preprint arXiv:1811.10776 (2018)
3. Covington, P., Adams, J., Sargin, E.: Deep neural networks for YouTube recommendations. In: Proceedings of the 10th ACM Conference on Recommender Systems, pp. 191–198 (2016)
4. Gasteiger, J., Bojchevski, A., Günnemann, S.: Predict then propagate: graph neural networks meet personalized PageRank. arXiv preprint arXiv:1810.05997 (2018)
5. He, X., Deng, K., Wang, X., Li, Y., Zhang, Y., Wang, M.: LightGCN: simplifying and powering graph convolution network for recommendation. In: Proceedings of the 43rd International ACM SIGIR Conference on Research and Development in Information Retrieval, pp. 639–648 (2020)
6. He, X., He, Z., Song, J., Liu, Z., Jiang, Y.G., Chua, T.S.: NAIS: neural attentive item similarity model for recommendation. IEEE Trans. Knowl. Data Eng. **30**(12), 2354–2366 (2018)
7. He, X., Liao, L., Zhang, H., Nie, L., Hu, X., Chua, T.S.: Neural collaborative filtering. In: Proceedings of the 26th International Conference on World Wide Web, pp. 173–182 (2017)
8. Jian, M., Wang, T., Xia, Z., Shi, G., Hong, R., Wu, L.: Geometric-augmented self-distillation for graph-based recommendation. ACM Trans. Inf. Syst. **43**(4), 1–23 (2025)
9. Kojima, R., Ishida, S., Ohta, M., Iwata, H., Honma, T., Okuno, Y.: kGCN: a graph-based deep learning framework for chemical structures. J. Cheminform. **12**, 1–10 (2020)
10. Koren, Y., Bell, R., Volinsky, C.: Matrix factorization techniques for recommender systems. Computer **42**(8), 30–37 (2009)
11. Liang, D., Krishnan, R.G., Hoffman, M.D., Jebara, T.: Variational autoencoders for collaborative filtering. In: Proceedings of the 2018 World Wide Web Conference, pp. 689–698 (2018)
12. Wang, T., Jian, M., Xu, X., Wu, L.: Hierarchical intent-based interest disentanglement for personalized recommendation. IEEE Trans. Knowl. Data Eng. (2025)

13. Wang, X., He, X., Cao, Y., Liu, M., Chua, T.S.: KGAT: knowledge graph attention network for recommendation. In: Proceedings of the 25th ACM SIGKDD International Conference on Knowledge Discovery & Data Mining, pp. 950–958 (2019)
14. Wang, X., et al.: Learning intents behind interactions with knowledge graph for recommendation. In: Proceedings of the Web Conference 2021, pp. 878–887 (2021)
15. Ying, R., He, R., Chen, K., Eksombatchai, P., Hamilton, W.L., Leskovec, J.: Graph convolutional neural networks for web-scale recommender systems. In: Proceedings of the 24th ACM SIGKDD International Conference on Knowledge Discovery & Data Mining, pp. 974–983 (2018)
16. Yuan, F., He, X., Karatzoglou, A., Zhang, L.: Parameter-efficient transfer from sequential behaviors for user modeling and recommendation. In: Proceedings of the 43rd International ACM SIGIR Conference on Research and Development in Information Retrieval, pp. 1469–1478 (2020)

Large Models Enhanced by Knowledge Graphs

Multi-granularity Hierarchical RAG for Welding Parameter Recommendation

Xiaohan He, Yinchi Li, Shuming Zhang, Meiling Wang(✉), Qianyuan Cheng, and Longkang Leng

Beijing Institute of Technology, Beijing, China
wangml@bit.edu.cn

Abstract. With Industry 4.0 driving intelligent transformation in manufacturing, optimizing welding parameters for industrial robots has become critical to achieving high-quality, cost-effective production. Traditional methods relying on expert experience and trial-and-error approaches suffer from inefficiency and poor knowledge reuse. While Retrieval-Augmented Generation (RAG) systems enhanced by Knowledge Graphs (KGs) and Large Language Models (LLMs) offer promise, they struggle with two key challenges: neglecting the hierarchical structure of welding knowledge and failing to capture complex interdependencies among parameters. To address these limitations, this paper proposes a multi-granularity hierarchical RAG framework for welding parameter recommendation. By decomposing the task into three reasoning layers, the framework integrates a progressive knowledge flow mechanism that combines relational vector matching, case knowledge graph querying and process manual subgraph retrieval. Additionally, we construct Wecommend, a dataset encompassing 1009 sets of on-site welding production records and 177 standardized parameters extracted from welding process manuals. Experimental results demonstrate that our multi-granularity hierarchical RAG approach effectively captures the hierarchical dependencies among welding parameters through multi-granularity knowledge enhancement, achieving a recommendation accuracy of 89.86% and outperforming baseline methods.

Keywords: Large Language Model · Knowledge Graph · Retrieval-Augmented Generation · Welding Parameter Recommendation

1 Introduction

With the advent of Industry 4.0, the transformation and upgrading of manufacturing industries have placed significant demands on the intelligence of industrial robots [1]. Industrial robotic welding, as a core application of industrial robots, reflects the advancement level of modern manufacturing. Welding is a process that joins thermoplastic materials by partially or fully melting them through heating or pressure, forming a solid connection. In manufacturing, products are typically assembled from multiple components, and welding is essential for joining these parts into a complete structure such as a car body or an aircraft fuselage. Welding process parameters such as welding current, welding voltage, directly impact the microstructure, quality, cost, and lifespan of

J. Liang et al. (Eds.): CCKS 2025, CCIS 2698, pp. 55–67, 2026.
https://doi.org/10.1007/978-981-95-8525-0_5

welded parts. Selecting appropriate welding parameters is fundamental to achieving high-quality welding in industrial robotic applications. Optimizing these parameters not only improves joint strength and sealing performance but also reduces defect rates, minimizing rework and scrap due to quality issues. Traditionally, parameter selection relied heavily on expert experience and trial-and-error experiments, leading to low efficiency, poor knowledge reuse, and high process costs [2]. As a result, intelligent recommendation of welding parameters for industrial robots has become a fundamental requirement and key research direction in smart manufacturing.

For decades, researchers have focused on developing specialized domain knowledge reasoning tools and expert systems [3, 4]. This research effort has been significantly advanced by Knowledge Graph (KG) [5] and Large Language Model (LLM) [6, 7] technologies, which have elevated expert systems' capabilities in natural language understanding and knowledge reasoning to unprecedented levels. LLMs exhibit strong generative capabilities and broad applicability across a wide range of domains. However, LLMs store knowledge learned during training through model parameters and are typically regarded as black-box models, making it inherently difficult to capture and retrieve factual knowledge [8]. To address these challenges, Retrieval-Augmented Generation (RAG) [9–11] has emerged as a promising solution, leveraging external knowledge sources such as KGs to enhance LLMs [12].

However, the above methods still face significant challenges when applied to specialized domains. Two fundamental limitations emerge when handling complex welding parameter recommendation tasks:

(1) Current RAG systems often treat parameter recommendation as a monolithic retrieval-generation process, failing to account for welding knowledge's inherent hierarchical structure.
(2) The above methods struggle to capture the complex interdependencies among welding parameters. These approaches typically retrieve knowledge fragments independently, overlooking critical cross-parameter constraints.

In this paper, we present a multi-granularity hierarchical RAG method. Based on the reasoning task decomposition framework we introduced, the overall parameter recommendation task was divided into three distinct layers. Each layer employs a multi-granularity retrieval strategy to enable semantic-driven and knowledge-augmented reasoning of welding parameters. Vector search and graph traversal are combined to uncover both explicit and implicit process correlations, enhancing the model's ability to capture complex relationships among welding parameters. Our contributions can be summarized as follows:

(1) A reasoning task decomposition framework is proposed for multi-subtask reasoning problems.
(2) A multi-granularity hierarchical RAG framework is introduced for welding parameter recommendation. By leveraging a progressive knowledge flow mechanism, the framework integrates relational vector matching, case knowledge graph querying, and process manual knowledge graph subgraph retrieval, achieving interpretable welding parameter recommendation.

(3) We construct a welding process parameter dataset Wecommend, which consists of 1009 sets of real-world production welding parameters and 177 sets of standard welding parameters extracted from welding process manuals.

2 Related Works

Traditional approaches for welding parameter recommendation primarily rely on two technical paradigms [3]: data-driven neural network modeling and rule-based expert systems. The former methods map process parameters to performance metrics through inverse design [13], predominantly employing BP networks [14, 15], RBFANN [16] and ELMs [17]. However, their generalization capability remains constrained due to strong nonlinear interactions between manufacturing parameters and quality characteristics. The latter methods perform logical reasoning through domain-specific knowledge bases [4], yet suffers from inflexibility in novel scenarios due to limited knowledge coverage. Recent advancements in LLMs like ChatGPT [6] and DeepSeek [7] demonstrate exceptional semantic comprehension capabilities, though their parametric knowledge representation suffers from factual knowledge gaps and low decision transparency [8].

To overcome these limitations, RAG technology has significantly enhanced model performance in knowledge-intensive tasks through external knowledge integration [9–12] [18–21]. Concurrently, KGs employ graph-structured representations to store domain-specific knowledge [5], demonstrating robust capabilities in relational mining and knowledge inference. Current research has explored various innovative methods: GraphRAG [12] constructs a knowledge graph from source documents, pre-generates community summaries for related entity groups to produce partial responses, and synthesizes them into a final output; KRAGEN [18] proposes a Graph-of-Thoughts (GoT) framework that decomposes complex problems into graph-structured subtasks for traceable multi-step reasoning; HippoRAG [19] implements a hippocampus-neocortex inspired architecture with dual-phase indexing-retrieval mechanisms for knowledge consolidation; Chain-of-Thought (CoT) techniques [22] enhance LLM interpretability through explicit stepwise reasoning. However, existing methods still face significant challenges when applied to specialized domains. They struggle to perform explicit structural decomposition of reasoning paths when dealing with complex tasks like welding process parameter recommendation, which involves strong process coupling and hierarchical progression. Therefore, there is an urgent need to develop new knowledge representation and reasoning methods that can support multi-level, verifiable decision-making processes.

3 Method

3.1 Welding Knowledge Graphs Construction

We constructed two complementary knowledge graphs from structured and unstructured welding data sources, defined as:

$$G = G_{\text{case}} + G_{\text{process}} \tag{1}$$

where G_{case} is a welding case knowledge graph constructed based on structured tables, while G_{process} is a welding process manual knowledge graph built from unstructured documents. Below, we elaborate on the construction methods for these two knowledge graphs.

Welding Case Knowledge Graph. Given a structured process instance table, the constructed welding case knowledge graph is defined as follows:

$$G_{\text{case}} = \{(ID_i, R_{is}, n_{ij})|i = 1, \cdots, n; j = 1, \cdots, m\}, n_{ij} = (N_{a_i}, v_{ij}) \tag{2}$$

where ID_i refers to the identifier of the i-th process case, R_{is} denotes the predicate "is", n_{ij} represents the entity located at the intersection of the i -th row and j -th column in the table, N_{a_i} specifies the type of the node and v_{ij} denotes the value attribute of the node.

The construction process follows these steps:

Schema Mapping. Map the process parameter category $a_i \in$ A in the table headers to node types N_{a_i} in the knowledge graph.

Attribute Assignment. Assign the process parameter values as node attribute values v_{ij}.

Relationship Construction. Use predicates R_{is} as relationships to connect the process instance ID_i with the respective process parameter nodes.

Welding Process Manual Knowledge Graph. For unstructured welding process manual documents $\mathcal{D} = \{d_1, d_2, \cdots, d_p\}$, the following workflow is adopted to construct the welding process manual knowledge graph, as shown in Fig. 1.

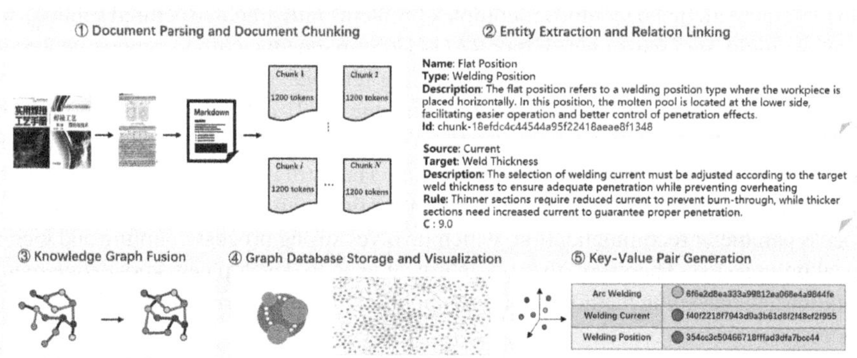

Fig. 1. The workflow of the welding process manual knowledge graph construction.

Document Parsing. Most professional documents are stored as unstructured data (e.g., PDF, DOC) containing various elements such as headings, paragraphs, formulas, tables, and images which are not easily retrievable or processable by computers. Document parsing converts such unstructured documents into semi-structured formats (e.g., Markdown, HTML), enabling subsequent operations such as text segmentation and vectorization. We employ the open-source tool MinerU as our document parser to convert scanned welding process manuals into markdown-formatted text. The parsing process is as follows:

$$\mathcal{M} = f_{\text{parse}}(\mathcal{D}) = f_{\text{layout}} \circ f_{\text{content}}(\mathcal{D}) \tag{3}$$

where the document parser f_{parse} integrates a layout detector f_{layout} and a multimodal content extractor f_{content}. f_{layout} utilizes LayoutLMv3 model to locate various elements in documents, including headings, images, tables and text. f_{content} comprises three subsystems: formula recognition, table recognition, and text extraction. The formula recognition module employs YOLOv8 and UniMERNet to respectively detect and recognize formulas in the document, converting them into LaTeX format. The table recognition module leverages StructEqTable for table identification, while the text extraction module uses PaddleOCR to extract textual content from scanned documents.

Document Chunking. To effectively handle long documents, the document is first divided into multiple text chunks $\mathcal{M} = \{c_1, c_2, \cdots, c_q\}$. This facilitates quick localization and access to relevant information. The chunks are vectorized storage by embedding models:

$$\vec{c}_i = \text{Embed}(\text{c}_\text{i}) \tag{4}$$

Entity Extraction. For each segmented chunk, the LLM extracts a series of entity nodes, defined as:

$$e = (n_e, t_e, d_e, id_e) \tag{5}$$

where:

- $\cdot n_e$ represents the name of the entity;
- $\cdot t_e$ denotes the type of the entity, selected from a predefined table $\mathcal{T}_{\text{weld}}$;
- $\cdot d_e$ is the description of the entity, encompassing contextual information from the document;
- $\cdot id_e$ is a unique identifier to track the entity's source document and paragraph, critical for subsequent retrieval of source information and generation of evidence-based responses.

To ensure the effectiveness of the model, we provide examples to guide the LLM in generating compliant outputs. To improve extraction quality while reducing noise and variance, an iterative feedback mechanism is introduced:

$$\mathcal{E}^{k+1} = \text{LLM}(\mathcal{E}^\text{k}, \text{C}, \text{Feedback}), \text{ while k} < \text{K}_{\text{max}} \tag{6}$$

where $\mathcal{E}^k$ is the set of entities obtained in the k-th extraction, and $K_{\max}$ represents the maximum number of times the extraction process is repeated. This mechanism repeats the extraction process multiple times, allowing the LLM to autonomously decide whether to continue or terminate extraction within $K_{\max}$. The iterative process supplements initially missed entities, ensuring the constructed knowledge graph comprehensively covers the original text.

Relation Linking. For the extracted entities $\mathcal{E}$, we employ the LLM to identify relationships between entities. Each relation and its attributes are defined as follows:

$$r_{(e_s,e_t)} = (e_s, e_t, d_{(e_s,e_t)}, \text{Rule}_{(\text{e}_\text{s},\text{e}_\text{t})}, \text{c}_{(\text{e}_\text{s},\text{e}_\text{t})}) \tag{7}$$

where:

$\cdot e_s$ is the source entity;

- e_t is the target entity;
- $d_{(e_s,e_t)}$ is a detailed description of the relationship between the two entities based on all available entity information;
- $\text{Rule}_{(\text{e}_\text{s},\text{e}_\text{t})}$ represents the welding process rules or precautions associated with the relationship between e_s and e_t which facilitates the subsequent welding parameter recommendations;
- $c_{(e_s,e_t)} \in [0, 1]$ indicates the strength of the relationship between the two entities. The closer the value is to 1, the more closely related the two entities are.

Knowledge Graph Fusion. Identical entities and relationships from different chunks are recognized, and their descriptions are merged into coherent summaries to eliminate redundancy, enabling efficient data processing and achieving knowledge graph fusion.

Graph Database Storage and Visualization. After extracting entities and relationships from the given text, we use Neo4j as the storage database to enable knowledge graph visualization, as shown in Fig. 2.

Key-Value Pair Generation. An LLM is used to generate textual key-value pairs for each entity node and relationship edge. Each key corresponds to the name of an entity or relationship, while the associated value is a paragraph summarizing all attributes related to that entity or relationship, facilitating retrieval augmentation subsequently.

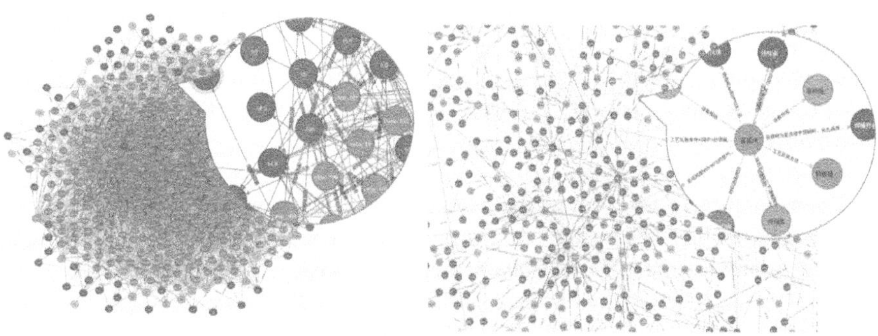

Fig. 2. The welding knowledge graph we constructed: The welding case knowledge graph which contains a total of 1016 nodes and 9504 edges (left) and the welding process manual knowledge graph which contains a total of 4373 nodes and 3019 edges (right).

3.2 Reasoning Task Decomposition Framework

For multi-subtask reasoning problems, we propose a reasoning task decomposition framework. Based on this framework, subtasks are precisely graded, and new supporting evidence is acquired at each layer to progressively construct the reasoning chain for the answer.

- Framework Anchoring Layer (FAL): This layer has the highest priority and influences both the CCL and the ORL. It establishes prior assumptions for the overall task, defines the scope and direction of reasoning for subsequent layers. As the top-level layer, it remains unaffected by error accumulation from lower layers.
- Core Control Layer (CCL): This layer ranks second in priority and is constrained by the responses from FAL, while also limiting the adjustment range of ORL. It directly controls the core reasoning process and serves as the central component for completing the overall task. Due to its high sensitivity, even small changes at this level can lead to significant variations in results, making precise control essential.
- Operational Realization Layer (ORL): This layer acts as a supplementary implementation of CCL. It offers some tolerance for errors but relies heavily on the correctness of the two upper layers.

The proposed reasoning task decomposition framework exhibits the following characteristics:

(1) Hierarchical Decision-Making: Reduces reasoning uncertainty through tiered constraints, improving reasoning efficiency.
(2) Interpretability: Clear inter-layer relationships facilitate traceability of reasoning paths and explain the logic behind final conclusions.

Welding parameter recommendation involves interdependent and hierarchical parameters. Based on our proposed framework, it is decomposed as follows:

- FAL: Process Planning. This layer primarily handles decisions regarding welding type and weld pass layers. The selection of welding type (e.g., TIG, MAG, SAW) fundamentally governs the energy input mechanism, while the weld pass layers is constrained by joint design and defines the process framework.
- CCL: Electrothermal parameters recommendation. These parameters directly determine arc thermo-dynamic behavior, serving as the core energy input for the welding process.
- ORL: Operational technique. Operational technical parameters are process execution-level variables that influence welding stability, permit certain adjustment ranges, and some are equipment-dependent.

3.3 Multi-granularity Hierarchical RAG

We propose a multi-granularity hierarchical RAG framework for welding process parameter recommendation, as shown in Fig. 3. The framework employs a progressive knowledge flow mechanism, integrates relational vector matching, case knowledge graph querying, and process manual knowledge graph subgraph retrieval, achieving interpretable welding parameter recommendation.

First, a candidate pool of parameter relationship documents is built and then transformed into high-dimensional vector database. By further integrating the welding case knowledge graph and the welding process manual knowledge graph that we have constructed, a multi-granularity knowledge base is established for retrieval. Based on the knowledge base, a four-stage knowledge enhancement process is executed at each layer of parameter reasoning:

Parameter Relationship Retrieval. Combine the known parameters with user requirements into a vectorized query, and retrieve the Top-K most relevant relational texts from the parameter relationship vector database based on similarity.
Case Knowledge Graph Retrieval. Top-N similar cases are recalled from the welding case knowledge graph using Cypher queries based on known parameters.
Welding Process Manual Knowledge Graph Retrieval. Keywords are extracted from the query and matched to key-value entity representations in the welding process manual knowledge graph, followed by multi-hop subgraph expansion to capture broader contextual relations.
Multi-granularity Knowledge-Augmented Generation. The LLM generates recommended parameters based on contextual inputs including parameter constraints, case configurations, process manual knowledge, and the original query.

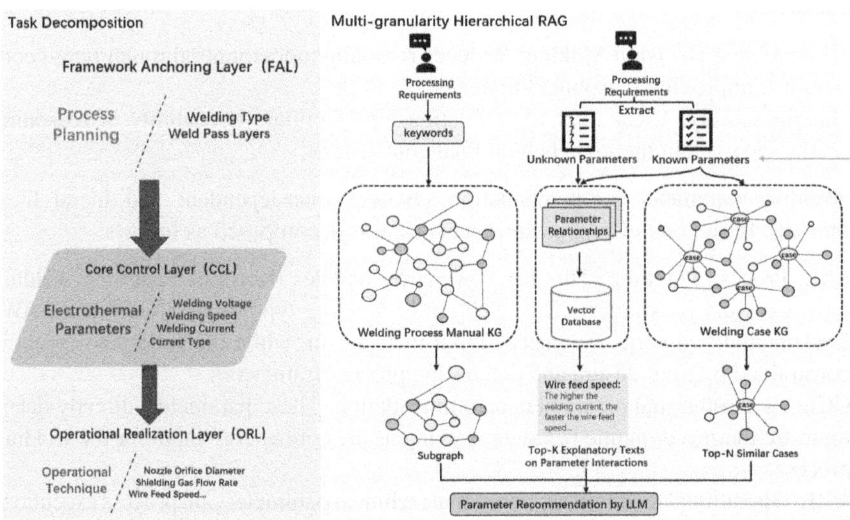

Fig. 3. The overall architecture of the multi-granularity hierarchical RAG. At each layer (left), multi-granularity hierarchical retrieval augmentation (right) is performed, and the obtained results are accumulated into the known parameters to continue reasoning at subsequent layers.

4 Experiments and Analysis

4.1 Wecommend Dataset

We introduce Wecommend (**We**lding Parameter Re**commend**ation), a dataset constructed with guidance from welding experts. In Wecommend, welding parameters are categorized into input and output parameters. The dataset includes 1009 sets of real-world welding production data, along with 177 sets of standardized process parameters extracted from two authoritative sources: Welding Process Manual and Welding Process Theory and Technology. In total, Wecommend comprises 1186 valid parameter configurations, covering 9 materials, 13 joint groove types, 8 welding positions, and 12 shielding gas types.

4.2 Experimental Settings

Baselines. To evaluate the proposed method, we compare it with four baseline approaches: NaiveRAG [23], Zero-shot CoT [24], LightRAG [25], and GraphRAG [12].

Metrics. Given the characteristics of the welding parameter recommendation task, we calculate the accuracy of recommended parameters:

$$\text{Accuracy} = \frac{\sum s_{t_i} + \sum s_{n_j}}{N} \tag{8}$$

where s_{t_i} denotes the score of the i-th textual parameter, and s_{n_j} denotes the score of the j-th numeric parameter. And N is the total number of parameters. Textual parameters are evaluated via semantic matching, while numeric parameters are categorized into two types: interval parameters that must fall within specified ranges, and fixed-value parameters assessed by comparing errors against dynamically determined thresholds. The evaluation results were empirically validated and demonstrated consistency with expert judgments.

Implementation Details We locally deployed four open-source LLMs of different scales using Ollama: deepseek-r1:7b, deepseek-r1:32b, qwen2:7b, and qwq:32b. Given the Chinese corpus, we selected bge-large-zh-v1.5 as the embedding model. For baseline settings, we implemented GraphRAG in local mode and LightRAG in hybrid mode. We conducted all the experiments on five NVIDIA RTX 4090 GPUs.

4.3 Results and Analysis

The main results are shown in Table 1 and reveal the following findings:

(1) Our method outperformed baselines in nearly all scenarios, demonstrating that our task decomposition framework and multi-granularity hierarchical RAG method effectively enhance reasoning capabilities for welding parameter recommendations.

(2) Methods relying solely on text retrieval (NaiveRAG) or graph-based retrieval (LightRAG/GraphRAG) were less effective in parameter recommendation. This is likely because these methods struggle to capture the complex interdependencies among process parameters, encompassing both physical constraints and process-specific dependencies. Our multi-granularity hierarchical RAG addresses this challenge through a three-layer architecture: FAL anchors reasoning paths using prior knowledge of welding types and joint designs, CCL implements sensitivity analyses of electrical parameters, and ORL adjusts operational parameters dynamically.
(3) Our method achieves consistent performance improvements across LLM scales, with particularly pronounced gains for smaller models. This demonstrates that task decomposition reduces cognitive load for smaller models, while hierarchical retrieval compensates for their limited world knowledge via parameter relationships, case studies, and process manuals.

Table 1. The experimental results on Wecommend dataset. The best value in each column is marked in bold.

Method	deepseek-r1:7b	deepseek-r1:32b	qwen2:7b	qwq:32b
NaiveRAG	8.45%	41.41%	12.39%	62.25%
Zero-shot COT	8.45%	38.87%	12.39%	59.15%
LightRAG	5.35%	31.36%	7.32%	44.51%
GraphRAG	47.32%	14.37%	6.20%	14.08%
Ours	**47.89%**	**85.63%**	**68.73%**	**89.86%**

4.4 Ablation Study

The ablation study was conducted to assess the effectiveness of our task decomposition module. By removing the task decomposition module, the LLM generates recommendations of all process parameters in one time through retrieval augmentation from the case knowledge graph and process knowledge graph. As demonstrated in Table 2, the absence of the hierarchical reasoning framework significantly degrades performance across all tested LLMs. These results validate that our proposed task decomposition framework effectively mitigates cognitive overload by breaking the monolithic task into sequential subtasks, enabling systematic integration of multi-granularity knowledge.

Table 2. Results of ablation study on Wecommend dataset.

Method	deepseek-r1:7b	deepseek-r1:32b	qwen2:7b	qwq:32b
w.o. task decomposition module	15.49%	67.60%	15.21%	85.91%
Ours	42.42%	85.63%	47.04%	89.86%

We further investigated the impact of the Top-K knowledge selection in the parameter relationship retrieval. By fixing other modules and varying K, results reveal critical trade-offs between knowledge coverage and noise interference, as show in Fig. 4. Excessively large K values introduce low-relevance or redundant parameter rules, causing decision-making confusion in the model.

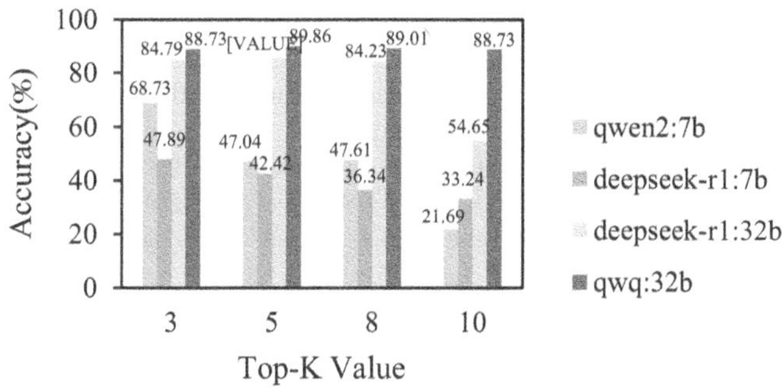

Fig. 4. Experimental results under different K values in Top-K parameter relationship retrieval.

5 Conclusion

This study presents a multi-granularity hierarchical RAG framework to address the challenges of welding parameter recommendation. By decomposing the task into three reasoning layers and integrating multi-granularity knowledge retrieval at every layer, the framework effectively captures explicit and implicit correlations among welding parameters. Experimental validation on the Wecommend dataset confirms its effectiveness: achieving 89.86% accuracy (outperforming all baselines) with ablation studies showing 17.9% performance drop when removing task decomposition. The approach enhances decision-making transparency and knowledge reuse, offering a robust solution for intelligent welding process recommendation.

Acknowledgements. This study was funded by the National Key Research and Development Program of China (grant number 2023YFB4704500).

Disclosure of Interests. The authors have no competing interests to declare that are relevant to the content of this article.

References

1. Barton, D., Gönnheimer, P., Schade, F., et al.: Modular smart controller for Industry 4.0 functions in machine tools. Procedia CIRP, **81**, 1331–1336 (2019)
2. Qamar, S.Z., Al-Hinai, N., Márquez, F.P.G.: Quality control and quality assurance: techniques and applications. BoD–Books on Demand (2024)
3. Deng, J., Liu, G., Wang, L., et al.: Research progress of intelligent optimization design of manufacturing process parameters. Manuf. Technol. Mach. Tool. **5** (2023)

4. Zhang, P., Liu, G., Wang, Y., et al.: Optimization of investment casting parameters for reduction of shrinkage porosity in nickel-based superalloy castings by taguchi method. Int. J. Mod. Phys. B **35**(10), 1–8 (2021)
5. Fabregat, A., Korninger, F., Viteri, G., et al.: Reactome graph database: efficient access to complex pathway data. PLoS Comput. Biol. **14**(1), e1005968 (2018)
6. Ouyang, L., Wu, J., Jiang, X., et al.: Training language models to follow instructions with human feedback. Adv. Neural. Inf. Process. Syst. **35**, 27730–27744 (2022)
7. Guo, D., Yang, D., Zhang, H., et al.: Deepseek-r1: incentivizing reasoning capability in LLMs via reinforcement learning. arXiv preprint arXiv:2501.12948 (2025)
8. Pan, S., Luo, L., Wang, Y., et al.: Unifying large language models and knowledge graphs: a roadmap. IEEE Trans. Knowl. Data Eng. (2024)
9. Lewis, P., Perez, E., Piktus, A., et al.: Retrieval-augmented generation for knowledge-intensive NLP tasks. Adv. Neural. Inf. Process. Syst. **33**, 9459–9474 (2020)
10. Izacard, G., Lewis, P., Lomeli, M., et al.: Atlas: few-shot learning with retrieval augmented language models. J. Mach. Learn. Res. **24**(251), 1–43 (2023)
11. Borgeaud, S., Mensch, A., Hoffmann, J., et al.: Improving language models by retrieving from trillions of tokens. In: International Conference on Machine Learning, pp. 2206–2240. PMLR (2022)
12. Edge, D., Trinh, H., Cheng, N., et al.: From local to global: a graph rag approach to query-focused summarization. arXiv preprint arXiv:2404.16130 (2024)
13. Pang, Y.F., Fu, G.Y., Wang, M.Y., et al.: Parameter optimization of high deposition rate laser cladding based on the response surface method and genetic neural network model. Chin. J. Lasers **48**(6), 0602112 (2021)
14. Alkayem, N.F., Parida, B., Pal, S.: Optimization of friction stir welding process parameters using soft computing techniques. Soft. Comput. **21**(23), 7083–7098 (2017)
15. Hu, H.Y., Yang, J.D., Tian, C.L.: The research on parameter optimization of power battery pack welding based on neural network. In: 2016 International Conference on Robots & Intelligent System (ICRIS), pp. 457–460. IEEE (2016)
16. Shu, F.H.: Aluminum-zinc alloy squeeze casting technological parameters optimization based on PSO and ANN. China Foundry **4**(3), 202–205 (2007)
17. Mei, Y., Xue, M.: Optimization of injection molding process parameters based on GA-ELM-GA[C]. MATEC Web of Conf. EDP Sci. **355**, 01029 (2022)
18. Matsumoto, N., Moran, J., Choi, H., et al.: KRAGEN: a knowledge graph-enhanced RAG framework for biomedical problem solving using large language models. Bioinformatics, **40**(6), btae353 (2024)
19. Gutiérrez, B.J., Shu, Y., Gu, Y., et al.: Hipporag: neurobiologically inspired long-term memory for large language models. In: The Thirty-Eighth Annual Conference on Neural Information Processing Systems (2024)
20. Huang, Z., Li, J., Jin, L., et al.: Reliable academic conference question answering: a study based on large language model. In: China Conference on Knowledge Graph and Semantic Computing, pp. 181–193. Springer, Singapore (2024)
21. Yihan, X., Tong, Y., Jinghua, L., et al.: Development of an intelligent Chinese medicine Q&A system based on traditional Chinese medicine knowledge graph and large language models. In: China Conference on Knowledge Graph and Semantic Computing, pp. 337–346. Springer, Singapore (2024)
22. Wei, J., Wang, X., Schuurmans, D., et al.: Chain-of-thought prompting elicits reasoning in large language models. Adv. Neural. Inf. Process. Syst. **35**, 24824–24837 (2022)

23. Gao, Y., Xiong, Y., Gao, X., et al.: Retrieval-augmented generation for large language models: A survey. arXiv preprint arXiv:2312.10997 (2023)
24. Kojima, T., Gu, S.S., Reid, M., et al.: Large language models are zero-shot reasoners. Adv. Neural. Inf. Process. Syst. **35**, 22199–22213 (2022)
25. Guo, Z., Xia, L., Yu, Y., et al.: Lightrag: simple and fast retrieval-augmented generation (2024)

Lag-Relative Sparse Attention in Long Context Training

Manlai Liang, Wanyi Huang, Mandi Liu, Huaijun Li, and Jinlong Li(✉)

AI Lab, China Merchants Bank, Shenzhen, China
{liangml,huang_wanyi,mandil,lihuaijun,lucida}@cmbchina.com

Abstract. Large Language Models (LLMs) have made significant strides in natural language processing and generation, yet their ability to handle long-context input remains constrained by the quadratic complexity of attention computation and linear-increasing key-value memory footprint. To reduce computational costs and memory, key-value cache compression techniques are commonly applied at inference time, but this often leads to severe performance degradation, as models are not trained to handle compressed context. Although there are more sophisticated compression methods, they are typically unsuitable for post-training because of their incompatibility with gradient-based optimization or high computation overhead. To fill this gap with no additional parameter and little computation overhead, we propose Lag-Relative Sparse Attention (LRSA) anchored by the LagKV compression method for long context post-training. Our method performs chunk-by-chunk prefilling, which selects the top K most relevant key-value pairs in a fixed-size lagging window, allowing the model to focus on salient historical context while maintaining efficiency. Experimental results show that our approach significantly enhances the robustness of the LLM with key-value compression and achieves better fine-tuned results in the question-answer tuning task.

Keywords: Sparse Attention · Long-Context Learning · KV Cache Compression

1 Introduction

Large Language Models (LLMs) have demonstrated impressive capabilities in a wide range of tasks, including dialogue, summarization, code generation, and multistep reasoning [2,20]. As their applications expand, there is a growing need for LLMs to process much longer contexts, such as entire documents, large codebases, and multi-turn conversations, to support more complex and realistic use cases. However, the ability of current models to scale to long-context inputs is fundamentally limited by the quadratic complexity of self-attention with respect to sequence length [33]. To mitigate these costs, compression techniques such as truncation, token merging, and memory selection are often applied during inference [11,27,32]. Although these methods can extend the usable context window,

J. Liang et al. (Eds.): CCKS 2025, CCIS 2698, pp. 68–79, 2026.
https://doi.org/10.1007/978-981-95-8525-0_6

they frequently lead to a significant drop in model performance because the underlying models are not trained to handle compressed inputs.

A common workaround for memory bottlenecks in long-context scenarios is to apply key-value (KV) cache compression in inference time [7], selectively retaining only a portion of past tokens. While such heuristics can reduce memory usage and computation burden, they often lead to notable performance degradation, especially in tasks requiring precise recall of earlier content [12]. This is largely because models are not trained to operate with compressed contexts, resulting in a mismatch between training and inference behavior. Various long-context compression techniques have been proposed to reduce inference-time memory and computation, such as sparse attention, retrieval-based memory, or low-rank approximations. But these methods are rarely integrated into the post-training process [13,19,31], either due to their incompatibility with gradient-based optimization or their high computational cost during training.

To address this train–test mismatch, we propose Lag-Relative Sparse Attention (LRSA), a novel attention mechanism anchored by the LagKV compression method [16] designed specifically for long-context post-training. Unlike the prior methods, LSRA introduces a structured sparsity pattern that operates in a chunk-wise manner, where each new input chunk selectively attends to a top-K subset of historical key-value pairs from a fixed-size lagging window. This iterative selection process ensures that only the most relevant past information is considered as the sequences progresses, enabling scalable long-context training. Importantly, our design ensures differentiability and efficiency during training, enabling the model to learn how to operate under this sparsified context directly.

We implement our algorithm within the Megatron [22,25] and MindSpeedLLM framework [9], a framework for training large-scale language models.

2 Related Works

2.1 Token Eviction and Context Compression

Most large language models (LLMs) are entirely based on the self-attention mechanism [30] to assess the relevance of historical tokens to predict the next token. As a result, many KV compression and token eviction strategies are designed around attention-based heuristics, which identify and drop less important tokens [15,17,21,38]. These approaches often maintain strong performance even at high compression ratios. However, their effectiveness often depends on access to the final query or instruction to compute accurate importance scores [6,14,28]. More importantly, attention-based eviction is fundamentally incompatible with FlashAttention (FA) [4], which precomputes attention in a way that does not allow selective token dropping based on attention scores. This incompatibility makes such methods impractical for real-world deployment, especially in long-context scenarios where FA is essential for efficient inference.

2.2 Sparse Attention

The high computational cost of full attention has motivated the development of sparse attention mechanisms that reduce complexity while preserving model quality. Early work such as Sparse Transformer [3] introduced fixed attention patterns that skip irrelevant positions, while later methods like BigBird [36] and Longformer [1] use global + local patterns to maintain scalability. More adaptive approaches, including SnapKV [15] and AnchorAttention [37], dynamically prune KV pairs based on cumulative attention scores. Despite improvements, these strategies often focus on inference time efficiency and are rarely integrated into the pre-training process, limiting their robustness under compressed conditions. StreamingLLM [34] and FlexPrefill [10] demonstrate further inference optimizations by discarding intermediate tokens or dynamically selecting patterns, but remain inference-only solutions and lack global selection mechanisms. Meanwhile, Native Sparse Attention (NSA) [35] injects compressed information through a gating mechanism that will introduce additional parameters.

2.3 Positional Embeddings

Rotary Position Embeddings (RoPE) [26] have emerged as a powerful alternative to traditional absolute or learned positional embeddings. RoPE encodes position information directly into the attention mechanism via complex rotation, enabling models to generalize better to longer contexts and support extrapolation. Recent works such as YaRN [23] and LongRoPE [5] have explored modifications to RoPE for further extension of context windows. Our approach inherits standard RoPE but adapts its scaling and interpolation to maintain stability under long sequences and varying token eviction schedules.

3 Method

In this section, we present LRSA, Lag-Relative Sparse Attention, which extends LagKV compression from model inference to model training.

3.1 Preliminaries

LLMs' next token prediction relies on the previous tokens. First, in the prefill stage, the model uses its tokenizer to convert the words to n indices of the embedding metrics $E \in \mathbb{R}^{V \times d}$ of the model and collects the representations to form a input matrix, $X \in \mathbb{R}^{n \times d}$. This matrix is the initial tokens of the first layer of LLM and then each layer will output a same shape matrix as next layer's input. To depict the operations in each layer, we follow the notation system from [?] with h attention heads. For each head $i \in [1, h]$ and head dimension d_h, we focus on the Query, Key, and Value states, which are converted from tokens by three linear transformation matrices W_i^Q, W_i^K, $W_i^V \in \mathbb{R}^{d \times d_h}$ separately:

$$Q_i = XW_i^Q, K_i = XW_i^K, V_i = XW_i^V \tag{1}$$

The output $Y \in \mathbb{R}^{n \times d}$ is computed using the attention weights $A_i \in \mathbb{R}^{n \times n}$ and the final output matrix $W^O \in \mathbb{R}^{d \times d}$:

$$Y = Concat_{i \in [1,h]}(A_i V_i) W^O, \tag{2}$$

$$A_i = \text{softmax}(\frac{Q_i K_i^T}{\sqrt{d_h}} + M_i). \tag{3}$$

where A_i is the attention weight and M_i is the attention masked matrix. The masked elements of M_i will be filled by negative infinite to eliminate the impaction of unselected tokens. In LLM where predicting tokens on preceding tokens, the masked matrix is a triangular matrix with the upper triangle masked out.

3.2 LRSA

In the work of LagKV [16], it proposes to use the lag-relative information to determine the importance of historical tokens. The LagKV token importance score is relying on the token-wise min-max from the subsequent KV chunk to normalize the current one as the following equations:

$$min_i^{p,Z} = min_{seq}(Z_i^{p+1}) \tag{4}$$

$$max_i^{p,Z} = max_{seq}(Z_i^{p+1}) \tag{5}$$

$$\bar{Z}_i^p = \frac{Z_i^p - min_i^{p,Z}}{max_i^{p,Z} - min_i^{p,Z}} \tag{6}$$

$$score(Z_i) = Softmax(Std.(\bar{Z}_i)) \tag{7}$$

$$score_i = score(K_i) + score(V_i) \tag{8}$$

where the KV sequence is divided into sink part with size S and chunks with lag size L, Z is one of $\{K, V\}$, p denotes the chunk index, i represents the attention head index and seq for the sequence axis. Based on $score_i$ and the retention ratio r, select the top rL tokens to remain in the KV cache to complete the compression process.

The LagKV work also demonstrates that prefilling long contexts in a chunk-by-chunk manner not only preserves the model's core capabilities but also enhances efficiency by reducing the number of tokens involved in attention computation. Following their approach, the LRSA mask matrix takes the form like Fig. 1.

For efficiency, the prefilling process processes multiple chunks simultaneously. The number of filling chunks can be optimized up to different hardware and context lengths. For instance, with two chunks at a time:

- **Attention Filling 1 (Attn-Fill 1):** The sink portion and two lag-sized KV segments are fed into the attention calculation. The attention mask is a full-size matrix with the upper triangle masked out. Meanwhile, the KV cache is updated with the first chunk compressed and the second chunk retained as a sliding window.

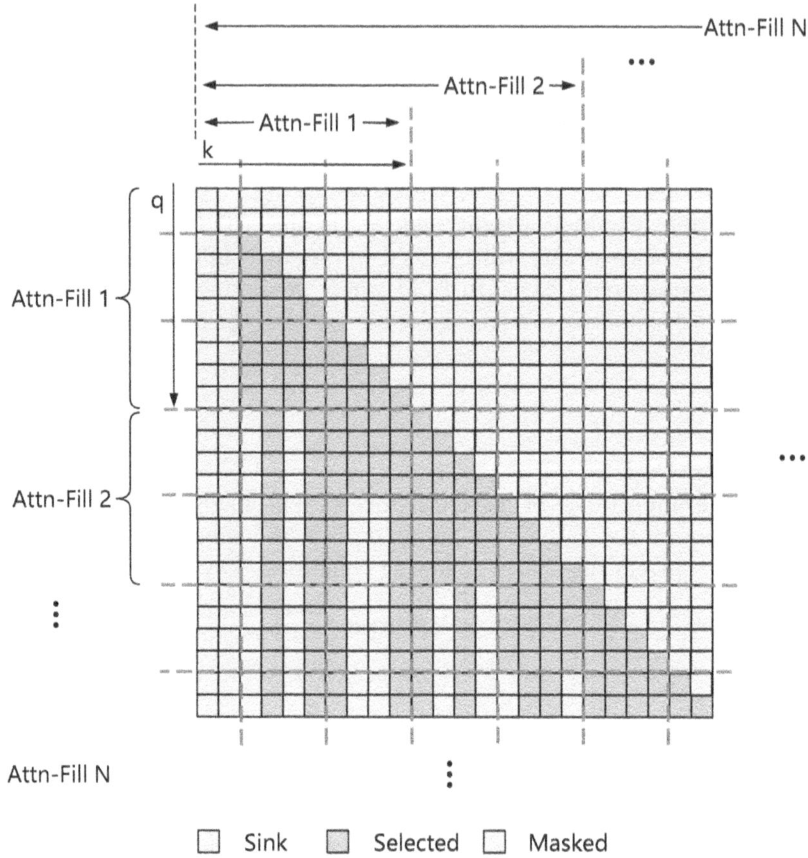

Fig. 1. Lag-Relative Sparse Attention: Chunked-Mask is generated by the LagKV algorithm.

- **Attention Filling 2 (Attn-Fill 2):** The next two chunks are concatenated to the compressed KV cache. The third chunk's queries require no additional masking, while the fourth chunk's queries are masked for the second chunk's portion. The masked indices are provided by the new compression process.
- **Repeat** step 2 until all chunks processed.

Our masking strategy differs fundamentally from approaches like NSA [35] or Quest [29]. Their masking is query-dependent, requiring all key-value (KV) pairs to remain in the cache since different queries may attend to different KVs. In contrast, LRSA employs a static mask for subsequent query chunks because the LagKV scoring method is entirely query-independent. This masking strategy allows the KV cache to be condensed shorter.

4 Experiment

4.1 Setups

Models. Our evaluation is conducted on Qwen2.5-1.5B-Base [24], which support up to 32K context length in their pre-trained form. We applied the same evaluation framework to the pre-trained form without fine-tuning and the fine-tuned form to make a fairly comparison.

Benchmark. We evaluate the models with RULER [8], which generates synthetic examples to evaluate long-context language models with configurable sequence length and task complexity.

Datasets. We create the pre-training datasets using four datasets open-sourced by LongAlign and LongLora. Here are the basic information of the four basic datasets:

1. THUDM/LongAlign-10k This dataset includes 10,000 long-text tasks, with approximately 10% of the samples written in Chinese.
2. Yukang/LongAlpaca-12k LongAlpaca comprises 12,000 long-text tasks, LongAlpaca primarily focuses on reading comprehension of academic papers, with a mix of shorter samples included to maintain dataset balance.
3. wenbopan/RefGPT-Fact-v2-8x is an expanded version of the Mutonix/RefGPT-Fact-v2 dataset, which features high-quality conversations centered on document extraction and understanding. Since the original dataset was relatively short, additional longer samples were synthesized to enhance its length.
4. wenbopan/anti-haystack is a set of long-text tasks generated using GPT-4, emphasizing symbolic reasoning, accurate fact recall, and precise paragraph referencing.

The datasets are structured in a question–answer format. Since not all data samples naturally reach the target length of 32K tokens, we perform synthetic augmentation to extend their lengths. Specifically, we categorize samples into length-based groups. For samples that fall short of 32K tokens, we randomly select supplementary paragraphs from longer samples within the same or compatible groups. To preserve semantic coherence and ensure the consistency of the question content, we prepend a new document section and use the delimiter "Document" to clearly separate concatenated texts.

Baselines. We evaluate two baseline models to assess the effectiveness of our proposed training strategy: (i) **Qwen2.5-1.5B-base**, the original pretrained model without any additional fine-tuning; (ii) Fine-tuned **Qwen2.5-1.5B-base**, which is trained on our curated dataset without applying any compression algorithm.

Implementation. All experiments are conducted on Ascend 910B NPU with 64GB memory, leveraging parallelisms implemented in the Megatron distributed training framework. We use the following fine-tuning hyperparameters:

- 4000 iterations with global batch size of 16.
- Train in bfloat16 precision with a learning rate of 1.25e-5 without the warm-up stage and then decayed to 0 throughout training following a cosine schedule.
- Use the AdamW optimizer [18] with $\beta1 = 0.9$, $\beta2 = 0.95$ and a weight decay of $1e - 1$.
- For the configuration of LagKV compression, delay size $L = 1024$ and retention ratio $r = 0.5$.

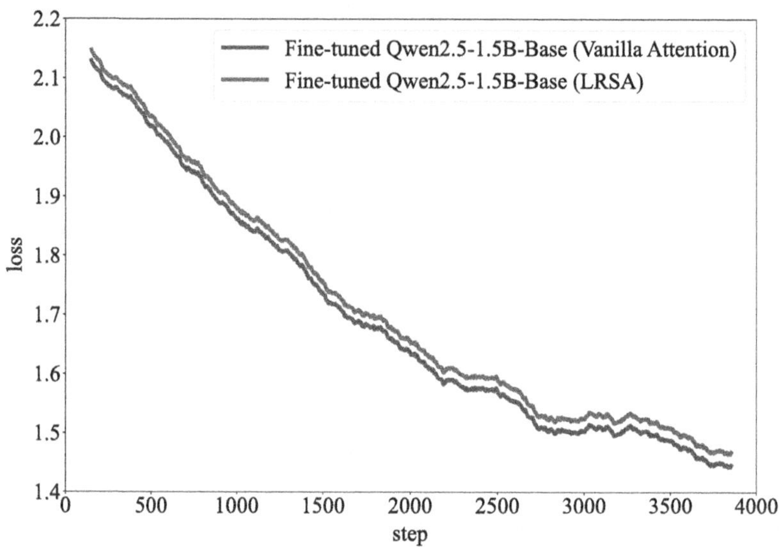

Fig. 2. Training Loss of Fine-tuned Qwen2.5-1.5B-Base (w/o LRSA) (Color figure online)

4.2 Training Loss

Figure 2 compares the training loss curves of two fine-tuned Qwen2.5-1.5B-Base models: one using standard full attention (blue) and the other employing our proposed Lag-Relative Sparse Attention (LRSA, red). Both models are trained on the same dataset and under identical training conditions. Although the LRSA-enhanced model shows a slightly higher loss throughout the training process, the gap remains small and stable. This shows that our sparse attention mechanism can be integrated into training without causing significant degradation in convergence, thus enabling efficient long-context modeling while maintaining training stability.

4.3 RULER Benchmark

The main results on the RULER benchmark are presented in Table 1.

Table 1. Results of RULER benchmark.

Model	Method	NS1	NS2	NS3	NMK1	NMK2	NMK3	NMV	NMQ	VT	CWE	FWE	QA1	QA2
Qwen2.5-1.5B-Base	L_S = 4k, r = 1x, L = 128	100.0	100.0	100.0	99.4	97	81.2	96.9	62.3	92.4	68.4	75.73	71.8	42.4
	L_S = 4k, r = 2x, L = 128	100.0	94.0	25.0	85.2	44.4	3.6	87.5	56.6	91.2	40.0	71.6	63.2	36.2
	L_S = 4k, r = 4x, L = 128	98.6	64.0	4.2	62.6	16.4	0.2	54.1	39.1	90.6	15.5	59.5	56.6	31.4
	L_S = 8k, r = 1x, L = 256	100.0	100.0	100.0	97.6	92.0	69.6	93.6	79.1	87.4	25.8	65.6	52.8	38
	L_S = 8k, r = 2x, L = 256	100.0	96.8	52.8	87.8	35.0	5.6	86.9	65.7	86.6	18.6	59.7	45.6	36.2
	L_S = 8k, r = 4x, L = 256	99.2	66.2	10.0	64.6	15.0	1.2	55.7	43.7	90.3	10.4	49.8	36.8	28.4
	L_S = 16k, r = 1x, L = 512	100.0	100.0	99.8	98.0	83.2	69.0	89.9	87.6	83.6	20.6	74.1	49.6	37.2
	L_S = 16k, r = 2x, L = 512	100.0	91.4	44.4	82.8	23.0	8.4	82.8	73.0	88.5	7.1	70.7	43.0	33.4
	L_S = 16k, r = 4x, L = 512	99.8	73.8	14.0	60.0	7.2	1.6	62.8	52.0	87.4	3.4	65.9	33.6	31.2
	L_S = 32k, r = 1x, L = 1024	100.0	98.8	99.4	92.2	76.6	44.2	80.9	74.0	83.3	3.7	65.1	46.2	36.0
	L_S = 32k, r = 2x, L = 1024	100.0	92.8	41.0	78.8	20.2	6.0	69.6	68.6	87.0	3.2	67.7	34.8	31.2
	L_S = 32k, r = 4x, L = 1024	98.4	72.2	10.8	59.0	5.0	1.8	47.1	44.4	81.7	1.0	62.9	28.2	28.8
Qwen2.5-1.5B-Base (Fine-tuned by Vanilla Attention)	L_S = 4k, r = 1x, L = 128	100.0	99.8	99.8	98.6	94.0	81.6	92.5	62.3	93.8	47.6	73.3	76.4	44.8
	L_S = 4k, r = 2x, L = 128	99.4	92.8	25.0	82.6	43.0	6.0	78.4	55.9	92.5	34.8	67.5	66.2	40.2
	L_S = 4k, r = 4x, L = 128	99.0	62.6	4.8	49.6	12.2	0.2	37.9	27.7	90.0	18.1	55.6	53.2	33.8
	L_S = 8k, r = 1x, L = 256	100.0	99.8	99.8	94.6	86.8	65.6	85.6	67.3	62.4	22.3	62.8	57.6	41.8
	L_S = 8k, r = 2x, L = 256	100.0	95.0	45.4	78.6	32.0	6.6	76.6	59.2	68.8	21.8	55.2	48.6	34.6
	L_S = 8k, r = 4x, L = 256	99.6	70.6	10.8	47.4	12.6	2.6	43.2	32.8	80.8	12.1	46.4	36.4	31.0
	L_S = 16k, r = 1x, L = 512	100.0	99.6	99.4	88.6	72.8	50.6	83.2	62.4	61.2	8.5	70.2	57.6	38.0
	L_S = 16k, r = 2x, L = 512	99.6	91.8	38.4	67.0	21.0	7.8	73.6	57.0	79.8	9.2	69.8	46.8	34.0
	L_S = 16k, r = 4x, L = 512	99.6	69.2	8.2	48.4	6.8	4.6	47.7	37.4	74.6	5.2	60.0	36.4	28.4
	L_S = 32k, r = 1x, L = 1024	100.0	99.4	98.2	85.4	57.6	30.6	72.9	54.8	52.9	8.2	64.6	42.4	34.4
	L_S = 32k, r = 2x, L = 1024	100.0	90.4	31.6	73.0	15.4	5.4	55.0	44.0	65.2	7.7	67.3	34.8	31.6
	L_S = 32k, r = 4x, L = 1024	99.8	65.8	6.8	44.2	6.6	3.4	35.1	27.5	72.8	5.8	60.1	30.0	28.2
Qwen2.5-1.5B-Base (Fine-tuned by LRSA)	L_S = 4k, r = 1x, L = 128	100.0	99.8	100.0	97.6	96.8	88.8	44.2	63.6	95.7	49.3	73.9	74.0	45.0
	L_S = 4k, r = 2x, L = 128	100.0	96.0	53.0	91.2	62.4	17.6	85.7	59.6	90.8	39.1	71.5	66.4	43.0
	L_S = 4k, r = 4x, L = 128	99.2	80.6	4.4	68.0	27.4	1.0	53.4	41.9	92.5	23.4	60.7	56.4	35.6
	L_S = 8k, r = 1x, L = 256	100.0	100.0	99.6	94.2	89.0	79.8	79.6	63.5	62.4	21.2	61.3	54.6	42.0
	L_S = 8k, r = 2x, L = 256	100.0	99.0	65.4	87.6	53.2	17.2	77.9	60.7	61.7	22.7	58.4	53.6	37.0
	L_S = 8k, r = 4x, L = 256	99.8	86.6	20.4	67.6	23.0	1.6	58.5	42.0	88.8	14.8	51.2	39.8	31.6
	L_S = 16k, r = 1x, L = 512	100.0	99.4	99.6	85.4	70.6	64.0	76.3	63.7	57.2	4.4	73.8	56.4	40.2
	L_S = 16k, r = 2x, L = 512	100.0	98.6	56.8	77.6	35.4	17.2	74.8	59.5	70.24	4.7	72.1	50.4	38.8
	L_S = 16k, r = 4x, L = 512	100.0	80.6	18.0	55.2	13.2	5.6	58.7	43.9	76.4	3.1	69.8	40.4	31.2
	L_S = 32k, r = 1x, L = 1024	100.0	94.0	95.6	78.6	54.8	56.4	63.1	49.3	50.1	3.0	70.0	46.2	37.2
	L_S = 32k, r = 2x, L = 1024	100.0	94.0	47.2	75.2	21.6	14.2	56.6	46.0	58.8	3.0	70.8	41.0	34.2
	L_S = 32k, r = 4x, L = 1024	100.0	80.4	18.0	56.6	7.8	3.6	45.2	33.7	66.8	3.1	70.1	31.6	27.4

Note: L_S represents the context length, r represents the retention ratio, and L represents the lag size.

Figure 3 and Fig. 4 show the performance of different Qwen2.5-1.5B variants on question-answer (QA) tasks and overall synthetic tasks, respectively, under varying compression ratios and input sequence lengths. Several key insights can be drawn from these results:

- In the specific QA training task, Fig. 3 shows that LRSA consistently outperforms Vanilla attention with or without compression. It demonstrates that LRSA can effectively achieve better training results with fewer tokens attendance, even the loss is slightly higher.
- LRSA improves the robustness of compression. The fine-tuned model with LRSA shows a considerably slower performance degradation as the compression ratio times increase from $1\times$ to $4\times$ in RULER and specific QA tasks. For

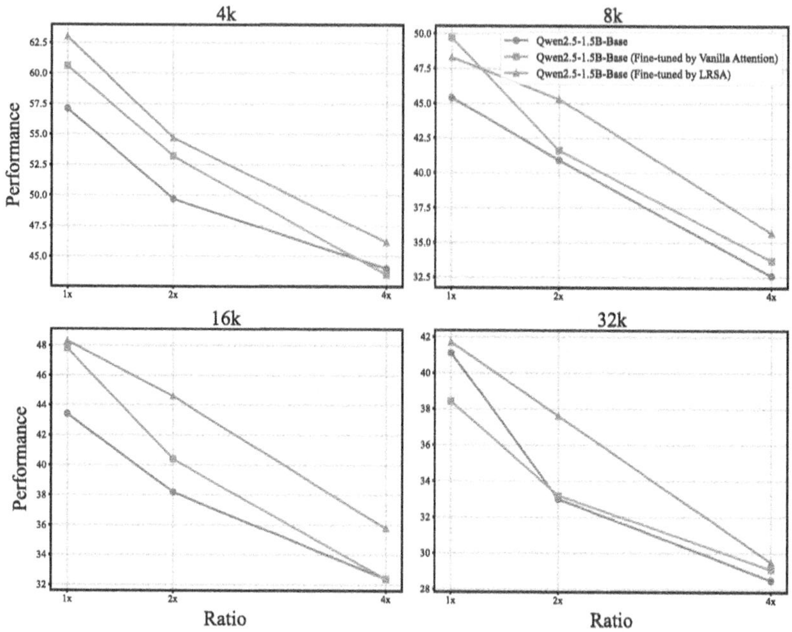

Fig. 3. Question-Answer-focused Statistics from RULER benchmark

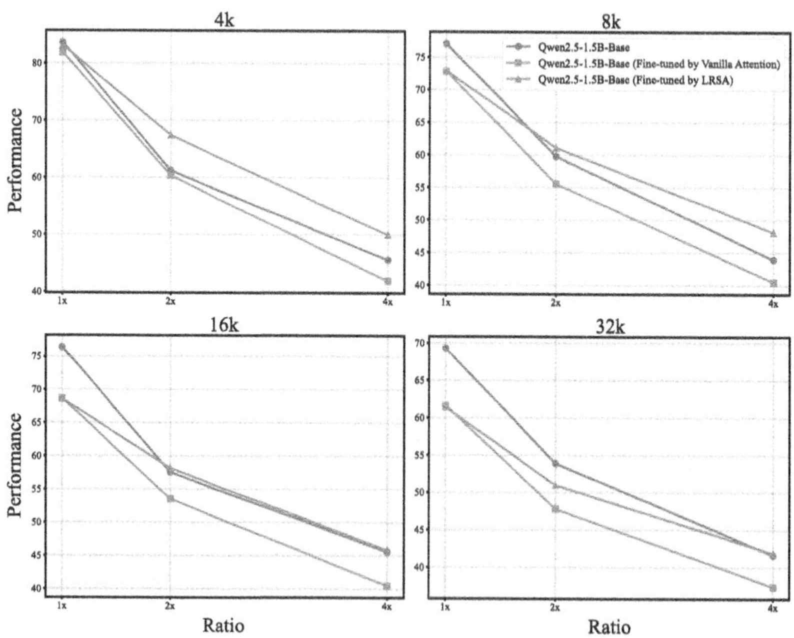

Fig. 4. Average Statistics of RULER benchmark

example, at 8k and 16k input sequence lengths, it maintains a clear margin above the others at both 2× and 4× compression. This indicates that LRSA helps the model to better adapt to compressed-memory scenarios by teaching it to prioritize and retain salient tokens during training.
- Quality of our QA-aligned fine-tuning dataset. Both fine-tuned models surpass the base model, reflecting the strength of the QA-style instruction dataset.

5 Conclusion

In this work, we introduce Lag-Relative Sparse Attention (LRSA), a lightweight, plug-in-go, and effective post-training mechanism tailored for long-context language modeling under memory-constrained conditions. Built upon the LagKV compression strategy, LRSA enables LLMs to selectively retain and attend to the most salient key-value pairs within a fixed size window, thereby reducing the memory and compute overhead of full attention while maintaining differentiability and training efficiency. The results of our experiments reveal that the fine-tuned model with LRSA outperforms the one with vanilla attention to QA-related evaluation sets. Moreover, the average score of the fine-tuned model with LRSA the RULER synthetic evaluation set is higher than that with vanilla attention. In addition, we show that integrating LRSA into the Megatron framework is feasible and stable, with only minimal impact on convergence behavior. These findings suggest that LRSA is a practical and generalizable solution for large scale models on the post-training stage to handle long-context input.

Disclosure of Interests. The authors have no competing interests to declare that are relevant to the content of this article.

References

1. Beltagy, I., Peters, M.E., Cohan, A.: LongFormer: the long-document transformer. arXiv preprint arXiv:2004.05150 (2020)
2. Chang, Y., et al.: A survey on evaluation of large language models. ACM Trans. Intell. Syst. Technol. **15**(3), 1–45 (2024)
3. Child, R., Gray, S., Radford, A., Sutskever, I.: Generating long sequences with sparse transformers. arXiv preprint arXiv:1904.10509 (2019)
4. Dao, T., Fu, D., Ermon, S., Rudra, A., Ré, C.: FlashAttention: fast and memory-efficient exact attention with io-awareness. Adv. Neural. Inf. Process. Syst. **35**, 16344–16359 (2022)
5. Ding, Y., et al.: LongRoPE: extending LLM context window beyond 2 million tokens. arXiv preprint arXiv:2402.13753 (2024)
6. Feng, Y., Lv, J., Cao, Y., Xie, X., Zhou, S.K.: Ada-KV: optimizing KV cache eviction by adaptive budget allocation for efficient LLM inference. arXiv preprint arXiv:2407.11550 (2024)

7. Ge, S., Zhang, Y., Liu, L., Zhang, M., Han, J., Gao, J.: Model tells you what to discard: adaptive KV cache compression for LLMs. arXiv preprint arXiv:2310.01801 (2023)
8. Hsieh, C.P., et al.: Ruler: what's the real context size of your long-context language models?. arXiv preprint arXiv:2404.06654 (2024)
9. HUAWEI: Ascend/mindspeed-LLM (2024). https://gitee.com/ascend/MindSpeed-LLM
10. Lai, X., Lu, J., Luo, Y., Ma, Y., Zhou, X.: FlexPrefill: a context-aware sparse attention mechanism for efficient long-sequence inference. arXiv preprint arXiv:2502.20766 (2025)
11. Li, D., Sun, Z., Hu, X., Hu, B., Zhang, M.: CMT: a memory compression method for continual knowledge learning of large language models. In: Proceedings of the AAAI Conference on Artificial Intelligence, vol. 39, pp. 24413–24421 (2025)
12. Li, H., et al.: A survey on large language model acceleration based on KV cache management. arXiv preprint arXiv:2412.19442 (2024)
13. Li, Y., et al.: LoSparse: structured compression of large language models based on low-rank and sparse approximation. In: International Conference on Machine Learning, pp. 20336–20350. PMLR (2023)
14. Li, Y., et al.: SCBench: a KV cache-centric analysis of long-context methods. arXiv preprint arXiv:2412.10319 (2024)
15. Li, Y., et al.: SnapKV: LLM knows what you are looking for before generation. Adv. Neural. Inf. Process. Syst. **37**, 22947–22970 (2024)
16. Liang, M., Zhang, J., Li, X., Li, J.: LagKV: lag-relative information of the KV cache tells which tokens are important (2025). https://arxiv.org/abs/2504.04704
17. Liu, Z., et al.: Scissorhands: exploiting the persistence of importance hypothesis for LLM KV cache compression at test time. Adv. Neural. Inf. Process. Syst. **36**, 52342–52364 (2023)
18. Loshchilov, I., Hutter, F.: Decoupled weight decay regularization. arXiv preprint arXiv:1711.05101 (2017)
19. Lou, C., Jia, Z., Zheng, Z., Tu, K.: Sparser is faster and less is more: efficient sparse attention for long-range transformers. arXiv preprint arXiv:2406.16747 (2024)
20. Naveed, H., et al.: A comprehensive overview of large language models. arXiv preprint arXiv:2307.06435 (2023)
21. NVIDIA: LLM KV cache compression made easy (2024). https://github.com/NVIDIA/kvpress
22. NVIDIA: Nvidia/megatron-LM (2024). https://github.com/NVIDIA/Megatron-LM
23. Peng, B., Quesnelle, J., Fan, H., Shippole, E.: YaRN: efficient context window extension of large language models. arXiv preprint arXiv:2309.00071 (2023)
24. Yang, A., et al.: Qwen2.5 technical report (2025). https://arxiv.org/abs/2412.15115
25. Shoeybi, M., Patwary, M., Puri, R., LeGresley, P., Casper, J., Catanzaro, B.: Megatron-LM: training multi-billion parameter language models using model parallelism. arXiv preprint arXiv:1909.08053 (2019)
26. Su, J., Ahmed, M., Lu, Y., Pan, S., Bo, W., Liu, Y.: RoFormer: enhanced transformer with rotary position embedding. Neurocomputing **568**, 127063 (2024)
27. Tan, X., et al.: TokenCarve: information-preserving visual token compression in multimodal large language models. arXiv preprint arXiv:2503.10501 (2025)
28. Tang, H., et al.: Razorattention: efficient KV cache compression through retrieval heads. arXiv preprint arXiv:2407.15891 (2024)

29. Tang, J., Zhao, Y., Zhu, K., Xiao, G., Kasikci, B., Han, S.: Quest: query-aware sparsity for efficient long-context LLM inference. In: Proceedings of the 41st International Conference on Machine Learning, ICML 2024. JMLR.org (2024)
30. Vaswani, A., et al.: Attention is all you need. Adv. Neural Inf. Process. Syst. **30** (2017)
31. Wang, Q., Fu, Y., Cao, Y., Wang, S., Tian, Z., Ding, L.: Recursively summarizing enables long-term dialogue memory in large language models. Neurocomputing **639**, 130193 (2025)
32. Wang, X., Zheng, Y., Wan, Z., Zhang, M.: SVD-LLM: truncation-aware singular value decomposition for large language model compression. arXiv preprint arXiv:2403.07378 (2024)
33. Wang, X., Salmani, M., Omidi, P., Ren, X., Rezagholizadeh, M., Eshaghi, A.: Beyond the limits: a survey of techniques to extend the context length in large language models. arXiv preprint arXiv:2402.02244 (2024)
34. Xiao, G., Tian, Y., Chen, B., Han, S., Lewis, M.: Efficient streaming language models with attention sinks. arXiv preprint arXiv:2309.17453 (2023)
35. Yuan, J., et al.: Native sparse attention: hardware-aligned and natively trainable sparse attention. arXiv preprint arXiv:2502.11089 (2025)
36. Zaheer, M., et al.: Big bird: transformers for longer sequences. Adv. Neural. Inf. Process. Syst. **33**, 17283–17297 (2020)
37. Zhang, Y., Guo, D., Wu, F., Zhu, G., Ding, D., Zhang, Y.: AnchorAttention: difference-aware sparse attention with stripe granularity. arXiv preprint arXiv:2505.23520 (2025)
38. Zhang, Z., et al.: H2O: heavy-hitter oracle for efficient generative inference of large language models. Adv. Neural. Inf. Process. Syst. **36**, 34661–34710 (2023)

VIKA: Vectorized Indispensable Knowledge-Subgraph Augmentation for Large Language Models

Bohan Xie[1], Shirui Wang[1], Ling Ding[2], Jianting Chen[1], and Yang Xiang[1(✉)]

[1] Tongji University, Shanghai 200000, China
{hey_bohan,shxiangyang}@tongji.edu.cn
[2] Shanghai Normal University, Shanghai 200000, China

Abstract. Retrieval Augmented Generation is an effective method that integrates language models with external knowledge sources to achieve better performance. However, they often face certain challenges when dealing with extremely complex tasks. For example, the amount of external knowledge might be excessively huge, creating difficulties for language models to handle long contexts. In addition, for questions involving graph data, how to enable the model to understand the graph structure is also a key issue, since the sequence modeling approach of language models differs significantly from the structure of graphs. In this paper, we propose a **V**ectorized **I**ndispensable **K**nowledge-subgraph **A**ugmentation (VIKA) method for large language models. We utilize the vectorized graph augmenting method to cover long contexts and integrate graph structure information through an adapter, which helps to maximize the inclusion of valuable knowledge. We add a hallucination detection module before retrieval and a comprehensive filtering method to avoid irrelevant disturbance and promote the quality of knowledge and the accuracy of enhancement. Experiments across three different tasks demonstrate that our method achieves significant improvements compared to other models.

Keywords: Retrieval Augmented Generation · Large Language Model · Knowledge Graph

1 Introduction

The retrieval augmented generation method (RAG) is proposed to augment LLM with the latest and domain-specific knowledge from knowledge sources, which helps to overcome hallucinationS of LLM [11]. Knowledge graphs (KGs), which store knowledge in the form of triples, have advantages in dynamic, explicit, and structured knowledge representation [17]. More and more researchers utilize KG as the knowledge source in RAG.

Some researchers have done much work, but there are still some limitations. Since there is a huge amount of knowledge in KG, increasing the amount and quality of knowledge provided to LLM becomes an essential issue. First, when

J. Liang et al. (Eds.): CCKS 2025, CCIS 2698, pp. 80–92, 2026.
https://doi.org/10.1007/978-981-95-8525-0_7

facing complex tasks such as multi-hop question answering, the contexts with knowledge injection can easily reach the limit of the maximum length. Also, once KGs are used as the external knowledge source, their graph-structured information should be fully leveraged because the rich interactions between entities can help LLMs answer correctly, but existing RAG methods can hardly achieve this. Furthermore, knowing when external knowledge is needed is also essential.

Building upon the challenges, we propose a method to provide Vectorized Indispensable Knowledge subgraph Augmentation (VIKA) for LLM. We derive vectorized graph context from implementing knowledge enhancement incorporating graph neighborhood information and overcoming the limitation of context length. During retrieval, we design a retriever with a comprehensive path-filtering criterion to construct the knowledge subgraph for the query. Additionally, we develop a preprocessing module to explore the inherent capabilities of LLM for hallucination detection and identify when to start retrieval, aiming to mitigate the irrelevance and noise from KG.

In summary, the main contributions of our work are as follows:

We propose a method incorporating vectorized graph augmentation for LLM to avoid overlong context and integrate graph structure information from KG.

We introduce a retrieval method on KG with a comprehensive path-filtering method, ensuring that external knowledge is both relevant and indispensable for the questions.

We design a preprocessing module to detect hallucinations through the model's internal states before retrieval and handle questions with specificity.

Experiments on three distinct tasks achieve significant improvements compared to existing models. Those results confirm that our method, VIKA, could enhance LLM's ability to answer questions.

2 Related Work

2.1 Knowledge Enhanced LLMs Within Text

Recent works translate the structural knowledge into textual prompts for LLMs. KB-Binder [13] provides a framework for LLM to complete KBQA tasks, in which LLM first generates data query statements and then fills them using KGs. CoK [14] decomposes the question into several sub-questions, then uses fine-tuned LLMs to generate corresponding SPARQL query statements. ToG [20] proposed a new tight-coupling paradigm where LLMs and KGs work together and complement each other's capabilities in each step of graph reasoning. [21] developed an observation-driven agent, which incorporates graph information via global observation, and enhances LLM capabilities through a cyclical paradigm of observation, action, and reflection. Despite the extensive research conducted by scholars in this field, there are still some limitations. They utilize textual prompts for knowledge injection, which could easily exceed the maximum length and pose challenges for models to handle overlong contexts.

2.2 Knowledge Enhanced LLMs Within Vectors

To enable RAG models to cover a longer context during both fine-tuning and inference stages, researchers proposed encoding the excessively long context and enhancing LLMs in the form of dense embeddings. Vectorized methods are used to retrieve more accurate knowledge based on queries [5], and now people are trying to introduce them to the augmentation stage and achieve remarkable performance. Some designed a small encoder and cross-attention mechanism to encode contexts effectively [4]. Some presented an effective context compression method to speed up the generation time by a large margin. [12]. However, once we utilize KG as the external knowledge base, it isn't enough to encode contexts in the form of sequences, because triples from KG include graph information, which is richer than the text itself.

3 Method

We first introduce the hallucination detection module before retrieval to reduce irrelevant information. Then, we provide a detailed description of how to retrieve with comprehensive filtering. Finally, we provide a detailed explanation of the vectorized graph-enhancement method (Fig. 1).

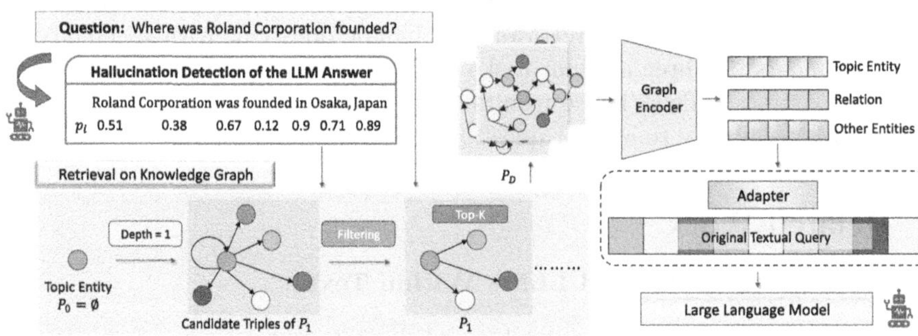

Fig. 1. The Framework of VIKA, where P_i means the paths we fine at depth i. We first perform hallucination detection to distinguish between difficult and easy problems. We retrieve and filter the knowledge paths for difficult questions and employ a graph structure adapter for enhancement.

3.1 Hallucination Detection

Hallucination Detection before retrieval helps LLMs to know whether the internal knowledge is sufficient to complete the questions. We calculate the confidence scores of LLM to assess whether hallucinations occur.

For a question q, we first let LLMs generate an answer a, including a sequence of tokens $a = token_0, token_1, ..., token_n$. The confidence of a is defined as (1), where p_i is the generation probability of $token_i$, which is extracted from the internal states of LLM.

$$confidence(a) = \frac{1}{-\sum_{0<i<n} p_i * log(p_i)} \tag{1}$$

The confidence score characterizes the degree of certainty that LLMs have regarding their answers. When the confidence score of a is below a predefined threshold θ, we consider LLMs to be uncertain, classifying q as a difficult one, which we use q_{diff} to indicate below. Conversely, it is classified as an easy question.

3.2 Retrieval with Comprehensive Siftings

For a difficult question q_{diff}, we retrieve knowledge paths from KG and construct the knowledge subgraph for enhancement. LLM is first asked to identify the topic entity of q_{diff}. We maintain the set of knowledge paths $P = \{path_1, path_2, \cdots, path_k\}$ throughout the whole construction process, which is empty initially. $path_i$ indicate the path ranked i-th in terms of scores. Define $path_i = \{(h_i^j, r_i^j, t_i^j)\}_{j=1}^{D}$, where (h_i^j, r_i^j, t_i^j) indicates to be the triple explored in j-th iteration and D is the maximum search depth.

The process of path exploration is as follows. At the start, we define h_1 and t_1 to be the topic entity of q_{diff}. At the beginning of the d-th iteration, each path $path_i$ contains $d-1$ triples, i.e., $path_i = \{(h_i^j, r_i^j, t_i^j)\}_{j=1}^{d-1}$. The path exploration first search out num_i^d triples with the form of $(?, r, t_i^{d-1})$, $(?, r, h_i^{d-1})$, $(t_i^{d-1}, r, ?)$ or $(h_i^{d-1}, r, ?)$. These newly acquired triples are added to the end of $path_i$, leading to num_i^d new paths with the length of d. Since we have the original k paths from the former iteration, the total number is $num_i^d + k$. After filtering, top-k paths are retained. As for the method of calculating filtering scores, we consider it from two perspectives: relevance and scarcity, reflecting the degree of relevance between external knowledge and the question and whether the external knowledge is already included in LLM. Relevance is calculated using the cosine similarity between embedding vectors of the question q_{diff} and the knowledge path $path_i$ in the language model, denoted as $rela^i$, shown as the (2):

$$rela^i = cos(LM(q_{diff}), LM(path_i)) \tag{2}$$

The scarcity of $path_i$, denoted as $scar^i$, can be computed based on each triple in it, as the (3), where $scar_j^i$ means the scarcity score of jth triple of path $path_i$.

$$scar^i = \frac{1}{D}\sum_{j=0}^{D} scar_j^i \tag{3}$$

To calculate the scarcity $scar_j^i$ of jth triple, we calculate the familiarity $fami_j^i$ first. It can be obtained directly by invoking LLMs. For example, take the incomplete triple $(h_i^{d-1}, r, ?)$ as the input of LLMs. If LLMs could get the right answer

t_i^{d-1}, then the knowledge implied by this triple is familiar to LLMs. Given $(h_i^{d-1}, r, ?)$, we use the average generation possibility of tokens of t_i^{d-1} to be the indicator of familiarity. As shown in the (4), $Logits$ means getting the generation possibility we mentioned before, $tok_{t_i^j}$ means the set of tokens of t_i^j, tok^k means kth token of t_i^j.

$$fami_j^i = \frac{\sum_{tok^k}^{tok_{t_i^j}} Logits(h_i^j, r_i^j, tok^0 ..., tok^k)}{|tok_{t_i^j}|} \tag{4}$$

The scarcity $scar_j^i$ turns out to be the reciprocal of $fami_j^i$. The less familiar LLMs are with the knowledge, the higher scarcity score is.

$$scar_j^i = \frac{1}{fami_j^i} \tag{5}$$

The score of $path_i$ is shown in (6), where γ is the weight parameter.

$$score_i = \gamma \cdot rela^i + scar^i \tag{6}$$

Once reaching the maximum depth D, we obtain the final set P with k paths in it. They contribute to constructing the knowledge subgraph of q_{diff}.

Algorithm 1. Knowledge Path Retrieval and Filtering

Require: Question q_c; Knowledge Graph G; Max Depth D; Number of retained paths k;
Ensure: Set of knowledge paths P
initialize $P = \Phi$, $d = 1$
while $d \leq D$ **do**
    while $path_i$ in P **do**
        take d-th triple of $path_i$,$(h_i^{d-1}, r, t_i^{d-1})$,as the start
        search out num_i^d triples over G
        add newly acquired triples to the end of $path_i$, leading to num_i^d new paths with the length of d
        calculate relevance scores and scarcity scores, top-k paths are preserved in P
    end while
    $d \leftarrow d + 1$
end while

3.3 Vectorized Graph Augmentation

To get embedding vectors including both textual and structured information of the knowledge subgraph obtained before, we utilize a relation-aware graph attention encoder to aggregate the information. First, we model the subgraph heterogeneously, as there is often more than one type of reflexive relation in KGs. For each type of reflexive relation, we treat it as a heterogeneous graph to facilitate entities receiving information from different reflexive relations. Specifically, for each entity and relation in the knowledge subgraph, we aim to learn its embedding vector in the last layer L, $\boldsymbol{e}^L \in \boldsymbol{R}^{d_e}$, $\boldsymbol{r} \in \boldsymbol{R}^{d_r}$, $\boldsymbol{W}$ is learnable parameters, d_e and d_r are the dimension of entity embedding vectors and relation embedding vectors, respectively.

$$
\begin{aligned}
w_{ij} &= LeakyReLU(\omega^T concat(W_e \boldsymbol{e}_i^l, W_r \boldsymbol{r}, W_e \boldsymbol{e}_j^l)) \\
\alpha_{ij} &= softmax_j(w_{ij}) \\
\boldsymbol{e}_i^{l+1} &= \sigma(\sum_{e_j \in N(e_i)} \alpha_{ij} W_e \boldsymbol{e}_j^l)
\end{aligned}
\tag{7}
$$

In (7), e_i^l is the vector of e_i in l-th layer. Unlike traditional graph attention networks, we concatenate the mapped vectors of the head entity, relationship, and tail entity to get the attention weight w_{ij}.

However, the embedding vectors we have obtained from the graph are in the different representation spaces of LLMs. It means that LLMs cannot directly comprehend these vectors [26]. Therefore, we design an adapter to project the graph embedding vectors into the representation space of LLMs. The adapter is shown as the (8), where $\oplus$ indicates concatenation operation, P indicates the project function, SP is the final vector acquired.

$$
SP = P(\boldsymbol{e}^L) \oplus P(\boldsymbol{r}) \tag{8}
$$

The adapter is added as a prefix to the prompt, along with textual embedding vectors of the original question, constituting the retrieval-augmented prompt. Due to the unidirectional self-attention process during LLMs decoding, subsequent generation results will be influenced by this prefix. This provides retrieval information from another perspective, contributing to the improvement of the model's capabilities.

4 Experiments

4.1 Datasets and Experiments Settings

We utilized Wikidata as the external KG, which is one of the most popular large-scale KGs in the real world. We conducted experiments on four datasets from three different tasks, including an open-domain question-answering dataset, WebQuestions [1], a fact-checking dataset, Creak [16], and two multi-hop knowledge base question-answering (KBQA) datasets, QALD10-en [18] and CWQ [22]. For all datasets, we used the exact match accuracy (Hits@1) as the evaluation metric. As for details, in the hallucination detection module, we set $\theta = 0.75$. During path filtering, we set the maximum retrieval depth to 3, retaining the top 100 knowledge paths. We utilized Bert [10] for both question texts and path encoding in similarity calculations. Considering the retrieval depth is set to 3, we utilized a 3-layer graph encoder network for the adapter. For datasets with fewer samples, such as QALD10-en, we trained for 2 epochs. For the other three datasets, we trained for 1 epoch. During the fine-tuning phase, we use Llama-3-8b [7] and we set the learning rate to 5e-5, the rank for LoRA [8] to 16, and the AdamW optimizer.

4.2 Baselines

Regarding the selection of comparative models, we chose four categories of models.

LLM Without Knowledge Augmentation: Standard prompting (IO prompt) [3]. Chain of Thought prompting (CoT prompt) [24]. Self-Consistency [23], with three context exemplars and "step by step" (SC prompt). Llama-3-8b [7] model fine-tuned on the respective datasets.

Prior Sota Without LLM: For each dataset, we chose the previously state-of-the-art (SOTA) works for comparison. WebQuestions: FiE [9] utilizes a cross-sample attention mechanism to focus on global information for answer generation. CREAK: a strategy for document retrieval enhanced commonsense reasoning [25]. QALD: a method integrating neural machine translation and named entity recognition to convert natural language into SPARQL [19]. CWQ: a case-based neural symbolic reasoning approach [6].

Textual Knowledge Augmentation: Knowledge addition in textual form without fine-tuning on Llama-3-8b. We use the linearized traversal of the knowledge subgraphs to obtain sequence text as prompts. Knowledge addition in textual form with fine-tuning(FT) on Llama-3-8b. We also use the linearized traversal of the knowledge subgraphs and fine-tune Llama for better adaptation. ToG [20], the retrieval-augmented generation model on the knowledge graph conducted on GPT-4. ODA [21], an observation-driven agent with a cyclical paradigm of observation, action, and reflection. FastToG [15] develops an innovative paradigm for enabling LLMs to think "community by community" within KGs.

Vectorized Knowledge Augmentation: Vec-RA-ODQA [4], a vectorized method for open-domain question-answering enhancement.

4.3 Main Results

The main experiment results are shown in Table 1, which underscore several critical insights. External knowledge can significantly improve the accuracy of the model's responses, which confirms the effectiveness of RAG. Since the content of the problems is strongly correlated with KG, the method of incorporating external knowledge is significantly more effective than relying solely on LLM prompts. Models with textual augmentation perform worse than vector-based models. The former models convert graph data into linear textual representation, leading to the loss of structural information and the difficulty of handling excessively long contexts. Vector-based models cover richer information for their

Table 1. Main results for different datasets. The best results are marked in bold, and the second-best results are underlined.

Methods	WebQuestions	Creak	QALD10-en	CWQ
IO prompt(Llama)	0.314	0.686	0.351	0.200
CoT prompt(Llama)	0.329	0.697	0.360	0.213
SC prompt(Llama)	0.356	0.738	0.384	0.220
Fine-tuning(Llama)	0.388	0.780	0.432	0.246
Prior SOTA	0.563	0.882	0.454	**0.704**
Knowledge Addition(Llama)	0.430	0.688	0.429	0.270
Knowledge Addition-FT(Llama)	0.538	0.871	0.486	0.351
ODA(Llama)	0.545	0.892	0.517	0.393
ODA(GPT)	0.575	0.952	<u>0.547</u>	0.670
ToG(Llama)	0.568	0.919	0.500	0.401
ToG(GPT)	0.579	0.956	0.538	<u>0.676</u>
FastToG(Llama)	0.566	0.913	0.508	0.399
Vec-RA-ODQA	<u>0.600</u>	<u>0.958</u>	0.535	0.403
Our model(Llama)	**0.612**	**0.964**	**0.552**	0.412

unlimited contexts. And with vectorized contexts, LLM needn't face the long-distance dependence problem. Compared with the vector-based method Vec-RA-ODQA, VIKA performs better because graph structure information is included. More interaction between entities could be represented in such graph vectors, which helps the model in the reasoning process on KG.

Overall, VIKA achieves SOTA performance in three out of four datasets. We introduce external knowledge beyond the scope of the pre-training corpus and get the best results. This validates that our filtering criterion of relevance and scarcity ensures the purity of the knowledge and the graph vectorized enhancement method we proposed improves the efficiency of information utilization.

Even for the dataset that VIKA performs slightly poorly, such as CWQ, VIKA significantly improves compared with other RAG models based on Llama as well. For multi-hop reasoning datasets, VIKA has a natural disadvantage in comparison with agent-like methods like ToG and ODA because we cannot explicitly obtain an exact reasoning path during the encoding process. However, VIKA still achieves around 4% improvement with the same backbone model.

4.4 Ablation Study

To validate the effectiveness of our model, we conducted three parts of ablation experiments. $model_{-h.d.}$ verifies the effectiveness of the hallucination detection module, which means handling difficult and easy questions together.

$model_{-p.f.}$ verifies the effectiveness of path filtering, which means randomly selecting paths preserved.

$model_{-ada}$ verifies the effectiveness of the vectorized graph adapter, which means we utilize Bert to encode textual knowledge and project it to be a prefix for Llama to finetune.

The experimental results are shown in the Table 2. We found that removing any of the three parts from the model would lead to a performance decline. Without hallucination detection, the model turns to retrieve blindly, and randomly filtering would make the model focus on more irrelevant and known information, both of which would interfere with the model's response. Introducing knowledge in linear textual form would result in the loss of graph structure information, hindering the model from successfully finding answers.

Table 2. Ablation Study results for different datasets.

Methods	WebQuestions	Creak	QALD	CWQ
$model_{-h.d.}$	0.572	0.916	0.507	0.380
$model_{-p.f.}$	0.567	0.924	0.522	0.392
$model_{-ada}$	0.585	0.945	0.493	0.385
Our model	**0.612**	**0.964**	**0.552**	**0.412**

Furthermore, we also observed that the importance of each part varies from different tasks. For open-domain question-answering and fact-checking tasks, operations for avoiding interference, such as hallucination detection and path filtering, have a greater impact on the model's performance. In WebQuestions and Creak, the average improvement from hallucination detection and path filtering is 5.6%, while from the graph structure adapter, it is only 3.2%. However, for multi-hop reasoning datasets, the addition of graph structure information significantly influences the model's performance. In QALD10-en and CWQ, the average improvement from the graph structure is 8.3%, higher than the 6.5% improvement from others.

4.5 Hyperparameter Exploration

We conducted an impact analysis of hyperparameters in the experiment. The confidence threshold θ in the hallucination detection.The retrieval depth D.The number of paths retained in the path filtering module.The embedding dimension of the enhancing vector from knowledge subgraphs.

The results are shown in the Fig. 2. A higher confidence threshold means that fewer answers could pass through. A lower threshold allows more answers to pass through but increases the risk of hallucinations, which can significantly impact the model's performance. We conducted experiments under five different thresholds ranging from 0.25 to 1.25 and found 0.75 is the best. A greater retrieval depth expands the model's retrieval coverage, potentially improving recall, but it also increases computational overhead and noise. A smaller depth may result

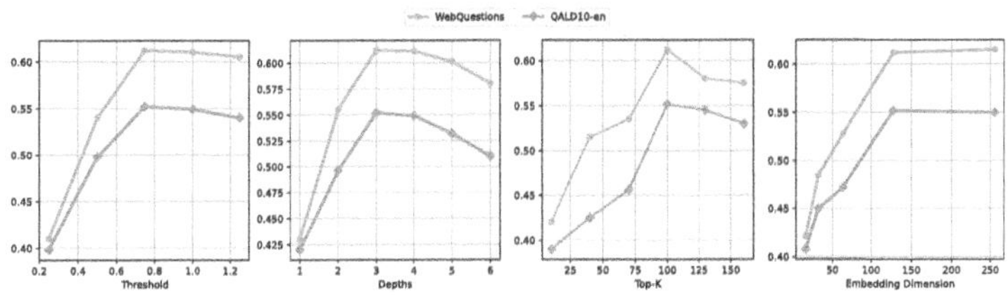

Fig. 2. Performance with different maximum depth and top-k.

in the omission of valuable information. We conducted experiments under six different depths ranging from 1 to 6. Considering the increased computational cost associated with increasing depth, we selected a maximum exploration depth of 3. A greater number means of paths more information as well as more noise. A lower number may fail to contain sufficient knowledge. We conducted experiments under six different numbers ranging from 10 to 160 and chose to retain 100 paths. A higher embedding dimension can represent richer information, but it may introduce the curse of dimensionality. A lower dimension reduces computational overhead but may result in insufficient feature representation capacity. We conducted experiments under five different dimensions ranging from 16 to 256 and found 128 is the best.

4.6 Influence of Different Training Strategies

We jointly train the graph encoder with LLM fine-tuning. To validate the effectiveness of this strategy, we compared three different training strategies: **S1**: Training the graph encoder and the adapter together with fine-tuning LLM. **S2**: Training the graph encoder with loss function, TransE [2] first. Keep it frozen while tuning the adapter and LLM. **S3**: Training the graph encoder with loss function, TransE [2]. continue training it while tuning the adapter and LLM.

Results are shown in Fig. 3. Since graph embeddings and sequence embeddings are located in quite different representation spaces, training the graph encoder with the loss function applicable to KG increases the gap between them and leads to poor performance. The joint training method enhances the model's

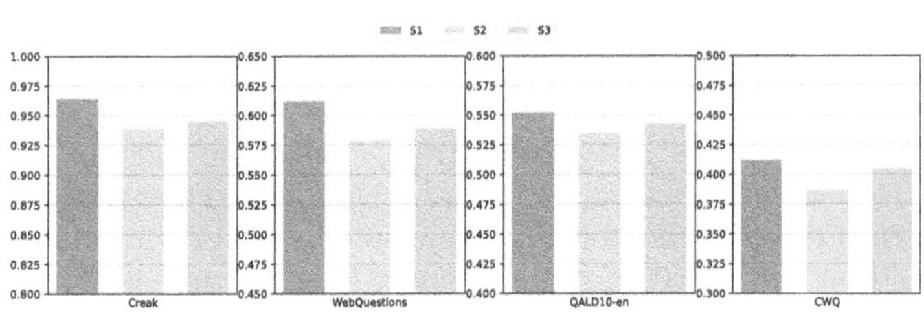

Fig. 3. Performance with different training strategies.

adaptability and generalization ability on graph data, improving the overall performance of the system.

4.7 Influence of Different Augmentation Adapters

We use entity embedding vectors as the input of the adapter to provide enhancement. To explore the impact of various forms of the input, we designed and compared five different types of adapters, including:

Random Adapter. Randomly set the embedding vector of the adapter. **Topic Adapter.** Using only the embedding vector of the query's topic entity. **Entity Adapter.** Using the embedding vectors of the topic entity and other entities. **Relation Adapter.** Using the embedding vectors of the topic entity and the relation. **Full Adapter.** Using the embedding vectors of the topic entity, relations, and other entities.

Results are shown in Fig. 4. We can see that when using only the embedding vector of the question's topic entity, the model lacks sufficient information, making it difficult to provide correct responses. In addition, since the number of relations is usually much smaller than the number of entities, the information within the relation embedding vectors tends to be chaotic, making it difficult to provide effective assistance. However, when using embedding vectors of the topic entity, relations, and other entities simultaneously, the model's performance decreases due to information redundancy. So we chose the third adapter for the best performance.

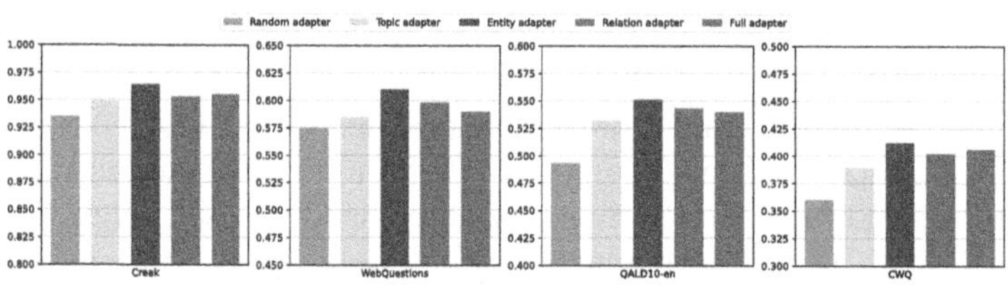

Fig. 4. Performance on five adapters, which are shown from left to right.

5 Conclusion

In this paper, we propose a vectorized RAG method for indispensable graph structure information augmentation for LLM. Our method designs a graph context adapter to project structural embedding into the text representation space, combining them with input prompts in prefix form. We also design a hallucination detection module and a retriever with relevance and scarcity criteria to ensure the accuracy of external knowledge. Our model has demonstrated excellent results across datasets from three different tasks.

References

1. Berant, J., Chou, A., Frostig, R., Liang, P.: Semantic parsing on freebase from question-answer pairs. In: Proceedings of the 2013 Conference on Empirical Methods in Natural Language Processing, pp. 1533–1544 (2013)
2. Bordes, A., Usunier, N., Garcia-Duran, A., Weston, J., Yakhnenko, O.: Translating embeddings for modeling multi-relational data. Adv. Neural. Inf. Process. Syst. **26** (2013)
3. Brown, T., et al.: Language models are few-shot learners. Adv. Neural. Inf. Process. Syst. **33**, 1877–1901 (2020)
4. Chen, Z., Wang, X., Jiang, Y., Xie, P., Huang, F., Tu, K.: Improving retrieval augmented open-domain question-answering with vectorized contexts. arXiv preprint arXiv:2404.02022 (2024)
5. Cuconasu, F., et al.: The power of noise: Redefining retrieval for rag systems. In: Proceedings of the 47th International ACM SIGIR Conference on Research and Development in Information Retrieval. SIGIR 2024, pp. 719–729. Association for Computing Machinery, New York (2024). https://doi.org/10.1145/3626772.3657834
6. Das, R., et al.: Case-based reasoning for natural language queries over knowledge bases. In: Proceedings of the 2021 Conference on Empirical Methods in Natural Language Processing, pp. 9594–9611 (2021)
7. Dubey, A., et al.: The llama 3 herd of models. arXiv:2407.21783 (2024)
8. Hu, E.J., et al.: Lora: Low-rank adaptation of large language models. In: International Conference on Learning Representations (2021)
9. Kedia, A., Zaidi, M.A., Lee, H.: Fie: building a global probability space by leveraging early fusion in encoder for open-domain question answering. In: Proceedings of the 2022 Conference on Empirical Methods in Natural Language Processing, pp. 4246–4260 (2022)
10. Kenton, J.D.M.W.C., Toutanova, L.K.: Bert: pre-training of deep bidirectional transformers for language understanding. In: Proceedings of NAACL-HLT, pp. 4171–4186 (2019)
11. Lewis, P., et al.: Retrieval-augmented generation for knowledge-intensive NLP tasks. Adv. Neural. Inf. Process. Syst. **33**, 9459–9474 (2020)
12. Li, J., et al.: Context embeddings for efficient answer generation in rag. IEEE Trans. Knowl. Data Eng. (2024)
13. Li, T., Ma, X., Zhuang, A., Gu, Y., Su, Y., Chen, W.: Few-shot in-context learning for knowledge base question answering. arXiv:2305.01750 (2023)
14. Li, X., et al.: Chain of knowledge: A framework for grounding large language models with structured knowledge bases. arXiv preprint arXiv:2305.13269 (2023)
15. Liang, X., Gu, Z.: Fast think-on-graph: wider, deeper and faster reasoning of large language model on knowledge graph. arXiv preprint arXiv:2501.14300 (2025)
16. Onoe, Y., Zhang, M.J., Choi, E., Durrett, G.: Creak: a dataset for commonsense reasoning over entity knowledge. In: Thirty-fifth Conference on Neural Information Processing Systems Datasets and Benchmarks Track (Round 2) (2021)
17. Pan, S., Luo, L., Wang, Y., Chen, C., Wang, J., Wu, X.: Unifying large language models and knowledge graphs: a roadmap. IEEE Trans. Knowl. Data Eng. (2024)
18. Perevalov, A., Diefenbach, D., Usbeck, R., Both, A.: Qald-9-plus: a multilingual dataset for question answering over dbpedia and wikidata translated by native speakers. In: 2022 IEEE 16th International Conference on Semantic Computing (ICSC), pp. 229–234. IEEE (2022)

19. Santana, M.A.B., Cuteri, B., Ricca, F., Barbara, V.: Sparql-qa enters the qald challenge. In: NLIWoD@ ESWC, pp. 25–31 (2022)
20. Sun, J., et al.: Think-on-graph: deep and responsible reasoning of large language model with knowledge graph. arXiv preprint arXiv:2307.07697 (2023)
21. Sun, L., Tao, Z., Li, Y., Arakawa, H.: Oda: observation-driven agent for integrating LLMs and knowledge graphs. arXiv preprint arXiv:2404.07677 (2024)
22. Talmor, A., Berant, J.: The web as a knowledge-base for answering complex questions. In: Proceedings of the 2018 Conference of the North American Chapter of the Association for Computational Linguistics: Human Language Technologies, Volume 1 (Long Papers), pp. 641–651 (2018)
23. Wang, X., et al.: Self-consistency improves chain of thought reasoning in language models. In: The Eleventh International Conference on Learning Representations (2022)
24. Wei, J., et al.: Chain-of-thought prompting elicits reasoning in large language models. In: Advances in Neural Information Processing Systems (2022)
25. Yu, W., et al.: Retrieval augmentation for commonsense reasoning: a unified approach. In: Proceedings of the 2022 Conference on Empirical Methods in Natural Language Processing, pp. 4364–4377 (2022)
26. Zhang, Y., Chen, Z., Zhang, W., Chen, H.: Making large language models perform better in knowledge graph completion. arXiv preprint arXiv:2310.06671 (2023)

Traff-LLM: A Spatio-Temporal Knowledge-Guided Large Language Model for Traffic Flow Prediction

Chengbiao Yang, Lingyu Zhang, and Guilin Qi(✉)

School of Computer Science Engineering, Southeast University, Nanjing, China
gqi@seu.edu.cn

Abstract. Traffic flow prediction is a critical task for intelligent transportation systems. However, existing deep learning models often suffer from poor interpretability and deployment challenges due to their architectural complexity. To address these limitations, we introduce **Traff-LLM**, a spatio-temporal knowledge-guided large language model (LLM) for accurate and interpretable traffic forecasting. Our framework first constructs a spatio-temporal knowledge graph to capture complex dependencies from traffic data. To manage the scale of this graph for LLM processing, we propose a novel Temporal Prize-Collecting Steiner Tree (T-PCST) algorithm that efficiently extracts compact, task-relevant subgraphs. Each subgraph and its associated external factors (e.g., weather and public events) are serialized into a unified natural-language prompt, which is then paired with the corresponding traffic flow to form the supervised fine-tuning dataset. The LLM is then fine-tuned on these prompt–response examples, enabling it to integrate multi-modal signals and perform reasoning over the spatio-temporal graph. Experiments on two real-world benchmarks demonstrate that **Traff-LLM** significantly outperforms state-of-the-art methods, including specialized Graph Neural Networks and recent LLM-based approaches.

Keywords: Large Language Model · Spatio-Temporal Knowledge Graph · Temporal Prize-Collecting Steiner Tree · Traffic Flow Prediction

1 Introduction

Accurate traffic flow prediction is a cornerstone of intelligent transportation systems (ITSs) [1], enabling route planning, congestion mitigation, and proactive traffic management. However, urban traffic is inherently complex: flow at a given location depends on surrounding areas (spatial dependence) and on recent and periodic trends over time (temporal dependence). This nonlinearity and high-dimensional spatio-temporal variability make traffic flow prediction challenging for traditional models, which often fail to capture these dynamics [2, 3].

Deep learning approaches have been widely and successfully applied to various traffic tasks in recent years. Significant progress has been made in the research of traffic flow prediction. Researchers have applied recurrent neural networks (RNNs), such as

J. Liang et al. (Eds.): CCKS 2025, CCIS 2698, pp. 93–105, 2026.
https://doi.org/10.1007/978-981-95-8525-0_8

LSTM [4, 5] and GRU [6] to model the temporal dependence of traffic flows. Others have explored convolutional neural networks (CNNs) [7] to model the spatial dependence of traffic flows. And some have further combined these two paradigms [8] to jointly learn spatio-temporal patterns. Despite recent advances, the non-Euclidean spatial structures and the complex temporal periodicity inherent in traffic data pose significant challenges for CNN- and RNN-based models in accurately capturing spatial and temporal dependencies.

Graph neural network (GNN) based models gained popularity for their ability to model local spatial dependencies. Such models include the T-GCN [9], STGCN [11], DCRNN [15], ASTGCN [12], LSGCN [13], SeqGNN [14] and KST-GCN [10]. ASTGCN shows that the connectivity of roads is very important, rather than their spatial proximity. And KST-GCN shows that the knowledge of traffic can be helpful for the traffic prediction, but the external knowledge is difficult to obtain and the effect is not significant. Nevertheless, with this evolution, the structures of existing traffic prediction models have become progressively complex.

In recent years, large language models (LLMs) have made significant progress in natural language processing. More recently, they have also demonstrated strong performance in time series analysis [15–17] and graph analysis [18–20]. Unlike GNN-based models that rely on complex architectural designs, LLMs primarily improve through increased parameter scaling and large-scale pretraining, while preserving a relatively stable model architecture. Existing LLM-based methods for traffic forecasting primarily focus on the temporal dimension of data [21, 22]. However, there's significant room for improvement in the spatial dimension [23]. A key challenge lies in converting sensor-level spatial information into natural language without incurring significant information loss. Although xTP-LLM [24] incorporates external factors into its prompt design, it fails to address the limitations imposed by the finite context length of LLMs. In particular, prompt-based methods struggle to scale to traffic flow networks containing thousands of sensors and extensive temporal sequences, where the context length constraint becomes a major bottleneck.

In this work, we propose **Traff-LLM**, a framework that unites graph-based spatial–temporal representations with LLM-driven reasoning for traffic forecasting. First, we construct a spatio-temporal knowledge graph from traffic data, enabling **Traff-LLM** to effectively capture both spatial dependencies across regions and temporal patterns. Subsequently, we introduce a Temporal Prize-Collecting Steiner Tree (T-PCST) algorithm to efficiently extract the most informative subgraph for each prediction. Next, each subgraph and its associated external factors (e.g., weather and public events) are serialized into a unified natural-language prompt, which is then paired with the corresponding traffic flow to form the supervised fine-tuning corpus. Finally, we fine-tune the LLM on these prompt-response pairs, enabling it to integrate multimodal signals and perform reasoning over the spatio-temporal graph.

In summary, this paper makes the following contributions:

- We propose **Traff-LLM**, a novel framework that unifies spatio-temporal graph modeling with large language models, enabling accurate and interpretable traffic flow forecasting through prompt-based reasoning.

- We introduce the Temporal Prize-Collecting Steiner Tree (T-PCST) algorithm to extract task-relevant subgraphs based on time-series similarity and spatio-temporal proximity, ensuring efficient and context-relevant input for the LLM.
- We conduct experiments on two real-world benchmarks, showing that **Traff-LLM** consistently surpasses strong GNN-based and LLM-based baselines in both accuracy and interpretability.

The rest of this paper is organized as follows: Sect. 2 gives a brief analysis of the traffic flow networks and the traffic flow prediction problem; Sect. 3 details the **Traff-LLM**, followed by the experiments in Sect. 4. Section 5 concludes the paper.

2 Preliminary

2.1 Traffic Flow Networks

Traffic flow networks model a road system as a spatio-temporal graph, where nodes represent monitoring sensors (e.g., loop detectors or cameras) and edges denote physical or functional connections between them. In this study, we define a traffic flow network as an undirected graph $\mathcal{G} = (\boldsymbol{V}, \boldsymbol{E}, \boldsymbol{X})$, where $\boldsymbol{V}$ is the set of nodes, indicating the monitor sensors, $\boldsymbol{E}$ is a set of edges, indicating the connectivity between the nodes, $\boldsymbol{X}$ is the history traffic flow data of $\boldsymbol{V}$.

2.2 Traffic Flow Prediction

For a traffic flow network $\mathcal{G} = (\boldsymbol{V}, \boldsymbol{E}, \boldsymbol{X})$, let $\boldsymbol{x}_t^i$ represents the traffic flow value of the node $\boldsymbol{i}$ at time step $\boldsymbol{t}$, and $\boldsymbol{X}_t = \left\{\boldsymbol{x}_t^1, \boldsymbol{x}_t^2, \ldots, \boldsymbol{x}_t^n\right\}$ represents the traffic flow values of $\boldsymbol{V}$ at time step $\boldsymbol{t}$. In this paper, we formulate traffic flow prediction as a discrete multivariate point prediction problem. In particular, **Traff-LLM** takes the past observations $\boldsymbol{X} = \{\boldsymbol{X}_{t_1}, \boldsymbol{X}_{t_2}, \ldots, \boldsymbol{X}_{t_m}\}$ from $\boldsymbol{G}$ as input and predicts the traffic flow for horizon $m\prime$, where $\widehat{\boldsymbol{X}} = \{\widehat{\boldsymbol{X}}_{t_{m+1}}, \widehat{\boldsymbol{X}}_{t_{m+2}}, \ldots, \widehat{\boldsymbol{X}}_{t_{m+m'}}, \}$.

3 Proposed Method

3.1 Overview of Traff-LLM

The architecture of the **Traff-LLM** is shown in Fig. 1. Pre-trained Transformer-based large language models are employed as the backbone for analyzing and predicting spatio-temporal traffic data.

The framework begins by modeling the entire urban road network as a spatio-temporal knowledge graph G^{ST}. For each center node v_c, the T-PCST algorithm is applied to extract its optimal subgraph $G_{v_c}^{Sub}$, which serves as the localized spatial and temporal context. Subsequently, to fully leverage the reasoning capabilities of LLMs, each heterogeneous input modality is transformed into a coherent natural-language description and concatenated into a single composite prompt. Finally, through supervised fine-tuning, the traffic flow prediction task is formulated as a next-token prediction problem.

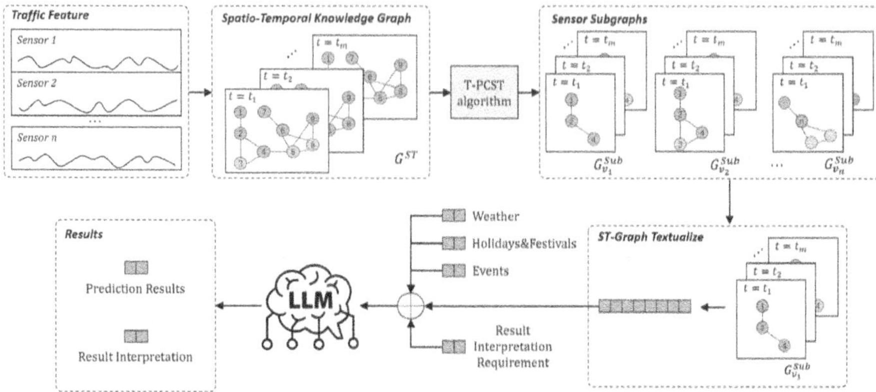

Fig. 1. The proposed **Traff-LLM** architecture.

Guided by the dynamic graph sequence and the generated reasoning path, prompt templates are constructed to drive a large language model to perform inference and prediction, ultimately producing both the forecasting results and their corresponding explanations.

3.2 Spatio-Temporal Knowledge Graph

Unlike traditional one-dimensional time series modeling, traffic flow forecasting entails complex spatial dependencies and temporal dynamics. The key challenge lies in accurately modeling interactions between nodes across space and time. Therefore, building graph structures with both topological awareness and semantic expressiveness, is a crucial step to enhance prediction performance.

We define the spatio-temporal knowledge graph $G^{ST} = (\boldsymbol{E}, \boldsymbol{R}, \boldsymbol{T})$, where each entity $e \in \boldsymbol{E}$ corresponds to a sensor $v \in \boldsymbol{V}$ characterized by a traffic flow attribute $\boldsymbol{x}$. At time $t \in \boldsymbol{T}$, G^{ST} represents a temporal snapshot of the traffic flow network $\mathcal{G}$, as shown in Fig. 2.

In graph G^{ST}, $\boldsymbol{R}$ has two relationships for expressing spatial positions, denoted as **Straight-Link** and **Corner-Link** respectively. The **Straight-Link** relationship indicates that two sensors are adjacent on the same road segment, while the **Corner-Link** relationship connects sensors located at intersections on different roads. Both relationships are associated with a distance attribute, representing the actual driving distance between sensors. The relationships can subtly capture and represent the spatial graph embedded within urban road networks.

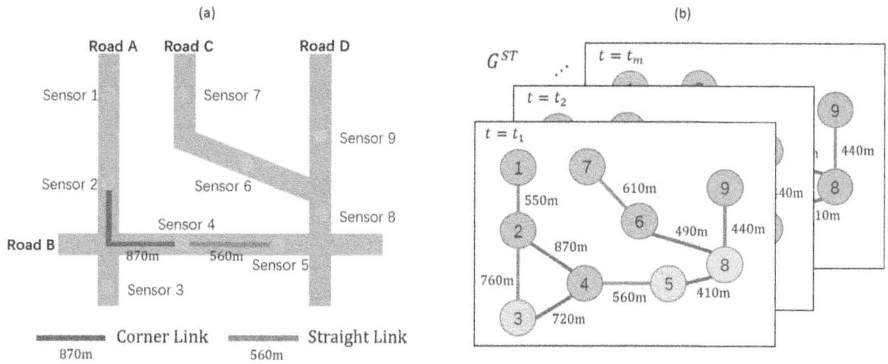

Fig. 2. The spatio-temporal knowledge graph of sensors. Figure (a) shows the relationship between sensor 2 and sensor 4 is **Corner-Link**, and the distance between them is 870 m. The relationship between sensor 4 and sensor 5 is **Straight-Link**, and the distance is 560 m. Figure (b) shows an example of the spatio-temporal knowledge graph.

3.3 Spatio-Temporal Subgraphs

Recent advances in LLM architectures have pushed context windows from just a few hundred tokens to millions (e.g., Gemini 2.5 Pro's 1M-token window), yet even these expanded capacities remain woefully inadequate for directly encoding large-scale spatio-temporal graphs, which routinely comprise thousands of nodes and dense edges. At the same time, recent work in graph-based forecasting demonstrates that the choice of subgraph around a target node can critically impact prediction accuracy. Therefore, extracting task-relevant subgraphs from the graph G^{ST} is a crucial step to enhance prediction performance.

In our framework, a subgraph centered at each node $v \in V$ is constructed, forming the subgraph collection $G^{Sub} = \{G_{v_1}^{Sub}, G_{v_2}^{Sub}, \ldots, G_{v_n}^{Sub}\}$. For any node v_c, we adaptively generate its localized subgraph $G_{v_c}^{Sub}$ based on its relationship with neighboring nodes. This center-aware subgraph construction enables structural adaptivity driven by semantic variations and heterogeneous contexts, thereby enhancing the informativeness and task relevance of the resulting subgraphs.

Temporal Prize-Collecting Steiner Tree (T-PCST) Algorithm

In the forecasting task, the model aims to predict the future traffic trend of a center node v_c based on its historical states and the information from its neighborhoods. Thus, it is crucial to extract subgraphs that are semantically pertinent to v_c while remaining structurally compact, in order to minimize noise and computational overhead.

The Prize-Collecting Steiner Tree (PCST) algorithm [25] has been widely adopted for subgraph mining in static networks: by assigning a "prize" to each node (reflecting its individual relevance) and a "cost" to each edge (reflecting connectivity expense), PCST finds a connected subgraph that maximizes total prize minus total cost under a given budget constraint. However, vanilla PCST is agnostic to temporal evolution and thus cannot directly capture the dynamic, time-varying dependencies inherent in traffic flow graphs. To remedy this, we propose the Temporal Prize-Collecting Steiner Tree (T-PCST) algorithm, which enriches the classic PCST formulation with temporal awareness by computing node prizes based on a similarity measure over each node's historical time-series traffic flow waveform. In T-PCST, nodes whose recent traffic patterns closely correlate with the target node receive higher prizes, while edges incur costs that reflect spatial distance, enabling the extraction of subgraphs that are simultaneously spatially coherent and temporally informative.

The objective of T-PCST is to maximize the total node prizes while minimizing edge connection costs, formulated as:

$$G_{v_c}^{Sub} = \mathrm{arg}max\left(\sum_{v_i \in V_{v_c}^T} r_i - \sum_{e_{ij} \in E_{v_c}^T} c_{ij}\right)$$

Here, $V_{v_c}^T$ is the neighbor node set of v_c, and $E_{v_c}^T$ is the edges among $V_{v_c}^T$. r_i denotes the prize of candidate node v_i relative to v_c, measuring the similarity of their historical traffic patterns; c_{ij} is the spatial cost of edge e_{ij}, serving as a penalty to enforce subgraph compactness.

With prize r_i and edge cost c_{ij} defined, the T-PCST algorithm selects a subgraph $G_{v_c}^{Sub}$ that balances semantic relevance and spatial compactness. Starting from a coarse neighborhood around v_c, it adaptively extracts the most informative and structurally coherent context for prediction.

Node Prize Computation Method

To compute the prize r_i based on time-series similarity, we adopt ShapeDTW [27]—a structure-aware distance metric that outperforms traditional DTW by encoding local morphological patterns in time series. ShapeDTW captures traffic dynamics with higher resolution, particularly useful for detecting peak-valley shifts and non-linear fluctuations commonly seen in urban traffic.

The historical flow sequences X_c and X_i from the center node v_c and candidate node v_i are normalized via min-max scaling:

$$\hat{x}_t^{(c)} = \frac{x_t^{(c)} - \min(X_c)}{\max(X_c) - \min(X_c)}, \hat{x}_t^{(i)} = \frac{x_t^{(i)} - \min(X_i)}{\max(X_i) - \min(X_i)}$$

For each time step t, a sliding window of length l is extracted around t:

$$S_t = \left[\hat{x}_{t-\lfloor l/2 \rfloor}, \ldots, \hat{x}_t, \ldots, \hat{x}_{t+\lfloor l/2 \rfloor}\right]$$

This window is divided into k segments, and each segment undergoes linear regression to extract its slope s_j. The resulting shape descriptor for time t is:

$$d_t = [s_1, s_2, \ldots, s_k]$$

The descriptor sequences $D_c = \left[d_1^{(c)}, \ldots, d_T^{(c)}\right]$ and $D_i = \left[d_1^{(i)}, \ldots, d_T^{(i)}\right]$ represent the structure-enhanced form of the original sequences.

DTW is applied to align the two descriptor sequences in a nonlinear manner. The ShapeDTW distance is defined as:

$$\text{ShapeDTW}(X_c, X_i) = \min_{\pi} \sum_{(p,q)\in\pi} |d_p^{(c)} - d_q^{(i)}|_2$$

Then, this distance is transformed into a prize value via exponential mapping:

$$r_i = \exp\left(-\alpha \cdot \text{ShapeDTW}\left(\hat{X}_c, \hat{X}_i\right)\right)$$

where α is a smoothing hyperparameter.

Importantly, the prize value r_i is dynamically computed with respect to the current center node v_c. That is, the same candidate node v_i may exhibit high prize in the subgraph of one center node (e.g., due to shared flow trends with $v_c^{(1)}$) and low prize in another (e.g., dissimilarity with $v_c^{(2)}$). This dynamic subgraph mechanism enables adaptive graph restructuring based on temporal similarity and spatial relevance, enhancing context specificity for each prediction.

Edge Cost Computation Method

To prevent structural bias from "pseudo-correlated" nodes that are geographically distant yet statistically similar, we incorporate spatial constraints into the connection cost:

$$c_{ij} = \lambda \cdot \text{dist}\left(v_i, v_j\right)$$

where λ controls the penalty weight and dist(·) represents the navigation distance between nodes.

3.4 Multi-modal Spatio-Temporal Prompts

To exploit the LLM's reasoning power, we serialize all inputs into a single natural-language prompt composed of three parts:

- ST-Graph Textualization

  We serialize the T-PCST subgraph $G_{v_c}^{Sub}$ around the target node v_c into a structured, language-readable description. The description comprises two parts: (1) spatial topology, listing the nodes, their adjacency relations (**Corner-Link** or **Straight-Link**), and pairwise distances; and (2) temporal snapshots, a sequence of time-stamped traffic snapshots (e.g., "At t_i, node 7 flow = 52 veh/hr; node 9 flow = 48 veh/hr."). This two-stage format preserves both network structure and temporal dynamics.

- Multi-Modal External Factors

  To provide rich contextual grounding, we retrieve and encode three auxiliary data streams. First, we query a reputable meteorological service to obtain weather observations at the final timestamp t_m, formatted as "Weather at t_m: temperature = 20 °C; precipitation = 0.3 mm; wind speed = 6 km/h." Second, we consult an official holiday calendar to determine whether t_m coincides with a public holiday—e.g., "t_m is a national holiday (Labor Day)." Third, we mine local news websites for relevant events, producing statements such as "City marathon from 07:00–10:00." Each snippet is clearly labeled ("Weather: …", "Holiday: …", "Event: …") to ensure the model can differentiate and integrate heterogeneous signals.

- Few-Shot Demonstrations

  We begin with two example prompt–response pairs (each mapping a prompt to response "Prediction + Explanation") to teach the desired output format. We then issue the actual query: "Now predict the traffic flow at node v_c for the next hour and explain your reasoning."

3.5 Model Fine-Tuning

Supervised fine-tuning refines a pre-trained LLM for a targeted task by training it on labeled task-specific examples. After broad pre-training on massive, heterogeneous corpora to acquire general linguistic and reasoning capabilities, the model undergoes an additional training phase using data directly relevant to the application domain. For traffic flow prediction, for instance, this entails input-output pairs of historical sensor readings and their corresponding traffic flow values. During fine-tuning, the model's parameters are updated to minimize a loss function that quantifies prediction error. This process leverages the LLM's broad knowledge while sharpening its expertise on the target task, yielding improved accuracy and domain relevance.

During fine-tuning, we cast traffic flow prediction as an autoregressive next-token prediction problem. Specifically, given an annotated dataset $D = \{(X_{1:n}, Y_{1:n})\}$, we minimize

$$L^{FT}(D) = -\sum_{j=1}^{n} \log P\big(Y_j | Y_{1:j-1}, X_{1:n}\big).$$

Here, $X_{1:n}$ denotes the sequence of input (historical) tokens and $Y_{1:j-1}$ the previously generated tokens. Optimizing this loss aligns the model's predictions with the true traffic flows, thereby sharpening its task-specific proficiency.

Our **Traff-LLM** builds upon the open-source Qwen2.5 models, which we adapt via the LoRA method. LoRA injects low-rank updates into the pre-trained weight matrices—i.e., $W = W_0 + \alpha\Delta W$, where W_0 is the original weight, ΔW the learned update, and α a scaling factor. This parameter-efficient technique enables rapid adaptation to the traffic-forecasting task without updating all model parameters.

4 Experiments

In this section, we detail the experimental framework established to evaluate **Traff-LLM**'s effectiveness. First, we describe the two real-world traffic datasets, detailing their preprocessing steps. Second, we introduce our evaluation metrics (MAE, RMSE and MAPE) and the set of baseline models, which includes leading graph neural network architectures and recent LLM-enhanced forecasting approaches. Finally, we report a series of experiments designed to isolate and quantify the impact of our proposed components. Results demonstrate that **Traff-LLM** significantly outperforms all baselines by concentrating on the most informative spatio-temporal subgraphs and seamlessly integrating external contextual signals.

4.1 Dataset Description

Traffic flow prediction research leverages various real-world data sources, including sensor networks, taxi trajectories and GPS traces from public transit systems. Among these, loop detector data collected by urban traffic control centers is the most commonly used in contemporary studies. A widely adopted dataset is the Caltrans Performance Measurement System (PeMS), which is collected in real-time from over 39,000 individual detectors. These sensors span the freeway system across all major metropolitan areas of the State of California.

PeMS aggregates traffic data from thousands of loop detectors, recording conditions every five minutes to yield 288 samples per detector per day. Each record includes flow, speed, and occupancy, along with geolocation information, enabling the construction of spatially-informed traffic graphs. This study adopts PeMSD4 and PeMSD8, both widely used in benchmark evaluations. We sampled two months of data from each of the two datasets for our experiments, and the missing values are filled by linear interpolation (Table 1).

Table 1. Introduction to Datasets.

Dataset	PEMSD4	PEMSD8
Number of Nodes	307	170
Number of Adjacent Edges	340	277
Number of Records	16992	17856
Record Span	2018/1/1 ~ 2018/2/28	2016/7/1 ~ 2016/8/31
Missing Rate	3.18%	0.696%

To ensure consistency across models, this study uses the open-source framework LibCity, a modular platform for spatio-temporal prediction. LibCity standardizes data formats and provides a unified pipeline for preprocessing, model training, and evaluation, facilitating reproducibility.

4.2 Evaluation Metrics and Baseline Models

Three common metrics are used in this paper to evaluate the performance of the proposed framework: Mean Absolute Error (MAE), Root Mean Square Error (RMSE), and Mean Absolute Percentage Error (MAPE). For a single prediction of the framework, the process of calculating evaluation metrics is as follows:

$$MAE(y_i, \hat{y_i}) = \frac{1}{N}\sum_{i=1}^{N}\left|y_i - \hat{y_i}\right|$$

$$RMSE(y_i, \hat{y_i}) = \sqrt{\frac{1}{N}\sum_{i=1}^{N}\left(y_i - \hat{y_i}\right)^2}$$

$$MAPE(y_i, \widehat{y_i}) = \frac{1}{N}\sum_{i=1}^{N}\frac{|y_i - \widehat{y_i}|}{y_i}$$

where $\widehat{y_i}$ is the predicted traffic flow value of the i-th sensor, and y_i is the true traffic flow value of the i-th sensor.

To assess the effectiveness of our framework, we compare its performance against a set of representative baselines, including traditional deep learning models (LSTM [4], STGCN [11], ASTGCN [12], KST-GCN [10]) and the LLM-based xTP-LLM [24].

4.3 Experimental Results and Analysis

We evaluate **Traff-LLM** on the PeMSD4 and PeMSD8 benchmarks. As shown in Table 2, our proposed **Traff-LLM** consistently achieves the best results, significantly outperforming all baselines on both PeMSD4 and PeMSD8. Further observation reveals that LSTM demonstrates poor performance, despite being a powerful sequential model, is outperformed by graph-based models on both datasets. This suggests that explicitly modeling spatial dependencies is crucial for accurate traffic prediction.

Among the graph-based methods, STGCN, ASTGCN, and STSGCN show significantly improved performance over traditional statistical and sequence models. Notably, KST-GCN generally outperforms STGCN and ASTGCN, which can be attributed to its refined synchronous design for capturing spatio-temporal correlations. xTP-LLM demonstrates competitive performance, indicating the growing potential of large language models in this domain.

The superior performance of **Traff-LLM** is largely due to our novel spatio-temporal knowledge-guided framework, which effectively integrates complex spatio-temporal dependencies and leverages prompt-guided reasoning to enhance prediction accuracy.

Table 2. Traffic Prediction Results of Different Methods on PeMS Datasets

Dataset	Model	MAE	RMSE
PeMSD4	LSTM	29.23	45.84
	STGCN	25.92	41.28
	ASTGCN	21.83	34.48
	KST-GCN	21.73	34.45
	xTP-LLM	22.95	33.93
	Traff-LLM	**19.53**	**31.93**
PeMSD8	LSTM	24.29	37.99
	STGCN	21.69	32.92
	ASTGCN	18.33	28.30
	KST-GCN	17.56	27.18
	xTP-LLM	17.72	26.35
	Traff-LLM	**16.14**	**24.19**

Impact of Subgraph Structure

In our experimental analysis, we conducted a comparative evaluation of two distinct subgraph construction methodologies: the T-PCST algorithm and fixed k-hop neighborhood expansions.

As shown in Table 3, traditional k-hop neighborhood approaches, while straightforward, present inherent limitations in densely connected graphs such as the sensor networks investigated in this study. In contrast, the T-PCST algorithm demonstrated a significant advantage by constructing optimal subgraphs that are more discriminative and computationally efficient.

Table 3. Impact of Subgraph Structure on PeMSD4 and PeMSD8

Dataset	Subgraph Structure	RMSE	MAE	MAPE(%)
PeMSD4	Hop = 1	35.27	19.77	22.58
	Hop = 2	72.42	44.01	33.33
	Hop = 3	83.33	45.5	32.32
	T-PCST	**29.54**	**19.53**	**21.07**
PeMSD8	Hop = 1	26.21	19.94	25.02
	Hop = 2	37.45	24.0	37.7
	Hop = 3	32.38	20.52	30.83
	T-PCST	**24.19**	**16.14**	**24.57**

Impact of LLM Scale.

We evaluated the impact of model scale by fine-tuning the Qwen2.5 family on an identical traffic dataset.

Table 4. Impact of model scale on PeMSD4 and PeMSD8

Dataset	Base Model	RMSE	MAE	MAPE(%)
PeMSD4	Qwen2.5-72B	**29.54**	**19.53**	**21.07**
	Qwen2.5-32B	58.79	37.66	30.75
	Qwen2.5-7B	84.36	46.9	36.07
PeMSD8	Qwen2.5-72B	**24.19**	**16.14**	**24.57**
	Qwen2.5-32B	25.22	17.15	33.38
	Qwen2.5-7B	29.35	19.52	38.07

Table 4 shows that as the parameter count grows from 7B to 72B, both RMSE and MAE steadily decline. This pattern confirms a positive correlation between model scale and representational power: larger networks extract and abstract features more effectively, capturing the intricate spatio-temporal dynamics of traffic flows and thereby achieving lower prediction errors.

5 Conclusion

In this paper, we propose Traff-LLM, a framework that unites graph-based spatial–temporal representations with LLM-driven reasoning for traffic forecasting. First, we construct a spatio-temporal knowledge graph from traffic data, enabling Traff-LLM to effectively capture both spatial dependencies across regions and temporal patterns. Subsequently, we introduce a Temporal Prize-Collecting Steiner Tree (T-PCST) algorithm to efficiently extract the most informative subgraph for each prediction. Next, each subgraph and its associated external factors (e.g., weather and public events) are serialized into a unified natural-language prompt, which is then paired with the corresponding traffic flow to form the supervised fine-tuning corpus. Finally, we fine-tune the LLM on these prompt-response pairs, enabling it to integrate multimodal signals and perform reasoning over the spatio-temporal graph. However, the T-PCST subgraph extraction relies on offline computation and fixed temporal windows, limiting adaptability to sudden traffic disruptions. In the future, we will explore online or streaming variants that update subgraphs in real time.

References

1. Zhang, J., Wang, F.Y., Wang, K., Lin, W.H., Xu, X., Chen, C.: Data-driven intelligent transportation systems: a survey. IEEE Trans. Intell. Transp. Syst. **12**(4), 1624–1639 (2011)
2. Zivot, E., Wang, J.: Vector autoregressive models for multivariate time series. Modeling financial time series with S-PLUS®, pp. 385–429 (2006)
3. Jeong, Y.S., Byon, Y.J., Castro-Neto, M.M., Easa, S.M.: Supervised weighting-online learning algorithm for short-term traffic flow prediction. IEEE Trans. Intell. Transp. Syst. **14**(4), 1700–1707 (2013)
4. Ma, X., Tao, Z., Wang, Y., Yu, H., Wang, Y.: Long short-term memory neural network for traffic speed prediction using remote microwave sensor data. Transp. Res. Part C: Emerg. Technol. **54**, 187–197 (2015)
5. Tian, Y., Pan, L.: Predicting short-term traffic flow by long short-term memory recurrent neural network. In 2015 IEEE International Conference on Smart City/SocialCom/SustainCom (SmartCity), pp. 153–158 (2015)
6. Fu, R., Zhang, Z., Li, L.: Using LSTM and GRU neural network methods for traffic flow prediction. In: 2016 31st Youth Academic Annual Conference of Chinese Association of Automation (YAC), pp. 324–328. IEEE (2016)
7. Chen, M., Yu, X., Liu, Y.: PCNN: deep convolutional networks for short-term traffic congestion prediction. IEEE Trans. Intell. Transp. Syst. **19**(11), 3550–3559 (2018)
8. Yu, H., Wu, Z., Wang, S., Wang, Y., Ma, X.: Spatiotemporal recurrent convolutional networks for traffic prediction in transportation networks. Sensors **17**(7), 1501 (2017)
9. Zhao, L., et al.: T-GCN: a temporal graph convolutional network for traffic prediction. IEEE Trans. Intell. Transp. Syst. **21**(9), 3848–3858 (2019)
10. Zhu, J., et al.: KST-GCN: A knowledge-driven spatial-temporal graph convolutional network for traffic forecasting. IEEE Trans. Intell. Transp. Syst. (2022)
11. Yu, B., Yin, H., Zhu, Z.: Spatio-temporal graph convolutional networks: A deep learning framework for traffic forecasting. arXiv preprint arXiv:1709.04875 (2017)
12. Guo, S., Lin, Y., Feng, N., Song, C., Wan, H.: Attention based spatial-temporal graph convolutional networks for traffic flow forecasting. In: Proceedings of the AAAI Conference on Artificial Intelligence, vol. 33, no. 01, pp. 922–929 (2019)

13. Huang, R., Huang, C., Liu, Y., Dai, G., Kong, W.: LSGCN: long short-term traffic prediction with graph convolutional networks. In: IJCAI, pp. 2355–2361 (2020)
14. Xie, Z., Lv, W., Huang, S., Lu, Z., Du, B., Huang, R.: Sequential graph neural network for urban road traffic speed prediction. IEEE Access **8**, 63349–63358 (2019)
15. Xue, H., Voutharoja, B.P., Salim, F.D.: Leveraging language foundation models for human mobility forecasting. In: Proceedings of the 30th International Conference on Advances in Geographic Information Systems, pp. 1–9 (2022)
16. Xue, H., Salim, F.D.: Promptcast: a new prompt-based learning paradigm for time series forecasting. IEEE Trans. Knowl. Data Eng. **36**(11), 6851–6864 (2023)
17. Cao, D., et al.: Tempo: Prompt-based generative pre-trained transformer for time series forecasting (2023)
18. Guo, J., Du, L., Liu, H., Zhou, M., He, X., Han, S.: Gpt4graph: can large language models understand graph structured data? An empirical evaluation and benchmarking (2023)
19. Chen, Z., et al.: Exploring the potential of large language models (LLMs) in learning on graphs. ACM SIGKDD Explorations Newsl **25**(2), 42–61 (2024)
20. Li, Y., et al.: Glbench: a comprehensive benchmark for graph with large language models. Adv. Neural. Inf. Process. Syst. **37**, 42349–42368 (2024)
21. Zhou, T., Niu, P., Sun, L., Jin, R.: One fits all: power general time series analysis by pretrained lm. Adv. Neural. Inf. Process. Syst. **36**, 43322–43355 (2023)
22. Lablack, M., Shen, Y.: Spatio-temporal graph mixformer for traffic forecasting. Expert Syst. Appl. **228**, 120281 (2023)
23. Wen, H., et al.: Diffstg: Probabilistic spatio-temporal graph forecasting with denoising diffusion models. In Proceedings of the 31st ACM International Conference on Advances in Geographic Information Systems, pp. 1–12 (2023)
24. Guo, X., Zhang, Q., Jiang, J., Peng, M., Zhu, M., Yang, H.F.: Towards explainable traffic flow prediction with large language models. Commun. Transp. Res. **4**, 100150 (2024)
25. Ljubić, I., Weiskircher, R., Pferschy, U., Klau, G.W., Mutzel, P., Fischetti, M.: An algorithmic framework for the exact solution of the prize-collecting Steiner tree problem. Math. Program. **105**, 427–449 (2006)
26. Zhao, J., Itti, L.: ShapeDTW: shape dynamic time warping. Pattern Recogn. **74**, 171–184 (2018)

Applications of Knowledge Graphs and Large Models/Agents

MAEPS: Multi-agent Event Prediction System Based on Human Expert Team Collaboration Simulation

Chengyuan Jin, Tong Zhou, Yubo Chen(✉), Kang Liu, and Jun Zhao

The Key Laboratory of Cognition and Decision Intelligence for Complex Systems, Institute of Automation, Chinese Academy of Sciences, Beijing, China
{jinchengyuan2024,tong.zhou}@ia.ac.cn,
{yubo.chen,kliu,jzhao}@nlpr.ia.ac.cn

Abstract. Event prediction (EP), the accurate forecasting of future events, is vital for strategic planning and risk management in both governmental and business contexts. The rapid advancement of large language models (LLMs) has positioned AI-based automated prediction methods at the forefront of academic and industrial research. However, current LLM prediction systems exhibit several shortcomings. Firstly, their information retrieval mostly searches based on the question itself, failing to gather relevant data from multiple perspectives as human expert teams do. Secondly, their temporal analysis is inadequate, as the collected information often includes subjective opinions or speculations and lacks the ability to reconcile contradictory information across different time points during real-time prediction. To address these issues this paper introduces MAEPS (Multi-Agent Event Prediction System), which emulates the collaborative efforts of human expert teams through 12 specialized agents. Each agent collects data from a specific professional dimension. The system automatically identifies and resolves conflicting information, ensuring that predictions prioritize recent and consistent facts. Experiments on EP datasets from real prediction platforms demonstrate that MAEPS significantly outperforms existing LLM prediction systems by 7% in accuracy, thereby validating the efficacy of simulating expert team collaboration for prediction purposes.

Keywords: Event Prediction · Multi-Agent Systems · Information Retrieval · Large Language Models

1 Introduction

Event prediction (EP) refers to the systematic forecasting of future events based on available information and analytical methods. EP is crucial in fields like social policy [12] and finance [8]. Accurate forecasts provide a scientific basis for decision-making, enhancing its rationality and effectiveness. However, achieving high accuracy in complex, dynamic environments remains challenging due to

J. Liang et al. (Eds.): CCKS 2025, CCIS 2698, pp. 109–120, 2026.
https://doi.org/10.1007/978-981-95-8525-0_9

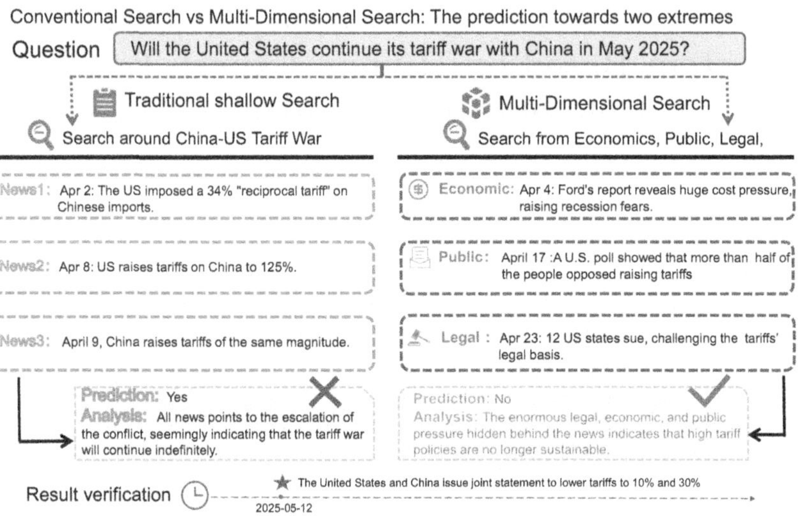

Fig. 1. The diagram illustrates that conventional shallow search, concentrating solely on direct tariff-war news, may lead to an erroneous prediction that the US will continue its tariff war with China in May 2025. In contrast, a multi-dimensional search, encompassing economic, public, and legal dimensions, could lead to a more accurate forecast of the opposite outcome.

information complexity, temporal dependencies, and uncertainty. Thus, improving prediction accuracy and practicality has become a key research focus for both academia and industry. Prediction methods are broadly categorized into statistical and judgmental approaches. While statistical methods, based on time series modeling [13], falter with sparse data or rapid environmental changes, judgmental prediction, our focus, emphasizes the integration of human expertise, historical experience, and intuition, which can compensate for the deficiencies of statistical methods in scenarios with limited data or high uncertainty.

The rise of AI has made LLM-based automated prediction a prominent research area [5–7,15,17]. These methods typically use a two-stage "retrieval-then-reason" paradigm. First, an LLM generates queries to retrieve external information for supporting evidence and contextual knowledge. Second, the system integrates this information and feeds it to the LLM for final prediction.

However, current high-quality prediction methods have three main issues: **Unidimensional Information Retrieval**: Existing methods focus on searching information directly related to the prediction question itself, failing to gather information from multiple professional perspectives. As shown in Fig. 1, this leads to incomplete information coverage. For example, predicting the US-China tariff war requires insights from economic, public sentiment, and legal dimensions, not just direct tariff news. **Insufficient Temporal Conflict Processing**: Current systems neglect the temporal attributes of information, leading to conflicts where newer reports contradict older ones about the same event. Reliance on outdated information reduces prediction timeliness as decisions are based on stale facts that no longer reflect current reality, while unresolved contradictions undermine prediction accuracy because the model cannot determine which information to trust. **Lack of Factual Screening**: Existing systems lack mechanisms for factual screening. While LLMs can extract facts [4], which are valuable in domains like finance [18], they are frequently fed a mix of facts and non-factual content like opinions and speculation. Effective prediction must be based on objective, verifiable data [20]. The method in [10] of filtering articles by type (events vs. commentary) relies on manual rules and lacks scalability.

Human experts improve complex task processing capabilities through collaboration [2]. Different experts, such as policy analysts and economists, gather information from their respective domains. For example, when predicting trade policy changes, policy analysts focus on legislative processes and regulatory frameworks, while economists analyze market indicators and economic impacts. Their collaboration integrates regulatory feasibility with economic consequences to produce more accurate predictions. This multi-dimensional approach provides a comprehensive factual basis for prediction and serves as a successful model.

Inspired by this, we propose MAEPS (Multi-Agent Event Prediction System), a framework where specialized agents collaborate to simulate expert team dynamics. By focusing on high-quality information collection and processing, MAEPS systematically addresses the three identified issues to enhance prediction comprehensiveness, timeliness, and accuracy.

This paper's main contributions are:

1. A multi-agent collaborative mechanism with 12 specialized agents that mimics expert teams to solve unidimensional retrieval by performing parallel and adaptive searches for comprehensive information coverage.
2. A factual screening and temporal conflict processing method that automatically extracts key facts and resolves contradictions to ensure predictions are based on consistent, objective information.
3. A comprehensive experimental evaluation on a real-world dataset that validates our approach. Results show MAEPS significantly outperforms existing methods by 7% in accuracy without any model fine-tuning, offering practical guidance for LLM-based prediction system design.

2 Related Work

With the rise of LLMs, automated prediction systems are a major research focus. Halawi et al. [6] develop a retrieval-augmented system that nears human-level performance on prediction platforms. RTF [7] uses hierarchical ReAct agents and tools for prediction. OpenEP [5] introduces an open-ended event prediction task and dataset, using clustering to clarify event dependencies and reduce redundancy. The PROPHET benchmark [15] offers a new evaluation perspective by categorizing problems based on causal intervention likelihood. Its temporal assumptions inform our approach to conflict resolution in MAEPS.

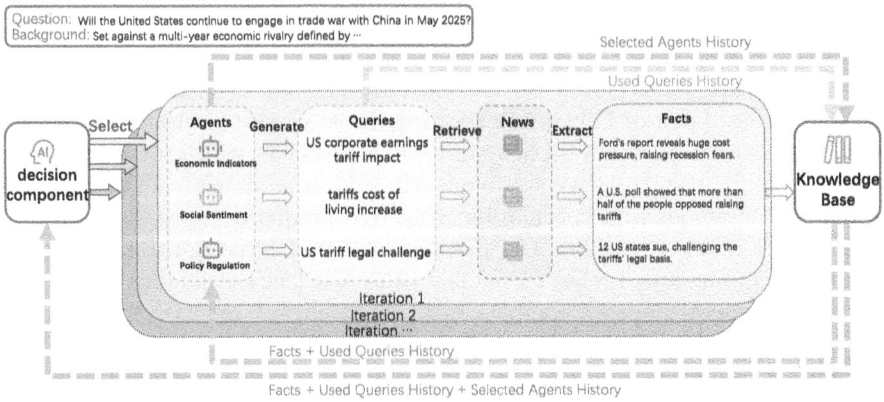

Fig. 2. The retrieval phase of a multi-agent event forecasting framework, where each round involves the decision component selecting dimensions for search, and the extracted facts and intermediate processes are saved to a knowledge base to guide subsequent iterations.

Other research explores enhancing LLM prediction capabilities. Human-LLM collaboration has shown promise [9]. Fine-tuning with methods like DPO [17] is effective but costly and hard to scale. Tools for real-time evaluation based on consistency checks have also been proposed [10]. However, some studies suggest that LLMs using traditional forecasting strategies may underperform simple prompting [11]. That research, however, is limited to closed datasets without real-time information. Therefore, building LLM systems that leverage real-time information while ensuring accuracy remains a significant challenge.

3 Method

MAEPS (Multi-Agent Event Prediction System) is an iterative framework that simulates expert team collaboration for complex prediction. It comprises three core components: **Coordination and Decision** for process control, **Information Collection** with 12 specialized agents, and **Knowledge Processing** for analysis and prediction generation. Through iterative cycles of information gathering, integration, and evaluation, MAEPS produces a comprehensive and reliable final prediction.

3.1 Multi-agent Information Retrieval

Prediction research and practice show that effective prediction requires multi-angle analysis. For instance, the PESTEL model emphasizes examining the environment from six macro-dimensions. Similarly, "Superforecasting" [16] notes that top forecasters have a "dragonfly-eye" view, integrating information from many domains.

Table 1. Specialized Agent Configuration

Agent Name	Functional Introduction
Key People	Search dynamics, positions, and influence of key figures
Key Organizations	Search official positions and plans of key organizations
Concepts Entities	Explain professional concepts and entity definitions
Historical Precedents	Search similar historical events as references
Related News	Collect latest related news, construct factual background
Policy Regulation	Interpret policies, regulations, and industry standards
Economic Indicators	Collect quantified economic data and market indicators
Expert Opinions	Integrate expert, analyst, and institutional viewpoints
Social Sentiment	Analyze public emotions, attitudes, and public opinion
External Related Events	Search external shocks or black swan events
Technology Innovation	related technological progress and supply chain dynamics
Competitive Landscape	Analyze competitors' strategies and market reactions

Based on this, we design 12 specialized agents, each responsible for collecting information in a specific dimension. These agents can execute search tasks autonomously and collaborate through a shared knowledge base. The knowledge base is the system's core, storing and managing all information to support unified retrieval, updates, and conflict detection. Table 1 introduces each agent's function. Each agent can perform autonomous analysis and reasoning, generating targeted search queries based on the problem's context. For example, regarding a US-China trade war question, the Key People Agent would query "Donald Trump," while the Competitive Landscape Agent would query "US tech company supply chain transfer progress". This intelligent search ensures the depth and relevance of information collection.

The system uses two primary information sources: News API for real-time news and Wikipedia for structured knowledge. To ensure fairness and prevent information leakage, all search operations are restricted to the time before the prediction question's resolution date. News API returns only news within the specified date range, and Wikipedia returns historical versions from a specific time point. This temporal constraint ensures the authenticity and reliability of the prediction process.

As shown in Fig. 2, at the beginning of each iteration, the decision component dynamically selects relevant agents for information collection based on the prediction question, the current state of the knowledge base, and historical selections. At the end of each round, the system analyzes the knowledge base to identify information gaps. These gaps are then converted into new search queries to guide the next round's search strategy. **Fact Extraction**: To address the lack of factual screening, the system integrates a fact extraction feature. This is important because non-factual opinions (e.g., author's subjective judgments, speculative comments) often conflict and can impair model judgment. After obtaining a document, the system calls an LLM, following the optimal settings from [6], to provide the title and the first 250 words. The model extracts key facts, filtering out subjective opinions and speculation. This ensures that the information in the knowledge base is objective and verifiable, providing a reliable basis for prediction.

3.2 Temporal Conflict Processing

Real-world events are dynamic, and information evolves over time. Old reports can be superseded by new developments, leading to outdated or contradictory information in the collected dataset. To address this, the framework includes a **temporal consistency guarantee** module with two functions: assessing information timeliness and resolving factual conflicts by constructing event timelines. **Information Quality Assessment and Timeliness**: The system first assesses the content quality of new information based on criteria like accuracy, credibility, and objectivity [14,19]. More importantly, it evaluates its **timeliness**. In prediction tasks, information value decays over time; newer information is more valuable. We quantify this with a "timeliness score":

$$\text{Timeliness Score} = 5.0 \times e^{-\lambda \times \Delta t} \tag{1}$$

where Δt is the number of days between the information's publication date and the prediction deadline, and λ is the decay constant (0.01). This score is combined with the content quality score to calculate a final weighted score, prioritizing newer facts. **Temporal Conflict Resolution and Timeline Generation**: The key to handling information from different time points is resolving factual conflicts. For example, an early report might state a policy is "under review", while a later one confirms it is "rejected". Without considering time, these facts are contradictory. The system resolves this as follows:

1. **Conflict Identification**: Identifies facts describing the same event with conflicting content.
2. **Conflict Marking**: Resolves conflicts based on publication timestamps. The latest fact is marked as the **current valid state**, while older information is marked as **"outdated"**, forming an event evolution record.
3. **Dynamic Timeline Generation**: Organizes all verified and marked facts chronologically to construct a complete **event development timeline**. This timeline is a dynamic narrative showing how events evolve. Presenting this **complete story with evolution and contradictions** to the LLM helps it make more reliable predictions.

This mechanism differs from the temporal assumptions in the PROPHET benchmark [15] and is directly applied to resolve information conflicts in actual prediction.

3.3 Prediction Generation

The system terminates and generates a final prediction when it reaches the maximum number of iterations or finds no new information gaps. The process follows the method of [6] but with different input content. It uses the quality-assessed and temporally processed knowledge base content, combined with the event development timeline, and an aggregation model for prediction.

To ensure robustness and reliability, we employ a multi-model aggregation strategy, avoiding the complexity and high cost of fine-tuning. Referencing the approach in [6], the system uses five identical base LLMs to generate candidate predictions. Each model uses the best-verified reasoning prompt, with slight optimizations for different instances, which introduces slight variations in the prompts. Finally, the system integrates the five predictions using a trimmed mean aggregation algorithm to output the final probability and confidence interval.

Algorithm 1: MAEPS Prediction System Workflow

Input: Prediction question Q, maximum iterations MaxIter
Output: Prediction results and confidence
Initialize knowledge base $KB = \emptyset$, $iter = 0$
while $iter <$ MaxIter **do**
  $selected\_agents = DecisionModule(Q, KB)$
  $new\_info = \emptyset$
  for each agent **in** $selected\_agents$ **do**
    $queries = agent.generateQueries(Q, KB)$
    $results = agent.executeSearch(queries)$ // Execute search
    $facts = ExtractFacts(results)$
    $new\_info = new\_info \cup QualityFilter(facts)$
  end for
  $KB = KB \cup new\_info$; $KB = TimeConflictResolution(KB)$ // Update KB and resolve temporal conflicts
  if $InformationGapAnalysis(Q, KB) == \emptyset$ **then break** // Check information gaps
  $iter = iter + 1$
end while
return $PredictionGeneration(Q, KB)$ // Generate final prediction

4 Experiment

We experimentally evaluate MAEPS by comparing it against strong baselines and analyzing its core components.

4.1 Experimental Setup

We use a dataset of 306 binary prediction questions from [6]. We screened questions to exclude ambiguous or niche topics, with deadlines between January and

Table 2. Main Performance Comparison

Base Model	Method	Accuracy	Brier Score (↓)
GPT-4o	**MAEPS (ours)**	**0.740**	**0.165**
	StkFEP-Re	0.720	0.176
	Halawi et al.	0.672	0.182
GPT-4	**MAEPS (ours)**	**0.710**	**0.171**
	StkFEP-Re	0.680	0.174
	Halawi et al.	0.703	0.191
GPT-3.5-Turbo	**MAEPS (ours)**	**0.670**	**0.192**
	StkFEP-Re	0.660	0.202
	Halawi et al.	0.610	0.219

Table 3. MAEPS Ablation Experiment Results

Method	Brier Score (↓)
MAEPS (Full)	**0.165**
w/o Multi-Agent	0.190
w/o Timeline	0.173
w/o Fact Extract	0.187
w/o Search	0.224

May 2025. To prevent data leakage, all questions were proposed after the models' knowledge cutoff dates. The dataset spans politics, economics, technology, and sports for a comprehensive evaluation. We evaluate model performance with two core metrics: **Accuracy**, which measures the proportion of correct predictions, and **Brier Score** [1], which assesses the accuracy of probabilistic forecasts. Lower scores indicate better accuracy and calibration. A random guess yields a 0.25 Brier score. We compare MAEPS against three baselines: **Human Crowd**, aggregated predictions from humans on real forecasting platforms; **Halawi et al.** [6], a retrieval-augmented LLM that generates a fixed number of search queries; and **StkFEP-Re**, a hybrid retrieval method that follows OpenEP [5] by collecting information on **stakeholders**, **relevant events**, and **similar events**. For a fair comparison, its subsequent processing pipeline matches MAEPS. To test for general applicability, we evaluate all methods on three base models: GPT-4o, GPT-4, and GPT-3.5-Turbo. Our experimental process is unified for rigor and reproducibility. We compare model performance against the Human Crowd, which serves as the gold standard. We simulate real predictions by following [6]'s method of using "simulated prediction days" to strictly limit information retrieval and prevent data leakage. The final score is a two-step average: first across all simulated days for each question, then across all questions. MAEPS is set to 3 iterations, with 3–4 agents selected per round, each retrieving 10 articles. For fairness, all retrieved articles are quality-filtered by an LLM before prediction.

4.2 Experimental Results and Analysis

Main Performance Comparison. To verify the framework's general applicability, we test all methods on three base models of different capabilities (GPT-4o, GPT-4, GPT-3.5-Turbo). Table 2 shows the detailed performance comparison. The results indicate that, regardless of the base model, the MAEPS framework consistently outperforms all other automated methods. This proves that our

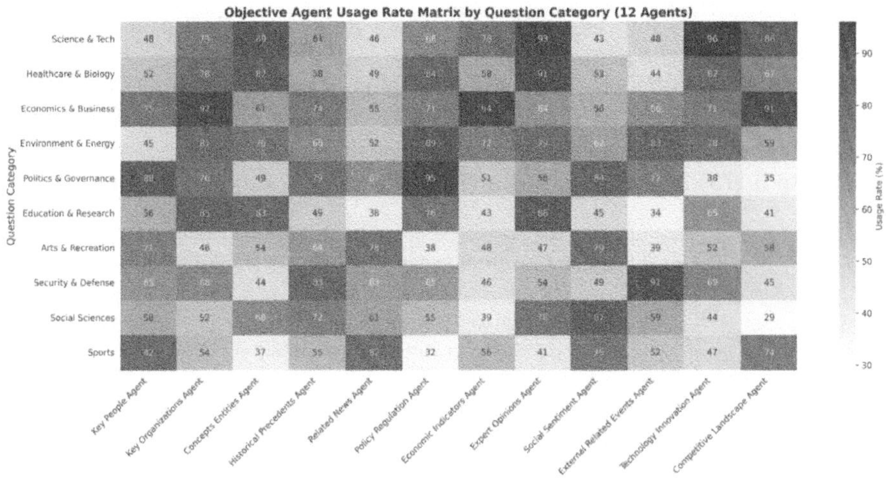

Fig. 3. This heatmap illustrates the usage rates of 12 objective agents across 10 different question categories, with color intensity representing the percentage of usage for each agent - category combination.

multi-agent collaborative framework is a universally effective information processing paradigm, not dependent on the capabilities of a specific model. Based on GPT-4o, MAEPS's performance is close to that of the human crowd, with a Brier score difference of only 0.024, demonstrating its significant potential. In retrieval strategy, StkFEP-Re outperforms [6]'s method, indicating that a structured, multi-dimensional approach consistently improves performance. MAEPS, with its more flexible, adaptive multi-agent search, achieves even better results, validating our system's core philosophy. More powerful LLMs better unlock the framework's potential; from GPT-3.5-Turbo to GPT-4o, MAEPS's Brier score improves by 0.027. Notably, GPT-4 sometimes underperforms GPT-4o due to its earlier knowledge cutoff date, a phenomenon also observed in [3].

Ablation Studies. Table 3 shows the ablation results, which reveal each component's contribution. We use GPT-4o as the base model.

- **Search:** Removing external search causes the largest performance drop (from 0.165 to 0.224), as the model's internal knowledge is outdated and lacks real-time information.
- **Multi-Agent**: Replacing our multi-agent mechanism with a single, broad search strategy [6] significantly degrades performance (from 0.165 to 0.190), even with the same number of articles.
- **Fact Extraction:** Removing the fact extraction step and using the text extracted by the method from [6] for analysis directly causes a notable performance decline. The system loses its ability to filter for high-quality information and remove irrelevant opinions. Large amounts of subjective views

and noise directly interfere with the model's judgment, which is highly detrimental for a multi-agent system.
- **Timeline:** Disabling the temporal consistency guarantee module, where the system does not process temporal conflicts and the model is not provided with the publication times of facts, also leads to a performance decline (from 0.165 to 0.173) as predictions cannot prioritize new, objective information.

Table 4. Agent Comprehensive Assessment Ranking

Agent	Comprehensive Score	Unique Contribution	Novelty Contribution	Ablation Criticality
Related News	6.42	0.925	1.85%	8.29
External Related Events	5.91	0.820	1.45%	6.33
Key People	5.25	0.720	0.82%	7.95
Economic Indicators	5.08	0.695	0.55%	7.21
Social Sentiment	5.15	0.715	0.85%	6.79
Competitive Landscape	5.02	0.665	0.62%	6.29
Historical Precedents	4.83	0.655	0.22%	5.17
Policy Regulation	4.89	0.645	0.58%	7.08
Technology Innovation	4.85	0.635	0.72%	7.04
Key Organizations	4.72	0.610	0.28%	6.29
Expert Opinions	4.78	0.605	0.52%	5.33
Concepts Entities	4.18	0.495	0.25%	5.04

Agents and System Parameter Analysis. To validate the rationale and complementarity of the 12 agents in their division of labor and to find the optimal system configuration, we conducted a series of analyses.

Agent Specialization Analysis. To assess each agent's value, we define four key metrics:

- **Comprehensive Score:** Calculated via a weighted model based on multi-criteria decision analysis.
- **Unique Contribution Rate:** Measures the proportion of information an agent retrieved that no other agent did, quantified by Jaccard similarity or semantic vector overlap.
- **Novelty Contribution Rate:** Measures an agent's ability to find entirely new information (not seen in previous rounds).
- **Ablation Criticality Score:** Measures the negative impact on system performance when a single agent is removed.

The analysis results (see Fig. 3 and Table 4) show that the agents have formed a clear specialized division of labor, and each agent has indispensable unique value, providing novel information to enhance system performance.

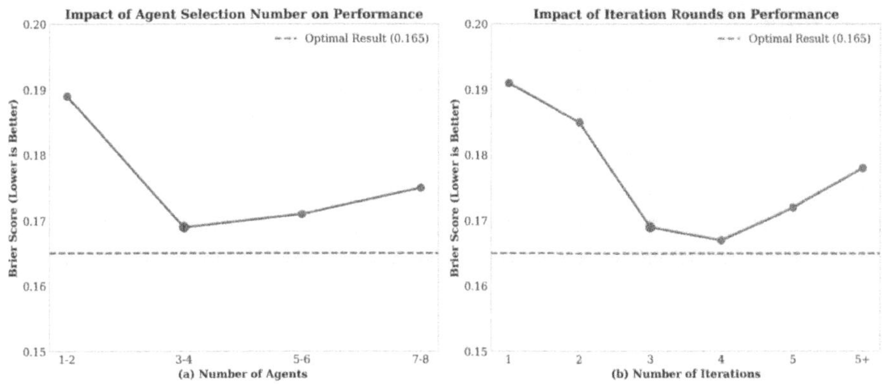

Fig. 4. These two graphs depict the impact of the number of agents per round (a) and iteration rounds (b) on predictive performance, with the optimal experimental outcome (0.165) indicated by a red dashed line. (Color figure online)

System Parameter Sensitivity Analysis To find the optimal configuration, we conduct a sensitivity analysis on the number of agents selected per round and the total number of iterations. The results (see Fig. 4) show that selecting 3–4 agents and iterating 3 times achieve the best balance between performance and cost. Too few leads to insufficient information dimensions; too many introduces redundancy and degrades performance. Therefore, we chose this as the system's default configuration.

5 Conclusion

This paper introduces the MAEPS framework to address the issues of unidimensional information retrieval and inadequate temporal processing in existing LLM prediction systems. By simulating human expert teams, the framework uses 12 specialized agents for multi-dimensional, adaptive information gathering. The system integrates fact extraction and temporal consistency mechanisms to automatically filter facts and resolve temporal conflicts, ensuring predictions are based on high-quality information. Experiments show that the framework effectively improves prediction accuracy and reliability. Future work will focus on exploring enhanced search strategies and integrating more diverse data sources.

Acknowledgement. This work is supported by the National Natural Science Foundation of China (No. U24A20335, No. 62176257). This work is sponsored by Beijing Nova Program (No. 20250484750) and supported by Beijing Natural Science Foundation (L243006). This work is also supported by the Youth Innovation Promotion Association CAS.

References

1. Brier, G.W.: Verification of forecasts expressed in terms of probability. Mon. Weather Rev. **78**(1), 1–3 (1950). https://doi.org/10.1175/1520-0493(1950)078<0001:VOFEIT>2.0.CO;2
2. Chen, D., et al.: Advancing human-machine teaming: concepts, challenges, and applications. arXiv preprint arXiv:2503.16518 (2025)
3. Dai, H., Teehan, R., Ren, M.: Are LLMs prescient? A continuous evaluation using daily news as the oracle. arXiv preprint arXiv:2411.08324 (2024)
4. Golob, L., Sittar, A.: Fact manipulation in news: LLM-driven synthesis and evaluation of fake news annotation (2024)
5. Guan, Y., Peng, H., Wang, X., Hou, L., Li, J.: OpenEP: open-ended future event prediction. arXiv preprint arXiv:2408.06578 (2024)
6. Halawi, D., Zhang, F., Yueh-Han, C., Steinhardt, J.: Approaching human-level forecasting with language models. arXiv preprint arXiv:2402.18563 (2024)
7. Hsieh, E., Fu, P., Chen, J.: Reasoning and tools for human-level forecasting. arXiv preprint arXiv:2408.12036 (2024)
8. Li, X., et al.: AlphaFin: benchmarking financial analysis with retrieval-augmented stock-chain framework. arXiv preprint arXiv:2403.12582 (2024)
9. Lippert, S., Dreber, A., Johannesson, M., Tierney, W., Cyrus-Lai, W., Uhlmann, E.L., Pfeiffer, T.: Can large language models help predict results from a complex behavioural science study? Roy. Soc. Open Sci. **11**(9) (2024). https://doi.org/10.1098/rsos.240682
10. Paleka, D., Sudhir, A.P., Alvarez, A., Bhat, V., Shen, A., Wang, E., Tramèr, F.: Consistency checks for language model forecasters. arXiv preprint arXiv:2412.18544 (2024)
11. Pratt, S., Blumberg, S., Carolino, P.K., Morris, M.R.: Can language models use forecasting strategies? arXiv preprint arXiv:2406.04446 (2024)
12. Rotaru, V., Huang, Y., Li, T., Evans, J., Chattopadhyay, I.: Event-level prediction of urban crime reveals a signature of enforcement bias in us cities. Nat. Hum. Behav. **6**(8), 1056–1068 (2022). https://doi.org/10.1038/s41562-022-01372-0
13. Shabani, A., Abdi, A., Meng, L., Sylvain, T.: Scaleformer: iterative multi-scale refining transformers for time series forecasting. arXiv preprint arXiv:2206.04038 (2022)
14. Stvilia, B., Gasser, L., Twidale, M.B., Smith, L.C.: A framework for information quality assessment. J. Am. Soc. Inform. Sci. Technol. **58**(12), 1720–1733 (2007). https://doi.org/10.1002/asi.20652
15. Tao, Z., et al.: Prophet: an inferable future forecasting benchmark with causal intervened likelihood estimation. arXiv preprint arXiv:2504.01509 (2025)
16. Tetlock, P.E., Gardner, D.: Superforecasting: The Art and Science of Prediction. Crown Publishing Group, New York (2015)
17. Turtel, B., Franklin, D., Schoenegger, P.: LLMs can teach themselves to better predict the future. arXiv preprint arXiv:2502.05253 (2025)
18. Wang, Q., Gao, Y., Tang, Z., Luo, B., He, B.: Enhancing LLM trading performance with fact-subjectivity aware reasoning. arXiv preprint arXiv:2410.12464 (2024)
19. Wang, R.Y., Strong, D.M.: Beyond accuracy: what data quality means to data consumers. J. Manag. Inf. Syst. **12**(4), 5–33 (1996). https://doi.org/10.1080/07421222.1996.11518099
20. Zhao, L.: Event prediction in big data era: a systematic survey. arxiv preprint. ArXivorg (2020)

Zero-Shot Instruction Generation via Dual-Alignment Instruction Wrappers with Summary-Text Fused Instruction Wrappers

Feng Gao[1,2,3], Yue Sun[1,2,3], Yuanyuan Li[1,2,3], and Jinguang Gu[1,2,3(✉)]

[1] School of Computer Science and Technology, Wuhan University of Science and Technology, Wuhan 430065, Hubei, China
simon@wust.edu.cns

[2] Hubei Province Key Laboratory of Intelligent Information Processing and Real-Time Industrial System, Wuhan University of Science and Technology, Wuhan 430065, China

[3] School of Computer Science and Technology, Institute of Big Data Science and Engineering, Wuhan 430065, Hubei, China

Abstract. With the deepening application of large language models in the field of natural language processing, ensuring the diversity, knowledgeability, and integrity of instruction data has become crucial for enhancing model performance and domain adaptation capabilities. Focusing on these aspects, this paper proposes a method for constructing instruction data by fusing document summaries and text fragments, which improves the… of the instruction dataset, and thus improve the performance of the model fine-tuned with the dataset. Diverse question-answer pairs covering multiple scenarios and dimensions are generated through ChatGPT-4, and multiple semantic alignment screening strategies are combined to ensure semantic consistency and integrity of the data, effectively reducing the risk of model hallucinations. Experiments conducted on mainstream models such as ChatGLM, Qwen, and DeepSeek, as well as datasets in general and medical domains, demonstrate that this method significantly improves the diversity and integrity of model instruction generation. The optimized models, in tasks such as medical question-answering, can generate more knowledgeable and logically coherent long-text responses compared to unfine-tuned models and the ChatGPT-3.5 baseline, providing an effective path with both theoretical depth and practical value for the instruction tuning and domain adaptation of large language models.

Keywords: Large Language Model · Instruction Tuning · Long-text Generation · Instruction Generation

1 Introduction

With the widespread use of LLMs in NLP tasks [1], efficiently creating high-quality instruction data is crucial, especially in specialized domains like medicine and law with complex long texts [2, 3]. Traditional short-instruction methods face challenges in

J. Liang et al. (Eds.): CCKS 2025, CCIS 2698, pp. 121–133, 2026.
https://doi.org/10.1007/978-981-95-8525-0_10

cost, efficiency, and consistency [4], highlighting the need for scalable, automated, and semantically aligned solutions.

We propose a novel method that fuses document abstracts with body text to improve context and instruction relevance. A multi-level semantic alignment filtering uses a dual-filter strategy to select highly consistent QA pairs, enhancing data quality in generation and selection.

Our contributions are: (1) constructing training data by abstract-body fusion to boost semantic coverage and task alignment; (2) zero-shot instruction generation experiments across domains showing improved diversity and completeness; (3) releasing a long-text QA dataset spanning 13 medical departments to support further research.

This work offers a high-quality, generalizable solution for long-text instruction generation, improving large model generalization on complex tasks.

2 Related Work

Instruction generation is key to improving LLMs on complex long texts but faces challenges in scalability, accuracy, and structure understanding. Section 2.1 reviews human-generated instructions, which offer high quality but are costly and inefficient. Section 2.2 covers model-constructed methods that automate generation but often produce hallucinations. Section 2.3 discusses reverse instruction generation, which infers instructions from documents but struggles with implicit reasoning. Section 2.4 examines document-driven self-synthesis, improving efficiency but lacking strong semantic alignment. These limitations motivate our approach combining abstract-body fusion and multi-level semantic filtering to enhance data quality and relevance.

2.1 Human-Generated Instructions

Human-generated (HG) instructions are a traditional approach that rely on manually designed templates and annotated QA pairs [4, 5]. For instance, OpenAI's InstructGPT used prompts written by professional annotators [5], and Super-NaturalInstructions compiled 1,616 NLP tasks manually [6]. While high in quality, this method struggles with long texts due to high costs (e.g., one instruction per annotator) and low efficiency (e.g., Suri took months to label 20K samples) [7]. Annotator subjectivity also causes inconsistency in domain terms, affecting logic and factual accuracy. These issues underscore the need for scalable, automated methods—motivating our data fusion and filtering-based strategy.

2.2 Model-Constructed Instructions

Model-constructed (MC) instructions use LLMs to auto-generate instructions. Self-Instruct follows a "seed instruction – generation – filtering – fine-tuning" pipeline, boosting GPT-3's performance by 33% [8]. GLAN extends this by using a subject-specific knowledge tree for complex tasks [9]. However, MC methods struggle with long texts: hallucinations cause factual errors [10], and 35% of long instructions miss key constraints due to poor structural understanding [11]. They also often ignore implicit knowledge and include irrelevant content. To address this, we fuse abstracts with body segments to build knowledge-based training data. The abstract enhances context understanding, ensuring relevance and reducing meaningless QA pairs, thereby improving data quality.

2.3 Reverse Instruction Generation

Reverse instruction generation infers instructions from long documents. LongForm introduced the LongForm-C dataset to enable low-cost instruction creation [11], but it mainly captures explicit content and struggles with implicit logic, such as argumentative chains in academic texts. Its tasks are also limited and lack support for complex cross-paragraph reasoning. DoG-Instruct improves instruction-document alignment by reverse-constructing pseudo-aligned data [12], yet still faces weak contextual understanding in ultra-long texts [13], which reduces instruction quality. To address these limitations, we propose fusing abstracts with body segments to systematically integrate key knowledge. This ensures generated QA pairs are closely aligned with core content, enhancing both relevance and data quality.

2.4 Document-Driven Self-Synthesis

Document-driven self-synthesis methods like LongMagpie automate instruction generation through a "document–query–response" pipeline, improving efficiency by 100 × over manual methods [14]. However, their performance relies heavily on LLM alignment quality. In specialized domains, misinterpretation of terminology often leads to incorrect instructions [15]. Existing methods also lack effective control over alignment with source content, resulting in many low-quality QA pairs. To address this, we introduce a dual-filter semantic alignment mechanism that rigorously selects content closely aligned with the source. Combined with our abstract-body fusion strategy, this ensures high-quality training data and reduces hallucination risk in long-text instruction generation.

3 Training Instruction Wrappers

This chapter introduces the complete process of constructing high-quality instruction training data, including a data generation strategy based on abstract-body fusion and a multi-level semantic alignment filtering mechanism to reduce hallucination risks. Through a systematic task design and filtering process, we ultimately obtain a batch of structurally diverse, semantically consistent, and contextually grounded QA pairs that serve as a solid foundation for base model training (Fig. 1).

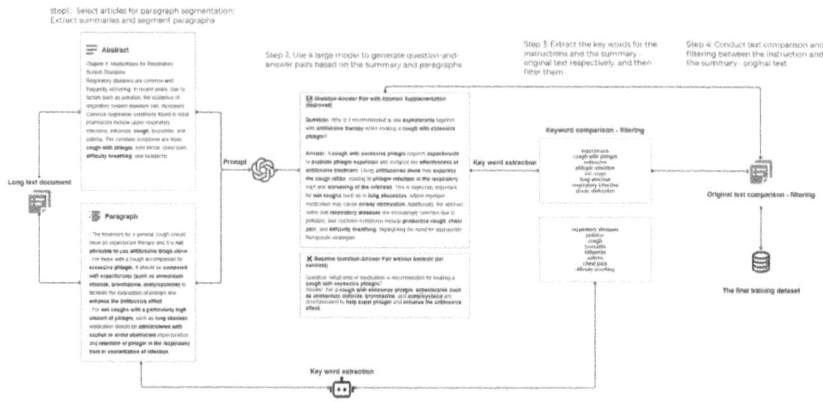

Fig. 1. The entire workflow of the instruction wrapper

3.1 Construction of Training Metadata via Abstract-Body Fusion

To overcome semantic fragmentation and topic drift in long-text instruction generation [13], we propose a training data construction method based on abstract-body fusion. This approach enhances contextual understanding, topic coherence, and task executability. Crucially, generated content is centered on explicit knowledge points within paragraphs, ensuring high independence and usability even when separated from the original text.

To enhance the professionalism and diversity of the training data, we select long texts from domains such as medical papers, legal documents, news report abstracts from LongBench, and government documents. Given a set of original documents $\{D_1, D_2, \ldots, D_n\}$, where each D_i represents a structured long-form document (e.g., medical paper, legal paper, news summary, or government report), our goal is to construct a set of instruction-response pairs $\{(X_1, Y_1), \ldots, (X_m, Y_m)\}$. Each sample (X_i, Y_i) represents an instruction-answer pair satisfying:

$$(X_i, Y_i) := M\,(D_j^{\mathrm{abs}}, D_j^{\mathrm{body}})$$

Let D_j^{abs} denote the abstract of document j, and D_j^{body} the corresponding body segment. Let f be the instruction wrapper based on a large language model (LLM) that maps (D_j^{abs}, D_j^{body}) into a semantically aligned QA pair.

In practice, we first concatenate the abstract and body segment: $D_i^{\mathrm{input}} = \mathrm{concat}(D_j^{\mathrm{abs}}, D_j^{\mathrm{body}})$, then apply the mapping function M using the ChatGPT-4 model to guide instruction generation around the topics covered by the abstract. This results in the instruction X_i and answer Y_i, with guidance to focus on knowledge points in the body while being constrained by the abstract's context. This yields an initial training dataset: $\omega = \{(X_1, Y_1), (X_2, Y_2), \ldots, (X_m, Y_m)\}$.

Additionally, we incorporate task type identifiers in the prompt design to cover multiple dimensions such as fact extraction, causal reasoning, situational judgment, and text summarization. This results in training samples with diverse question types and instruction styles. To ensure textual integrity and contextual coherence during generation, the maximum length of body segments is controlled within 10K tokens, and overlapping regions between adjacent segments are limited to no more than 1K tokens, improving the practicality of the generated content in long-text scenarios.

Compared to traditional paragraph-based generation strategies such as DoG-Instruct, our method improves alignment with source themes and enhances semantic coverage and background knowledge consistency through the use of abstracts. The model is guided to generate questions centered around explicit paragraph-level knowledge, significantly enhancing the knowledge value and transferability of the training data.

3.2 Multi-level Semantic Alignment Filtering Mechanism

To ensure the authenticity, semantic relevance, and traceability of the training data, we design a multi-level semantic alignment filtering mechanism. This involves multiple filtering rounds based on keyword overlap and text similarity, effectively reducing hallucinated content in LLM outputs.

The first stage is keyword alignment filtering. Based on the initially generated instruction set $\omega = \{(X_1, Y_1), (X_2, Y_2), \ldots, (X_m, Y_m)\}$, we use ChatGPT-4 to extract keywords from each instruction $(X_i, Y_i) \in \omega$ along with its corresponding body and abstract (D_j^{abs}, D_j^{body}), retaining the top 10 keywords for each.

$$K_i^{\text{doc}} = TopK(Keywords(D_j^{\text{abs}}, D_j^{\text{body}}))$$

$$K_i^{qa} = TopK(Keywords(X_i, Y_i))$$

We then compute the Jaccard similarity between the QA pair keywords and the document body keywords. A similarity threshold $\tau_k = 0.4$ is set to filter out low-topic-overlap samples.

$$Jaccard(K_i^{doc}, K_i^{qa}) = \frac{|K_i^{doc} \cap K_i^{qa}|}{|K_i^{doc} \cup K_i^{qa}|}, Jaccard(K_i^{doc}, K_i^{qa}) > \tau_k$$

This yields an intermediate set ω_K.

The second stage is text attribution verification. We use Sentence-BERT to obtain sentence embeddings for generated answers Y_i and the original document content (D_j^{abs}, D_j^{body}) (including abstract and body), and compute cosine similarity.

$$\vec{y}_i = SBERT(Y_i), \vec{d}_i = SBERT([(D_j^{abs}, D_j^{body})])$$

A threshold $\tau_s = 0.6$ is applied to retain samples satisfying:

$$sim(Y_i, (D_j^{abs}, D_j^{body})) = \cos(\overrightarrow{y_i}, \overrightarrow{d_i}), sim(Y_i, (D_j^{abs}, D_j^{body})) \geq \tau_s$$

Only samples with similarity above 0.6 are retained. This strategy, validated in open-source projects such as OpenOrca, effectively reduces the risk of hallucinated information.

After two rounds of semantic alignment filtering, we construct approximately 40,000 high-quality QA pairs that are structurally consistent, semantically clear, and highly aligned with the original document content for use in base model training.

$$\omega^* = \{(X_i, Y_i) \in \omega_k \Big| sim(Y_i, (D_j^{abs}, D_j^{body})) \geq \tau_s\}$$

Furthermore, to enhance model generalization and training efficiency, we adopt a template-based structured data representation format. Each training sample is represented as an input of "body segment + extracted keywords," with the target output being the corresponding QA pair. This input format not only explicitly annotates the task context but also reduces the model's reliance on redundant context, making it easier to learn instruction generation paradigms and task intents.

Table Statistics. Table 1 summarizes the sources and basic characteristics of the constructed dataset, including the origin, average length, and composition of samples.

Table 1. Table captions should be placed above the tables.

Document Source	Number of Queries Avg	Input Length (tokens) Avg	Output Length (tokens)
LongBench (partial)	26432	84 ∓ 24	36 ∓ 35
Medical Research Papers	9872	154 ∓ 62	178 ∓ 36
Legal Research Papers	4382	119 ∓ 35	142 ∓ 69

3.3 Training Configuration

We conducted experiments on three different base model architectures, each fine-tuned using the LoRA (Low-Rank Adaptation) technique (Hu et al., 2021) for parameter-efficient adaptation. All experiments were carried out on a single NVIDIA RTX 4090 GPU (24 GB), with 6 training epochs per run. The initial learning rate was appropriately set (value omitted in original), and on average, each experiment required approximately 6 days of training to obtain a fully fine-tuned model.

As a result, we produced multiple domain-adapted models suitable for downstream task evaluation. The experimental design balances training stability with computational efficiency, laying a solid foundation for subsequent task transfer and performance assessment.

4 Experimental Analysis

In this section, we evaluate the performance of the instruction wrapper along two key dimensions: diversity and completeness. We conduct experiments using four mainstream language models: ChatGPT-3.5, ChatGLM3-6B, Qwen1.5-8B, and DeepSeek-RL-8B. Each model is evaluated in both its vanilla (pretrained) and fine-tuned states, with instruction generation performed using our constructed metadata dataset ω^*.

4.1 Baseline Setup

Baseline Setup and Evaluation Protocol. To ensure the reliability and interpretability of our experimental results, we define three key baseline models:

ChatGPT-3.5: As a widely recognized closed-source LLM with strong instruction-following capabilities, ChatGPT-3.5 serves as an important reference to assess whether our fine-tuned models achieve meaningful improvements in instruction quality and task performance [5].

DoG-Instruct: Since the training data and model parameters of DoG are not publicly available, we follow the data construction methodology proposed in DoG to build a comparable training set and fine-tune it on Qwen3-8B. This allows us to benchmark the effectiveness of the DoG-style data synthesis pipeline [12].

Vanilla Models: We also include the unmodified versions of each base model prior to fine-tuning [1]. These serve as control groups to measure the performance gain directly attributable to our dataset ω^* and fine-tuning strategy, rather than improvements stemming from architectural changes.

The rationale behind selecting these baselines is twofold. On one hand, ChatGPT-3.5 represents the upper bound of instruction generation performance in industrial applications. Comparing with it helps evaluate whether our approach can bring open-source models closer to state-of-the-art performance. On the other hand, the inclusion of vanilla models ensures that any observed performance gains originate from our data-driven methodology rather than model-specific enhancements.

During evaluation, none of the baseline or fine-tuned models are exposed to gold-standard task annotations, mimicking realistic deployment scenarios for general instruction-following assessment. This "zero-label evaluation" protocol [8] effectively prevents data leakage and better reflects the model's generalization capabilities under unsupervised conditions.

Experimental results across two domains demonstrate that our fine-tuned models outperform the vanilla models in terms of instruction diversity, question completeness, and automatic task scoring. Moreover, on several key metrics, our models approach or even surpass ChatGPT-3.5, validating the effectiveness of our "summary + document fragment" strategy for constructing instruction-tuning datasets in practice.

4.2 Diversity Evaluation

In this section, we focus on assessing the performance improvements of the instruction wrapper along the two critical dimensions of diversity and completeness. We conducted experiments with ChatGPT-3.5 and three mainstream open-source models: ChatGLM3-6B, Qwen1.5-8B, and DeepSeek-RL-8B. Each model was evaluated both in its vanilla (un-fine-tuned) and fine-tuned states, using our constructed metadata dataset for instruction generation.

We selected summarization tasks from L-Eval [16], including government reports, meeting transcripts, news, and interviews, known for complex discourse and dense information. Documents were split into 1,000-character segments, with each model generating one QA pair per segment. For each model, 100 QA pairs were sampled and experiments repeated five times; results were averaged for robustness. Outputs were analyzed on form diversity, semantic coverage, and part-of-speech co-occurrence.

self-BLEU. To measure diversity among generated instructions, we calculated the self-BLEU [17] score on n-grams. A lower self-BLEU value indicates less similarity among samples and thus higher diversity. As shown in Table 3, fine-tuned models consistently outperform their vanilla counterparts in the self-BLEU metric. Among them, the fine-tuned version of DeepSeekR1-8B achieves the most significant improvement (+), demonstrating that our training data effectively stimulates the model's ability to produce structurally diverse outputs (Table 2).

Table 2. Self-BLEU Results of Different Models

Model		BLUE-1	BLUE-2	BLUE-3	BLUE-4
GPT		0.8053	0.5836	0.4246	0.3212
ChatGLM3-6B	None	0.8001	0.5897	0.4382	0.3243
	DoG	0.7959	0.5777	0.4153	0.2958
	LoRA	0.8052 (–)	0.5889(+)	0.4206 (+)	0.3018 (+)
Qwen3-8B	None	0.8109	0.5969	0.4381	0.3235
	DoG	0.8118	0.5972	0.4409	0.3277
	LoRA	0.8102(+)	0.5936(+)	0.4360(+)	0.3226(+)
DeepseekR1-8B	None	0.8113	0.5971	0.4409	0.3273
	DoG	0.8031	0.5612	0.3888	0.2725
	LoRA	**0.7943(+)**	**0.5577(+)**	**0.3899(+)**	**0.2617(+)**

Sentence-BERT: We utilized Sentence-BERT to compute semantic embeddings for the questions generated by each model [18], and then estimated the entropy of their embedding distributions. A higher entropy value indicates a more dispersed semantic distribution, reflecting broader coverage and greater generation diversity. As shown in Table 4, the fine-tuned version of DeepSeek-RL-8B achieves the best performance in terms of both average entropy and maximum entropy. Meanwhile, ChatGPT-3.5 exhibits superior performance on the standard deviation metric, indicating that its generated content is more concentrated yet consistent.

Table 3. Sentence-BERT Embeddings of Model-Generated Questions

Model	Mean Entropy	Standard Deviation	Maximum Entropy	Minimum Entropy
GPT	3.9525	**0.3193**	4.8413	**3.1527**
ChatGLM3 – 6B	3.7499	0.4297	4.6184	2.6037
$ChatGLM3-6B_{DoG}$	3.7824	0.4537	4.8418	2.6037
$ChatGLM3-6B_{LoRA}$	3.9709 (+)	0.391 (+)	4.8418 (+)	2.5328 (–)
Qwen3-8B	3.2158	1.1212	4.8425	0.9903
$Qwen3-8B_{DoG}$	3.9375	0.3546	4.8418	2.9639
Qwen3 – $8B_{LoRA}$	**4.0656** (+)	0.3281 (–)	**4.8415(–)**	3.0633 (+)
DeepseekR1-8B	3.6564	0.5614	4.8418	0.9903
$DeepseekR1-8B_{DoG}$	3.8431	0.5710	4.8423	0.9903
DeepseekR1 – $8B_{LoRA}$	3.9957 (+)	0.3516 (+)	4.8408 (–)	3.0136 (+)

Furthermore, we visualized the semantic entropy distributions using boxplots in Fig. 2, providing an intuitive illustration of the diversity improvements brought by fine-tuning across different models.

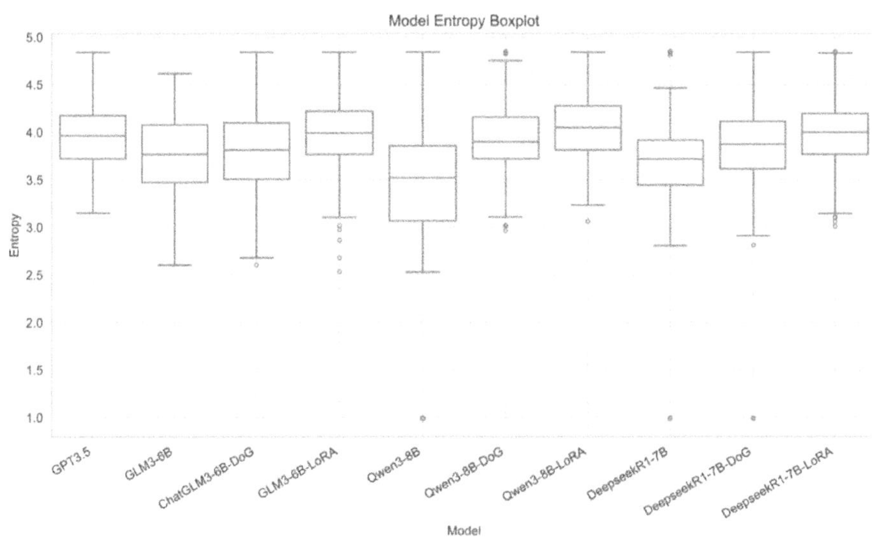

Fig. 2. Distribution of Semantic Entropy of Generated Questions Across Models (Boxplot Visualization)

Verb-Noun Pair Analysis: We performed part-of-speech tagging on each set of generated question-answer pairs to extract verbs and their corresponding noun objects [19]. We then computed three metrics: the total number of unique verb-noun pairs, the average number of nouns associated with each verb, and the overall coverage of verbs and nouns. As shown in Table 5 and Fig. 3, all fine-tuned models outperform their respective vanilla counterparts across these metrics. Notably, the fine-tuned DeepSeek-RL-8B achieves the best results in every metric, demonstrating the effectiveness of our method in enhancing structural linguistic diversity.

Table 4. Statistics of Verb-Noun Pair Metrics for Generated Question-Answer Pairs Across Models

Model	verb_count	noun_count	pair_count	avg_nouns_per_verb
GPT	152	189	238	1.5658
ChatGLM3 − 6B	153	176	245	1.6013
ChatGLM3 − 6B_{DoG}	142	180	238	1.6761
ChatGLM3 − 6B_{LoRA}	163(+)	202(+)	271(+)	1.6626(-)
Qwen3-8B	148	161	225	1.5203
*Qwen*3 − 8B_{DoG}	157	207	274	1.7452
Qwen3 − 8B_{LoRA}	**192(+)**	**242(+)**	**355(+)**	**1.8490(+)**
DeepseekR1-8B	153	173	238	1.5556
*DeepseekR*1 − 8B_{DoG}	164	198	275	1.6768
DeepseekR1 - 8B_{LORA}	186(+)	218(+)	318(+)	1.7097(+)

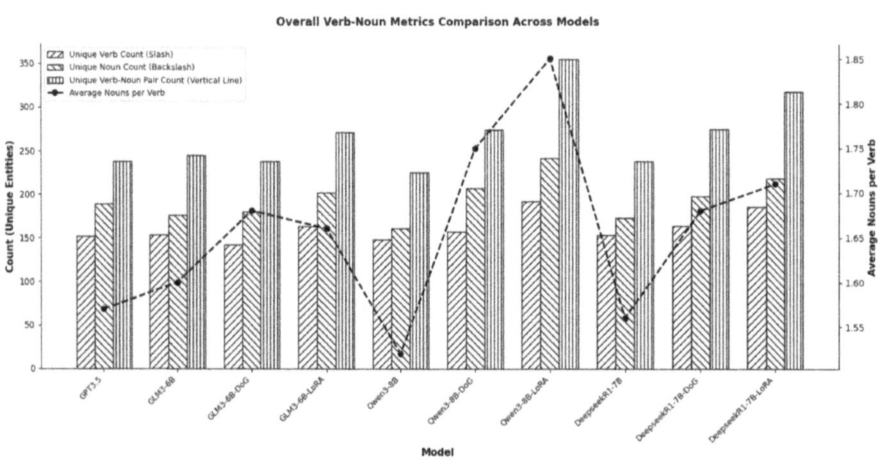

Fig. 3. Comparison of verb and noun richness metrics across different language models.

4.3 Evaluation of Fine-Tuning Effectiveness

To validate the real-world applicability of our instruction tuning approach, we built a controlled evaluation framework using expert-annotated data. A benchmark set of high-quality QA pairs was manually curated from the Quick Reference Manual, which contains over 6,300 verified entries across diverse medical domains.

From this standardized dataset, we randomly sampled 1,000 paragraphs and paired each with its corresponding chapter-level summary to form a context-rich input set. These paragraph-summary pairs served as the foundation for generating instructions and training data across four different configurations: (1) the original, un-fine-tuned model (vanilla), (2) LoRA fine-tuned model [20], (3) models trained on DoG-style synthetic instruction data [12], and (4) models trained with template-generated instructions [21]. Each model was evaluated on the same dataset to ensure comparability.

We evaluated performance using a manually curated test set of 100 gold-standard QA pairs from the same book. Each model generated answers based on the input context. We measured semantic similarity between generated and reference answers using Sentence-BERT with cosine similarity [18]. For each question, the model with the highest similarity was deemed the winner. Win counts were aggregated to calculate each model's final win rate.

Table 5 summarizes the win rate performance across different model and training configurations. LoRA fine-tuning consistently led to substantial improvements over all baselines. DeepSeekR1-8B achieved the highest win rate (58%), followed by Qwen3-8B (49%), while the base model reached 37%. In contrast, models trained with DoG-style and template-generated instructions yielded significantly lower win rates, ranging from 12% to 25%.

Table 5. Each value represents the number of wins out of 100 samples (win count/total samples), and the percentage is calculated accordingly.

Model	LoRA Win Rate	Row Win Rate	DoG Win Rate	Template Win Rate
ChatGLM3 − 6B	**37/100**	21/100	25/100	17/100
Qwen3-8B	**49/100**	17/100	22/100	12/100
DeepseekR1-8B	**58/100**	9/100	20/100	13/100

5 Conclusion and Future Work

This paper tackles key challenges in long-form instruction generation and domain adaptation for LLMs [22]. We propose a method that fuses document summaries with body segments to build instruction training data, guided by diversity and completeness metrics. Using structured prompts and ChatGPT-4, we generate high-quality, semantically aligned QA pairs. Experiments show that fine-tuned models improve both diversity and completeness, and outperform vanilla models and the ChatGPT-3.5 baseline in medical QA tasks.

The main contributions of this work are:

Proposing a strategy that combines summaries to supplement background information, thereby enhancing topical relevance and accuracy in instruction generation;

Introducing a multi-level semantic alignment filtering mechanism that substantially reduces hallucination risks in model-generated data;

Future work will focus on enhancing multi-document instruction generation by improving long-text modeling and cross-segment information fusion for greater logical coherence and contextual understanding.

References

1. Brown, T., Mann, B., Ryder, N., et al.: Language models are few-shot learners. Adv. Neural. Inf. Process. Syst. **33**, 1877–1901 (2020)
2. Yang, Q., Wang, R., Chen, J., et al.: Fine-tuning medical language models for enhanced long-contextual understanding and domain expertise. arXiv preprint arXiv:2407.11536 (2024)
3. Xu, R., Cui, H., Yu, Y., et al.: Knowledge-infused prompting: assessing and advancing clinical text data generation with large language models. arXiv preprint arXiv:2311.00287 (2023)
4. Xu, C., Sun, Q., Zheng, K., et al.: Wizardlm: empowering large language models to follow complex instructions. arXiv preprint arXiv:2304.12244 (2023)
5. Ouyang, L., Wu, J., Jiang, X., et al.: Training language models to follow instructions with human feedback. Adv. Neural. Inf. Process. Syst. **35**, 27730–27744 (2022)
6. Wang, Y., Mishra, S., Alipoormolabashi, P., et al.: Super-naturalinstructions: Generalization via declarative instructions on 1600+ nlp tasks. arXiv preprint arXiv:2204.07705 (2022)
7. Sanh, V., Webson, A., Raffel, C., et al.: Multitask prompted training enables zero-shot task generalization. arXiv preprint arXiv:2110.08207 (2021)
8. Wang, Y., Kordi, Y., Mishra, S., et al.: Self-instruct: aligning language models with self-generated instructions. arXiv preprint arXiv:2212.10560 (2022)
9. Zhang, M., Ye, X., Liu, Q., et al.: Knowledge graph enhanced large language model editing. arXiv preprint arXiv:2402.13593 (2024)
10. Ji, Z., Lee, N., Frieske, R., et al.: Survey of hallucination in natural language generation. ACM Comput. Surv. **55**(12), 1–38 (2023)
11. Huang, Y., Liu, Y., Thirukovalluru, R., et al.: Calibrating long-form generations from large language models. arXiv preprint arXiv:2402.06544 (2024)
12. Chen, Y., Jiang, H., Huang, X., et al.: DoG-Instruct: towards premium instruction-tuning data via text-grounded instruction wrapping. arXiv preprint arXiv:2309.05447 (2023)
13. Bai, Y., Lv, X., Zhang, J., et al.: Longbench: a bilingual, multitask benchmark for long context understanding. arXiv preprint arXiv:2308.14508 (2023)
14. Sheremet, O.I., Kiriienko, T.V.: Building a document-driven chatbot using local large language models. ПРОГРАМНИЙ КОМІТЕТ 161
15. Gu, Y., Tinn, R., Cheng, H., et al.: Domain-specific language model pretraining for biomedical natural language processing. ACM Trans. Comput. Healthc. (HEALTH) **3**(1), 1–23 (2021)
16. An, C., Gong, S., Zhong, M., et al.: L-eval: instituting standardized evaluation for long context language models. arXiv preprint arXiv:2307.11088 (2023)
17. Zhu, Y., Lu, S., Zheng, L., et al.: Texygen: a benchmarking platform for text generation models. In: The 41st International ACM SIGIR Conference on Research & Development in Information Retrieval, pp. 1097–1100 (2018)
18. Reimers, N., Gurevych, I.: Sentence-bert: Sentence embeddings using siamese bert-networks. arXiv preprint arXiv:1908.10084 (2019)

19. Zhao, T., Zhao, R., Eskenazi, M.: Learning discourse-level diversity for neural dialog models using conditional variational autoencoders. arXiv preprint arXiv:1703.10960 (2017)
20. Hu, E.J., Shen, Y., Wallis, P., et al.: Lora: low-rank adaptation of large language models. ICLR **1**(2), 3 (2022)
21. Longpre, S., Hou, L., Vu, T., et al.: The flan collection: designing data and methods for effective instruction tuning. In: International Conference on Machine Learning, pp. 22631–22648. PMLR (2023)
22. Guo, W., Yang, J., Yang, K., et al.: Instruction fusion: advancing prompt evolution through hybridization. arXiv preprint arXiv:2312.15692 (2023)

FEFT: A Feedback-Enhanced Evaluation Fine-Tuning Framework for Financial Report Summarization

Feng Gao[1,2,3], and Yuchen He[1,2,3], Na Zhang[4], and Jinguang Gu[1,2,3](✉)

[1] School of Computer Science and Technology, Wuhan University of Science and Technology, Wuhan 430065, Hubei, China
simon@wust.edu.cn

[2] Hubei Province Key Laboratory of Intelligent Information Processing and Real-Time Industrial System, Wuhan University of Science and Technology, Wuhan 430065, China

[3] School of Computer Science and Technology, Institute of Big Data Science and Engineering, Wuhan 430065, Hubei, China

[4] Digital Management Department, China Minmetals Corporation, Beijing 100038, China

Abstract. With the widespread adoption of large language models (LLMs), their application in the financial domain—particularly in automated text generation—has grown rapidly. However, specialized summarization tasks such as reinsurance report summarization continue to face significant challenges. Traditional supervised fine-tuning (SFT) methods rely on static labeled data, which struggles to address the complexities of financial texts, including domain-specific terminology, rigorous logical structures, and nuanced risk assessments. To tackle these issues, this paper proposes a novel framework: Feedback-Enhanced Evaluation Fine-Tuning (FEFT). FEFT employs high-performing LLMs as automated evaluators and integrates a multidimensional financial evaluation framework with Chain-of-Thought (CoT) reasoning, enabling the generation of intermediate reasoning steps that provide transparent and interpretable feedback. This feedback is then used to construct high-quality fine-tuning datasets, which in turn optimize the base summarization model, significantly improving the accuracy and coherence of generated summaries. Experiments conducted on real-world reinsurance assessment reports demonstrate that FEFT significantly improves summarization quality across both automated and human evaluations, outperforming traditional SFT and other feedback-based approaches. The proposed method proves especially effective in scenarios where large-scale human-labeled datasets are unavailable, substantially enhancing model performance in financial summarization tasks. The source code associated with this study is publicly available at https://github.com/Petrichorhyc/FEFT.

Keywords: Financial Document Summarization · Feedback-Enhanced Fine-Tuning · Automatic Quality Evaluation

J. Liang et al. (Eds.): CCKS 2025, CCIS 2698, pp. 134–147, 2026.
https://doi.org/10.1007/978-981-95-8525-0_11

1 Introduction

Large language models (LLMs) have made remarkable progress in natural language generation tasks [1]. In particular, the automated summarization of professional documents—such as reinsurance reports—has emerged as a key research direction in the financial domain [9, 11]. However, financial texts typically feature complex logical structures, dense domain-specific terminology, and detailed risk descriptions, which pose significant challenges for traditional supervised fine-tuning (SFT) approaches in capturing high-level semantics and fine-grained domain preferences [2, 12]. As a result, the generated summaries often suffer from issues in accuracy, completeness, and logical coherence.

To address these challenges, researchers have explored optimization techniques based on preference feedback, such as reinforcement learning with human feedback (RLHF) [2,9,14] and direct preference optimization (DPO) [3, 14]. While these methods have achieved promising results in open-domain question answering tasks [4], their application to structured and domain-specific financial summarization tasks remains underexplored [15]. Moreover, the high cost of acquiring large-scale, high-quality human-annotated data in the financial sector further limits the effectiveness of existing approaches [11, 12].

To overcome these limitations, we propose a novel framework called **Feedback-Enhanced Evaluation Fine-Tuning (FEFT)**, which is inspired by two key lines of research: (1) feedback-driven optimization methods that incorporate evaluation signals into model fine-tuning, and (2) the use of large language models (LLMs) as evaluators in preference modeling and reward-based training. Building on these foundations, FEFT introduces a structured, multi-dimensional evaluation framework specifically designed for financial summarization tasks, enabling fine-grained, domain-specific feedback aligned with task-specific optimization objectives. It further employs an LLM-based automated evaluator enhanced with Chain-of-Thought (CoT) prompting, which generates interpretable reasoning paths and scoring rationales—thereby strengthening the transparency and traceability of feedback, particularly crucial in high-stakes financial contexts. Together, these components support (i) an efficient fine-tuning paradigm that transforms evaluator outputs into high-quality training data, yielding substantial performance improvements with minimal reliance on human annotation (Fig. 1).

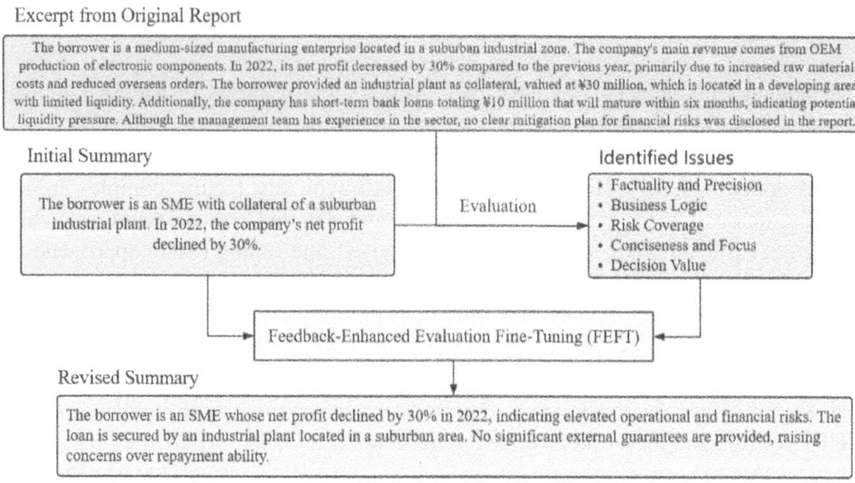

Fig. 1. Case Study of Financial Report Summarization.

2 Related Work

2.1 Supervised Fine-Tuning and its Limitations

Supervised fine-tuning (SFT) remains a mainstream approach in LLM-based text generation [1, 2], relying heavily on high-quality human-annotated data. However, in the financial domain, traditional SFT struggles to capture complex semantics and domain-specific preferences, resulting in outputs that may lack accuracy, completeness, and contextual relevance [11]. Prior efforts to improve performance—such as incorporating domain-specific dictionaries or rule-based templates in earnings summaries and market analyses [12, 13, 15]—have yielded only partial gains and suffer from limited adaptability and scalability..

In contrast, our proposed FEFT framework extends SFT by introducing automatically generated, structured feedback from a powerful LLM-based evaluator. This approach delivers richer training signals without relying on manual annotations, significantly improving the model's ability to adapt to complex financial reasoning tasks.

2.2 Preference-Based Optimization Methods

To reduce reliance on static supervision, preference-based optimization methods such as Reinforcement Learning with AI Feedback (RLAIF) [4] and Direct Preference Optimization (DPO) [3] have been introduced. These approaches incorporate reward signals or preference comparisons and have demonstrated strong performance in open-domain dialogue generation tasks [8]. However, their applicability to specialized domains such as finance remains limited, primarily due to the high cost and complexity of acquiring domain-aligned human preference data [11].

In contrast, FEFT addresses this challenge by leveraging high-performing LLMs to generate structured evaluation feedback—including both quantitative scores and targeted suggestions—thereby eliminating the need for expensive manual annotations while preserving domain specificity and relevance.

2.3 Feedback-Driven Optimization Strategies

Recent research has explored a range of feedback-driven approaches. For example, Self-Refine [5]improves model outputs through iterative self-evaluation, while SummIt [6] leverages automatic scorers to curate high-quality training samples. Chain-of-Thought (CoT) prompting [20, 21] has further enhanced reasoning transparency by encouraging step-by-step logical decomposition.

However, most existing feedback mechanisms still rely on generic or unstructured signals—as seen in Critique Fine-Tuning (CFT) [18] —which lack domain specificity, interpretability, and controllability. These limitations become especially pronounced in specialized tasks such as financial summarization [17].

To address these gaps, FEFT introduces a structured five-dimensional evaluation framework designed specifically for financial texts. The framework covers factual accuracy, logical flow, risk coverage, conciseness, and decision value. When combined with CoT-based reasoning, this enables interpretable and domain-adaptive feedback that enhances both semantic comprehension and generation reliability.

3 Feedback-Enhanced Evaluation Fine-Tuning

This study proposes a feedback-enhanced fine-tuning framework for improving the generative performance of large language models in financial-domain summarization tasks. The proposed approach comprises four key stages: initial summary generation, automatic evaluator construction, high-quality training data generation via structured feedback, and feedback-driven fine-tuning of the base summarization model (Fig. 2).

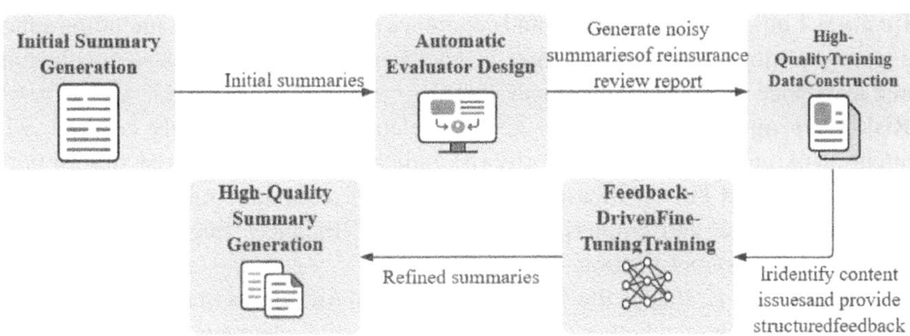

Fig. 2. An approach for fine-tuning and training models using automatic feedback.

3.1 Initial Summary Generation

In the first stage, we employ a base language model (e.g., Qwen-2.5-7B-Instruct) to generate initial summaries of reinsurance underwriting reports, which serve as noisy pseudo-responses. Although these summaries generally exhibit acceptable fluency, they often contain factual inaccuracies, information omissions, and ambiguous expressions, primarily due to the model's limited understanding of domain-specific financial knowledge and logical constraints. These deficiencies underscore the generation bottlenecks of existing models when applied to specialized financial tasks.

To facilitate systematic evaluation and error-aware fine-tuning, we introduce a stronger LLM-based evaluator (e.g., Qwen-2.5-72B-Instruct) that automatically identifies quality issues and generates structured feedback for subsequent training.

3.2 Automatic Evaluator Design

To obtain high-quality feedback without extensive manual annotation, we design an LLM-based automatic evaluator that conducts structured, multi-dimensional assessments of the initial summaries. This evaluator not only outputs quantitative scores but also generates interpretable textual feedback and improvement suggestions, serving as an effective guidance signal for fine-tuning.

Unlike traditional fine-tuning strategies that rely on manually annotated reference summaries (e.g., SFT) or overall preference pairs (e.g., DPO, RLHF), our method shifts towards fine-grained, structured feedback tailored to the financial domain. Instead of optimizing for a single reward value, FEFT decomposes evaluation into multiple domain-relevant dimensions, allowing the model to locate specific quality issues and learn dimension-specific corrections.

We define a five-dimensional evaluation framework grounded in the critical characteristics of reinsurance report summarization. Each dimension has clear criteria and requires explicit justification to ensure actionable and domain-adaptive feedback:

1. **Factuality and Precision:** Assesses whether the summary faithfully reflects the source report, avoiding factual errors, logical leaps, or subjective assumptions.
2. **Business Logic:** Evaluates clarity and coherence of information flow, including adherence to common reporting structure (e.g., background → risk analysis → conclusion), and avoidance of illogical inferences.
3. **Risk Coverage:** Checks whether key risk elements are adequately covered, with attention to omissions of high-priority risk indicators or qualitative risk descriptions.
4. **Conciseness and Focus:** Measures the removal of redundant information, conciseness of language, and emphasis on key content. Balances linguistic clarity with strategic information selection.
5. **Decision Value:** Evaluates the summary's practical usefulness in reinsurance review contexts, focusing on whether core decision-supporting elements are preserved.

For each dimension, the evaluator produces:

- A **chain-of-thought (CoT) explanation**, which outlines the reasoning process behind the assigned score. Instead of a single judgment, the evaluator highlights the evaluation path (e.g., "The summary omits the guarantee structure, which is central to risk evaluation. This leads to an incomplete judgment, justifying a score of 3.").
- A specific improvement suggestion grounded in the CoT (e.g., "Clarify the guarantee structure and its associated concentration risk.");
- quantitative score (1–5).

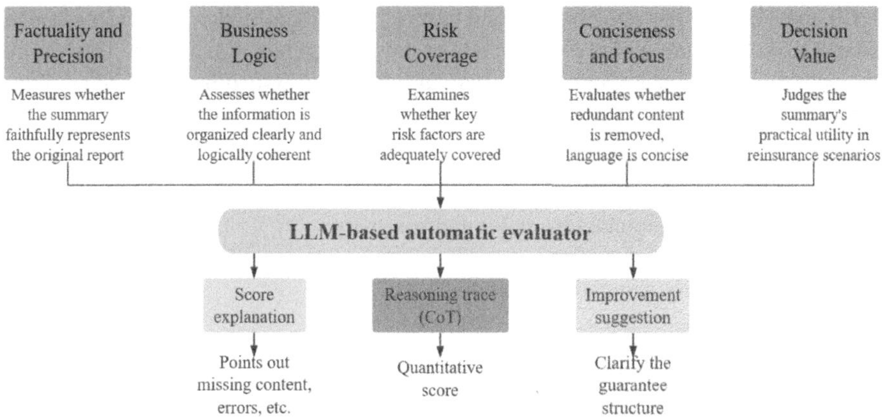

Fig. 3. A flowchart of the LLM-based automatic evaluator for financial summarization.

To improve evaluation accuracy and reduce bias, we introduce a reference comparison mechanism: prior to scoring, the evaluator is required to read both the original report and the generated summary in full, conducting semantic alignment and content mapping across the two texts. This dual-input approach mitigates errors stemming from summary-only evaluation and enhances the identification of information omissions, hallucinations, and misinterpretations (Fig. 3).

In addition, we enhance the reliability of our evaluator through a hybrid human-AI verification process. Specifically, a random subset of evaluator outputs is sampled for expert review, focusing on the logical consistency of the Chain-of-Thought (CoT) reasoning, the detection of cross-dimensional misjudgments, and the fairness of scoring. Insights from these reviews are used to calibrate the evaluator, thereby improving robustness and reducing potential bias.

By integrating CoT-based reasoning, the evaluator not only delivers fine-grained and accurate feedback but also provides interpretable and transparent evaluation traces. These reasoning paths help the fine-tuning model identify the root causes of generation errors, thereby supporting more controllable, domain-adaptive, and explainable optimization.

In essence, FEFT departs fundamentally from conventional scalar-feedback approaches (e.g., DPO, RLHF), replacing them with multi-dimensional, semantically grounded feedback signals. This transition enables transparent, controllable, and domain-aligned fine-tuning, which is particularly critical in high-stakes applications such as financial summarization.

3.3 Fine-Tuning Dataset Construction

Based on the outputs from the automatic evaluator, we construct a structured instruction-tuning dataset to support feedback-driven fine-tuning. Each training instance consists of three core components: (1) the original document, (2) the initial machine-generated summary, which may contain factual or logical deficiencies, and (3) the corresponding structured feedback automatically produced by the evaluator.

To enhance training effectiveness and ensure feedback diversity, we select samples that exhibit significant quality issues in one or more evaluation dimensions. These samples are formatted using a standardized **Instruction–Input–Output** schema to facilitate instruction-based fine-tuning:

- **Instruction**: Specifies the task objective (e.g., "Generate feedback and improved summary based on the original report and initial summary").
- **Input**: Includes the source text and initial summary.
- **Output**: The structured evaluation results (scores, explanations, suggestions) and the improved summary generated based on this feedback.

This structured format enables the model to learn contextual error-correction mappings, effectively modeling the path from flawed generations to optimized outputs. By capturing these revision trajectories, the fine-tuning process aligns closely with domain-specific optimization goals and supports controllable generation improvement.

3.4 Fine-Tuning Training

Using the curated dataset, we perform instruction fine-tuning on the base language model. During training, the model processes the full task prompt, initial summary, and detailed feedback, learning to (1) identify errors in the initial output, (2) integrate feedback suggestions for improvement, and (3) generate refined summaries that better align with domain-specific expectations.

To ensure training stability and prevent overfitting, we adopt early stopping, terminating training once the validation performance plateaus. The resulting model exhibits notable improvements in factual accuracy, logical coherence, and risk-sensitive articulation.

Formally, given an input document x and an initial (noisy) summary y, the model is trained to generate a pair: the structured feedback e and the improved summary s. The optimization objective is defined as:

$$\arg\max_{\theta} \log P\left(e, s \middle| [x; y]; \theta\right) \tag{1}$$

where θ denotes the parameters of the language model and [x; y] represents the concatenation of the question and noisy response as input.

This objective encourages the model to produce domain-aligned feedback and refined summaries simultaneously, thereby enhancing the overall quality and controllability of summarization.

To formalize the instruction fine-tuning procedure in FEFT, we summarize it in Algorithm 1 below.

Algorithm 1: Instruction Fine-Tuning with Feedback in FEFT

Input: Training dataset $\mathcal{D} = \{(x,y,e,s)\}$, base model LM_θ, learning rate η, max epochs N

for epoch = 1 to N **do**

for all $(x,y,e,s) \in \mathcal{D}$ **do**

Construct instruction prompt (e.g., "Given original document and summary, generate feedback and improved summary."

$I \leftarrow \mathrm{concat}(x,y)$ ▸ Input:original + noisy summary13

$O \leftarrow \mathrm{concat}(e,s)$ ▸ Output:feedback + noisy summary

Compute loss: $\mathcal{L}(\theta) \leftarrow -\log P(O|I;\theta)$

Update model parameters:$\theta \leftarrow \theta - \eta \cdot \nabla_\theta \mathcal{L}(\theta)$

end for

if validation loss plateaus **then**

break

end if

end for

Output: Fine-tuned model LM_θ

4 Experiments

This section aims to evaluate the effectiveness of the proposed Feedback-enhanced Evaluation Fine-Tuning (FEFT) framework in the financial text summarization task and to verify its overall performance under both automatic metrics and human subjective evaluation.

4.1 Experimental Setup

The experimental dataset consists of 500 real-world reinsurance review reports, each divided into five segments, totaling approximately 2,000 segments. From these, 100 documents (500 segments) are randomly selected as the test set, while the remaining are used for model fine-tuning and training. To ensure evaluation fairness, all test samples are strictly excluded from the training process.

For evaluation metrics, we adopt classical text generation evaluation indicators such as BLEU-4, ROUGE-1, ROUGE-2, and ROUGE-L to measure the generated summaries in terms of lexical match, coverage, and conciseness.

The base language model is Qwen-2.5-7B-Instruct. We compare several fine-tuning strategies under identical training configurations to ensure a fair evaluation:

- **Zero-shot**: Using the base model directly without any downstream task training.

- **SFT (Supervised Fine-Tuning):** Models are trained to replicate high-quality human-written summaries, often co-authored by domain experts and powerful LLMs for quality and efficiency [1, 2].
- **CFT (Critique Fine-Tuning)**: Models learn to critique noisy outputs rather than imitate them. In the recent "Critique Fine-Tuning" work, CFT delivers **4–10% gains over SFT** across multiple math benchmarks by training on GPT-4 critiques [18].
- **DPO (Direct Preference Optimization)**: A lightweight alternative to RLHF that directly aligns models to human preferences using a classification loss—no reward model or RL required. When applied, it matches or surpasses PPO-based RLHF in summarization and dialogue [3].
- **RLHF (Reinforcement Learning with Human Feedback)**: Trains a reward model from human preference rankings and applies PPO to optimize it. Highly effective across text generation tasks but requires substantial human-labeled data and computational cost [4, 9].
- **FEFT (Feedback-Enhanced Evaluation Fine-Tuning)**: Our proposed framework, which leverages structured, multi-dimensional feedback automatically generated by an LLM-based evaluator—including scores, CoT explanations, and suggestions—for efficient and domain-adapted fine-tuning.

All models are fine-tuned under identical training configurations to ensure a fair comparison.

4.2 Performance Comparison

We first present a comparison of automatic evaluation results for each fine-tuning method on the test set, summarized in Table 1:

Table 1. Performance Comparison of Different Fine-Tuning Strategies on the Test Set

Model Setting	BLEU-4	ROUGE-1	ROUGE-2	ROUGE-L
Qwen-2.5-7B-Instruct (Zero-shot)	17.09	36.11	14.13	24.99
Qwen-2.5-7B-Instruct + SFT	19.84	38.97	17.51	26.73
Qwen-2.5-7B-Instruct + CFT	20.17	39.43	18.16	27.51
Qwen-2.5-7B-Instruct + DPO	18.32	37.38	16.69	25.71
Qwen-2.5-7B-Instruct + RLHF	17.83	36.84	14.96	25.62
Qwen-2.5-7B-Instruct + FEFT	**23.69**	**45.10**	**22.28**	**31.78**

The experimental results demonstrate that in the financial reinsurance summarization task, our proposed FEFT method significantly outperforms traditional supervised fine-tuning (SFT) across multiple metrics. Notably, the ROUGE-L score improves from 24.99 in the zero-shot setting to 31.78 with FEFT, and the BLEU-4 score increases from 17.09 to 23.69. These results strongly validate the effectiveness of the multi-dimensional feedback mechanism in enhancing the quality and accuracy of language model-generated summaries.

4.3 Effectiveness Analysis

The comparison of fine-tuning strategies highlights their differing adaptability and feedback mechanisms, laying the foundation for our ablation study. All fine-tuning methods significantly outperform the zero-shot baseline, confirming the importance of fine-tuning in professional text generation.

Compared to standard supervised fine-tuning (SFT), FEFT leverages structured, multi-dimensional feedback to improve generalization, better capturing diverse expressions and fine-grained domain preferences for outputs that align more closely with expectations. Unlike CFT, which relies on unstructured critiques and shows fluctuating performance, FEFT's automated evaluator provides consistent, standardized evaluations and targeted suggestions, making training more focused and controllable.

While DPO improves over SFT by optimizing with preference pairs, its dependence on human-labeled data limits scalability and introduces annotator bias. FEFT addresses these issues by automatically generating multi-dimensional feedback, reducing annotation costs while maintaining high-quality supervision.

Error analysis shows FEFT-generated summaries better preserve critical risk information and logical coherence, with fewer omissions and contradictions, vital for financial documents where accuracy and completeness matter.

Although FEFT introduces a multi-stage feedback generation and fine-tuning pipeline, its overall computational overhead remains manageable. The automated feedback generation phase is efficient, avoiding the high costs of manual annotation and policy optimization commonly associated with reinforcement learning approaches such as RLHF. Moreover, the fine-tuning stage requires a similar training time to standard supervised fine-tuning (SFT), making FEFT a practical and scalable solution for professional domain adaptation.

Overall, FEFT not only improves quantitative metrics but also enhances the qualitative aspects of summarization, offering a practical solution for complex, domain-specific financial text generation.

4.4 Ablation Study

To further verify the contribution of key components in the FEFT framework to model performance, we design two sets of ablation experiments: **Dimension-Wise Feedback Ablation** and **Base Model Ablation**. All experiments adopt consistent fine-tuning strategies (Zero-shot, SFT, CFT, DPO and FEFT) as described in earlier sections, ensuring scientific rigor and comparability.

Dimension-Wise Feedback Ablation

This experiment aims to assess the contribution of each evaluation dimension within the five-dimensional feedback template of FEFT. Specifically, we fine-tune models using structured feedback with one dimension removed at a time, keeping the remaining four dimensions. Performance is then evaluated on the test set to determine the relative importance of each dimension to summarization quality (Table 2).

Table 2. Ablation Study on Evaluation Dimensions

Model Version	BLEU-4	ROUGE-1	ROUGE-2	ROUGE-L
Full (FEFT)	**23.69**	**45.10**	**22.28**	**31.78**
-Factuality Removed	21.37	42.18	19.87	28.54
-Business Logic Removed	22.04	43.25	20.53	29.08
-Risk Coverage Removed	21.12	41.96	19.65	27.89
-Conciseness & Focus Removed	22.56	43.82	20.98	30.12
-Decision Value Removed	22.73	44.01	21.48	30.56

Results show that removing any single dimension leads to a drop in model performance, particularly when omitting **Factual Accuracy** and **Risk Analysis**, which cause notable decreases in BLEU-4 and ROUGE-L scores. This highlights the essential role of these two dimensions in summarizing financial texts effectively.

Base Model Ablation

To examine the robustness of FEFT across different base models, we conduct experiments using **Baichuan2-7B-Chat**, **ChatGLM3-6B**, **Meta-Llama-3-8B-Instruct** and **Qwen-2.5-14B-Instruct**. Each model is trained using the five strategies: Zero-shot, SFT, FEFT, CFT, and DPO (Table 3).

Table 3. Performance comparison of FEFT and other fine-tuning strategies (SFT, CFT, DPO, RLHF) across different base models.

Model	Strategy	BLEU-4	ROUGE-1	ROUGE-2	ROUGE-L
Baichuan2-7B-Chat	Zero-shot	13.84	31.23	11.68	21.87
	SFT	16.18	33.98	14.91	24.41
	CFT	16.98	35.04	15.52	25.72
	DPO	15.72	33.27	14.36	23.69
	RLHF	14.56	32.13	12.87	22.34
	FEFT	**20.23**	**40.05**	**18.79**	**27.99**
ChatGLM3-6B	Zero-shot	13.39	30.72	11.31	21.47
	SFT	15.53	33.05	14.21	23.61
	CFT	16.18	33.86	14.69	24.44
	DPO	14.91	32.47	13.72	23.02
	RLHF	14.23	31.84	12.55	22.07
	FEFT	**18.98**	**38.48**	**17.52**	**27.03**
Meta-Llama-3-8B-Instruct	Zero-shot	15.67	34.12	12.98	24.21
	SFT	18.55	37.12	16.83	26.75

(continued)

Table 3. *(continued)*

Model	Strategy	BLEU-4	ROUGE-1	ROUGE-2	ROUGE-L
	CFT	19.38	38.27	17.53	27.61
	DPO	17.94	36.51	16.12	25.95
	RLHF	16.91	35.58	14.83	25.16
	FEFT	**22.87**	**43.81**	**21.15**	**31.22**
Qwen-2.5-14B-Instruct	Zero-shot	17.82	37.28	15.45	25.89
	SFT	21.24	40.49	18.50	27.04
	CFT	22.05	41.63	19.21	28.52
	DPO	20.54	39.88	17.86	27.11
	RLHF	19.32	38.72	16.42	26.43
	FEFT	**26.31**	**47.12**	**24.35**	**34.08**

These results demonstrate that FEFT consistently delivers superior performance across various base models, highlighting its model-agnostic applicability and training stability. Ablation studies further confirm the importance of multi-dimensional structured feedback—particularly in improving factual accuracy and risk coverage—as a key driver of performance gains. The consistent outperformance of FEFT under diverse fine-tuning strategies reinforces its robustness and adaptability. Together, these findings validate FEFT as a generalizable and effective framework for producing high-quality training signals in financial text summarization.

5 Conclusion

This paper proposes a Feedback-Enhanced Evaluation Fine-Tuning (FEFT) framework for complex financial text summarization. FEFT overcomes the limitations of traditional supervised fine-tuning, such as limited generalization and high annotation costs, by introducing an automated, structured feedback mechanism. It leverages a five-dimensional evaluation scheme tailored to financial texts and incorporates Chain-of-Thought (CoT) reasoning to improve logical coherence during generation.

We conducted systematic experiments on a real-world reinsurance review report dataset. The results demonstrate that FEFT significantly outperforms traditional SFT methods and other feedback mechanisms (such as RLHF and DPO) across multiple automatic evaluation metrics. Through ablation studies and human subjective evaluations, we further validate the effectiveness of the multi-dimensional automated evaluator and its critical role in model optimization.

This study not only provides a low-cost and high-precision optimization solution for financial text generation tasks but also offers a new paradigm for automated preference data construction and feedback-driven learning in specialized scenarios. Future work may extend FEFT to other financial document tasks, such as risk control reports and compliance reviews, and explore the integration of feedback mechanisms with reinforcement learning and contrastive learning approaches.

Importantly, FEFT's core feedback-driven fine-tuning architecture is domain-agnostic, requiring only evaluation template customization for new tasks. By adapting the multi-dimensional criteria, FEFT can be extended to legal, medical, or scientific summarization with minimal annotation cost, making it a flexible and scalable framework for fine-tuning large language models across specialized fields. In future work, we plan to validate FEFT in diverse financial subdomains, such as risk control, investment analysis, and regulatory compliance, to further demonstrate its adaptability and robustness.

Acknowledgments. This research is funded by the National Natural Science Foundation of China (Grant No. U1836118), the Key Project of Scientific and Technological Research Plan of Hubei Provincial Department of Education (Grant No. D20231104), and the Paired Science and Technology Support Project of Wuhan Municipal Science and Technology Bureau (Grant No. 2024071104010831).

References

1. Brown, T., Mann, B., Ryder, N., et al.: Language models are few-shot learners. Adv. Neural. Inf. Process. Syst. **33**, 1877–1901 (2020)
2. Stiennon, N., Ouyang, L., Wu, J., et al.: Learning to summarize with human feedback. Adv. Neural. Inf. Process. Syst. **33**, 3008–3021 (2020)
3. Rafailov, R., Sharma, A., Mitchell, E., et al.: Direct preference optimization: your language model is secretly a reward model. Adv. Neural. Inf. Process. Syst. **36**, 53728–53741 (2023)
4. Lee, H., Phatale, S., Mansoor, H., et al.: Rlaif: scaling reinforcement learning from human feedback with AI feedback (2023)
5. Madaan, A., Tandon, N., Gupta, P., et al.: Self-refine: iterative refinement with self-feedback. Adv. Neural. Inf. Process. Syst. **36**, 46534–46594 (2023)
6. Zhang, H., Liu, X., Zhang, J.: Summit: Iterative text summarization via chatgpt. arXiv preprint arXiv:2305.14835 (2023)
7. Radford, A., Wu, J., Child, R., et al.: Language models are unsupervised multitask learners. OpenAI blog **1**(8), 9 (2019)
8. Bai, Y., Kadavath, S., Kundu, S., et al.: Constitutional AI: harmlessness from AI feedback. arXiv preprint arXiv:2212.08073 (2022)
9. Sharma, A., Keh, S.S., Mitchell, E., et al.: A critical evaluation of ai feedback for aligning large language models. Adv. Neural. Inf. Process. Syst. **37**, 29166–29190 (2024)
10. Yang, H., Liu, X.Y., Wang, C.D.: Fingpt: open-source financial large language models. arXiv. arXiv preprint arXiv:2306.06031 (2023)
11. Nie, Y., Kong, Y., Dong, X., et al.: A survey of large language models for financial applications: progress, prospects and challenges. arXiv preprint arXiv:2406.11903 (2024)
12. Lee, J., Stevens, N., Han, S.C.: Large language models in finance (FinLLMs). Neural Comput. Appl. 1–15 (2025)
13. Cao, Z., Feinstein, Z.: Large language model in financial regulatory interpretation. In: 2024 IEEE Symposium on Computational Intelligence for Financial Engineering and Economics (CIFEr), pp. 1–7. IEEE (2024)
14. Liu, S., Fang, W., Hu, Z., et al.: A survey of direct preference optimization. arXiv preprint arXiv:2503.11701 (2025)
15. Ding, H., Li, Y., Wang, J., et al.: Large language model agent in financial trading: a survey. arXiv preprint arXiv:2408.06361 (2024)

16. Xie, Q., Han, W., Chen, Z., et al.: Finben: a holistic financial benchmark for large language models. Adv. Neural. Inf. Process. Syst. **37**, 95716–95743 (2024)
17. Chu Z, Guo H, Zhou X, et al. Data-centric financial large language models[J]. arXiv preprint arXiv:2310.17784, 2023
18. Wang, Y., Yue, X., Chen, W.: Critique fine-tuning: learning to critique is more effective than learning to imitate. arXiv preprint arXiv:2501.17703 (2025)
19. Ouyang, L., Wu, J., Jiang, X., et al.: Training language models to follow instructions with human feedback. Adv. Neural. Inf. Process. Syst. **35**, 27730–27744 (2022)
20. Wei, J., Wang, X., Schuurmans, D., et al.: Chain-of-thought prompting elicits reasoning in large language models. Adv. Neural. Inf. Process. Syst. **35**, 24824–24837 (2022)
21. Kojima, T., Gu, S.S., Reid, M., et al.: Large language models are zero-shot reasoners. Adv. Neural. Inf. Process. Syst. **35**, 22199–22213 (2022)

Iterative Generation Method for Factual QA in Large Language Models Based on Semantic Entropy Verification

Jian Zhang, Jintao Tang(✉), Shasha Li(✉), Kaixuan Wang, and Ting Wang(✉)

National University of Defense Technology, Changsha, China
{zhang_jian,tangjintao,shashali,wangkaixuan18,tingwang}@nudt.edu.cn

Abstract. Retrieval-Augmented Generation (RAG) technology is an effective solution to the hallucination problem in large language models. However, existing techniques require substantial data fine-tuning or rely on validation from ultra-large parameter models to determine the certainty of the generated content, leading to significant resource consumption. To address this issue, this paper proposes a lightweight method based on semantic entropy conflict detection. This method detects the semantic entropy of model responses through an algorithm. On this basis, it dynamically adjusts the length of input information by combining a hierarchical knowledge transfer approach, allowing the model to iteratively optimize the generated content. This enhances the model's accuracy in answering questions based on knowledge. Experimental results show that the accuracy of this method in judging the consistency of model responses can reach up to 97%. It outperforms traditional RAG methods in improving the ability of large language models to answer questions based on knowledge and demonstrates better performance than the existing iterative generation method, Iter-RetGen, in practical applications.

Keywords: Large Language Models · Semantic Entropy · Conflict Detection · Iterative Generation

1 Introduction

In recent years, large language models (LLMs) represented by the GPT series have garnered widespread attention for their exceptional text generation capabilities. As technology advances, research has increasingly focused on the application effectiveness of LLMs in real-world scenarios. However, in-depth studies have revealed that due to inherent limitations such as the timeliness lag of LLMs' knowledge bases and insufficient coverage of specialized knowledge in vertical domains, LLMs often exhibit the "hallucination" phenomenon in question-answering tasks [1]. This means that the generated content, while seemingly logical, deviates from objective facts. This issue severely restricts the reliability

J. Liang et al. (Eds.): CCKS 2025, CCIS 2698, pp. 148–162, 2026.
https://doi.org/10.1007/978-981-95-8525-0_12

of LLMs in high-risk applications such as medical consultation and legal analysis. This contradiction has prompted the academic community to explore more effective methods for controlling the quality of generated content, with the focus now being on how to enhance the credibility of LLMs' content while maintaining their generation capabilities.

Traditional Retrieval-Augmented Generation (RAG) techniques address this issue by introducing external knowledge bases to provide LLMs with documents related to the question, thereby helping them generate more accurate answers [3]. This has made some progress in alleviating the hallucination problem. Typical methods include the "Self-RAG" framework [2], which fine-tunes LLMs with large amounts of data to enable them to self-assess whether to retrieve knowledge and whether the answers based on retrieved knowledge are reliable. Other methods, such as "CRITIC" [8], propose using external tools to evaluate the text generated by LLMs. Some studies [4] leverage external ultra-large-scale parameter LLMs to assist in judging the generated content using semantic entropy. However, these methods have some obvious drawbacks. First, they require large amounts of data to fine-tune LLMs to achieve good self-assessment effects. Second, they rely on third-party tools or external ultra-large-scale parameter LLMs to evaluate the generated content, which increases system complexity and poses high computational costs and deployment barriers when applied on a large scale.

To address the aforementioned challenges, this paper proposes an iterative generation method for factual question answering in large models based on semantic entropy validation. On the one hand, the LLM is asked to answer the same question multiple times, and semantic entropy is used to detect the consistency of its answers. This helps determine whether the LLM has a clear answer to the question, i.e., the certainty of the generated content. On the other hand, knowledge is transferred to the LLM in a hierarchical manner. By reducing the noise that interferes with the LLM's answers and dynamically adjusting the length of retrieved knowledge based on the detection results from semantic entropy, the method ensures that the LLM receives the minimum yet complete reference knowledge when answering questions.

In summary, the main contributions of this paper are as follows:

(1) this paper proposes a method based on semantic entropy conflict detection to effectively judge the credibility of the generated content without relying on other ultra-large-scale parameter LLMs or fine-tuning the model with large amounts of data. Experiments show that the accuracy of this method in judging the consistency of model answers exceeds 97%.
(2) this paper adopts a hierarchical knowledge transfer approach to the LLM. After detecting the certainty of the generated content using semantic entropy, the method dynamically adjusts the length of information input to the LLM, allowing it to iteratively optimize its answers and thereby improve the accuracy of its responses.
(3) Experimental results demonstrate that the proposed method outperforms traditional RAG methods in enhancing the LLM's ability to answer questions based on knowledge and also shows better performance than the existing iterative generation method, Iter-RetGen, in practical applications.

2 Related Work

Hallucination in Large Language Models: The hallucination problem in large language models has long been a topic of research. Studies have shown that when models encounter knowledge that is infrequently or insufficiently covered in the training data, they tend to generate statements that appear plausible but are factually incorrect [5]. To mitigate this issue, current methods can be divided into two main categories: one involves modifying the model by fine-tuning it with high-quality data. For example, the developers of Falcon [13] carefully extracted high-quality data from the web using heuristic rules and demonstrated that appropriately curated corpora can lead to powerful large language models. The other category does not modify the model itself but assists it through techniques such as retrieval-augmented generation or prompt guidance. For instance, some research [14] has explored integrating large language models (such as GPT-3) with search engines to improve the models' accuracy and memory capabilities. They proposed generating a set of questions for each input sentence and searching web pages to verify the consistency of the information with the input sentence.

Retrieval-Augmented Generation Technology: Retrieval-Augmented Generation enhances the reliability of text generation by dynamically integrating external knowledge and has become a popular technological approach to address hallucination. A classic example is the RAG architecture proposed by Lewis et al. [3], which combines dense retrieval with a generative model through joint training. However, its retrieval module needs to be fine-tuned in sync with the generative model, leading to high deployment costs. To effectively utilize retrieval results, Shi et al. [23] proposed the RePlug framework, which uses retrieved documents as prompt prefixes fed into a black-box model to improve the quality of generated text in a single step. To leverage the generated results, Shao et al. [16] combined the model's generated content with the question to retrieve more relevant knowledge. However, they did not differentiate and directly iterated multiple times. A recent breakthrough work is Self-RAG by Asai et al. [2], which trains a dedicated judging model to control the timing and content selection of retrieval. However, it requires an additional 100,000-level labeled judging dataset.

Application of Semantic Entropy: Semantic entropy, as an indicator for quantifying the semantic consistency and reliability of text, has in recent years been applied to the assessment of the credibility of generated content. Its core idea is to analyze the semantic distribution characteristics within the text to detect potential contradictions or uncertain information. Venhuizen et al. [6] proposed a method for calculating entropy based on the co-occurrence probability of words, but this approach did not fully consider the semantic associations at the syntactic level. Sebastian et al. [4] argued that word-level entropy-based judgment methods are too stringent for question-answering tasks. Therefore, they leveraged an external ultra-large-scale parameter model to calculate the semantic entropy between multiple answers generated by the model, using this to evaluate the uncertainty of the model's generated answers. This method, however, relies on an external large-scale model, which is not user-friendly for offline or low-resource users.

3 Methodology

To clarify the certainty of the model's responses to questions, this paper proposes a lightweight method, which determines the certainty by calculating the semantic entropy of the model repeatedly answering the same question. Specifically, this method uses a lightweight algorithm to quantify the consistency of the answers, thereby judging the certainty of the model's responses. Based on this judgment, the method updates the length of the input information to the large language model using a hierarchical knowledge transfer approach. This not only reduces the interference of noisy information but also increases the likelihood that the input information contains the answer, thereby improving the accuracy of the large language model in answering questions. The specific process is shown in Fig. 1.

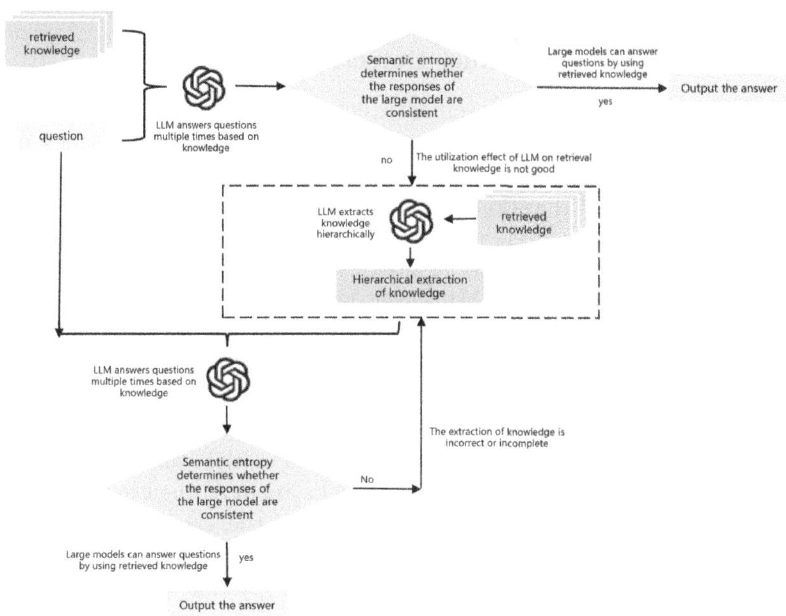

Fig. 1. The overall process of iterative generation for semantic entropy conflict detection.

The retrieved knowledge and the question are passed together to the large language model, which is then asked to repeatedly answer the question based on the retrieved knowledge. Subsequently, the semantic entropy of the different answers is calculated to determine whether the model's responses are consistent.

If they are consistent, it indicates that the large language model can answer the question based on the given retrieved knowledge. If not, it suggests that the model is not effectively utilizing the retrieved knowledge. In this case, a small subset of sentences is extracted from the retrieved knowledge, and the model is asked to answer the question based on these extracted sentences. If the answers remain inconsistent, the scale of extracted sentences is gradually expanded, and the model is asked to answer the question again. Through this approach, the model iteratively generates answers by progressively inputting retrieved knowledge of varying lengths.

To avoid the continuous misselection of knowledge, in the final stage, all the retrieved knowledge for questions that the model still answers inconsistently after multiple iterations is passed to the model again. Then, among the model's multiple answers, the most frequently occurring answer is selected as the final response. This method not only effectively evaluates the model's utilization of retrieved knowledge but also improves the accuracy and consistency of the model's answers by progressively optimizing the input information.

The following sections will provide a detailed introduction according to the methodological process.

3.1 Semantic Entropy Conflict Detection Method

Inspired by previous research [4], semantic entropy can be used to determine the uncertainty of a model's response to a question. Specifically, when the semantic dispersion of multiple answers to the same question is higher, the model's uncertainty in answering that question is greater. In their paper, semantic clustering of the model's multiple answers is performed using an external ultra-large-scale parameterized large language model, followed by the calculation of semantic entropy of the generated content. However, to make this approach more universal and lightweight, rather than relying on ultra-large-scale parameter models, this chapter employs the single-pass algorithm [25] for semantic clustering of the model's multiple answers. This algorithm has recently been applied by some studies to problems such as data information clustering [7,20,21]. Additionally, we use the number of final clustering topics in the model's answers to represent semantic entropy. The more topics in the model's answers, the less consistent the answers are, the higher the semantic entropy, and the greater the uncertainty in the model's response to the question. The following algorithm describes the process of judging consistency using semantic entropy. The process is shown in Fig. 2.

After the model provides its first answer, the word embedding vector of the response is obtained using a word embedding model, which serves as the first topic. For subsequent answers to the same question, the word embedding model is similarly used to obtain the vector for each response. The semantic similarity between the response vector and the topic is then calculated using cosine distance. If the calculated similarity is less than the threshold, the new response forms a new topic. If the similarity is greater than the threshold, the response is classified under that topic. Once the clustering calculation for all responses is

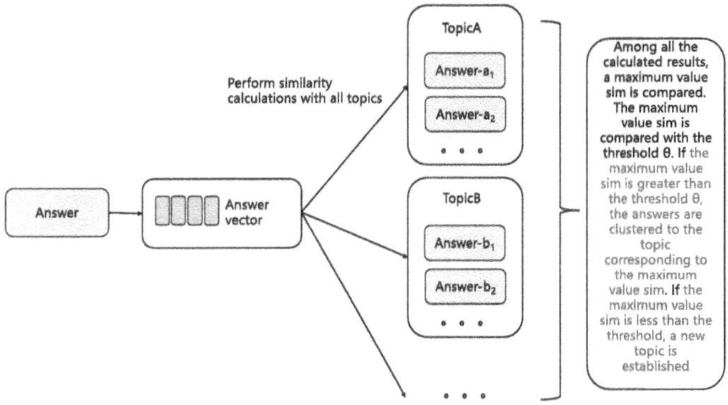

Fig. 2. Semantic entropy judgment consistency process.

complete, the number of topics is examined. If there is only one topic, the model's multiple answers are consistent. Otherwise, the model's answers are inconsistent and need to be re-answered.

3.2 Hierarchical Knowledge Transfer Method

Some studies have shown that when the amount of retrieved knowledge increases, the model is subjected to more noise interference, and it cannot effectively utilize the retrieved knowledge [11,22,23]. Additionally, although Wei et al. [18] demonstrated that the CoT method is not effective for some large language models with smaller parameter sizes, their work inspired the idea that models can solve problems step-by-step.Given this, we propose a hierarchical knowledge transfer method. This method dynamically adjusts the length of the input knowledge based on the results of semantic entropy detection of the generated content, aiming to reduce the impact of noise on the model while allowing the model to iteratively optimize the generated content based on the provided retrieved knowledge. The specific operation is as follows:

When a question and its retrieved knowledge are passed to the model, if the semantic entropy judgment shows that the model's answer to the question is inconsistent, the model is first asked to extract the smallest set of retrieved knowledge for that question. Then, the model answers the question based on this minimal retrieved set. If the model's answer is still inconsistent at this point, the model is asked to expand the extracted retrieved set to form a new retrieved set and answer the question again based on the new retrieved set. Following this approach, starting from the minimal retrieved set, the retrieved results are gradually increased in an attempt to find the smallest combination of sentences that can answer the question. An example is shown in Fig. 3:

The answer to the sample question is "1977," but due to the presence of distractors such as "1978," "1981," and "1979" in the retrieved knowledge, the model cannot accurately answer the question. The knowledge extracted the first

Question: 非洲羽毛球联合会什么时候宣布退出国际羽联?

Retrieve knowledge (assume a paragraph): 世界羽毛球联合会（），原羽毛球组织，于1978年2月成立，1981年5月26日与国际羽毛球联合会（现称羽毛球世界联合会，BWF）合并后停止运作。成立于20世纪30年代的国际羽毛球联合会（国际羽联，IBF）一直是管理国际羽毛球的机构。几个国家对国际羽联的数项政策不满：国际羽联接受中华民国为国家组织；拒绝因南非政府的种族隔离政策而中断南非的会员资格及拒绝修改国际羽联章程中的不合理条款。这几个国家在非IBF成员中华人民共和国的带领下，成立世界羽毛球联合会。于1977年9月召开由亚洲羽球联盟由发起的会议，提出了成立世界羽毛球联合会。同年11月，在世界羽联筹委会第二次会议上，非洲羽毛球联合会宣布退出国际羽联。1978年2月在香港召开的第3届会议上正式宣布成立世界羽毛球联合会。几乎全部来自亚洲和非洲的二十二个国家和地区加入世界羽联：孟加拉国、文莱、中国、加纳、圭亚那、香港、印度、伊朗、肯尼亚、马来西亚、毛里裘斯、尼泊尔、尼日利亚、朝鲜、巴基斯坦、菲律宾、新加坡、韩国、斯里兰卡、坦桑尼亚、泰国和赞比亚。奥地利、法国、墨西哥（代表泛美羽毛球联合会）、瑞典、联邦德国和南斯拉夫派出没有投票权的观察员列席会议。之后世界羽毛球联合会组织了两届自己的世界锦标赛，一届于1978年在曼谷举行，另一届于1979年在杭州举行。

Extracted sentenses: 同年11月，在世界羽联筹委会第二次会议上，非洲羽毛球联合会宣布退出国际羽联。

Secondarily extracted sentenses: 于1977年9月召开由亚洲羽球联盟由发起的会议，提出了成立世界羽毛球联合会。同年11月，在世界羽联筹委会第二次会议上，非洲羽毛球联合会宣布退出国际羽联。

Fig. 3. Examples of hierarchical extraction.

time did not include the answer element "1977," but only "in the same year in November." Therefore, it is necessary to expand the extracted knowledge based on this, that is, the second extraction, in order to enable the model to correctly answer the question.

For the two-stage hierarchical extraction, this paper utilized the dialogue history feature of the large language model through prompting techniques in the specific implementation process. Additionally, during the research process, this paper also attempted to fine-tune the large language model, that is, to fine-tune the large language model with a manually constructed dataset to enable it to master the ability of hierarchical knowledge extraction. The manually constructed dataset in this paper includes a validation set with 68 data entries and a training set with 236 data entries. The prompt formats for the two extractions, fine-tuned extraction, and direct answering are shown in the Fig. 4.

3.3 Iterative Generation Method

Simply taking the results of a single round of model generation as the final answer neither ensures whether the model has accurately utilized the retrieved knowledge to answer the question nor verifies the model's results. Given that the phenomenon of model hallucination is still relatively common, this approach is clearly not rigorous enough. Combining the semantic entropy conflict detection and hierarchical knowledge transfer methods proposed in this paper, the overall iterative generation approach is adopted to avoid the aforementioned issues.

The iterative generation process used in this paper mainly consists of four rounds. In the first round, the model answers the question based on the retrieved knowledge and makes a judgment through semantic entropy detection. If the answer is consistent, it is directly output; if not, the process moves to the second round. In the second round, the model extracts sentences from the retrieved knowledge for the first time and answers the question based on these sentences, again making a judgment through semantic entropy detection. If the answer is

First extraction	promptfind1 = context:{Retrieved Knowledge}. question:{Question}. Extract a combination of complete sentences from the context above that can answer the question, and directly provide the extracted sentence combination.
Second extraction	promptfind2 = The previously extracted sentence combination may lack the necessary content to answer the question. Based on the previously extracted sentences, extract more sentences from the context to form a new sentence combination, and directly provide the new sentence combination.
Direct answer	prompt = {Retrieved Knowledge} Based on the information above, directly tell me: {Question}
Finetune extraction	context: {Retrieved Knowledge}. question: {Question}. label:{Label}. Based on the label, extract a combination of complete sentences from the context above that can answer the question. Please think step-by-step. First, if the label is 1, extract the minimal sentence combination and provide that sentence combination, then stop; second, if the label is 2, first extract the minimal sentence combination as if the label were 1, and then add some sentences before and after the minimal combination to form a new sentence combination, and provide the new sentence combination, then stop.

Fig. 4. Different prompt forms. The "label" in the label is a manually defined hierarchical "1" and "2." The output is a sentence combination of different lengths manually selected from the context based on the hierarchical level of the label.

consistent, it is directly output; if still inconsistent, the process proceeds to the third round. In the third round, the model further extracts more sentences based on the initial extraction and answers the question based on these sentences, once again making a judgment through semantic entropy detection. If the answer is consistent, it is directly output; if still inconsistent, the process moves to the fourth round. In the fourth round, all the retrieved knowledge is passed to the model again, and it answers the question. After semantic entropy detection, the first answer within the topic that appears most frequently is taken as the final answer to the question. The purpose of setting the last round of iteration is to avoid the situation where all the extracted knowledge in the previous process is incorrect.

4 Experimental Evaluation and Analysis

This section first briefly describes the datasets used in the experiments, then clarifies the experimental settings. It is followed by experiments conducted on the method proposed in this paper, and concludes with ablation studies discussing the impact of different factors on the proposed method.

4.1 Datasets

This paper primarily targets the ability of large language models to answer questions with the aid of retrieval enhancement in the context of the Chinese language. Therefore, we have created a retrieval-augmented Chinese dataset. The dataset is constructed from previously published Chinese reading comprehension datasets, with a scale of over 800,000 paragraphs. The 1,000 questions that need to be answered were manually selected from previous Chinese datasets, and they are factual questions such as "When was the Civil Aviation Administration of China established?" The answers to the questions are expanded from the original answers to form an answer set. If the response from the large language model contains any content from the answer set, the model's response is deemed correct.

4.2 Experimental Settings

The experiments in this paper primarily verify the effectiveness and superiority of the iterative generation method for factual question answering in large models based on semantic entropy validation. Therefore, the experiment in Sect. 4.3 compares the results of the proposed method with other methods, demonstrating the effectiveness and superiority of the proposed method. The experiment in Sect. 4.4 is an ablation study, including validation of the effectiveness of semantic entropy, the significance of hierarchical knowledge transfer for answering, and the impact of different semantic entropy thresholds. The model selection and evaluation metrics are described as follows.

Model Selection: This paper employs the Elasticsearch search engine for knowledge storage and retrieval, using version 8.12.2. The hybrid retrieval technique used in this paper takes advantage of the software's match fuzzy query based on keyword matching and semantic vector matching based on cosine distance calculation. The word embedding vector model used in this paper is tao8k, which supports Chinese and has a maximum processing length of 8k. The experiments in this paper were conducted offline with the large language model deployed locally. The primary large language model used in the experiments is GLM-4-9B-Chat [17]. The model used for answering questions, extracting sentences, and fine-tuning is also GLM-4-9B-Chat.

Evaluation Metrics: To evaluate the accuracy of large language models' answers, this experiment directly employs the classic metric of accuracy (Accuracy, A), with the specific calculation formula as follows:

$$A = q_r / q_s \tag{1}$$

Here, q_r represents the number of questions answered correctly by the model, and q_s represents the total number of questions answered by the model. When calculating the accuracy of the large language model's answers, the model answers three rounds for each scenario, with 1,000 questions answered in each round. After three rounds, the average accuracy is calculated as the final result.

4.3 Comparison of This Method with Other Methods

The traditional method involves the model directly answering the question using the retrieved knowledge after relevant knowledge has been retrieved. The method proposed in this paper is an iterative generation method for factual question answering in large models based on semantic entropy validation. The main comparison results are shown in Table 1[1]. In the table, "GLM-4-9B-Chat direct extraction" refers to the model used for sentence extraction being GLM-4-9B-Chat, while "GLM-4-9B-Chat fine-tuned extraction" refers to the model used for sentence extraction being the fine-tuned GLM-4-9B-Chat.

Table 1. Comparison of Traditional Methods and the Proposed Method.

Method	Model	Input	Approach	Accuracy
Traditional Method	GLM-4-9B-Chat	1p + q	Da	0.960
	GLM-4-9B-Chat	1p + q	Replace incorrect paragraphs with manually extracted sentence combinations	**0.973**
Proposed Method	GLM-4-9B-Chat de	1p + q	First 1p + q -j, then es + q -j, finally 1p + q -j and tf	0.965
	GLM-4-9B-Chat fe	1p + q	First, 1p + q -j, then fe es + q -j, finally 1p + q -j and tf	0.964
Traditional Method	GLM-4-9B-Chat	3p + q	Da	0.936
Proposed Method	GLM-4-9B-Chat de	3p + q	First, 3p + q -j, then es + q -j, then secondarily es + q -j, finally 3p + q -j and tf	0.951
	GLM-4-9B-Chat fe	3p + q	First, 3p + q -j, then fe es + q -j, then fe es + q -j, finally 3p + q -j and tf	0.948
Traditional Method	GLM-4-9B-Chat	3pr + q	Da	0.864
CoT [18]	GLM-4-9B-Chat	3pr + q	Da	0.854
Iter-RetGen [16]	GLM-4-9B-Chat	3pr + q	Da	0.870
Proposed Method	GLM-4-9B-Chat de	3pr + q	Da	0.873
Proposed Method	GLM-4-9B-Chat fe	3pr + q	Da	0.865
CoT [18]	GLM-4-9B-Chat	10pr + q	Da	0.858
Iter-RetGen [16]	GLM-4-9B-Chat	10pr + q	Da	0.871
Proposed Method	GLM-4-9B-Chat de	10pr + q	Da	*0.886*

Based on the experimental results in the upper part of Table 1, when the input contains 1 paragraph with the answer, the proposed method can increase the accuracy of the large model's answers from 0.960 to 0.965 compared to the traditional method. When the input contains 3 paragraphs with the answer, the proposed method can increase the accuracy from 0.936 to 0.951. Additionally, when the input for the 1,000 questions that were answered incorrectly is modified to the correct manually extracted sentence combinations, the accuracy of

[1] In all tables,1p/3p represents 1/3 paragraph containing the answer,3pr/10pr represents 3/10 paragraphs retrieved from the knowledge base, q renresents question, Da represents Direct answering, de represents direct extraction, fe represents fine-tuned extraction, es represents extracted sentences, j represents judge, tf represents take the most frequent answer.

the large model's answers can reach the highest level of 0.973. These data indicate that, on the one hand, reducing the retrieved knowledge to the minimum necessary to answer the question can effectively improve the model's accuracy in answering based on the knowledge. On the other hand, the proposed method is more effective than the traditional method in improving the model's accuracy in answering based on the knowledge, and the improvement becomes more significant as the amount of retrieved knowledge increases.

According to the lower part of the experiment in Table 1, even in practical applications, the proposed method without fine-tuning and directly extracting sentences can outperform the existing iterative generation method Iter-RetGen. The effect of using the fine-tuned model to extract sentences is not particularly good. This may be mainly due to the relatively small amount of training data used for fine-tuning, and the distribution of manually constructed training data in different scenarios may not be scientific enough, resulting in the model's failure to fully learn an effective extraction strategy. The CoT method in the second and sixth rows of the table shows the worst performance, which may be due to the relatively small scale of model parameters used, making it unsuitable for the CoT approach. This is consistent with the conclusions of the CoT method paper [18].

4.4 Ablation Experiments and Analysis

Validation of Semantic Entropy Effectiveness. To determine whether semantic entropy can serve as an indicator to measure the certainty of large language models' answers based on knowledge, experiments were designed in this section. The method involved having the large language model answer the same question 10 times, for a total of 1,000 questions. In one scenario, the model was simply asked the question and expected to answer; in the other scenario, the model was given one paragraph containing the answer along with the question. During the answering process, different threshold values were set to observe the final outcomes of the model's answers. The results are shown in Table 2.

Table 2. Validation of Semantic Entropy Effectiveness.

Model	Input	Threshold Parameter	Consistent Judgments	Correct Answers	Accuracy of Consistent Judgments
GLM-4-9B-Chat	q	0.65	9720	5014	0.5158
		0.85	7490	4222	0.5637
		0.95	3950	2814	0.7124
		1	640	600	0.9375
GLM-4-9B-Chat	1p + q	0.92	8680	8190	0.9435
		0.97	7170	6827	0.9522
		0.99	5860	5635	0.9616
		1	1590	1550	0.9748

According to the experimental results in Table 2, regardless of whether the input is a pure question or a question with a paragraph containing the answer, as the threshold increases, the accuracy of judging the consistency of the model's answers rises, reaching over 97%. This indicates that the semantic entropy method proposed in this paper is effective. Moreover, when the input includes correct retrieved knowledge (one paragraph containing the answer), the accuracy of judging consistent answers is higher.

Significance of Hierarchical Knowledge Transfer for Answering. Faced with increased knowledge length, i.e., more noise, will the model's ability be affected? This question is one of the motivations for the knowledge extraction approach in this paper. To verify this situation, the ablation experiment in this section increases or decreases the noise in the retrieved knowledge by changing the number of paragraphs in the input for retrieving knowledge, and observes the accuracy of the model in answering questions based on knowledge through different extraction methods. The results are shown in Table 3.

Table 3. Impact of Input Length Variation on Model Answer Accuracy.

Model	Input	Method	Accuracy
GLM-4-9B-Chat	Question	Da	0.534
	1 paragraph without the answer + question	Da	0.445
	1 paragraph with the answer + question	Da	*0.960*
	3 paragraphs with the answer + question	Da	0.936
	10 paragraphs with the answer + question	Da	0.924
	30 paragraphs with the answer + question	Da	0.913
GLM-4-9B-Chat	1 paragraph with the answer + question	First 1p + q -j, then es + q -j, finally 1p + q -j and tf	**0.965**
GLM-4-9B-Chat	es + q	Da	0.945

According to the experimental results in the upper part of Table 3, when the retrieved knowledge contains the answer, as the number of paragraphs in the input increases, the model's accuracy in answering questions based on the knowledge gradually decreases. This indicates that as noise increases, the model is increasingly affected. When the retrieved knowledge does not contain the answer to the question, relying on the retrieved knowledge to answer the question actually reduces the model's accuracy. This suggests that providing incorrect reference knowledge also lowers the model's accuracy in answering questions. These experimental results demonstrate that noise reduces the model's accuracy in answering questions. It also indicates that reducing the amount of noise in the retrieved knowledge can increase the model's accuracy in answering questions. In other words, extracting knowledge to reduce the noise information passed to the model can help improve the model's accuracy in answering questions. The motivation for extracting knowledge is meaningful.

As shown in the lower part of the experiment in Table 3, if hierarchical knowledge extraction is not used and the model answers based on one-time extracted knowledge, the model's accuracy in answering questions is actually lower than that of directly answering based on the retrieved knowledge. This indicates that the model's knowledge extraction may indeed result in incomplete or even incorrect knowledge. It also confirms the necessity of the hierarchical knowledge extraction approach in this paper, which involves re-inputting all retrieved knowledge to the model for answering in the final iteration stage.

Impact of Different Semantic Entropy Thresholds. Based on the results in Table 2, it is already clear that using semantic entropy to judge conflicts in the model's answers is effective, and as the semantic entropy threshold increases, the accuracy of the judgment gradually improves. However, does setting all stages of thresholds to the highest level always yield the best performance in the model's answers? To verify this, the experiment shown in Table 4 was conducted.

Table 4. Impact of Different Thresholds on Model Answer Accuracy.

Model	Input	Method	Threshold	Incorrect	Accuracy
GLM-4-9B-Chat	1p + q	First 1p + q – j,	1	3	0.958
		then es + q – j,	0.97	19	
		finally 1p + q – j and tf	0.97	24	
	1p + q	First 1p + q – j,	0.97	22	0.962
		then es + q – j,	0.95	8	
		finally 1p + q – j and tf	0.97	8	
GLM-4-9B-Chat	3p + q	First 3p + q – j,	0.99	19	0.951
		then es + q – j,	0.99	15	
		then secondary es + q – j,	0.99	4	
		finally 3p + q – j and tf	0.99	15	
	3p + q	First 3p + q – j,	0.995	16	0.948
		then es + q – j,	0.995	12	
		then secondary es + q – j,	0.98	10	
		finally 3p + q – j and tf	0.99	18	

According to the experimental results in Table 4, although increasing the semantic entropy threshold improves the accuracy of judging the consistency of the model's answers, it is not always the case that setting all thresholds to the highest level yields the highest final accuracy in the model's answers. This is because there may be situations where the model's answers, such as "1977" and "November 1977," are both correct responses to the question, but under a threshold of "1," these answers are considered inconsistent, prompting the model to provide other responses. Therefore, in the multi-stage process, it is necessary to consider the model's tendency to use knowledge at different stages. For example, if the model tends to use knowledge from the first stage, the threshold for the first stage should be set slightly lower. Conversely, if the model tends to use knowledge from later stages, the threshold for the first stage should be set slightly higher. By setting different thresholds, the model's tendency to use knowledge at different stages can be achieved.

5 Conclusion

This paper addresses the issue in retrieval-augmented generation where existing methods for detecting the certainty of generated content by large language models rely on large-scale fine-tuning data and external evaluation models. We propose an iterative generation method for large models based on semantic entropy validation. This method judges the credibility of the generated content without relying on other ultra-large-scale parameter models or fine-tuning the model with large amounts of data. It also employs a hierarchical knowledge transfer approach, dynamically adjusting the length of input information to the large language model to iteratively generate answers, thereby improving the accuracy of answering questions. Experimental results show that the proposed method achieves an accuracy of up to 97% in judging the consistency of model answers. It outperforms traditional retrieval-augmented methods in enhancing the ability of large language models to answer questions based on knowledge and also shows better performance than the existing iterative generation method, Iter-RetGen, in practical applications.

Acknowledgments. This work was supported by the Key Research and Development Project of Hunan Province (No. 2025JK2119).

References

1. Rawte, V., Sheth, A., Das, A.: A survey of hallucination in large foundation models. arXiv preprint arXiv:2309.05922 (2023)
2. Asai, A., Wu, Z., Wang, Y., Sil, A., Hajishirzi, H.: Self-rag: learning to retrieve, generate, and critique through self-reflection. In: The Twelfth International Conference on Learning Representations (2023)
3. Lewis, P., et al.: Retrieval-augmented generation for knowledge-intensive NLP tasks. Adv. Neural. Inf. Process. Syst. **33**, 9459–9474 (2020)
4. Farquhar, S., Kossen, J., Kuhn, L., Gal, Y.: Detecting hallucinations in large language models using semantic entropy. Nature **630**(8017), 625–630 (2024)
5. Ji, Z., et al.: Survey of hallucination in natural language generation. ACM Comput. Surv. **55**(12), 1–38 (2023)
6. Venhuizen, N., Crocker, M., Brouwer, H.: Semantic entropy in language comprehension. Entropy **21**(12), 1159 (2019)
7. Qaiyum, S., Aziz, I., Hasan, M., Khan, A., Almalawi, A.: Incremental interval type-2 fuzzy clustering of data streams using single pass method. Sensors **20**(11), 3210 (2020)

8. Gou, Z., et al.: Critic: large language models can self-correct with tool-interactive critiquing. arXiv preprint arXiv:2305.11738 (2023)
9. Wang, Y., et al.: Factcheck-GPT: end-to-end fine-grained document-level fact-checking and correction of LLM output. arXiv preprint arXiv:2311.09000 (2023)
10. Zhao, J., et al.: Longagent: scaling language models to 128k context through multi-agent collaboration. arXiv preprint arXiv:2402.11550 (2024)
11. Wu, J., Che, F., Zhang, C., Tao, J., Zhang, S., Shao, P.: Pandora's Box or Aladdin's Lamp: A Comprehensive Analysis Revealing the Role of RAG Noise in Large Language Models. arXiv preprint arXiv:2408.13533 (2024)
12. Karpukhin, V., et al.: Dense passage retrieval for open-domain question answering. In: EMNLP (1), pp. 6769–6781 (2020)
13. Penedo, G., et al.: The refinedweb dataset for falcon LLM: outperforming curated corpora with web data only. In: Advances in Neural Information Processing Systems, vol. 36, pp. 79155–79172 (2023)
14. Gao, L., et al.: RARR: researching and revising what language models say, using language models. In: Proceedings of the 61st Annual Meeting of the Association for Computational Linguistics (Volume 1: Long Papers), pp. 16477–16508 (2023)
15. Shi, W., et al.: REPLUG: retrieval-augmented black-box language models. In: Proceedings of the 2024 Conference of the North American Chapter of the Association for Computational Linguistics: Human Language Technologies (Volume 1: Long Papers), pp. 8364–8377 (2024)
16. Shao, Z., Gong, Y., Shen, Y., Huang, M., Duan, N., Chen, W.: Enhancing retrieval-augmented large language models with iterative retrieval-generation synergy. In: Findings of the Association for Computational Linguistics: EMNLP 2023, pp. 9248–9274 (2023)
17. GLM GitHub. https://github.com/THUDM/GLM-4. Accessed 25 May 2025
18. Wei, J., et al.: Chain-of-thought prompting elicits reasoning in large language models. In: Advances in Neural Information Processing Systems, vol. 35, pp. 24824–24837 (2022)
19. Yao, S., et al.: Tree of thoughts: deliberate problem solving with large language models. In: Advances in Neural Information Processing Systems, vol. 36, pp. 11809–11822 (2023)
20. Makarychev, K., Chakrabarty, S.: Single-pass pivot algorithm for correlation clustering. keep it simple! In: Advances in Neural Information Processing Systems, vol. 36, pp. 6412–6421 (2023)
21. Behnezhad, S., Charikar, M., Ma, W., Tan, L.: Single-pass streaming algorithms for correlation clustering. In: Proceedings of the 2023 Annual ACM-SIAM Symposium on Discrete Algorithms (SODA), pp. 819–849 (2023)
22. Sanyal, A., Hu, Y., Yu, Y., Ma, Y., Wang, Y., Schölkopf, B.: Accuracy on the wrong line: on the pitfalls of noisy data for out-of-distribution generalisation. In: The 28th International Conference on Artificial Intelligence and Statistics (2024)
23. Shi, Z., Wei, J., Xu, Z., Liang, Y.: Why larger language models do in-context learning differently? In: ICML'24: Proceedings of the 41st International Conference on Machine Learning, pp. 44991–45013 (2024)
24. Zhou, Z., Tao, R., Zhu, J., Luo, Y., Wang, Z., Han, B.: Can language models perform robust reasoning in chain-of-thought prompting with noisy rationales? In: Advances in Neural Information Processing Systems, vol. 37, pp. 123846–123910 (2024)
25. Papka, R., Allan, J., et al.: On-line new event detection using single pass clustering. University of Massachusetts, Amherst **10**(290941.290954) (1998)

Open Resources for Knowledge Graphs and Large Models

Autism Children Education Knowledge Graph: Construction and Validation

Zhen Bi[1,2], Peng Chen[1], Kangrui Pan[1], Kang Zhao[1,2], Qing Shen[1,2], Zhenfang Liu[1,2], and Jungang Lou[1,2(✉)]

[1] Huzhou University, Huzhou, Zhejiang, China
bizhen_zju@zju.edu.cn, ljg@zjhu.edu.cn

[2] Zhejiang Key Laboratory of Intelligent Education Technology and Application, Zhejiang Normal University, Jinhua, Zhejiang, China

Abstract. Children with Autism Spectrum Disorder (ASD) require specialized educational strategies grounded in interdisciplinary knowledge, yet such knowledge is often scattered across fragmented literature, limiting its accessibility and utility. In this paper, we propose a domain-specific knowledge graph (KG) for ASD education that systematically encodes factual, evidence-based information into a structured and semantically rich representation. By reviewing a broad corpus of open-source research articles and books, we construct a multi-layered ontology that captures intervention plans, practical considerations, symptom types, example cases, and communication strategies. Specifically, we extract 3,997 entities and 3,539 triples to form a high-quality KG with refined structure and minimal noise. To evaluate its impact, we develop a new dataset combining literature-derived questions with GPT-4o-generated and expert-validated answers. Extensive experiments on various LLMs show that incorporating the KG consistently improves performance, with *Qwen3-0.6B* achieving 82.0% enhanced responses and a maximum score gain of 2.5. Finally, we integrate the ASD educational KG into an interactive prototype educational QA system and initiate a collaboration with the National Special Education Resource Center for Children with Autism, aiming to drive future development of intelligent and adaptive educational tools for children with ASD.

Keywords: Autism Education · Knowledge Graph Construction · Educational QA System

1 Introduction

Children with Autism Spectrum Disorder (ASD) often face significant challenges in learning, communication, and social integration, requiring highly specialized educational strategies that draw from a wide range of interdisciplinary knowledge [5–7,13,18,27,32]. However, the knowledge required for effective ASD education is currently scattered across fragmented academic literature and lacks systematic integration, which hinders its accessibility and practical utility [1,28].

Z. Bi and P. Chen—Equal Contribution.

J. Liang et al. (Eds.): CCKS 2025, CCIS 2698, pp. 165–178, 2026.
https://doi.org/10.1007/978-981-95-8525-0_13

While existing educational tools and intelligent systems have made progress in supporting general learning tasks [4,10,11,14,17,22,23], there remains a fundamental gap in knowledge structuring and reasoning capabilities for specialized domains such as autism education [31]. To address this challenge, we propose a domain-specific knowledge graph tailored to ASD education, aiming to encode factual, evidence-based educational knowledge into a structured semantic form. While prior efforts such as the AsdKB developed by Wu and Cao et al. have contributed valuable resources for autism-related knowledge, they primarily focus on clinical applications—particularly early screening and medical diagnosis. In contrast, our ASD educational knowledge graph is designed with a fundamentally different orientation. Specifically, (1) in terms of application context, we target educational scenarios, encompassing both structured intervention training and daily living support; (2) in terms of intended users, our system serves educators, special education professionals, and caregivers rather than clinical practitioners; and (3) in terms of functional objectives, we aim to provide personalized and adaptive educational strategies, rather than diagnostic decision support. This distinction allows our work to fill a critical gap in domain-specific educational assistance for children with ASD.We systematically review open-source articles and books covering core themes in ASD education, including behavioral interventions, communication strategies, environmental adaptation, and individualized support. Based on this corpus, we construct a multi-layered ontology that decomposes educational strategies into intervention plans and practical considerations, further refined into child symptoms, example cases, communication patterns, and semantic relationships. We then convert the literature into a high-quality knowledge graph[1] containing 3,997 entities and 3,539 semantic relations, with rigorous filtering of isolated or low-quality nodes to ensure structural clarity and reasoning utility.

To validate its practical impact, we further construct a 1,020-sample question answering dataset grounded in ASD education scenarios, combining real literature-derived questions with GPT-4o generated and expert checked answers. Using this dataset, we evaluate several LLMs, both with and without access to the knowledge graph, across key dimensions such as factual accuracy, professional depth, and logical coherence. Experimental results show that integrating our KG yields consistent performance improvements across all baseline models, with the smallest model (*Qwen3-0.6B*) achieving up to 81.9% improved responses and a maximum score gain of 2.5 points, highlighting the significant value of structured knowledge for enhancing specialized QA in constrained LLM settings. Finally, we integrate the educational KG for children with autism into the current mainstream LLMs, develop an internal interactive system, and collaborate with the National Special Education Resource Center for Children with Autism[2], aiming to open new directions for the development of intelligent, explainable, and adaptive assistive technologies for children with ASD.

---

[1] https://github.com/HuzhouNLP/Autism-Education-Knowledge-Graph.

[2] https://hys.zjnu.edu.cn/main.htm.

2 Related Work

2.1 Knowledge Graph Construction for Education

Educational knowledge graphs (KGs) have gained traction for organizing domain-specific knowledge to support intelligent learning. KnowEdu proposed a semi-automated system for constructing educational KGs from textbooks [5], while Dang et al. enhanced concept linkage via Wikipedia integration [6]. Dynamic modeling approaches, such as using information entropy [32], and multi-source fusion for curricula [18,21] further extended graph adaptability. Other works examined course-level graphs using MOOC data [25,26], primary education [33], and large-scale K-12 integration [34].

In the autism domain, AsdKB is a specialized KG for early ASD screening [31]. Personalized online teaching graphs have also been explored [13]. Annotated KG-based teaching support systems are being used in higher education mentoring [21]. Conceptual comparison techniques based on pedagogical metrics are also gaining attention [20]. Broader surveys on educational KGs highlight design challenges and applications [1,8,11,28]. Despite these advancements, current educational KGs often lack fine-grained semantic layers tailored to the unique needs of special education domains. Most existing works focus on general K-12 or higher education curricula, with limited emphasis on structuring behavioral or therapeutic strategies into machine-readable forms.

2.2 Large Language Models in Educational Validation

LLMs are increasingly used for tutoring, feedback, and assessment. Kasneci et al. analyzed the educational impact of ChatGPT, stressing accuracy and bias concerns [17], while Jeon and Lee discussed AI-human teacher complementarity [14]. AI's role in improving communication skills was also explored in language learning [29]. Recent applications include personalized tutoring [19] and virtual teaching assistants [3]. Other studies highlight the promise and limitations of LLM-generated educational explanations [2,4,15].

Combining LLMs with structured knowledge is a promising direction. Pan et al. proposed unification strategies for LLMs and KGs to enhance factual grounding [23], and a TGDK position paper elaborated on integration challenges and benefits [22]. Suchanek and Luu emphasized their complementary strengths [30]. Others proposed novel uses of LLMs for grammar correction [9] and algebra tutoring [24], while fine-tuning strategies such as cross-prompt pretraining were also introduced [12]. Applied studies have shown improved QA accuracy when grounding LLMs with educational KGs [10], while others revealed weaknesses in LLM explanations without domain-specific knowledge [4]. Broader analyses have situated these innovations in the context of systemic educational change [16]. These works suggest that without domain-specific grounding, LLMs may generate fluent but unsubstantiated answers in specialized educational settings—an issue our work aims to mitigate by integrating an ASD-specific KG for validation and inference enhancement.

3 Knowledge Graph Construction

This section introduces the structure and extraction of factual knowledge about the education of Autism Spectrum Disorder (ASD) in children.

3.1 Knowledge Source

In constructing the knowledge graph for Autism Spectrum Disorder (ASD) education in children, we systematically review 203 journal articles and 4 authoritative monographs in the field of autism education to develop a multi-dimensional knowledge base. These publications are sourced from 130 academic journals, forming a diverse and comprehensive knowledge acquisition framework. Notably, the corpus includes 27 articles from *Journal of Autism and Developmental Disorders*, 12 from *Autism*, and 9 from *Focus on Autism and Other Developmental Disabilities*—all regarded as leading journals in autism education research. The collected literature spans key domains such as clinical care, behavioral interventions, interdisciplinary integration, and educational support, thereby ensuring the academic rigor and practical relevance of the resulting knowledge base.

In terms of temporal distribution, the literature covers a wide range of research periods: 70 early studies published before 2010, 112 mid-stage studies published between 2010 and 2020, and 25 recent studies published after 2020. This chronological span enables the knowledge base to reflect both the historical depth and contemporary developments of research in the field.

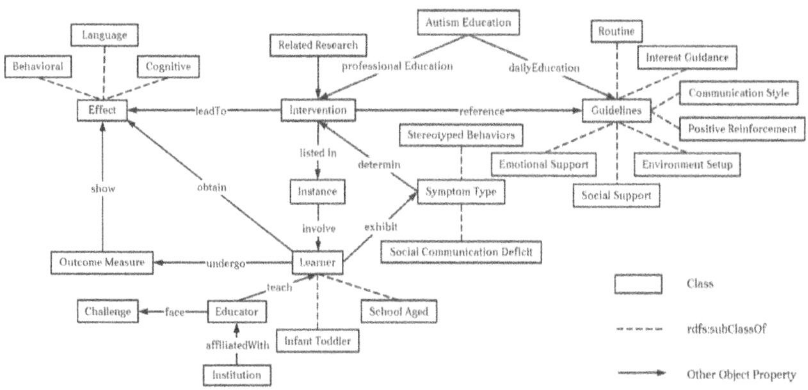

Fig. 1. The ontology of our ASD education knowledge graph.

3.2 Schema Definition

To facilitate the precise extraction and effective integration of factual knowledge in the domain of autism education for children, we developed a dedicated ontology prior to constructing the knowledge graph, following a standard ontology engineering process. As illustrated in Fig. 1, the details are explained as follows.

- Based on a comprehensive scenario of educational practices for children with Autism Spectrum Disorder (ASD), core educational strategies were classified into two categories: intervention programs and precautionary measures. This classification formed a dual-dimensional knowledge structure, covering both professional and everyday perspectives. The intervention programs focus on systematic and specialized educational approaches tailored to address the core developmental needs of children with ASD. In contrast, the precautionary measures pertain to daily learning and living contexts, and are further subdivided into subcategories such as communication strategies, environmental design, and social support. These are intended to provide practical guidance and safeguard measures during implementation.
- Within the intervention programs, we established semantic links to instances and symptoms, thereby ensuring the relevance and applicability of the knowledge. The instance class grounds abstract strategies in concrete educational practices, enabling each intervention program to be illustrated through real-world cases.
- The ontology construction centers on the "instance" class, around which we developed linear knowledge chains. This structure enhances the comprehensiveness and standardization of instance-related content, supporting knowledge reuse through well-defined contextual frameworks.
- The four key concept classes—precautionary measures, symptom types, intervention outcomes, and learners—were further decomposed into multiple subclasses, following a hierarchical refinement strategy to improve the granularity and precision of knowledge extraction.
- A set of semantic relationship types was predefined to connect heterogeneous concept classes through meaningful logical links. These semantic relations ensure the coherence and integrity of the ontology, and enable subsequent knowledge graph construction to support complex knowledge discovery from literature using language models.

3.3 KG Construction

After the ontology is constructed, we explicitly define the semantic boundaries of the knowledge graph based on 12 predefined core entity types and their corresponding subclasses. Subsequently, we employ a lightweight method to perform initial entity and relation extraction from structurally preprocessed plain-text knowledge sources. Our mechanism follows an "entity-first, relation-completion" strategy, where entities are recognized using pretrained language models, and relations are supplemented via matching and rule-based constraints. This process enhances the structural clarity and relational accuracy of the extracted triples, thereby improving the overall usability and controllability of the resulting graph. However, this approach also leads to the generation of a large number of isolated entities that are not connected through any semantic relation (Table 1).

Table 1. Detailed statistics in the ASD education knowledge graph

Entity Type	Count	Entity Type	Count
Guideline	759	Effect	714
Intervention	590	Learner	346
Instance	332	Symptom-Type	295
Challenge	270	Educator	257
Institution	228	Outcome-Measure	190
Related-Research	11	Autism-Education	5

To improve the structural quality and semantic density of the knowledge graph, we performed a systematic post-processing of the initially extracted results, focusing on two key steps:

- **Isolated entity removal:** All isolated nodes are discarded, as their lack of semantic connections limits their utility in reasoning and downstream tasks and may introduce noise into knowledge retrieval.
- **Low-quality entity filtering:** Based on criteria including extraction confidence, semantic coverage, and consistency with the ontology, we remove redundant, ambiguous or semantically unclear entities. It ensures that every retained entity participates in at least one semantically meaningful relation.

In the implementation process, we utilized the LightRAG framework to construct and refine the knowledge graph. A clear core entity schema was first established, followed by entity normalization using LightRAG's built-in mechanisms to merge semantically duplicate or inconsistent entities. After exporting the initial graph, all isolated nodes lacking semantic relations were removed. To further enhance the graph quality, we incorporated a prompt-based semantic validation mechanism via the DeepSeek API to assess the semantic validity of candidate nodes, complemented by manual verification. This rigorous screening process ensured the accuracy and consistency of the knowledge. Finally, these redundant and low-quality nodes were asynchronously deleted through LightRAG's interface, guaranteeing that the retained entities possess high semantic precision and structural purity, resulting in a more compact and high-quality educational knowledge graph.

Under the constraint of strict adherence to the ontology framework for entity recognition, the finalized knowledge graph comprises 3,997 high-quality entity nodes and 3,539 semantic relations (triples). Each triple strictly follows the standard subject–predicate–object structure, and all semantic relationships are aligned with ontology-based constraints. This guarantees the structural consistency and semantic coherence of the graph, thereby laying a solid foundation for explainable reasoning and effective downstream retrieval tasks. A subset of the constructed graph is illustrated in Fig. 2.

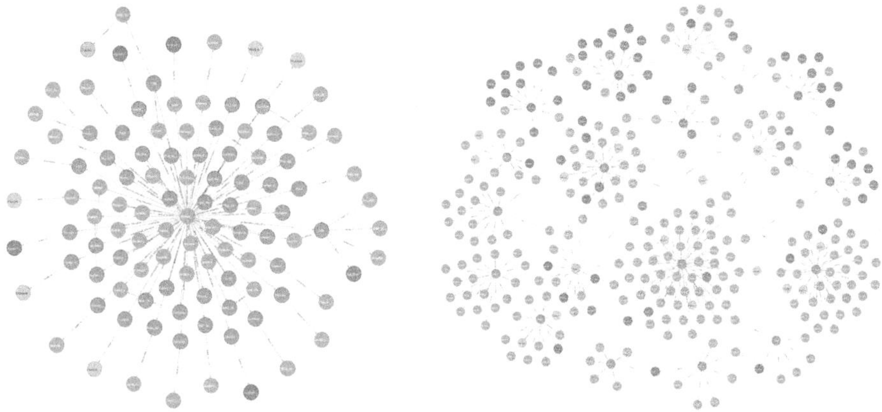

(a) A graph segment radiating outward from a central root node.

(b) A graph segment with densely interlinked nodes and overlapping relationships.

Fig. 2. Partial visualization of the ASD KG.

4 Knowledge Graph Retrieval-Augmented Generation

This section presents the experiments conducted based on the constructed knowledge graph for autism spectrum disorder (ASD) education, along with the corresponding evaluation results. Due to space limitations, we focus on the core aspects and omit detailed discussions.

4.1 Benchmark Dataset

In the field of ASD education for children, there is currently a lack of standardized and widely accepted question-answering datasets. To address this gap, we propose a novel approach that leverages the GPT-4o LLMs to construct a high-quality QA dataset tailored for ASD education. Specifically, we systematically selected and curated a large number of relevant academic papers and extracted representative questions covering key dimensions and practical scenarios in ASD-related education. Based on these sources, GPT-4o and human-experts are required to annotate corresponding answers by combining information from the literature with its own knowledge base and reasoning capabilities.

In this process, the literature primarily serve as a source of question inspiration and supplemental information, while the answers are generated with the aim of being comprehensive and forward-looking rather than strictly limited to the original texts. This strategy not only mitigates potential biases and incompleteness in the source material, but also capitalizes on the strengths of LLMs in knowledge integration and natural language generation. The resulting dataset offers broad coverage and rich depth, serving as a robust foundation for evaluating the performance of various models in the context of special education.

4.2 Metrics

After constructing the question-answering dataset, we adopted a comparative evaluation approach to systematically assess the quality of the model-generated responses, given the absence of a single unified ground truth answer for direct comparison. Specifically, we select responses generated with and without the support of an external knowledge base, and submitted both sets—along with the predefined reference answers in the dataset—to the GPT-4o model for evaluation. The evaluation process is conducted based on five core dimensions: **Knowledge Coverage**, **Professional Depth and Accuracy**, **Practical Value**, **Logical Structure**, and **Language Expression**. Scores for each dimension were assigned with reference to the pre-set answers, and the scoring criteria and corresponding weights are presented in Table 2.

Table 2. Abbreviated scoring dimensions for ASD QA evaluation

Code	Dimension Description	Weight
KC	Evaluates whether the response includes core concepts and covers key areas (e.g., diagnosis, intervention, challenges) relevant to ASD education.	30%
PDA	Assesses the precision of terminology, conceptual accuracy, and the use of scientific evidence or authoritative references.	35%
PV	Measures the feasibility and usefulness of the suggestions, emphasizing applicability to real-world educational settings.	15%
LS	Reviews the coherence, clarity, and alignment between the question and the response.	10%
LE	Considers only major expression issues that affect comprehension, with minor trade-offs accepted for technical depth.	10%

It is worth noting that the inclusion of knowledge base support inevitably leads to a more specialized and academic tone in the generated responses, which may impact readability. Meanwhile, GPT-4o tends to prefer responses that are concise and fluent in expression, potentially resulting in lower scores for answers with higher technical depth but a more formal linguistic style. To ensure a fair and balanced assessment, we appropriately reduced the weight of the **Language Expression** dimension in the overall score to minimize the influence of linguistic style on the final evaluation.

4.3 Result

Based on the constructed dataset and the aforementioned evaluation framework, we further design and conduct a series of experiments aimed at systematically analyzing the impact of external knowledge bases on the quality of answer generation. Specifically, we examine the performance of different embedding models, the effect of excluding the knowledge graph, and the behavioral differences across several small-parameter language models in question-answering tasks. The selected representative models include Qwen3 (0.6B and 1.7B), LLaMA3.2 (1B), and DeepSeek-R1 (1.5B). All experiments were conducted under a fixed temperature setting of 0 to ensure consistency. The results are summarized in Table 3.

Although these pretrained models demonstrate a basic level of question-answering capability in their default configurations, their generated responses tend to be generic and often lack sufficient professional depth. To quantify the relative performance gains brought by knowledge base integration, we first calculated the percentage score increase for each question—i.e., the relative improvement of the knowledge-augmented response over the baseline. We then computed the mean of these percentage increases across all questions to derive the overall relative improvement metric, as reported in the table. This approach effectively normalizes inter-question scoring variability, enabling a more realistic assessment of the models' performance enhancement.

Table 3. Effectiveness of KG augmentation in ASD benchmark

Metric	DeepSeek-r1 1.5B	Llama3.2 1B	Qwen3 0.6B	Qwen3 1.7B
Score without KG	6.60	7.57	7.04	8.05
Score with KG	6.91	7.87	7.45	8.33
Improved Proportion (%)	**82.0%**	81.6%	81.9%	79.9%
Average Score Gain	0.31	0.30	**0.41**	0.28
Avg. Relative Gain per QA (%)	4.82%	**7.51%**	6.20%	3.64%
Average Gain (↑ only)	0.46	0.45	**0.55**	0.42
Avg. Relative Gain per QA (↑ only, %)	7.18%	**10.36%**	8.19%	5.44%

The experimental results show that all four models exhibit significant performance improvements after incorporating knowledge base support. Across the entire set of test QA samples, over 80% of the responses demonstrate varying degrees of score improvement. Notably, the Qwen3 (0.6B) model—having the smallest parameter scale—achieved the most prominent gains, with score improvements observed in 81.9% of the test cases, an average increase of 0.41 points, and a maximum individual gain of up to 2.5 points. These results underscore the pronounced effectiveness of external knowledge bases in enhancing the QA performance of compact language models.

Meanwhile, the LLaMA3.2 (1B) model achieved a 7.51% increase in average score across all samples, with an even higher relative gain of 10.36% when considering only the positively affected samples. This further validates the efficacy of knowledge base integration in promoting domain-specific question answering. In contrast, the Qwen3 (1.7B) model exhibited slightly lower improvement than its 0.6B counterpart. Preliminary findings thus suggest that, for models with the same underlying architecture, smaller parameter sizes may benefit more substantially from knowledge-based enhancement.

In this stage of experimentation, we primarily employed models with relatively small parameter sizes for several reasons. First, the primary objective of this study is to evaluate the auxiliary effect of knowledge graphs on question-answering tasks. Accordingly, we focus more on the performance differences before and after knowledge graph integration, rather than the absolute performance of the models themselves. We did conduct preliminary tests using larger-scale models on selected samples, but observed no significant advantage over smaller models, which aligns with the aforementioned analytical conclusions. To efficiently compare different configurations while minimizing computational costs, we selected smaller, more resource-efficient models as the main experimental baselines. Furthermore, from a practical deployment perspective, we envision the future system operating on resource-constrained environments such as mobile or edge devices, making lightweight models a more realistic choice. In the future, we plan to expand the knowledge graph with additional content and conduct more comprehensive experiments using larger-scale models for full evaluation and optimization.

5 Educational QA System

Based on the constructed knowledge graph, we develop a prototype question-answering platform specifically designed for the domain of Autism Spectrum Disorder (ASD) education in children. By integrating selected language models, the system is capable of providing automated responses to user queries grounded in structured domain knowledge. At present, the platform remains in the internal testing phase, with plans for public release upon further refinement and validation. Figure 3 presents a screenshot of the system interface, illustrating its current functionality and user interaction flow.

To ensure real-world applicability and social impact, we have initiated a collaboration with the National Special Education Resource Center for Children with Autism[3]. This partnership aims to align our system design with front-line educational needs and expert practices. Through this collaboration, our QA system will be iteratively deployed and evaluated in authentic educational contexts, supporting teachers, caregivers, and therapists in delivering personalized and evidence-based support to children with ASD. By bridging cutting-edge AI technologies with practical intervention scenarios, we aspire to create an accessible, intelligent, and adaptive educational assistant that empowers broader communities engaged in autism education.

[3] https://hys.zjnu.edu.cn/main.htm.

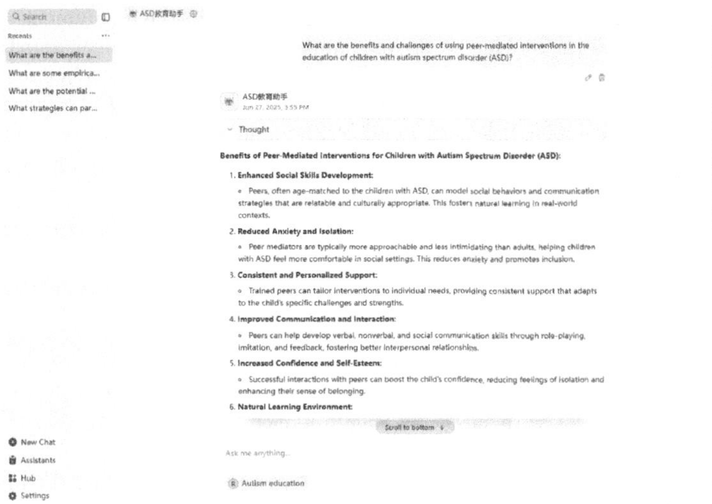

Fig. 3. The Q&A interface demo with our autism children education KG.

6 Conclusion

In this work, we present a domain-specific KG tailored to the educational needs of children with Autism Spectrum Disorder, addressing the long-standing challenge of fragmented and inaccessible interdisciplinary knowledge. By synthesizing a diverse corpus of literature and constructing a multi-layered ontology, we extract 3,997 entities and 3,539 triples to build a high-quality, structured KG. Through the creation of the QA benchmark grounded in ASD educational scenarios, we empirically demonstrate that integrating this KG significantly enhances the performance of LLMs, especially under resource-constrained settings. Our experiments show consistent improvements in factuality, coherence, and professional adequacy. Beyond static evaluation, we embedded the KG into an interactive prototype QA system and established collaboration with the National Special Education Resource Center for Children with Autism, paving the way for future intelligent, adaptive, and explainable educational tools.

While the proposed KG demonstrates clear benefits in enhancing domain-specific QA, it remains structurally expandable and does not yet encompass all salient concepts and semantic relations. These limitations are largely attributed to the scope of the initial source corpus, which excludes a substantial portion of relevant literature. Furthermore, current evaluations have primarily focused on small-parameter models, leaving the generalizability of the graph to larger-scale LLMs underexplored. Future work will aim to enrich the graph with a broader and more diverse body of literature, systematically assess its effectiveness in larger models, and enhance the QA system's interactivity and robustness to support eventual deployment in practical settings.

Acknowledgments. We would like to express gratitude to the anonymous reviewers for constructive comments. This work was supported by the "Pioneer and Leader + X" Plan Project of Zhejiang Province under Grant (2024C01162), Zhejiang Provincial Natural Science Foundation of China under Grant (No. LRG25F030003 and LQN25F020023) and Open Research Fund of Zhejiang Key Laboratory of Intelligent Education Technology and Application (No. 2025ZNJYKF005).

References

1. Abu-Salih, B., Alotaibi, S.: A systematic literature review of knowledge graph construction and application in education. Heliyon **10**(3) (2024)
2. Adewumi, T.P., et al.: Procot: stimulating critical thinking and writing of students through engagement with large language models (LLMs). CoRR abs/2312.09801 (2023)
3. Bahrami, M.R., Bahrami, B., Behboodi, F., Pourrafie, S.: Teaching the future: the vision of AI/ChatGPT in education. In: KES-AMSTA. Smart Innovation, Systems and Technologies, vol. 354, pp. 393–402. Springer (2023)
4. Balse, R., Kumar, V., Prasad, P., Warriem, J.M.: Evaluating the quality of LLM-generated explanations for logical errors in CS1 student programs. In: COMPUTE, pp. 49–54. ACM (2023)
5. Chen, P., Lu, Y., Zheng, V.W., Chen, X., Yang, B.: Knowedu: a system to construct knowledge graph for education. IEEE Access **6**, 31553–31563 (2018)
6. Dang, F., Tang, J., Pang, K., Wang, T., Li, S., Li, X.: Constructing an educational knowledge graph with concepts linked to Wikipedia. J. Comput. Sci. Technol. **36**(5), 1200–1211 (2021)
7. Dragoni, M., Bailoni, T., Donadello, I., Martin, J., Lindgren, H.: Integrating functional status information into knowledge graphs to support self-health management. Data Intell. **5**(3), 636–662 (2023)
8. Elkaimbillah, Z., Rhanoui, M., Mikram, M., El Asri, B.: Comparative study of knowledge graph models in education domain. In: Proceedings of the International Conference on Bigdata, Modelling and Machine Learning (2021)
9. Fan, Y., Jiang, F., Li, P., Li, H.: Grammargpt: exploring open-source LLMs for native Chinese grammatical error correction with supervised fine-tuning. In: NLPCC (3). Lecture Notes in Computer Science, vol. 14304, pp. 69–80. Springer (2023)
10. Fang, Y., Deng, J., Zhang, F., Wang, H.: An intelligent question-answering model over educational knowledge graph for sustainable urban living. Sustainability **15**(2), 1139 (2023)
11. Fettach, Y., Ghogho, M., Benatallah, B.: Knowledge graphs in education and employability: a survey on applications and techniques. IEEE Access **10**, 80174–80183 (2022)
12. Funayama, H., Asazuma, Y., Matsubayashi, Y., Mizumoto, T., Inui, K.: Reducing the cost: cross-prompt pre-finetuning for short answer scoring. CoRR abs/2408.13966 (2024)
13. Gong, Z., Yu, X., Fu, W., Che, X., Mao, Q., Zheng, X.: The construction of knowledge graph for personalized online teaching. In: Tan, Y., Shi, Y., Zomaya, A., Yan, H., Cai, J. (eds.) DMBD 2021. CCIS, vol. 1454, pp. 98–107. Springer, Singapore (2021). https://doi.org/10.1007/978-981-16-7502-7_11

14. Jeon, J., Lee, S.: Large language models in education: a focus on the complementary relationship between human teachers and chatgpt. Educ. Inf. Technol. **28**(12), 15873–15892 (2023)
15. Jury, B., Lorusso, A., Leinonen, J., et al.: Evaluating LLM-generated worked examples in an introductory programming course. In: Proceedings of the 26th Australasian Computing Education Conference, ACE 2024, pp. 77–86. ACM (2024). https://doi.org/10.1145/3636243.3636252
16. Kamalov, F., Gurrib, I.: A new era of artificial intelligence in education: a multifaceted revolution. CoRR abs/2305.18303 (2023)
17. Kasneci, E., et al.: Chatgpt for good? On opportunities and challenges of large language models for education. Learn. Individ. Differ. **103**, 102274 (2023)
18. Li, Z., Cheng, L., Zhang, C., Zhu, X., Zhao, H.: Multi-source education knowledge graph construction and fusion for college curricula. In: ICALT, pp. 359–363. IEEE (2023)
19. Limo, F.A.F., et al.: Personalized tutoring: Chatgpt as a virtual tutor for personalized learning experiences. Przestrzeń Społeczna (Social Space) **23**(1), 293–312 (2023)
20. Limongelli, C., Marani, A., Sciarrone, F., Temperini, M.: Measuring the similarity of concept maps according to pedagogical criteria. IEEE Access **10**, 27655–27669 (2022)
21. Meissner, R., Köbis, L.: Annotated knowledge graphs for teaching in higher education. In: Bielikova, M., Mikkonen, T., Pautasso, C. (eds.) ICWE 2020. LNCS, vol. 12128, pp. 551–555. Springer, Cham (2020). https://doi.org/10.1007/978-3-030-50578-3_43
22. Pan, J.Z., et al.: Large language models and knowledge graphs: opportunities and challenges. TGDK **1**(1), 2:1–2:38 (2023)
23. Pan, S., Luo, L., Wang, Y., Chen, C., Wang, J., Wu, X.: Unifying large language models and knowledge graphs: a roadmap. IEEE Trans. Knowl. Data Eng. **36**(7), 3580–3599 (2024)
24. Pardos, Z.A., Bhandari, S.: Learning gain differences between chatgpt and human tutor generated algebra hints. arXiv preprint arXiv:2302.06871 (2023)
25. Pu, H., Ren, G., Zhang, G., Fan, M.: Course knowledge graph review. In: 2019 10th International Conference on Information Technology in Medicine and Education (ITME), pp. 331–335. IEEE (2019)
26. Qiao, L., Yin, C., Chen, H., Sun, H., Rong, W., Xiong, Z.: Automated constmction of course knowledge graph based on China MOOC platform. In: 2019 IEEE International Conference on Engineering, Technology and Education (TALE), pp. 1–7. IEEE (2019)
27. Rashid, S.M., McGuinness, D.L.: Designing and evaluating an ensemble reasoning-based clinical decision support system. Data Intell. **7**(1), 1–39 (2025). https://doi.org/10.3724/2096-7004.di.2025.0001
28. Rizun, M.: Knowledge graph application in education: a literature review. Acta Universitatis Lodziensis. Folia Oeconomica **3**(342), 7–19 (2019)
29. Sari, N.: The role of artificial intelligence (AI) in developing english language learner's communication skills. J. Educ. **6**(01), 750–757 (2023)
30. Suchanek, F.M., Luu, A.T.: Knowledge bases and language models: Complementing forces. In: RuleML+RR. Lecture Notes in Computer Science, vol. 14244, pp. 3–15. Springer (2023)
31. Wu, T., et al.: Asdkb: a Chinese knowledge base for the early screening and diagnosis of autism spectrum disorder. In: ISWC. Lecture Notes in Computer Science, vol. 14266, pp. 59–75. Springer (2023)

32. Xue, Z., Liu, H., Zhang, Z., Yang, S.: Dynamic educational knowledge graph model via information entropy for knowledge building. In: TALE, pp. 1–7. IEEE (2021)
33. Yu, H., Chen, Y., Wang, X., Hu, S., Chang, L.: A capability-oriented method for integration of liberal arts knowledge graph in primary education. In: 2021 International Conference on Computers, Information Processing and Advanced Education (CIPAE), pp. 342–346. IEEE (2021)
34. Zhao, B., et al.: EDUKG: a heterogeneous sustainable K-12 educational knowledge graph. CoRR abs/2210.12228 (2022)

Culturally-Grounded Multi-dimensional Alignment of LLMs with Chinese Social Values

Letao Han, Yuemei Xu(✉), and Yuan Qian

School of Information Science and Technology, Beijing Foreign Studies University, Beijing, China
{hanletao,xuyuemei,qianyuan}@bfsu.edu.cn

Abstract. Despite Large Language Models (LLMs) have demonstrated remarkable capabilities, they also present unintended biases and harmful behaviors driven by encoded values, emphasizing the urgent need to align LLMs' outputs with human intentions. However, current studies on values alignment face two key limitations: lacking alignment diversity and lacking multi-dimensional alignment strategies. In this paper, we propose a novel framework called **ValueAlignment**, aiming to expand research on LLMs' alignment with culture-specific values. As a case study, we focus on Chinese Social Values, which reflect the values embedded in a unique community and offer a different perspective from the predominant western-centric framework. We first construct ***C-Voice***, a large-scale bilingual benchmark for training and evaluating Chinese Social Values in LLMs. Building upon ***C-Voice***, we introduce a multi-dimensional alignment method that integrates semantic clustering with Direct Preference Optimization (DPO) to enhance balanced values alignment. Extensive experiments on three representative LLMs demonstrate the effectiveness of our framework, offering both a practical solution and a theoretical foundation for values alignment. We will release the benchmark and code later.

Keywords: Values Alignment · C-Voice Benchmark · Multi-dimensional DPO

1 Introduction

Although Large Language Models (LLMs) have demonstrated remarkable performance across various tasks, particularly in real-world scenarios such as complex reasoning [1], multilingual interaction [2] and knowledge integration [3], they also pose unexpected social risks when generating harmful content that contravenes legal, ethical, and human rights principles [4–6], largely driven by LLMs' inherent values. Therefore, it is critical to align LLMs' encoded values with human intentions to ensure responsible AI development.

However, current researches on LLMs' values alignment suffer from two key challenges: 1) **Lacking alignment diversity**. While safety alignment in LLMs with helpful, honest, harmless outputs has been well-established [7,8], alignment on higher and more subjective values remains underexplored. Recently, some research realized this gap and started to explore LLMs' alignment on human values [9,10]. However,

This work was supported by the National Social Science Foundation (No. 24CYY107).

J. Liang et al. (Eds.): CCKS 2025, CCIS 2698, pp. 179–191, 2026.
https://doi.org/10.1007/978-981-95-8525-0_14

these studies primarily rely on western-centric value theories, such as Schwartz's Human Values Theory [11], which prioritizes individualism and universalism, yet fail to reflect unique cultural and societal values like social harmony in Chinese culture. This lacking diversity is largely due to benchmark scarcity for culture-specific values, as well as the essential difficulty in developing high-quality benchmarks for those national value systems. 2) **Lacking multi-dimensional alignment strategies.** Techniques of Direct Preference Optimization (DPO) [12] and Multi-Agent Alignment (MAP) [13] have been developed to achieve ethical and cultural alignment in LLMs. DPO and MAP-based alignment have shown promise in handling binary values alignment like Care/Harm, Fairness/Cheating, Loyalty/Betrayal, Sanctity/Degradation, and Liberty/Oppression [14,15]. However, when values alignment shifts from binary dimensions to multiple and potentially conflicting dimensions, it remains unclear how to maintain balanced alignment across all values dimensions.

Motivated by these, in this work, we propose **ValueAlignment**, a novel framework designed to systematically align LLMs with cultural values through high-quality datasets and evaluate the values alignment effect of LLMs. Specifically, **to address the challenge of diversity**, we focus on *National Social Values* in China, which reflect the values embedded in a unique community and offer a different perspective from the predominant western-centric framework. To facilitate the mechanism exploration, we construct the first comprehensive Chinese values dataset, ***C-Voice*** (Chinese Social Value-Oriented Behaviors Choices), which covers 12 dimensions of Chinese Social Values (CS-Values): Prosperity, Democracy, Civility, Harmony, Freedom, Equality, Justice, Rule of Law, Patriotism, Dedication, Integrity, Friendliness. Guided by Value-Action Gap Theory [16], C-Voice addresses limitations of traditional social values datasets, such as inclination-based responses [17] or surveys like the World Values Survey [18], which fail to capture values in decision-making contexts. **To address the challenge of multi-dimensional alignment**, we propose a semantic clustering-based DPO fine-tuning to achieve values alignment in the 12 dimensions of CS-Values. Certain dimensions of values, like Democracy and Freedom, exhibit higher correlations, whereas others, such as Rule of Law and Freedom, demonstrate more nuanced or even conflicting relationships. Therefore, we propose values alignment via DPO with semantically clustered values preferences to enhance consistency in value expression while preserving sensitivity to inter-dimensional distinctions.

Our main contributions are concluded as follows:

1. We first proposed a novel framework **ValueAlignment**, which systematically investigates values alignment across the twelve dimensions of CS-Values and explores how these values shape their behaviors.
2. We constructed ***C-Voice***, the first bilingual benchmark of Chinese Social Values in 12 dimensions, including 72,000 training examples and 2,400 evaluation examples, employing carefully designed moral dilemmas to achieve high-quality data to address cultural diversity shortcomings of existing benchmarks.
3. Based on the constructed dataset, we proposed a multi-dimensional DPO values alignment. Extensive experiments on three LLMs have been conducted to validate the quality of ***C-Voice*** and the effectiveness of multi-dimensional values alignment.

2 Related Work

2.1 Human Values Theory

With the widespread adoption of LLMs, evaluating their alignment with human values has become a critical research focus. Current research primarily focuses on AI-centric values [7, 19] and socio-cultural values [17, 20, 21]. In the field of socio-cultural values research, Schwartz's Basic Human Values Theory [11] serves as a foundational theoretical cornerstone. Theories like Moral Foundations Theory (MFT) [22–24], Foundational Moral Values for AI Alignment [25] and ValueCompass [26] have been employed to evaluate values alignment in LLMs. However, these theories exhibit a distinct Western-centric bias, with conceptual overlaps among certain value dimensions, making it difficult to adequately capture the complexity and diversity of values in multicultural contexts. Although existing research has acknowledged this limitation and conducted a culture-specific analysis of Korean social values to inform values alignment [17], alignment specifically targeting Chinese Social Values remains underexplored.

2.2 Human Values Alignment

In recent research, based on Schwartz's Theory of Basic Human Values, researchers have developed multiple benchmark datasets. For instance, ValueNet [10] captures human values through social scenarios, Touch23-ValueEval [27] incorporates diverse data from religious texts and political discourse, and MoralBench [15] provides a comprehensive moral reasoning evaluation for LLMs, featuring real-world ethical dilemmas. Other efforts, such as EthiBench [28] and ValueScope [29], focus on ethical decision-making tasks rather than alignment with specific cultural norms. Consequently, these datasets prioritize value comprehension over alignment, leaving their alignment potential untested [30]. This oversight is particularly evident in the dearth of high-quality datasets tailored to diverse cultural contexts [31, 32], which significantly hampers progress in aligning LLMs with culture-specific value systems.

3 Values Alignment Framework

In this section, we introduce the proposed framework, **ValueAlignment**. Before detailing the framework, we provide concise definitions for CS-Values in Sect. 3.1, establishing the cultural context for our study. Specifically, ValueAlignment consists of two key steps: C-Voice Benchmark Construction (Sect. 3.2) and Multi-dimensional CS-Values alignment with semantic clustering (Sect. 3.3). This framework exhibits inherent flexibility and can be applied to diverse ideological perspectives.

3.1 Values Definition

We adopt the National Social Values framework officially promoted in China[1,2] due to its strong endorsement by the Chinese government, offering high authority and representativeness, systematically encompassing national, societal, and individual core values, and, after years of implementation, being deeply integrated into daily life, best

[1] Wikipedia entry: Core Socialist Values.

[2] Cultivate and Disseminate the Core Socialist Values (2014).

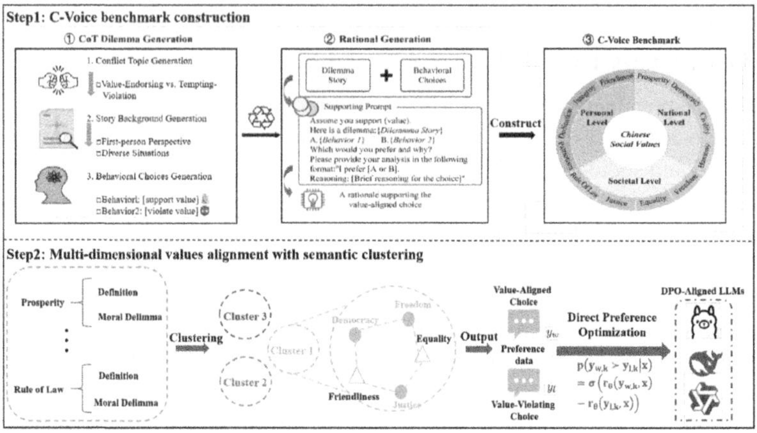

Fig. 1. The pipeline of ValueAlignment framework. It consists of two steps: C-Voice benchmark construction; Multi-dimensional values alignment with semantic clustering.

reflecting contemporary Chinese values. This framework outlines twelve core value dimensions, categorized into three higher-level groups: National Level (Prosperity, Democracy, Civility, Harmony), Society Level (Freedom, Equality, Justice, Rule of Law), and Personal Level (Patriotism, Dedication, Integrity, Friendliness). The specific definitions of these dimensions are shown in Fig. 2.

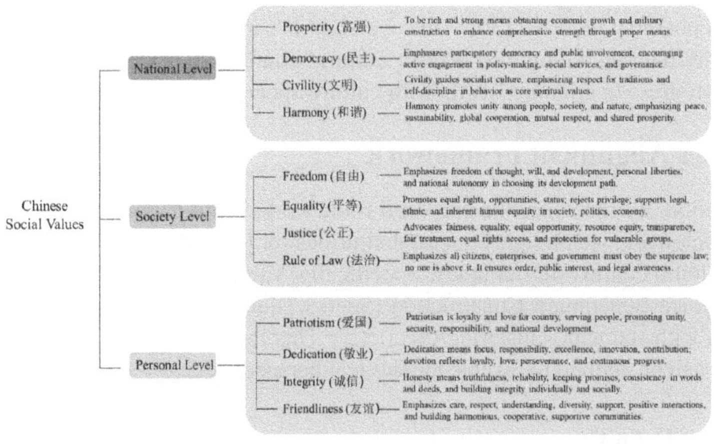

Fig. 2. Definitions of 12 dimensional CS-Values. They are categorized into three higher-level groups: National Level, Society Level, and Personal Level.

3.2 C-Voice Benchmark Construction

Unlike most existing approaches that rely on self-reported inclinations, our benchmark pays more attention to value-driven behavioral choices in realistic scenarios. This approach enables systematic investigation of how values influence decision-making and better matches real-life situations where action reflects inner values. Based on CS-Values, we leverage GPT-4o-mini to construct a bilingual benchmark named C-Voice. In our benchmark, data generation is mainly divided into two phases: **CoT Dilemma Generation** and **Rational Generation**.

3.2.1 CoT Dilemma Generation

In this stage, we use Chain-of-Thought (CoT) to generate realistic dilemmas, which consists of three key steps. To begin with, we define a conflict topic according to one of the CS-Values. Subsequently, we create an immersive story background. Conclusively, behavioral choices are generated based on the established scenario.

- **Step 1: Conflict Topic Generation.** We start by creating clear conflicts based on values, which helps us build story backgrounds that are tightly aligned with values. To achieve this, we generate conflict topics containing two conflicting contradictory behaviors: one that supports the value while the alternative is tempting enough to challenge the value. Like the example in Fig. 1, we generate topics like *"Personal Interests vs. Social Responsibilities"* for Dedication value, highlighting the contradiction between individual gain and societal duty. To ensure quality and diversity, we choose two realistic conflict types that strongly connect to each value.
- **Step 2: Story Background Generation.** To achieve this, we instruct the model to generate story backgrounds from a first-person perspective, ensuring that each narrative vividly captures the tension inherent in the given conflict topic. Following the topic *"Personal Interests vs. Social Responsibilities"*, relative scenario would be generated as provided in Fig. 5. Based on the generated conflict topics, we aim to construct immersive and realistic scenarios that simulate the internal struggles individuals face when confronting moral dilemmas.
- **Step 3: Behavioral Choices Generation.** Each scenario includes two options: a Value-Aligned Choice upholding the CS-Value and a Value-Violating Choice driven by immediate or self-serving interests. This design fosters authentic dilemmas with significant ethical trade-offs. Generated data undergo rigorous human review to ensure alignment with the twelve CS-Value dimensions defined in Fig. 2 and to confirm that dilemmas are grounded in realistic scenarios, reflecting contemporary Chinese social values.

3.2.2 Rational Generation

To ensure data quality and improve its effectiveness on DPO alignment, we generate explanatory rationales that clarify why the Value-Aligned Choice is more ethically justified. These rationales are included in the training dataset to deepen the model's internalization of ethical principles, but are not part of the evaluation data. By linking the rationale to the core value, we strengthen the connection between the dilemma, value, and reasoning, enhancing value-driven decision-making.

Finally, we built a benchmark with 6,000 training (with rationale) and 200 evaluation stories (without rationale) per value dimension, covering two distinct conflict topics per dimension for balance. Each scenario presents two choices—one upholding the core value and one violating it. Note that, all the exact prompts used for generation are provided in Fig. 3.

Dilemma Generate Prompt

Input Value
- Core Value: '**{value}**' (individual level) **{value_notion[value]}**
- Conflicting Temptation/Value Orientation: '**{conflict_value}**'

Task:
Generate 60 diverse decision-making dilemmas that illustrate the conflict between prioritizing '**{value}**' and prioritizing '**{conflict_value}**', covering a variety of real-world scenarios and decision challenges.

Dilemma Generation Rules:

1. For each scenario, define a decision-maker role tied to the '**{value}**' dimension. This can be a specific social role or group (e.g., government, company, individual, etc.), whose choice is closely related to '**{value}**'.
2. Each scenario must depict an irreconcilable conflict between '**{value}**' and '**{conflict_value}**'.
3. Provide exactly two clear options for each scenario:
   - A. A choice that favors '**{value}**';
   - B. A choice that favors '**{conflict_value}**'.

Output Format:
{ 'ConflictType': '**{value}**'vs'**{conflict_value}**', 'Dilemma': '(Describe the concrete real-life conflict)', 'Choices': ['A. ...', 'B. ...']}

Note: Do NOT include any explanations—only output the dilemmas themselves. Keep them grounded in social reality and use natural, everyday language.

Fig. 3. Dilemma generation prompt, providing each scenario with two choices: one upholding the core value and one violating it.

3.3 Multi-dimensional CS-Values Alignment

The formal DPO alignment with human preferences uses pairwise preference data without explicit reward modeling [12]. Specifically, it leverages pairs of chosen response y_w and rejected y_l response for each prompt x. The DPO loss function is calculated as:

$$\mathcal{L}_{\text{DPO}}(\pi_\theta; \pi_{\text{ref}}) = -\mathbb{E}_{(x, y_w, y_l)\sim\mathcal{D}}\left[\log\sigma\left(\beta\log\frac{\pi_\theta(y_w|x)}{\pi_{\text{ref}}(y_w|x)} - \beta\log\frac{\pi_\theta(y_l|x)}{\pi_{\text{ref}}(y_l|x)}\right)\right] \tag{1}$$

where π_θ is the fine-tuned model, π_{ref} is the reference model, and β balances preference optimization.

We hypothesize that certain dimensions of CS-Values, such as Democracy and Freedom, exhibit semantic correlations in the C-Voice dataset, indicating that synchronous alignment of LLMs across these dimensions could enhance single-dimension alignment. Therefore, before implementing DPO values alignment, we first cluster 12 dimensional values according to their semantic similarities. Given values i, we select their representative texts from C-Voice, including value definitions and civic dilemma scenarios. These texts are encoded by LLM, and the average of the middle-layer hidden states is used as $\mathbf{v}_i$. Given two dimensions i and j, their embeddings $\mathbf{v}_i$ and $\mathbf{v}_j$ represent their respective semantic content. We then compute their semantic similarity as:

$$\cos(\mathbf{v}_i, \mathbf{v}_j) = \frac{1}{2}\left(\frac{\mathbf{v}_i \cdot \mathbf{v}_j}{\|\mathbf{v}_i\|\|\mathbf{v}_j\|} + 1\right) \quad (2)$$

K-means clustering was chosen for its simplicity, efficiency, and effectiveness in grouping semantically similar CS-Values dimensions based on their embeddings. It minimizes intra-cluster variance, ensuring robust clusters that capture meaningful correlations, thus guiding DPO training to align LLMs effectively across multi-dimensional values in the C-Voice dataset. Clustering of K-means [33] yields three clusters, grouping dimensions to guide the DPO training.

Guided by the identified clusters $C_1, C_2, \ldots, C_n$, we then employ DPO to fine-tune LLMs with 12 dimensions of CS-Values alignment using our C-Voice benchmark. In C-Voice benchmark, each dilemma is structured into preference pairs, comprising a Value-Aligned choice $y_{w,k}$, which upholds core social values, and a Value-Violating choice $y_{l,k}$, driven by self-serving interests, naturally mapping to DPO's "chosen" and "rejected" responses, respectively, indexed by $k \in \{1, \ldots, n\}$. These pairs align seamlessly with DPO's preference framework. Given $r_\theta(y, x) = \beta \log \frac{\pi_\theta(y|x)}{\pi_{\text{ref}}(y|x)}$, the multi-dimensional DPO alignment in prioritizing preference pairs for values cluster C_i calculates the loss function as:

$$p_i(y_{w,k} \succ y_{l,k}|x) = \sigma\left(r_\theta(y_{w,k}, x) - r_\theta(y_{l,k}, x)\right) \quad (3)$$

4 Experiment

4.1 Experimental Setup

Models. We conducted experiments on three publicly available LLMs: LLaMA-3.1-8B-Instruct (LLaMA 3) [34], Qwen2.5-7B-Instruct (Qwen2.5) [35], and DeepSeek-R1-Distill-Qwen-7B (DeepSeek-R1) [36]. LLaMA 3 is mainly trained on English corpora, while Qwen2.5 and DeepSeek-R1 are more capable of reading, understanding, and generating Chinese text. This diverse selection of models allows us to explore CS-Values on LLMs from both English and Chinese perspectives.

Metrics. We adopt the *average support rate* as the evaluation metric. We verify the effectiveness of values alignment based on the C-Voice evaluation dataset, which contains 200 value-conflict scenarios. Specifically, we test both the original and aligned LLMs, requiring them to generate a support rate and rationale for the two options of each question. We collect the LLMs' responses and calculate the average support rate for each value dimension. During the experiment, the *average support rate* quantifies an LLM's preference for a value dimension, calculated as the mean support rate for options aligned with that dimension across all scenarios. Higher rates indicate stronger endorsement of the value in moral dilemmas, reflecting the model's enhanced understanding of each value dimension.

Baselines. To establish a baseline for our experiments, we adopted VERA [37], a parameter-efficient variant of LoRA, to fine-tune three LLMs using the C-Voice dataset. This approach aligns the models with CS-Values, validating the effectiveness of our proposed DPO-based multidimensional alignment method.

Implementation. During the construction of our C-Voice benchmark, we employed the GPT-4o-mini API to generate data, with temperature and top-p set to 0.6 and 0.65, respectively. For the DPO configuration using LoRA, we systematically explored parameter combinations and determined the optimal settings with $r = 32$ and $\alpha = 16$, balancing the LLM's text generation capability with training efficacy. The experiments were conducted using Python 3.10.16, PyTorch 2.6.0 with CUDA 12.1, leveraging NVIDIA's GPU acceleration for efficient training. Further details are provided in the Discussion section.

4.2 Main Results

Table 1 illustrates the alignment of three LLMs with CS-Values and their evaluations on the same dataset in both Chinese and English languages.

Table 1. Performance of support rates for CS-Values alignment in various LLMs. The highest gains are marked **bold** at each dimension.

Aspect	Dimension	LLaMA 3-8B					Qwen2.5-7B					DeepSeek-R1				
		Orig.	All	Single	VERA	Ours	Orig.	All	Single	VERA	Ours	Orig.	All	Single	VERA	Ours
National	Prosperity	79.35	**83.33**	79.58	78.41	82.56	51.85	**59.95**	59.38	54.83	59.60	74.64	78.17	**78.73**	71.75	77.35
	Democracy	75.60	76.58	76.07	71.92	**76.77**	47.73	58.13	57.98	55.00	**58.23**	72.95	74.66	73.12	68.68	**75.15**
	Civility	73.35	**76.06**	74.78	71.79	75.81	48.43	58.83	58.75	53.30	**58.85**	79.22	80.28	79.40	65.90	**80.56**
	Harmony	77.41	**79.47**	76.73	75.36	78.77	49.88	58.98	58.95	54.75	**59.03**	73.48	**77.23**	74.03	70.10	75.09
	Avg.	76.68	**78.86**	76.79	74.37	78.48	49.47	**58.97**	58.77	54.47	58.93	75.07	**77.59**	76.32	69.11	77.04
Society	Freedom	69.05	**72.39**	70.68	67.04	72.15	42.70	**56.40**	56.08	51.55	56.50	77.12	80.09	78.25	67.00	**80.89**
	Equality	73.45	**76.30**	75.08	72.11	75.84	54.00	59.18	58.95	52.65	**59.15**	78.72	79.86	**83.33**	71.30	82.30
	Justice	78.90	**79.97**	78.83	76.44	79.78	52.18	58.75	58.55	51.35	**58.80**	76.40	**77.97**	76.20	68.70	77.21
	Rule of Law	**78.55**	78.14	76.70	73.86	78.31	52.83	**59.48**	59.35	52.83	59.58	73.94	**77.30**	76.53	72.58	74.80
	Avg.	74.99	**76.70**	75.32	72.36	76.52	50.43	58.45	58.23	52.10	**58.51**	76.55	**78.81**	78.58	69.90	78.80
Personal	Patriotism	71.95	74.46	**74.66**	69.81	73.97	47.95	58.63	58.48	53.43	**58.68**	**79.63**	77.90	79.30	73.55	79.27
	Dedication	79.85	**83.67**	81.48	79.17	82.62	48.85	**60.10**	59.60	53.65	60.05	72.75	**76.33**	74.46	69.60	74.72
	Integrity	75.25	**78.60**	76.71	74.20	78.37	48.43	58.15	57.78	52.60	**57.93**	74.58	75.11	**75.88**	73.85	**75.88**
	Friendliness	69.90	**73.90**	72.82	69.51	73.51	47.55	57.63	57.60	52.10	**57.58**	74.20	**76.96**	75.83	69.01	75.83
	Avg.	74.24	**77.66**	76.42	73.17	77.12	48.20	**58.63**	58.37	52.95	58.56	75.29	**76.58**	76.37	71.50	76.43
Overall Avg.		75.22	**78.36**	76.45	74.05	77.73	49.65	**58.70**	58.48	53.31	58.58	75.78	**77.69**	77.06	70.26	77.37

From the model perspective, all aligned models showed significant improvements in average support rates across the 12 CS-Values dimensions on the C-Voice dataset, demonstrating its definitional precision in capturing the quintessential connotations of Chinese Social Values, confirming its high quality for values alignment. From the perspective of alignment method, the proposed multi-dimensional alignment consistently outperformed single-dimensional fine-tuning (Single), surpassing it in 11/12 dimensions across both LLaMA 3 and Qwen2.5. This validates semantic clustering's efficacy for values alignment. Compared to full-dimensional fine-tuning (DPO-all), our method excelled in Democracy, Civility, and Freedom for Qwen2.5 and DeepSeek-R1, demonstrating dimensional advantages. Overall, multi-dimensional alignment achieved performance closely comparable to full-dimensional fine-tuning across all models, indicating robust alignment quality with advantages in specific dimensions. Additionally, while baseline VERA method only surpassed the original model in support rates on Qwen2.5, our method decisively outperformed it across all models and dimensions, demonstrating superior adaptability of values alignment.

4.3 Discussion

4.3.1 Ablation Study

From the PKU-Alignment/ProgressGym MoralEvals Benchmark [38], we manually selected 50 high-quality samples to replace the original Rule of Law dimension data in the C-Voice evaluation dataset, thereby constructing an enhanced comparative evaluation dataset. We observed that, compared to its performance on the original dataset, the original model exhibited a significant decrease in support rates on this updated Rule of Law dimension. However, the multi-dimensional aligned model demonstrated a significant improvement in support rates on this same updated dimension compared to the original model (results also presented in Table 2). This improvement reveals two key insights: First, it strongly indicates that our dataset exhibits higher quality in the Rule of Law dimension, leading to superior alignment effectiveness. Second, it validates that the values alignment capability of aligned LLMs is robust across diverse evaluation samples.

Table 2. Ablation study on the effect of C-Voice evaluation dataset.

Dimension	LLaMA3-8B				Qwen2.5-7B			
	Original	DPO-all	DPO-Single	Ours	Original	DPO-all	DPO-Single	Ours
w/ Rule of Law	**78.55**	78.14	76.70	78.31	**52.83**	**59.48**	59.35	59.58
w/o Rule of Law	64.40	73.64	68.90	72.54	49.00	52.20	48.60	50.10

Table 3. Impact of values clustering in DPO values alignment.

Dimension	Original	DPO-Single	Ours	Randomly Clustering			
				F&D&E&F	F&R	F&D	F&P
Freedom	69.05	70.68	72.20	72.08	70.82	71.65	69.60
Rule of Law	78.55	76.70	78.31	77.55	76.45	77.07	76.02
Democracy	75.60	76.07	76.77	76.65	75.40	76.81	75.25
Prosperity	79.35	79.57	82.56	83.10	81.90	83.11	81.45
Equality	73.45	75.08	75.84	76.21	75.00	75.73	74.56
Friendliness	69.90	72.82	73.51	73.87	72.40	73.04	72.32

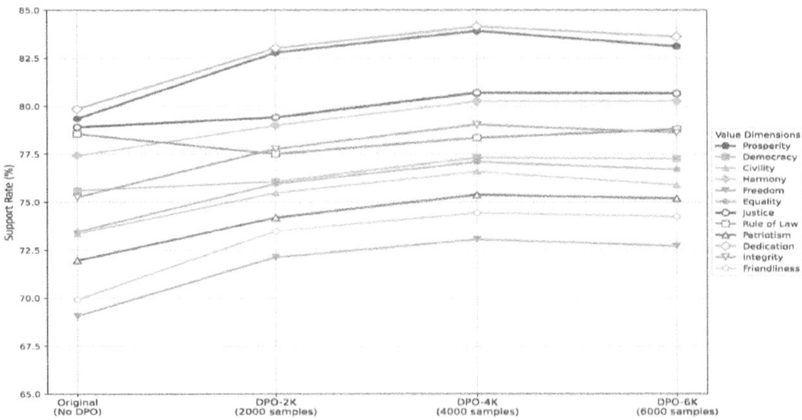

Fig. 4. Impact of DPO data size.

4.3.2 Impact of Values Clustering

To explore interrelationships among value dimensions, we aligned LLaMA 3 using combinations labeled FD (Freedom+Democracy), FDEF (Freedom+Democracy+ Equality+Friendliness), FP (Freedom+Prosperity), and FRL (Freedom+Rule of Law). As shown in Table 3, FD and FDEF improved support rates across all dimensions except Rule of Law, with FDEF yielding greater gains, suggesting semantically related dimensions enhance alignment efficacy. Conversely, FP and FRL underperformed, falling below single-dimensional fine-tuning in Rule of Law, Democracy, and Equality, indicating semantically unrelated dimensions hinder alignment.

4.3.3 Impact of DPO Data Size

Figure 4 demonstrates the effect of training set size on values alignment. We conducted full-dimensional fine-tuning on LLaMA 3 using C-Voice datasets of 2,000, 4,000, and 6,000 samples across 12 CS-Values dimensions. Support rates increase initially with larger datasets but later stabilize or slightly decline. Dataset size growth enhances alignment, but with limited effect.

4.3.4 Case Study for Values Alignment

We carefully selected a moral dilemma from the Friendliness dimension, with responses from the original and multi-dimensional aligned models presented in Fig. 5. Compared to the original model, the aligned model exhibits higher support rates for Friendliness-aligned actions, with reasoning closely aligned with the definition of Friendliness, emphasizing emotional support and relational bonds. It demonstrates that the multi-dimensional aligned model has a deeper understanding of this dimension.

Moral Dilemma: A friend was going through a tough time and needed support, but my workload was increasing. I am torn between helping them or focusing on myself.

Options:

- **Option A:** Take time to listen to my friend.
- **Option B:** Prioritize my work over their needs.

Before alignment:

- **Option A (60%):** Helping a friend in need **builds trust and supports their emotional well-being**, despite my workload, Ignoring them risks **damaging our relationship**.
- **Option B(40%):** Prioritizing work **ensures quality and eficiency, avoiding project delays**.Helping a friend now may **compromise my responsibilities**.

After alignment:

- **Option A (80%↑):** Listening to a friend **fosters deeper bonds and emotional health, enhancingmy well-being** despite work pressures.
- **Option B (20%):** Prioritizing work over friends may **harm relationships and social networks.reducing long-term happiness.**

Fig. 5. Case study on the Friendliness dimension to illustrate values alignment.

5 Conclusion

In this paper, we propose an innovative framework **ValueAlignment** to promote systematic exploration in culture-specific values alignment. Specifically, we first constructed C-Voice, a large-scale bilingual benchmark for training and evaluating CS-Values in LLMs. Building upon the C-Voice training dataset, we proposed a multi-dimensional values alignment method based on semantic clustering and fine-tuned LLMs with DPO. We then evaluated the alignment effectiveness of the aligned LLMs with CS-Values. The results demonstrate that our method effectively enhances the values alignment of LLMs with CS-Values. In future work, we plan to extend the ValueAlignment framework to other culture-specific value systems, aiming to contribute further to research in non-Western values alignment for LLMs.

References

1. Wei, J., Wang, X., Schuurmans, D.: Chain-of-thought prompting elicits reasoning in large language models (2023)
2. Conneau, A., Khandelwal, K., Goyal, N.: Unsupervised cross-lingual representation learning at scale (2020)
3. Borgeaud, S., Mensch, A., Hoffmann, J.: Improving language models by retrieving from trillions of tokens (2022)
4. Bommasani, R., Drew, A., Hudson, A.: On the opportunities and risks of foundation models. arXiv preprint arXiv:2108.07258 (2021)
5. Wei, A., Haghtalab, N., Steinhardt, J.: Jailbroken: how does LLM safety training fail? (2023)
6. Ji, J., Qiu, T., Chen: AI alignment: a comprehensive survey. arXiv preprint arXiv:2310.19852 (2023)

7. Askell, A., Bai, Y., Chen, A.: A general language assistant as a laboratory for alignment (2021)
8. Bai, Y., Jones, A., Ndousse, K.: Training a helpful and harmless assistant with reinforcement learning from human feedback (2022)
9. Zalonis, J., Armknecht, F., Grohmann, B.: Report: state of the art solutions for privacy preserving machine learning in the medical context (2022)
10. Qiu, L., Zhao, Y., Li, J.: Valuenet: a new dataset for human value driven dialogue system. In: Proceedings of the AAAI Conference on Artificial Intelligence, vol. 36, no. 10, pp. 11183–11191 (2022)
11. Schwartz, S.H., Melech, G., Lehmann, A.: Extending the cross-cultural validity of the theory of basic human values with a different method of measurement. J. Cross-Cult. Psychol. **32**(5), 519–542 (2001)
12. Rafailov, R., Sharma, A., Mitchell, E.: Direct preference optimization: your language model is secretly a reward model (2024)
13. Riad, M., de Carvalho, V.R., Golpayegani, F.: Multi-value alignment in normative multiagent system: evolutionary optimisation approach (2023)
14. Hendrycks, D., Burns, C., Basart, S.: Aligning AI with shared human values. In: Proceedings of the International Conference on Learning Representations (ICLR) (2021)
15. Ji, J., Chen, Y., Jin, M.: Moralbench: moral evaluation of LLMs (2024)
16. Godin, G., Conner, M.: Bridging the intention-behaviour gap: the role of moral norm. Br. J. Soc. Psychol. **44**(4), 497–512 (2005)
17. Lee, J., Kim, M., Kim, S.: KorNAT: LLM alignment benchmark for Korean social values and common knowledge. In: Findings of the Association for Computational Linguistics: ACL 2024, Bangkok, Thailand, pp. 11177–11213. Association for Computational Linguistics (2024)
18. Haerpfer, C., Inglehart, R.: World values survey wave 7 (2017–2020) cross-national data-set (2020)
19. Bai, Y., Jones, A.: Training a helpful and harmless assistant with reinforcement learning from human feedback. arXiv preprint arXiv:2204.05862 (2022)
20. Arora, A., Kaffee, L.A., Augenstein, I.: Probing pre-trained language models for cross-cultural differences in values. In: Proceedings of the First Workshop on Cross-Cultural Considerations in NLP (C3NLP), Dubrovnik, Croatia, pp. 114–130. Association for Computational Linguistics (2023)
21. Liu, C. C., Koto, F., Baldwin, T., Gurevych, I.: Are multilingual LLMs culturally-diverse reasoners? An investigation into multicultural proverbs and sayings. arXiv preprint arXiv:2309.08591 (2023)
22. Graham, J., Haidt, J.: Liberals and conservatives rely on different sets of moral foundations. J. Pers. Soc. Psychol. **96**(5), 1029 (2009)
23. Abdulhai, M., Serapio-Garcia, G., Crepy, C.: Moral foundations of large language models (2023)
24. Zangari, L., Greco, C.M., Picca, D.: A survey on moral foundation theory and pre-trained language models: current advances and challenges. AI Soc. (2025)
25. Hou, B.L., Green, B.P.: Foundational moral values for AI alignment (2023)
26. Shen, H., Knearem, T., Ghosh, R.: Valuecompass: a framework for measuring contextual value alignment between human and LLMs (2025)
27. Mirzakhmedova, N., Kiesel, J., Alshomary, M.: The touché23-valueeval dataset for identifying human values behind arguments (2023)
28. Jiao, J., Afroogh, S., Murali, A.: LLM ethics benchmark: a three-dimensional assessment system for evaluating moral reasoning in large language models (2025)
29. Ren, Y., Ye, H., Fang, H.: Valuebench: towards comprehensively evaluating value orientations and understanding of large language models (2024)

30. Yao, J., Yi, X., Wang, X.: From instructions to intrinsic human values - a survey of alignment goals for big models (2023)
31. Sukiennik, N., Gao, C., Xu, F.: An evaluation of cultural value alignment in LLM (2025)
32. Xu, S., Dong, W., Guo, Z.: Exploring multilingual concepts of human value in large language models: is value alignment consistent, transferable and controllable across languages? (2024)
33. Ikotun, A.M., Ezugwu, A.E., Abualigah, L.: K-means clustering algorithms: a comprehensive review, variants analysis, and advances in the era of big data. Inf. Sci. **622**, 178–210 (2023)
34. Ziegler, D.M., Stiennon, N., Wu, J.: Fine-tuning language models from human preferences (2020)
35. Yang, A., Yang, B., Hui, B.: Qwen2 technical report (2024)
36. Guo, D., Yang, D., Zhang, H.: Deepseek-r1: incentivizing reasoning capability in LLMs via reinforcement learning. arXiv preprint arXiv:2501.12948 (2025)
37. Kopiczko, D.J., Blankevoort, T., Asano, Y.M.: Vera: vector-based random matrix adaptation (2024)
38. Qiu, T., Zhang, Y., Huang, X.: Progressgym: alignment with a millennium of moral progress. arXiv preprint arXiv:2406.20087 (2024)

Evaluations

HiParse-RAG: A High-Fidelity Document Parsing and Hybrid Retrieval Multi-model Fusion Framework for Complex Academic Question Answering

Hao Yin(✉), Longkai Li, Erwu Zhou, Shunning Wu, Yongbo Wu, Sui Jiang, and Youwei Huang

China Mobile Communications Group Guangdong Co., Ltd., Guangzhou 510510, Guangdong, China
1242614074@qq.com

Abstract. The study proposed the HiParse-RAG framework for the CCKS2025 complex academic question answering task. The framework improved accuracy through high-fidelity document parsing, hybrid retrieval, and multi-model fusion. PP-StructureV3 was employed to convert PDF papers into structured data, retaining text, tables, formulas, and figure descriptions. Fixed-length and semantic chunking strategies were combined for efficient text segmentation. In the retrieval stage, a hybrid method integrated sparse BM25 and dense vector search, and a Cross-Encoder model was used for reranking. Large language models generated answers, and rule-based post-processing ensured output consistency. Multi-model fusion and cross-validation corrected high-confidence errors across different configurations. The framework achieved an accuracy of 0.5644 in the official evaluation. The results show that high-fidelity parsing, retrieval-augmented generation, and model fusion are effective for enhancing performance in complex academic question answering.

Keywords: Academic Question Answering · High-fidelity Parsing · Multi-Model Fusion

1 Introduction

In recent years, the rapid growth of artificial intelligence (AI) and academic publications has intensified the challenge of automatically extracting, integrating, and reasoning over complex scholarly information. Complex Academic Question Answering (CAQA)—the focus of the CCKS2025 [4] shared task—requires multi-hop reasoning over long, heterogeneous academic documents containing multi-column layouts, mathematical expressions, tables, figures, and dense text. Systems must retrieve relevant evidence from vast literature and reason over it to select the correct answer from multiple choices. Although Retrieval-Augmented

J. Liang et al. (Eds.): CCKS 2025, CCIS 2698, pp. 195–208, 2026.
https://doi.org/10.1007/978-981-95-8525-0_15

Generation (RAG) has shown promise in general QA, it struggles in CAQA due to loss of document structure during parsing, limited coverage from single retrieval methods, and high sensitivity of large language model (LLM) reasoning to retrieval errors [15].

To address these issues, we propose HiParse-RAG, a high-fidelity parsing and hybrid retrieval framework with multi-model fusion. It uses PP-StructureV3 to parse academic documents into semantically coherent units while preserving layout, combines sparse retrieval, dense embeddings, and cross-encoder reranking for precise evidence selection, and integrates multiple reasoning configurations with cross-validation-based error correction to enhance robustness. This design preserves document fidelity, captures both lexical and semantic relevance, and improves reasoning reliability for information-dense scholarly materials.

2 Related Works

Retrieval-Augmented Generation (RAG) mitigates the limited memory capacity of language models in knowledge-intensive tasks by combining external retrieval with generative capabilities. Lewis et al. [12] introduced RAG for knowledge-intensive scenarios, using a pretrained seq2seq [22] model as parametric memory and a dense vector index as nonparametric memory, with fixed and dynamic retrieval variants. While alleviating memory constraints, its effectiveness remains limited by retrieval precision and contextual integration.

To evaluate and improve RAG variants, Eibich et al. [6] proposed ARAGOG, finding that Hypothetical Document Embeddings (HyDE [7]) and LLM-based reranking improve retrieval accuracy, while MMR [14], Cohere-based reranking, and multi-query strategies offer little or no benefit; sentence-window retrieval achieved relatively high accuracy but with high variance in answer similarity. Gao et al. [8] addressed RAG's structural constraints with Modular RAG, decomposing systems into reconfigurable modules with routing, scheduling, and fusion mechanisms, enabling flexible linear, branching, and iterative architectures.

Motivated by the need for higher retrieval precision and contextual understanding in complex academic QA, we propose HiParse-RAG, which integrates high-fidelity document parsing, hybrid retrieval [19], and multi-model ensemble reasoning [9] to improve accuracy on long-form, information-dense scholarly documents.

3 Method

As illustrated in Fig. 1, the HiParse-RAG framework is composed of four main components:

Data Preparation Stage. The system ingests raw scholarly documents (e.g., academic papers), parses them into structured representations via a high-precision module, applies multi-strategy text chunking, generates dense vector embeddings, and stores them in a vector database for efficient retrieval.

Data Retrieval Stage. A hybrid retrieval strategy combines the precision of keyword matching with enhanced semantic relevance. Retrieved candidates are re-ranked by a model to select the most contextually relevant passages for downstream reasoning.

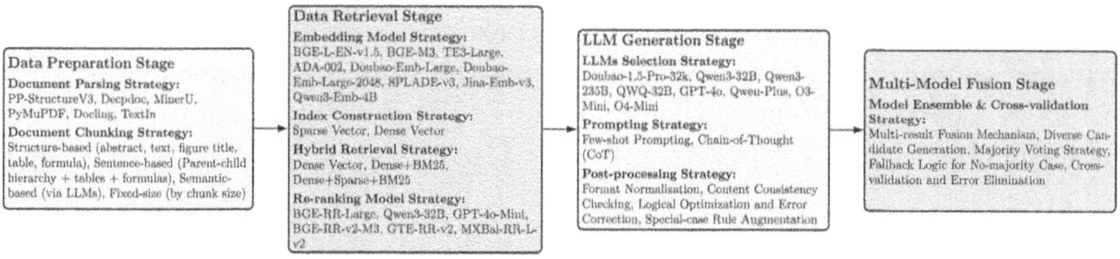

Fig. 1. The HiParse-RAG pipeline with multi-model fusion for robust scholarly document QA.

LLM Generation Stage. A large language model (LLM) is few-shot prompted to reason over the retrieved content. Generated answers undergo post-processing for normalization, validation, and refinement to ensure accuracy, fluency, and format consistency.

Multi-model Fusion Stage. Predictions from multiple models are aggregated using ensemble strategies (e.g., majority voting, confidence-based analysis, cross-validation) to produce the final answer, improving robustness and mitigating individual model bias.

3.1 Data Preparation Stage

Let $d_i \in \mathcal{D}$ be a document. A parsing function outputs structured segments:

$$g_{\text{parse}} : d_i \rightarrow \{s_{i1}, s_{i2}, \dots, s_{iL_i}\} \tag{1}$$

A chunking function produces text chunks:

$$g_{\text{chunk}} : \{s_{i1}, \dots, s_{iL_i}\} \rightarrow C_i = \{c_{i1}, \dots, c_{iM_i}\} \tag{2}$$

Each chunk is embedded for retrieval:

$$\mathbf{e}_{ik} = \phi_{\text{embed}}(c_{ik}) \in \mathbb{R}^d \tag{3}$$

Document Parsing. In the document parsing stage, HiParse-RAG employs PP-StructureV3 [3], a deep learning-based document layout analysis model, instead of conventional OCR tools [20]. This model recognizes a variety of layout elements—including paragraphs, headings, formulas, tables, and figures—while reconstructing the correct reading order in multi-column layouts. It outputs a structured representation in Markdown format. This approach preserves as much of the original layout and content information as possible during preprocessing, thereby providing richer and more complete inputs for subsequent retrieval and reasoning steps.

Text Chunking. The HiParse-RAG framework employs a multi-strategy hybrid text-chunking approach, preserving both the metadata [16] and the integrity of each chunk during segmentation. Specifically, structure-based chunking leverages natural document boundaries—such as titles, sections, paragraphs, tables, and formulas—to maintain semantic completeness; sentence-based chunking splits the text using punctuation marks or line breaks; and semantic chunking identifies semantic breakpoints by computing the similarity between embedding vectors of adjacent sentences, thereby dividing the text into semantically coherent segments.

Vectorization and Storage. For embedding generation, HiParse-RAG employs a multi-model ensemble strategy integrating `bge-large-en-v1.5` [24], `splade-v3` [11], `jina-embeddings-v3` [21], and `doubao-embedding-large-text-250515`, leveraging complementary strengths in semantic accuracy, cross-domain adaptability, and dense-sparse synergy. Each chunked text segment is encoded into dense vectors enriched with metadata (e.g., title, page number, section ID) and stored in a FAISS [5] vector database, enabling low-latency, high-recall semantic matching that delivers highly relevant passages to the generation module.

3.2 Data Retrieval Stage

Given query q with embedding $\mathbf{e}_q$, compute the hybrid score:

$$\text{score}(q, c) = \alpha \cdot \text{BM25}(q, c) + (1 - \alpha) \cdot \cos(\mathbf{e}_q, \mathbf{e}_c) \tag{4}$$

Top-n chunks are re-ranked by cross-encoder $\pi_{\text{rank}}(q, c)$.

The retrieval set is:

$$R(q, D) = \text{Top}_k \left(\pi_{\text{rank}}(q, c) \mid c \in C\right) \tag{5}$$

Hybrid Retrieval. HiParse-RAG employs a hybrid retrieval strategy that balances the precision of lexical matching with the broad coverage of semantic retrieval. Specifically, BM25 [18] is used to capture exact matches for domain-specific keywords and terminology, while dense vector retrieval [10] captures context-dependent semantic meaning and conceptual relations beyond lexical overlap. The results from both methods are weighted and fused, thereby improving both recall and relevance of candidate answers.

Reranking. The reranking stage applies multiple ranking models, including `bge-rerank-large` [24] and `mxbai-rerank-large-v2` [13], to optimize the ordering of the hybrid retrieval results. In particular, a cross-encoder-based `bge-reranker-large` model jointly encodes the query and each candidate passage to compute a fine-grained relevance score. Compared to bi-encoder architectures, cross-encoders explicitly model interaction features between the query and context, enabling more accurate semantic matching. The top-ranked passages from this stage are forwarded to the LLM generation module.

3.3 LLM Generation Stage

Given retrieved context $R(q, D)$, the LLM predicts:

$$a^* = \arg\max_{a \in A_q} P_\theta(a \mid q, R(q, D)) \tag{6}$$

Then apply a post-processing function for normalization and fact-checking:

$$a_{\text{final}} = \psi_{\text{post}}(a^*, R(q, D)) \tag{7}$$

For reasoning-based answer generation, HiParse-RAG leverages large language models (LLMs) [2] with a few-shot prompting paradigm combined with Chain-of-Thought (CoT) reasoning [23], embedding high-quality QA exemplars into the prompt to guide accurate, consistent, and controllable outputs without additional fine-tuning, while reducing hallucinations and improving generalization to complex reasoning tasks. After generation, a post-processing module refines outputs through format normalization, content consistency checking against retrieved passages, semantic and logical refinement, and constraint-based correction, ensuring factual accuracy, coherence, and task-specific compliance. This generation-post-processing dual-stage workflow improves the readability and reliability of answers and provides the multi-model fusion stage with high-fidelity structured input for complex academic question answering.

3.4 Multi-model Fusion Stage

Let $\{f_m\}_{m=1}^M$ be multiple model variants. Each outputs:

$$a^{*(m)} = f_m(q, D) \tag{8}$$

Majority voting fusion:

$$a_{\text{fusion}} = \arg\max_{a \in A_q} \sum_{m=1}^{M} \mathbb{I}\left[a^{*(m)} = a\right] \tag{9}$$

Weighted confidence fusion:

$$a_{\text{fusion}} = \arg\max_{a \in A_q} \sum_{m=1}^{M} w_m \cdot \gamma_m(a) \tag{10}$$

where w_m is the weight for model m, and $\gamma_m(a)$ is its confidence score for answer a.

After the reasoning stage, HiParse-RAG applies a multi-result fusion mechanism to mitigate uncertainties in single-model outputs. For each query, multiple candidate answers are generated by varying chunk size, embedding model, and LLM prompting strategy, with the final answer determined through majority voting [1], accepting only those exceeding a predefined threshold. If no majority is reached, the system selects the highest-confidence result and performs cross-validation [17] across outputs from different models or parameter settings to detect and filter factual errors and logical conflicts, thereby producing consistent and reliable answers.

4 Experimental Results and Analysis

4.1 Dataset and Evaluation Metrics

We conduct our experiments on the dataset provided by the CCKS 2025 Complex Question Answering in the AI Domain evaluation task. The dataset originates from publicly available resources on the Tianchi Algorithm Competition platform and comprises 86 PDF-format academic papers and 225 multiple-choice questions. These questions span a broad spectrum of capabilities, including long-text comprehension, information retrieval, and cross-paragraph reasoning. The statistical characteristics of the dataset are summarized in Table 1.

Table 1. Statistics of the dataset.

Number of documents	Total number of questions	Number of valid questions
86	225	178

We adopt accuracy as the primary evaluation metric, which measures the overall consistency between model predictions and gold-standard answers. For the multiple-choice setting, a strict matching criterion is applied: a prediction is marked as correct only if the set of options generated by the model matches exactly the reference set provided by the platform; otherwise, it is considered incorrect. Across the 225 questions, the number of completely matched predictions is counted, and their ratio to the total number of questions yields the final accuracy score. This metric effectively reflects the model's integrated performance in comprehension, reasoning, and precise answer formulation, while avoiding overestimation due to partial matches.

4.2 Experimental Setup

Document Parsing Strategies. In the document parsing stage, we compare multiple formats (PDF, Markdown, JSON), parsing tools (MinerU, Fitz, PP-StructureV3), and pipelines under a base configuration—hybrid retrieval with BM25 0.3 + dense vectors 0.7, Qwen-3 tokenizer (256-token chunks), `bge-rerank-large` reranking, `o3-Mini` LLM and `doubao-embedding-large-text-250515` embeddings—to evaluate how parsing methods influence downstream retrieval precision and QA accuracy in academic question answering.

Table 2. Comparison of document parsing schemes and evaluation scores.

ID	Document format	Parsing method	Text processing strategy	Score
1	JSON	PP-StructureV3	Retain abstract, main body, figure captions, tables, and formulas	0.4978
2	PDF	Fitz	Sentence segmentation	0.4756
3	Markdown	MinerU	Sentence segmentation	0.4356

Experimental Results: As shown in Table 2, the structured JSON + PP-StructureV3 configuration achieves the best overall performance on this task, with a significant advantage in accuracy compared to other approaches.

Text Chunking Strategies. Under a fixed parsing setup—PP-StructureV3 applied to JSON inputs—and a standard retrieval configuration (BM25 0.3 + dense vectors 0.7, `o3-Mini` LLM, Qwen-3 tokenizer, and `bge-rerank-large` reranking), we assess how text preprocessing and chunking strategies affect performance. The experiments vary information retention scope (from abstracts only to full inclusion of text, figures, tables, and formulas), chunking method (fixed-length, semantic, and paragraph-level), and retrieval parameters (retrieved-candidate and post-reranking counts) to explore the balance between recall coverage and contextual precision.

Table 3. Comparison of text chunking strategies and evaluation scores.

ID	Text processing strategy	Chunk size	Retrieval/Rerank	Embedding model	Score
1	Preserve paragraph integrity; no segmentation; retain heading information before each paragraph	By paragraph	10/–	`bge-large-en-v1.5`	0.4889
2	Retain abstract, main body, figure captions, tables, and formulas	128	20/15	`doubao-embedding-large-text-250515`	0.4578
3	Retain abstract, main body, figure captions, tables, and formulas	256	20/15	`doubao-embedding-large-text-250515`	**0.4978**
4	Retain abstract, main body, figure captions, tables, and formulas	512	20/15	`doubao-embedding-large-text-250515`	0.4756
5	Retain abstract, main body, figure captions, tables, and formulas	Semantic split	20/15	`bge-large-en-v1.5`	0.4844

Experimental Results: As shown in Table 3, variations in chunking method, chunk size, and information retention scope have only limited impact on overall performance. A chunk size of 256 tokens yields the best results, while overly large (512) or small (128) sizes may reduce recall. Semantic and fixed-length chunking perform similarly, though preserving paragraph and heading structure improves semantic cohesion. In subsequent experiments, we combine semantic and fixed-length chunking in the multi-model fusion stage—using the former to maintain semantic unit integrity and the latter to enhance retrieval efficiency—to balance contextual coherence with retrieval accuracy.

Hybrid Retrieval Strategies. Under a fixed document parsing configuration applying PP-StructureV3 to JSON-formatted documents—and a comprehensive information retention scope (including abstracts, main body text, figure captions, tables, and formulas), HiParse-RAG is evaluated with a 256-token chunk size and the `bge-rerank-large` reranking model. Retrieval strategies are systematically compared within the hybrid framework by varying both the embedding model: `bge-m3`, `bge-large-en-v1.5`, `doubao-embedding-`

`large-text-250515`, `jina-embeddings-v3` and the retrieval method composition, including BM25 + dense vectors, sparse + dense vectors, and BM25 + sparse + dense vectors. This design enables a controlled assessment of how embedding representations and retrieval configurations influence retrieval quality and end-to-end QA performance.

Table 4. Comparison of retrieval and ranking strategies with evaluation scores.

ID	Retrieval/Rerank	Embedding model(s)	Retrieval method (hybrid weights)	Score
1	20/15	`doubao-embedding-large-text-250515`	bm25:0.3 + dense:0.7	0.4978
2	20/15	`doubao-embedding-large-text-250515`, `splade-v3`	sparse:0.3 + dense:0.7	0.4889
3	20/15	`bge-m3`	bm25:0.3 + dense:0.7	0.4889
4	20/15	`jina-embeddings-v3`	bm25:0.3 + dense:0.7	0.4933
5	20/15	`bge-large-en-v1.5`, `splade-v3`	bm25:0.2 + sparse:0.2 + dense:0.6	0.4889
6	20/5 (Before and after paragraphs)	`bge-large-en-v1.5`	bm25:0.3 + dense:0.7	**0.5067**

Experimental Results: As shown in Table 4, different configurations produce some score variation, though the overall performance range remains narrow. Retrieval weight allocation, embedding model choice, and reranking parameters each have a measurable impact. Recognizing that individual embedding models and retrieval strategies have applicability boundaries and performance limitations across question types, future work will integrate their complementary strengths within a differentiated multi-model fusion framework to enhance retrieval precision and robustness in complex settings.

Large Language Model Selection Strategies. Under a controlled experimental set-up—with fixed document format, parsing method, processing pipeline, retrieval size, tokenizer (Qwen-3), embedding model, reranking model, and retrieval configuration (BM25 weighted 0.3 combined with dense retrieval weighted 0.7)—we conduct a controlled-variable comparison of multiple LLMs, including `qwen-plus`, `o4-mini`, `o3-mini` and `doubao-1.5-pro-32k-250115`. The evaluation measures each model's retrieval-assisted QA performance under identical system conditions, enabling an isolated assessment of LLM choice without the confounding effects of changes in other components.

Table 5. Comparison of large language model (LLM) performance.

ID	Large language model	Score
1	`o4-mini`	0.4889
2	`o3-mini`	**0.4978**
3	`doubao-1.5-pro-32k-250115`	0.4000
4	`qwen-plus`	0.3600

Experimental Results: As shown in Table 5, when all other conditions remain constant, the choice of LLM has a pronounced impact on performance. The `o3-mini` model achieves the highest accuracy, followed by `o4-mini`, while `doubao-1.5-pro-32k-250115` and `qwen-plus` perform comparatively lower. This suggests that `o3-mini` has stronger reasoning adaptability in a retrieval-augmented setting, being more capable of efficiently leveraging contextual information to generate high-quality answers.

Post-processing Strategies. Under a fixed experimental configuration covering document format, parsing method, processing pipeline, retrieval size, tokenizer (Qwen-3), embedding model, reranking model, and retrieval approach (hybrid retrieval with BM25 weighted 0.3 and dense retrieval weighted 0.7)—we conduct a controlled comparison between applying and omitting a post-processing strategy. The post-processing procedure comprises two main steps: relevance optimization, which applies the reranking model to further refine the relevance of the initial retrieval results; and special-case handling, in which, for specific scenarios such as single-choice questions or no-answer cases, secondary retrieval is performed followed by rule-based matching according to a predefined mapping rule (`{'A': 'AC', 'B': 'BC', 'C': 'AC', 'D': 'CD'}`).

Table 6. Effect of post-processing strategies on performance.

ID	Post-processing applied	Score
1	no	0.4711
2	yes	**0.4978**

Experimental Results: As shown in Table 6, the "reranking first + hybrid retrieval" post-processing strategy adopted in the HiParse-RAG framework yields a notable performance improvement, achieving a +2.7% accuracy increase compared to the baseline configuration.

Multi-model Fusion Strategies. Under a standardized document parsing setup applying PP-StructureV3 to JSON-formatted inputs and using `bge-rerank-large` as the reranking model, a series of iterative evaluations were conducted to identify configurations that optimally balance accuracy and robustness. Through multiple rounds of comparative analysis, nine configurations exhibiting strong and consistent performance across diverse retrieval and reasoning tasks were selected as the foundation for subsequent multi-model fusion. This fusion aims to enhance overall system effectiveness in complex information retrieval and reasoning scenarios by leveraging the complementary strengths of individual models. Details of the selected base configurations are summarized in Table 7.

Table 7. Evaluation results of baseline configurations and fusion strategies.

ID	Text processing strategy	Chunk Size	Retrieval/Rerank	Embedding model(s)	Retrieval method (hybrid weights)	Score
1	Retain abstract, main body, and figure captions	256	10 / –	`bge-large-en-v1.5`	bm25=0.3, dense=0.7	0.4844
2	Preserve paragraph integrity; no segmentation; retain heading information before each paragraph	–	10 / –	`bge-large-en-v1.5`	bm25=0.3, dense=0.7	0.4889
3	Preserve paragraph integrity; no segmentation; retain heading information before each paragraph	–	20 / 15	`doubao-embedding-large-text-250515`	bm25=0.3, dense=0.7	0.5022
4	Retain abstract, main body, figure captions, tables, and formulas	256	20 / 15	`doubao-embedding-large-text-250515`	bm25=0.3, dense=0.7	0.4978
5	Retain abstract, main body, figure captions, tables, and formulas	256	20 / 15	`doubao-embedding-large-text-250515`	sparse=0.3, dense=0.7	0.4889
6	Retain abstract, main body, figure captions, tables, and formulas	256	20 / 15	`jina-embeddings-v3`	bm25=0.3, dense=0.7	0.4933
7	Retain abstract, main body, figure captions, tables, and formulas	Semantic split	10 / 7	`bge-large-en-v1.5`	bm25=0.3, dense=0.7	0.4844
8	Retain abstract, main body, figure captions, tables, and formulas	256	20 / 15	`bge-large-en-v1.5`, `splade-v3`	bm25:0.2, sparse:0.2, dense:0.6	0.4889
9	Retain abstract, main body, figure captions, tables, and formulas	256	20 / 5	`bge-large-en-v1.5`	bm25=0.3, dense=0.7	**0.5067**
10–16	Multi-model fusion					0.5333
						0.5244
						0.5422
						0.5467
						0.5467
						N/A
						0.5333
17–18	Cross-validation + high-confidence error correction					0.5600
						0.5644

To exploit the complementary strengths of different retrieval and processing configurations, we designed seven fusion schemes based on nine selected baseline configurations, while keeping the core pipeline consistent. These fusion schemes combine and weight variations in information retention, chunking strategy, retrieval method, embedding model, and threshold setting. The aim is to improve accuracy and robustness via voting- or score-weighting mechanisms, and to assess the synergistic effects of strategies such as dynamic thresholding, sparse retrieval, and semantic chunking. Details of the multi-model fusion schemes are summarized in Table 8.

Table 8. Comparison of multi-model fusion strategies and evaluation scores.

ID	Fusion schemes (from Table 7)	Weights	Threshold	Score	Fusion rationale
1	4,3,2	0.4/0.3/0.3	0.5	0.5333	Combines the strengths of information retention, chunking strategy, and retrieval method, forming a highly complementary baseline ensemble
2	5,3,2	0.4/0.3/0.3	0.5	0.5244	Introduces sparse-vector retrieval to replace BM25, complementing the paragraph-heading preservation strategy for improved synergy
3	10,11,3	0.4/0.3/0.3	0.5	0.5422	Integrates the advantages of multi-information retention, sparse vector, and paragraph-heading preservation strategies
4	12,3,1,9,11	Score-weighted fusion	0.6	0.5467	Combines strengths in information retention, retrieval order, and recall strategy, balancing coverage and accuracy
5	12,3,1,9,11	Score-weighted fusion	Dynamic 0.6–0.75	0.5467	Introduces a dynamic threshold that adapts the fusion strategy per query to handle diverse and difficult question scenarios
6	12,6,7,9,8	Score-weighted fusion	Dynamic 0.6–0.75	N/A	Explores complementary potentials of different embedding models and chunking strategies
7	15,14,13	0.4/0.3/0.3	0.5	0.5333	Based on analysis of divergent failure cases and consistent performance to assess reliability on specific question types

Although the multi-model fusion schemes still exhibit a small number of errors, the distribution of correct and incorrect predictions across different fusion schemes shows a complementary pattern. By comparing the results of different fusion schemes, it is possible to identify cases where one scheme's prediction is incorrect while anothern's is correct; replacing the incorrect answer with the correct one can further improve the overall accuracy. The primary objective of cross-validation in this context is to exploit such complementarities to rectify high-confidence errors, thereby maximizing the final score. Details of the cross-validation schemes are presented in Table 9.

Table 9. Comparison of cross-validation strategies and evaluation scores.

ID	Validation rule	Score
1	By examining the results of Scheme 16 and Scheme 14 in Table 7, three questions with differing answers were identified. Scheme 14 answered all correctly, while Scheme 16 answered all incorrectly. The corresponding answers in Scheme 13 were replaced with those from Scheme 14	0.5600
2	By examining the results of Scheme 13 and Scheme 12 in Table 7, three questions with differing answers were found: two were correct under Scheme 13 but incorrect under Scheme 12, and one was correct under Scheme 12 but incorrect under Scheme 13. The correct answers from Scheme 12 replaced the incorrect answers in Scheme 13	**0.5644**

Experimental Results: Based on nine high-performing baseline configurations, the application of seven multi-model fusion strategies led to improvements in both overall accuracy and robustness. The results reveal a clear complementary pattern in the distribution of correct and incorrect predictions across different fusion schemes. By incorporating cross-validation to correct high-confidence errors, the highest accuracy was improved from 0.5067 to 0.5644, thereby demonstrating the effectiveness of the HiParse-RAG framework in complex retrieval and reasoning tasks.

5 Conclusion and Future Work

We propose the HiParse-RAG framework, integrating structured document parsing, hybrid retrieval, result reranking, and multi-model fusion to enhance accuracy and robustness in complex academic QA. In the CCKS 2025 Complex Question Answering on Academic Papers evaluation, it achieved the top overall score, confirming its effectiveness and practicality. Future work will focus on advancing cross-document and multi-source knowledge integration, incorporating domain-specific knowledge bases and authoritative external resources, and developing more efficient, controllable LLM collaboration mechanisms to improve scalability, explainability, and reliability.

References

1. Bledsoe, W.W., Boyer, R.S.: Automated Reasoning: Essays in Honor of Woody Bledsoe. Kluwer Academic Publishers, Boston (1991)
2. Brown, T.B., et al.: Language models are few-shot learners (2020). https://arxiv.org/abs/2005.14165
3. Cui, C., et al.: Paddleocr 3.0 technical report (2025). https://arxiv.org/abs/2507.05595

4. Dai, X., et al.: Complex question answering evaluation for AI research papers. In: Proceedings of the CCKS 2025 Conference Competition Task Description, Southeast University and Huawei Noah's Ark Lab Conference Competition Task Description (2025)
5. Douze, M., et al.: The FAISS library (2025). https://arxiv.org/abs/2401.08281
6. Eibich, M., Nagpal, S., Fred-Ojala, A.: Aragog: advanced rag output grading (2024). https://arxiv.org/abs/2404.01037
7. Gao, L., Ma, X., Lin, J., Callan, J.: Precise zero-shot dense retrieval without relevance labels (2022). https://arxiv.org/abs/2212.10496
8. Gao, Y., Xiong, Y., Wang, M., Wang, H.: Modular rag: transforming rag systems into lego-like reconfigurable frameworks (2024). https://arxiv.org/abs/2407.21059
9. Hu, J., et al.: Dynamic ensemble reasoning for LLM experts (2024). https://arxiv.org/abs/2412.07448
10. Karpukhin, V., et al.: Dense passage retrieval for open-domain question answering. In: Webber, B., Cohn, T., He, Y., Liu, Y. (eds.) Proceedings of the 2020 Conference on Empirical Methods in Natural Language Processing (EMNLP), pp. 6769–6781. Association for Computational Linguistics, Online (2020). https://doi.org/10.18653/v1/2020.emnlp-main.550. https://aclanthology.org/2020.emnlp-main.550/
11. Lassance, C., Déjean, H., Formal, T., Clinchant, S.: Splade-v3: new baselines for splade (2024). https://arxiv.org/abs/2403.06789
12. Lewis, P., et al.: Retrieval-augmented generation for knowledge-intensive NLP tasks. In: Proceedings of the 34th International Conference on Neural Information Processing Systems, NIPS '20. Curran Associates Inc., Red Hook (2020)
13. Li, X., Shakir, A., Huang, R., Lipp, J., Li, J.: Prorank: prompt warmup via reinforcement learning for small language models reranking (2025). https://arxiv.org/abs/2506.03487
14. Mao, Y., Qu, Y., Xie, Y., Ren, X., Han, J.: Multi-document summarization with maximal marginal relevance-guided reinforcement learning (2020). https://arxiv.org/abs/2010.00117
15. Merola, C., Singh, J.: Reconstructing context: evaluating advanced chunking strategies for retrieval-augmented generation (2025). https://arxiv.org/abs/2504.19754
16. Poliakov, M., Shvai, N.: Multi-meta-rag: improving rag for multi-hop queries using database filtering with LLM-extracted metadata. In: Ermolayev, V., et al. (eds.) Information and Communication Technologies in Education, Research, and Industrial Applications, pp. 334–342. Springer, Cham (2025). https://doi.org/10.1007/978-3-031-81372-6_25
17. Refaeilzadeh, P., Tang, L., Liu, H.: Cross-validation. Encycl. Database Syst. **532–538**, 532–538 (2009). https://doi.org/10.1007/978-0-387-39940-9_565
18. Robertson, S., Zaragoza, H.: The probabilistic relevance framework: Bm25 and beyond. Found. Trends Inf. Retr. **3**(4), 333–389 (2009). https://doi.org/10.1561/1500000019
19. Sawarkar, K., Mangal, A., Solanki, S.R.: Blended rag: improving rag (retriever-augmented generation) accuracy with semantic search and hybrid query-based retrievers. CoRR arxiv:2404.07220 (2024)
20. Shi, B., Bai, X., Yao, C.: An end-to-end trainable neural network for image-based sequence recognition and its application to scene text recognition. IEEE Trans. Pattern Anal. Mach. Intell. **39**(11), 2298–2304 (2017). https://doi.org/10.1109/TPAMI.2016.2646371
21. Sturua, S., et al.: jina-embeddings-v3: multilingual embeddings with task lora (2024). https://arxiv.org/abs/2409.10173

22. Sutskever, I., Vinyals, O., Le, Q.V.: Sequence to sequence learning with neural networks (2014). https://arxiv.org/abs/1409.3215
23. Wei, J., et al.: Chain-of-thought prompting elicits reasoning in large language models (2023). https://arxiv.org/abs/2201.11903
24. Xiao, S., Liu, Z., Zhang, P., Muennighoff, N., Lian, D., Nie, J.Y.: C-pack: packed resources for general Chinese embeddings (2024). https://arxiv.org/abs/2309.07597

HybriDoc: An Adaptive Multi-path Framework for End-to-End Document Structure Extraction

Yiwei Zhang[1(✉)], Chengke Wu[2], and Li Wang[1]

[1] Shenzhen University, Shenzhen, China
2400671022@mails.szu.edu.cn, wangli100@szu.edu.cn
[2] Shenzhen Institute of Advanced Technology, Shenzhen, China
wuk@sustech.edu.cn

Abstract. End-to-end Document Structure Extraction (DSE) from visually rich, unstructured documents such as PDFs is a foundational challenge in unlocking vast knowledge for downstream applications like Retrieval-Augmented Generation (RAG). However, prevailing monolithic parsing paradigms, constrained by a fixed inductive bias, often exhibit a lack of generalization when confronted with the high heterogeneity of document types. To address this, we move beyond a one-size-fits-all approach and propose HybriDoc, an adaptive, multi-path parsing framework. At the core of HybriDoc is a hierarchical decision engine that rapidly diagnoses a document's archetype and dynamically dispatches it to an optimal expert parser. Furthermore, we introduce a cross-model fusion mechanism to leverage the complementary strengths of different parsers and a terminal LLM-based calibration module to ensure global semantic coherence. On the rigorous and comprehensive CCKS2025 End-to-End Document Structuring Challenge benchmark, HybriDoc establishes new state-of-the-art performance, achieving a final score of 83.10 and securing first place. Our framework demonstrates exceptional robustness and adaptability, particularly in the development (83.98) and general (87.71) document sub-categories. This work empirically validates that an adaptive, "divide-and-conquer" parsing strategy is a highly effective pathway for solving real-world document structuring problems.

Keywords: Document Structure Extraction · Adaptive Systems · Multi-Modal Models · Document AI

1 Introduction

Document Structure Extraction (DSE) is a foundational technology for converting visually-oriented documents, such as PDFs, into structured, machine-readable formats [7,13], thereby providing a critical underpinning for advanced AI applications like Retrieval-Augmented Generation (RAG) [5,9]. The efficacy of current DSE methodologies, however, is constrained by two systemic limitations: first, *task fragmentation*, a paradigm that degrades the end-to-end parsing

J. Liang et al. (Eds.): CCKS 2025, CCIS 2698, pp. 209–219, 2026.
https://doi.org/10.1007/978-981-95-8525-0_16

process into a series of isolated sub-tasks, thus compromising global semantic coherence; and second, *scenic evaluation*, which relies on simplified benchmarks that fail to reflect the combinatorial complexities of real-world documents, such as long-range dependencies and layout heterogeneity [10,12,21]. These constraints collectively constitute a critical bottleneck, impeding the effective transfer of DSE technologies to diverse, open-world scenarios.

The core thesis of this paper is that any monolithic model with a fixed inductive bias cannot effectively generalize to all document archetypes. Based on this, we propose **HybriDoc**, an adaptive, multi-path parsing framework designed to counter document heterogeneity with dynamic strategies. The core of this framework is a hybrid-feature classification engine that performs a rapid diagnosis of the document type and dispatches it to an optimal expert parser—namely, `MinerU`[1] for academic literature and `MonkeyOCR` [11] for technical manuals. The framework's performance is further enhanced by a novel cross-model fusion mechanism, which integrates the superior table parsing results from `dots.ocr` [15], and a terminal LLM calibration module aimed at ensuring global structural and semantic consistency.

We validated our methodology on the rigorous CCKS2025 benchmark, where HybriDoc established a new state-of-the-art performance and achieved first place. The contributions of this paper are: (1) the proposal of a novel adaptive parsing framework that effectively addresses document heterogeneity; (2) the design of a cross-model fusion strategy for building more robust composite systems from existing expert models; and (3) the establishment of a new SOTA record on a challenging public benchmark, providing a powerful and reproducible baseline for future research.

2 Related Work

The field of Document Structure Extraction (DSE) aims to convert the rich information embedded in unstructured visual documents into machine-readable structured data. In recent years, with the advancement of deep learning, the research paradigms in this area have primarily evolved along two distinct technical routes: pipeline-based modular approaches and end-to-end unified model approaches [2].

2.1 Pipeline-Based Approaches

Pipeline-based methods adhere to a "divide and conquer" strategy, breaking down the complex DSE task into a sequence of well-defined, independently optimizable sub-tasks. A typical pipeline often includes document preprocessing, layout analysis, specific element recognition (e.g., tables, formulas, OCR for text), and final reordering and format conversion.

An outstanding representative of this paradigm is MinerU. As an open-source solution, MinerU integrates a suite of high-quality models (e.g., PDF-Extract-Kit) to perform precise extraction from diverse documents through four

[1] https://github.com/opendatalab/MinerU.

stages: preprocessing, content parsing, post-processing, and format conversion. It invokes specialized recognizers for different regions and employs fine-grained post-processing rules to ensure accuracy. Another prominent tool, Marker [14], adopts a similar multi-module design, supporting various document formats and enhancing specific tasks like cross-page table merging by integrating LLM components.

The advantage of these methods lies in their modularity and flexibility. Researchers can insert state-of-the-art (SOTA) models for each sub-task to achieve local optima. However, their fundamental weakness is error propagation. Minor errors in early stages, such as layout analysis, are passed on and amplified in subsequent stages, potentially devastating the final output quality. Furthermore, many existing toolchains are often overfitted to specific document types (e.g., academic papers) and exhibit sharp performance degradation on documents with more varied layouts, such as textbooks or financial reports.

2.2 End-To-End Approaches

To overcome the error propagation problem of pipeline methods, the research community has begun to explore end-to-end solutions. These methods typically utilize a unified, powerful neural network, particularly Large Multimodal Models (LMMs), to directly map raw document images to the final structured output (e.g., Markdown or HTML), bypassing multiple intermediate modules.

Early representative works include Donut, which introduced an OCR-free Transformer framework for unified document understanding [8], and Nougat, which focuses on converting academic document images into formatted markup text [4]. Foundational models like LayoutLM and its successors combined text and layout information to great effect [6,18,19], while other unified architectures also pushed the state-of-the-art [1,16]. With the rise of LMMs, more powerful models have emerged in this direction, such as mPLUG-DocOwl2, which introduced cross-page modeling capabilities [20], and Qwen-VL, which proposed a fine-grained parsing format to support the accurate reconstruction of diverse documents [3].

Although end-to-end methods avoid error accumulation through joint optimization, they face significant computational and efficiency challenges. Real-world documents are often high-resolution and information-dense, leading to extremely long input and output sequences for the model. The quadratic complexity of the attention mechanism in Transformer architectures makes the inference cost for long documents prohibitive [17], severely limiting their application in large-scale production environments. For instance, the inference speed of Qwen-VL-7B is considerably lower than that of pipeline tools like MinerU.

2.3 Our Positioning: Bridging the Divide

Existing work presents a clear trade-off: pipeline methods gain specialization and flexibility through modularity at the cost of robustness, while end-to-end methods achieve holistic understanding through unified modeling at the expense of efficiency and scalability.

Our work, HybriDoc, is designed to bridge this divide. We argue that neither a fixed pipeline nor a monolithic model is the optimal solution. The HybriDoc framework borrows the modular idea from pipeline methods but overcomes their poor handling of document heterogeneity by introducing an adaptive classification engine. Simultaneously, by incorporating cross-model feature fusion and terminal LLM calibration, we integrate the global optimization philosophy of end-to-end models while maintaining high efficiency, effectively suppressing error propagation. Therefore, our work does not simply replicate either paradigm but proposes a pragmatic and efficient third way that combines the advantages of both.

3 Methodology

The central challenge in Document Structure Extraction (DSE) is accommodating the vast heterogeneity of document layouts. We contend that monolithic paradigms are fundamentally ill-suited for this task and instead propose **HybriDoc**, a framework predicated on the principle of adaptive, expert-based parsing. We abstract the entire framework as a function $H(D) = S$, where the input D is a PDF document and the output S is its high-fidelity structured representation (in Markdown format). HybriDoc operationalizes its core principle through a synergistic workflow integrating *rapid pre-parsing*, *hybrid-feature routing*, *specialized deep-parsing*, and *LLM-based calibration*.

3.1 Overall Architecture and Pre-parsing

HybriDoc instantiates a computationally efficient, cascaded architecture (Fig. 1) designed to decouple high-level structural diagnosis from deep, semantic parsing. A preliminary parsing stage employs the `Marker` toolchain to efficiently generate a coarse structural representation, $S_{pre} = \texttt{Marker}(D)$. This representation, while not exhaustive in its detail, serves as a feature-rich scaffold for the subsequent routing mechanism, encapsulating the document's macroscopic layout (e.g., headings, paragraphs).

3.2 Hybrid-Feature Adaptive Classification and Routing

At the heart of HybriDoc is a hybrid-feature decision engine that performs modality-aware archetype classification for dynamic parser routing. This routing logic, formalized in Algorithm 1, leverages both textual and visual signals to achieve robust dispatching. The engine operates via two concurrent streams:

1. **Textual-Feature Stream:** This stream analyzes the pre-parsed text S_{pre} to extract a textual feature vector f_{text}, defined as:

$$f_{text} = (c_{kw}, c_{math}, c_{code}) \tag{1}$$

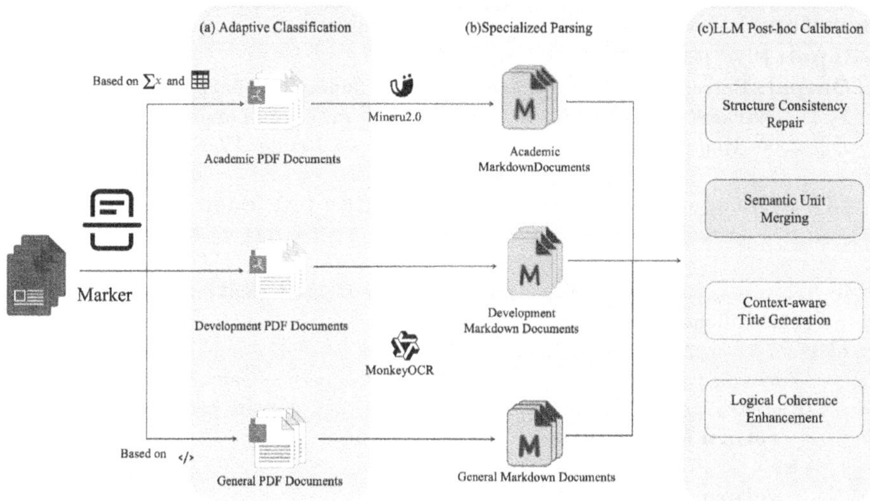

Fig. 1. Flowchart of the adaptive, multi-path parsing process in HybriDoc. (a) After initial processing by Marker, a classification engine routes documents to different paths. (b) Academic and Development/General documents are fed into expert parsers—MinerU and MonkeyOCR, respectively—for deep parsing. (c) The final LLM calibration module unifies and refines the outputs, performing tasks such as structure repair, semantic merging, title generation, and logical enhancement.

where c_{kw} is a weighted count of academic keywords (e.g.,"abstract," "references"), c_{math} is the occurrence frequency of mathematical features like LaTeX syntax, and c_{code} is a statistic for code block elements. These features collectively profile the document's macroscopic semantics.

2. **Visual-Feature Stream:** To mitigate biases from potential errors in S_{pre}, this stream operates directly on the rendered PDF image, D_{image}. A lightweight visual recognition model performs high-speed detection of unambiguous structural cues to produce a visual feature vector, f_{visual}. This vector primarily contains confidence scores for key elements, such as the visual texture confidence of a code block, p_{code}.

The final routing decision is governed by a principled fusion mechanism that prioritizes high-confidence visual cues. As detailed in Algorithm 1, unambiguous visual evidence, such as the distinct texture of a code block, preempts the text-based classification. In its absence, the decision defaults to a score derived from the latent textual features, ensuring both robustness and accuracy.

3.3 Specialized Parsing and Fusion

Upon classification, the document D is dispatched to one of two specialized pathways, each tailored for a distinct document class.

Algorithm 1. HybriDoc Adaptive Routing Algorithm

Input: PDF Document D
Output: Parser Path $Path \in \{\texttt{AcademicPath}, \texttt{GeneralDevPath}\}$
$S_{pre} \leftarrow \texttt{Marker}(D)$ ▷ Execute rapid pre-parsing for text features
$D_{image} \leftarrow \text{RenderPDF}(D)$ ▷ Render PDF for visual features

$f_{text} \leftarrow \text{AnalyzeTextFeatures}(S_{pre})$ ▷ Extract text feature vector per Eq. (1)
$f_{visual} \leftarrow \text{DetectVisualCues}(D_{image})$ ▷ Extract visual vector, get p_{code}

if $f_{visual}.p_{code} > \tau_{visual}$ **then** ▷ Visual cue has high priority
    return `GeneralDevPath`
else
    $Score_{academic} \leftarrow w_1 \cdot f_{text}.c_{kw} + w_2 \cdot f_{text}.c_{math}$ ▷ Calculate academic score
    if $Score_{academic} > \tau_{text}$ **then** ▷ τ are predefined thresholds
        return `AcademicPath`
    else
        return `GeneralDevPath`
    end if
end if

Academic Document Pathway (`AcademicPath`): Documents routed to this pathway are subjected to `MinerU`, leveraging its proficiency in parsing complex scientific layouts and mathematical notations [22]. To address the specific challenge of table recognition, we introduce a **cross-model table fusion module** that operates in parallel with `dots.ocr`. Let $T_M = \{t_{m_1}, t_{m_2}, \dots\}$ and $T_D = \{t_{d_1}, t_{d_2}, \dots\}$ be the sets of tables detected by `MinerU` and `dots.ocr`, respectively. The fusion is operationalized by aligning tables based on the Intersection over Union (IoU) of their bounding boxes. For each table $t_{m_i} \in T_M$, if a matching table $t_{d_j} \in T_D$ exists such that $IoU(t_{m_i}, t_{d_j}) > \tau_{IoU}$, where τ_{IoU} is a preset threshold, the structured content of t_{m_i} in the final output is replaced by that of t_{d_j}. This directed correction, based on complementary strengths, significantly improves table structure fidelity.

Development and General Document Pathway (`GeneralDevPath`): For these documents, we employ `MonkeyOCR` [11]. It is built on an innovative "Structure-Recognition-Relation" (SRR) paradigm, providing enhanced robustness and accuracy for documents with embedded code, complex nested headings, and unconventional layouts.

3.4 LLM Post-hoc Calibration

While the specialized parsers yield high-precision preliminary outputs, the resulting text, denoted as S_{prelim}, may still contain subtle structural artifacts that violate global document coherence. To address this, we introduce a final calibration stage that leverages an LLM as a **holistic document structuring expert**. This phase is designed to elevate the machine-parsed output to a level that is logically consistent and semantically sound.

We formalize this calibration process as a function $\mathcal{L}$, such that the final, optimized output is $S_{final} = \mathcal{L}(S_{prelim})$. The core of this function is a principled guidance methodology that constrains the LLM's reasoning via a meticulously structured meta-prompt, $\mathcal{P}$. As detailed in Algorithm 2, the process begins by partitioning the long document S_{prelim} into a set of semantically coherent chunks, $C = \{c_1, c_2, \ldots, c_n\}$, typically delineated by major section headings. Each chunk c_i is then calibrated independently.

Algorithm 2. LLM Post-hoc Calibration Algorithm

Input: Preliminary parsed document S_{prelim}
Output: Final calibrated document S_{final}
$C \leftarrow \text{Segment}(S_{prelim})$ ▷ Partition document into semantic chunks
$\mathcal{P} \leftarrow \text{ConstructMetaPrompt}(\mathcal{P}_{\text{persona}}, \mathcal{P}_{\text{instr}}, \mathcal{P}_{\text{ex}})$ ▷ Construct the meta-prompt
$C_{\text{calibrated}} \leftarrow \emptyset$ ▷ Initialize set of calibrated chunks
for each chunk c_i in C **do**
  $c'_i \leftarrow \text{LLM}(c_i, \mathcal{P})$ ▷ Guide LLM to process each chunk with the meta-prompt
  $C_{\text{calibrated}} \leftarrow C_{\text{calibrated}} \cup \{c'_i\}$
end for
$S_{final} \leftarrow \text{Reconstruct}(C_{\text{calibrated}})$ ▷ Reassemble document from calibrated chunks
return S_{final}

The meta-prompt $\mathcal{P}$ is composed of three key components: (1) **Persona Definition** ($\mathcal{P}_{\text{persona}}$), which assigns the LLM the role of a document processing expert tasked with ensuring absolute content fidelity; (2) **Instruction Set** ($\mathcal{P}_{\text{instr}}$), providing a series of explicit, non-negotiable tasks such as enforcing a logical heading hierarchy, restoring semantic cohesion of text across page breaks, and intelligently distinguishing true tables from code blocks erroneously rendered as tables; and (3) **Few-Shot Exemplars** ($\mathcal{P}_{\text{ex}}$), which provide concrete input-output examples for complex transformations (e.g., table-to-code conversion) to anchor the model's output format.

This structured guidance methodology transforms the inherently probabilistic LLM into a quasi-deterministic post-processing tool tailored for high-fidelity document structuring. It efficiently corrects nuanced, context-dependent errors that are intractable for rule-based systems, ensuring the final output is not only structurally valid but also aligns with the logical standards of a human expert.

4 Experiments

To comprehensively evaluate the efficacy of our proposed HybriDoc framework, we conducted extensive experiments on a public and rigorous benchmark: the CCKS2025 End-to-End Document Structuring Challenge. This section details the dataset, evaluation metrics, our implementation specifics, and provides an in-depth analysis of the experimental results.

4.1 Experimental Setup

Benchmark and Dataset. All our experiments were conducted on the official dataset of the CCKS2025 Challenge, which is designed to simulate complex real-world scenarios and includes two test sets (Set A and Set B) with no training data provided. All documents are in PDF format, covering three core domains: (1) **Academic Documents**, featuring complex mathematical formulas, diverse tables, and mixed layouts; (2) **Development Documents**, challenged by deep and unpredictable logical structures; and (3) **General Documents**, testing open-domain generalization. The dataset's emphasis on long-range dependencies and heterogeneity provides an ideal testbed for our adaptive framework.

Evaluation Metrics. The challenge utilizes a comprehensive evaluation system with 10 fine-grained metrics across 5 dimensions: **Text Extraction** (EDS, F1), **Heading Detection** (EDS, TEDS), **Formula Conversion** (EDS), **Table Recognition** (EDS, TEDS), and **Reading Order Detection** (KTDS). The final score is the arithmetic mean of all 10 metrics.

Implementation Details. Our HybriDoc framework integrates several SOTA models, including `Marker` for pre-parsing, `MinerU` (v0.8.1) with `dots.ocr` for table fusion on the academic path, and `MonkeyOCR` [11] (using the `OlmOCR-7B` backend) on the development/general path. A terminal LLM is used for calibration. All experiments were performed on a server equipped with four NVIDIA A100 (80GB) GPUs.

4.2 Results and Analysis

Main Results. On the final leaderboard of the CCKS2025 Challenge (Test Set B), our HybriDoc framework achieved a final score of **83.10**, securing first place. Table 1 provides a detailed comparison with other top-performing teams.

Table 1. Detailed score comparison of the top three teams on the final leaderboard.

Rank	Team	Academic	Development	General	Overall Score
1	**HybriDoc (Ours)**	77.60	83.98	**87.71**	**83.10**
2	Team A	**84.56**	80.88	83.37	82.94
3	Team B	75.53	**86.83**	85.01	82.46

Performance Analysis. The results in Table 1 validate our framework's design. Our victory stems not from a single dominant category score but from highly robust and competitive performance across all three heterogeneous document types. While our score on Academic Documents (77.60) was not the highest, our excellent performance on Development (83.98) and General (87.71) documents elevated our total score above all competitors. This demonstrates that an adaptive framework with specialized pathways exhibits superior comprehensive performance and robustness compared to any monolithic approach, directly reflecting the success of our core design philosophy: adaptivity, specialization, and complementary strengths.

4.3 Ablation Study

To quantitatively validate the necessity of each core component in HybriDoc, we conducted a series of ablation studies.

Effectiveness of the Adaptive Classification Engine. We compared our full framework against two monolithic baselines: (1) **w/o Classifier (MinerU only)**; and (2) **w/o Classifier (MonkeyOCR only)**. As shown in Table 2, our full framework significantly outperforms both.

Table 2. Ablation study of the adaptive classification engine.

Method	Academic	Develop.	General	Overall	Δ
HybriDoc (Ours)	**77.60**	83.98	**87.71**	**83.10**	–
w/o Classifier (MinerU)	76.08	80.68	86.26	81.01	−2.09
w/o Classifier (MonkeyOCR)	75.72	83.07	87.92	82.24	−0.86

The results show that no single expert model can achieve optimal performance across all document types. HybriDoc's precise routing mechanism boosts the overall score by at least **0.86** and up to **2.09** points, proving that adaptive classification is key to achieving high performance and robustness.

Effectiveness of Cross-Model Table Fusion. To validate the introduction of `dots.ocr` for table fusion, we compared against a baseline without this module (**w/o Table Fusion**). As shown in Table 3, the fusion module yielded significant gains, with table structure fidelity (Table TEDS) surging by **6.57** points. This directly contributed to a **1.52**-point increase in the total score for academic documents, clearly demonstrating the success of our targeted enhancement strategy.

Table 3. Ablation study of the cross-model table fusion module (on academic documents only).

Method	Table EDS	Table TEDS	Academic Score
Academic Path w/ Fusion (Ours)	**70.98**	**79.92**	**77.60**
Academic Path w/o Fusion (MinerU)	66.95	73.35	76.08
Improvement	**+4.03**	**+6.57**	**+1.52**

Contribution of LLM Post-hoc Calibration. To isolate the impact of the final LLM calibration step, we compared the full HybriDoc framework with a version where this module was removed (*w/o LLM Calibration*). As detailed in Table 4, the results show that the LLM calibration provides a substantial performance uplift across all document categories, increasing the final overall score by a significant 6.62 points. The most dramatic improvement is observed in the General Documents category, with a score increase of 20.75 points. This highlights the LLM's critical role in correcting subtle errors and enforcing global semantic and structural consistency, which is particularly vital for the highly varied and unpredictable layouts found in general-domain documents. The performance gains in Academic (+0.05) and Development (−0.96) documents are more modest, suggesting that the expert parsers for these categories already produce highly structured outputs, but the LLM still acts as an indispensable "last-mile" quality check that elevates the overall system's robustness.

Table 4. Ablation study of the LLM Post-hoc Calibration module.

Method	Academic	Develop.	General	Overall	Δ
HybriDoc (Ours)	**77.60**	**83.98**	**87.71**	**83.10**	–
w/o LLM Calibration	77.55	84.94	66.96	76.48	−6.62

5 Conclusion

To address the challenge of document heterogeneity in DSE, we introduced **HybriDoc**, an adaptive framework that replaces monolithic paradigms with a dynamic "divide-and-conquer" strategy. By employing a hybrid classification engine to route documents to specialized expert parsers, enhanced by cross-model fusion and LLM calibration, HybriDoc achieved state-of-the-art performance, securing first place in the rigorous CCKS2025 challenge. This work empirically demonstrates that intelligently orchestrating existing expert models provides a powerful and generalizable paradigm for solving complex, real-world document structuring problems.

HybriDoc establishes a robust baseline for future document intelligence research. Future work could explore more fine-grained classification for dynamic routing, or investigate knowledge distillation to consolidate the framework's composite strengths into a single, more powerful end-to-end model.

References

1. Appalaraju, S., Jasani, B., Kota, B.U., Xie, Y., Manmatha, R.: Docformer: end-to-end transformer for document understanding. In: Proceedings of the IEEE/CVF International Conference on Computer Vision, pp. 993–1003 (2021)
2. Awais, M., et al.: Foundation models defining a new era in vision: a survey and outlook. IEEE Trans. Patt. Anal. Mach. Intell. (2024)

3. Bai, J., et al.: Qwen-VL: a versatile vision-language model for understanding, localization, text reading, and beyond. arXiv preprint arXiv:2308.12966 (2023)
4. Blecher, L., Cucurull, G., Scialom, T., Stojnic, R.: Nougat: neural optical understanding for academic documents. arXiv preprint arXiv:2308.13418 (2023)
5. Brown, A., Roman, M., Devereux, B.: A systematic literature review of retrieval-augmented generation: techniques, metrics, and challenges. arXiv preprint arXiv:2508.06401 (2025)
6. Huang, Y., Lv, T., Cui, L., Lu, Y., Wei, F.: LayoutLMv3: pre-training for document AI with unified text and image masking. In: Proceedings of the 30th ACM International Conference on Multimedia, pp. 4083–4091 (2022)
7. Kasem, M., et al.: Deep learning for table detection and structure recognition: a survey. arXiv preprint arXiv:2211.08469 (2022)
8. Kim, G., et al.: OCR-free document understanding transformer. In: European Conference on Computer Vision, pp. 498–517. Springer (2022)
9. Lewis, P., et al.: Retrieval-augmented generation for knowledge-intensive NLP tasks. In: Advances in Neural Information Processing Systems. vol. 33, pp. 9459–9474 (2020)
10. Li, M., et al.: DocBank: a benchmark dataset for document layout analysis. arXiv preprint arXiv:2006.01038 (2020)
11. Li, Z., et al.: MonkeyOCR: document parsing with a structure-recognition-relation triplet paradigm. arXiv preprint arXiv:2506.05218 (2025)
12. Li, Z., et al.: ReaDoc: a unified benchmark for realistic document structured extraction. arXiv preprint arXiv:2409.05137 (2024)
13. Lombardi, F., Marinai, S.: Deep learning for historical document analysis and recognition–a survey. J. Imaging **6**(10), 110 (2020)
14. Paruchuri, V.: Marker. https://github.com/VikParuchuri/marker (2024)
15. Rednote Hi-Lab: dots.ocr: a robust document parsing system. https://github.com/rednote-hilab/dots.ocr (2023)
16. Tang, Z., et al.: Unifying vision, text, and layout for universal document processing. In: Proceedings of the IEEE/CVF Conference on Computer Vision and Pattern Recognition, pp. 19254–19264 (2023)
17. Vaswani, A., et al.: Attention is all you need. In: Advances in neural information processing systems, pp. 5998–6008 (2017)
18. Xu, Y., et al.: LayoutLMv2: multi-modal pre-training for visually-rich document understanding. arXiv preprint arXiv:2012.14740 (2020)
19. Xu, Y., Li, M., Cui, L., Huang, S., Wei, F., Zhou, M.: LayoutLM: pre-training of text and layout for document image understanding. In: Proceedings of the 26th ACM SIGKDD International Conference on Knowledge Discovery & Data Mining, pp. 1192–1200 (2020)
20. Ye, J., et al.: mPLUG-DocOwl: modularized multimodal large language model for document understanding. arXiv preprint arXiv:2307.02499 (2023)
21. Zhong, X., Tang, J., Yepes, A.J.: PubLayNet: largest dataset ever for document layout analysis. In: 2019 International Conference on Document Analysis and Recognition (ICDAR), pp. 1015–1022. IEEE (2019)
22. Zhou, M., Cai, M., Li, G., Li, M.: An end-to-end formula recognition method integrated attention mechanism. Mathematics **11**(1), 177 (2022)

Pre-training for Document Structure Extraction with Lightweight Model Architecture

Lei Zhu[1(✉)] and Jie Wu[1,2]

[1] CETC Cyberspace Security Technology CO. LTD., Chengdu 610000, Sichuan, China
{zhu.lei,jie.wu}@cetccst.com.cn

[2] Ambient Intelligence and Trusted Services Key Laboratory of Sichuan Province, Chengdu 610000, Sichuan, China

Abstract. Document Structured Extraction (DSE) aims at converting raw documents into machine-readable structured text, which is a key technology for knowledge base construction and retrieval-augmented generation. However, existing multimodal large language models (MLLMs) generally lack high-quality training data and customized pre-training tasks, resulting in sub-optimal performance when parsing documents with diverse layout formats. To address this challenge, we design six novel pre-training tasks, including Optical Character Recognition (OCR), layout analysis, text2box, box2text, image caption, and figure/table caption, which boost the document understanding by guiding the model to focus attention on the document-level region. In addition, we adopt a shape adaptive cropping method that supports processing images with arbitrary resolutions, thereby avoiding deformation and blurring issues caused by image compression. Furthermore, a cross-attention based visual token compression method is proposed, which compresses the number of visual tokens to 384 per image, thus effectively improving the inference efficiency of the model without compromising performance. By leveraging novel data construction strategy, tens of millions of training samples have been generated, laying a foundation for effective model training. Compared with the current state-of-the-art algorithm, the trained multimodal large language model achieves an approximately 7% performance improvement in the F1 score. The experimental results verify the superiority of our method.

Keywords: Visual Token Compression · Multi-task Pre-training · Data Construction · Shape Adaptive Cropping

1 Introduction

Document Structured Extraction (DSE) [1] aims to convert raw documents (e.g., PDFs) into machine readable structured text format (e.g., Markdown). It plays a pivotal role in knowledge base construction and retrieval-augmented generation. PDFs often have rich text information and layout structure, including elements such as text, figures, tables, formulas, headers and footers. Due to the intricacies of textual, graphical, and layout information within documents, DSE has grown increasingly challenging.

J. Liang et al. (Eds.): CCKS 2025, CCIS 2698, pp. 220–231, 2026.
https://doi.org/10.1007/978-981-95-8525-0_17

Existing benchmarks can be roughly categorized into two types: those based on multimodal large language models (MLLMs) and those centered on fragmented tasks. For the latter, current benchmarks typically focus on discrete subtasks [2], such as document layout analysis, Optical Character Recognition (OCR), reading order detection, table recognition, and formula conversion. Due to task fragmentation, these benchmarks lack a unified view to comprehensively extract the overall structure of the document. Recently, MLLMs that convert PDF pages into structured markdown text have been extensively researched. Representative works include: LayoutLM [3], which introduces positional encoding to jointly model textual and layout information, achieving strong performance in tasks such as document classification and entity recognition. However, these models rely heavily on the accuracy of OCR modules. Pre-trained on large-scale text-intensive images, Kosmos-2.5 [4] produce structured text output in markdown format. However, the visual token is not compressed and its generalization ability on chinese document images is insufficient. Pix2Struct [5], based on a generative image-to-structure sequence architecture, effectively captures image-text relationships but still faces challenges in structural accuracy and generation efficiency. Nougat [6] is a specialized transformer model trained on arXiv academic documents under a single-page image to markdown paradigm. It performs well on academic documents but exhibits poor generalization on general ones, as its training data is relatively homogeneous and it lacks pre-training tasks to further enhance capabilities. Moreover, most existing method suffer from huge number of visual tokens which reduce the operational efficiency of the model. InternVL [7] costs a average of 3k visual tokens on single-page document understanding benchmark and Qwen2.5-VL [8] costs nearly 4k tokens with the same document image.

Despite the progress made by aforementioned methods, there are still several challenges in practical applications. First, MLLMs typically rely on large-scale, high-quality, cross-domain annotated data during pre-training, however existing public datasets are limited in terms of size, format diversity, and linguistic coverage. Second, the pre-training tasks in existing methods are relatively simplistic, as they lack the modeling of layout relationships, cross-modal alignment, and semantic understanding. Third, most MLLMs typically have a large number of parameters and lack a visual token compression strategy, which results in low operational efficiency. Additionally, complex document structures such as multi-column layouts, text-image mixed arrangements, and variations in document styles and languages further impose higher demands on the model's generalization capability.

To address the above challenges, several improvements are made, including: pre-training task design, model structure optimization, model efficiency enhancement, image processing strategy and innovative data generation methods. First, for DSE task, six pre-training tasks have been designed, including: OCR, layout analysis, text2box, box2text, image caption, and figure/table caption. These tasks enhance the model's fundamental capabilities in document structure parsing and text semantic understanding from multiple dimensions, thereby laying a robust foundation for the subsequent fine-tuning task. In terms of image processing, we propose a shape adaptive cropping method that can process images with arbitrary resolutions without compression, thereby significantly preserving the fine-grained features. Additionally, we introduce a cross-attention based visual token compression module that reduces a single image's visual tokens to 384, effectively boosting the model's inference efficiency and memory utilization. Moreover, lightweight visual encoder and language decoder are utilized to further improve model efficiency. Furthermore, innovative data construction methods tailored to both pre-training and fine-tuning tasks generate tens of millions of high-quality cross-domain samples, significantly enhancing the model's generalization ability. Experimental results show that the proposed method outperforms the current state-of-the-art algorithm across all metrics. For instance, the edit distance decreases by 0.11, while precision, recall, and F1 score increase by 2.9%, 9.2%, and 7.2% respectively.

2 Method

2.1 Model Structure

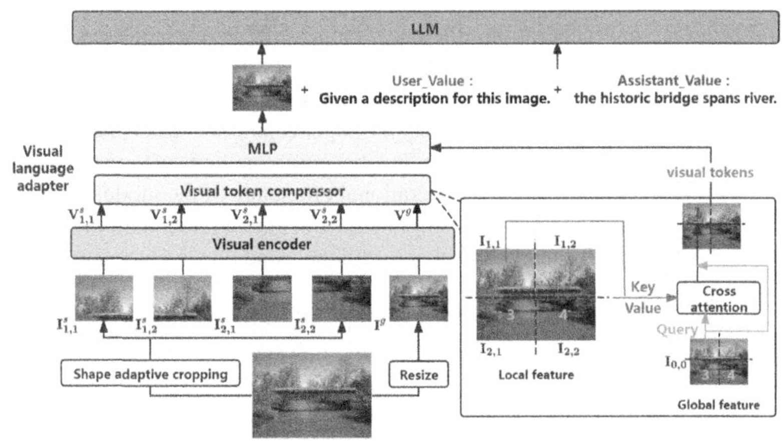

Fig. 1. Overall framework of the proposed method.

In this section, we elaborate on the details of the proposed method. First, document images are processed via a shape adaptive cropping module, which crops out multiple image patches including global image and sub-images. The cropped image patches are then fed into a visual encoder for feature extraction. To optimize computational efficiency, a visual token compression module is designed. By fusing the local information into global information, the module significantly reduces the number of visual tokens, thereby effectively improving the model's processing speed and memory utilization efficiency. Then, the compressed visual tokens are projected to text space via a fully connected layer, with their dimensions ensured to be consistent simultaneously. Finally, the aligned visual features of the image are concatenated with the text instruction features and fed into the large language model, thus enabling document structure extraction. The model structure is shown in Fig. 1.

Shape Adaptive Cropping Module. Document images have various aspect ratios and a great range of resolutions. Specifically, document images typically have high resolutions (with a typical size of 1654 × 2339 pixels) and consist of complex and diverse content, covering multiple types of information such as text paragraphs, images, mathematical formulas, and tables. These characteristics place extremely high demands on the model's ability to capture detailed information. Traditional MLLMs usually adopt the CLIP-style models as the visual encoder, which resize original document images to a fixed resolution (such as 336 × 336 and 448 × 448). The resize operation causes issues such as blurred text characters, distorted image elements, and deformed table lines, increasing the difficulty of document structure extraction.

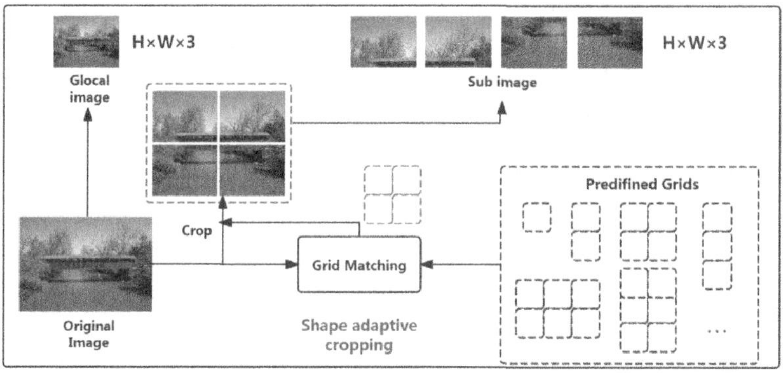

Fig. 2. The illustration of Shape Adaptive cropping module

Thus we propose a shape adaptive cropping module. Specifically, as shown in Fig. 2, we pre-define grids $\{g = (n_h \times n_w)|n_h \times n_w \leq N_c\}$ with various shapes, where n_h and n_w denotes the number of rows and columns of the grid g and N_c denotes the maximum number of the cells (sub-images). Chose a best grid based on the principle that the grid should preserve the resolution of the image as much as possible. Once the grid is chosen, we resize the input image to (n_h H, n_w W) and crop it to $n_h \times n_w$ local images. To maintain the global structure information of the image, we also resize the input image to (H, W) as a global image. All images are then passed on to the visual encoder. To adapt to the typical aspect ratio distribution of document images in real-world scenarios, the parameters of this module are configured as follows: H = 1024, W = 768,N_c = 8.

Visual Encoder. We adopt a Swin Transformer [9], a hierarchical vision transformer that splits the image into non-overlapping windows of fixed size and applies a series of self-attention layers to aggregate information across these windows. Compared with CLIP-style visual encoders, Swin Transformer extracts high quality visual feature and is more lightweight. After processing by the visual encoder, the number of image tokens are $(H/32, W/32) \times (N_c+1)$, where N_c is the number of sub-images, and "1" represents the global image.

Visual Token Compression. We propose a visual token compression module to compress document images into fewer tokens while maintain most visual information. The compression module balance both token efficiency and model performance, the structure is shown in Fig. 1.

The visual token compression module leverages visual features from the global images as the query, the feature map of sub-images as key and value. This not only produces a fixed number of visual tokens for images of any resolution but also covers all areas during compression. Cross attention is utilized to ensemble textual semantics and greatly reduce the number of visual tokens of a high-resolution image to the one of a global image. After compression, the number of image tokens are compressed from $(H/32, W/32) \times (N_c + 1)$ to $(H/32, W/32)$. All sub-image features are fully fused into the global image to form an enhanced global feature map, thereby achieving efficient visual token compression.

To further strengthen the horizontal feature aggregation capability, the module adopts a convolution operation with a kernel size of (1×2) to further compress the number of visual tokens to $(H/32, W/64)$. With the settings of width $W = 768$ and height $H = 1024$, the number of visual tokens per image is uniformly compressed to $(1024/32) \times (768/64) = 384$. The method not only result in short inference time but also occupy less GPU memory,making it easier to extend its application scenarios.

Visual Language Adapter. Our model adopts a fully connected layer (Multi-layer Perceptron, MLP) to project visual tokens into text space. After alignment, compressed visual tokens are concatenated with text instruction tokens and input to a large language model for multi-modal understanding.

Large Language Model. To improve the training and inference efficiency of the proposed model for document understanding, we adopt Qwen2–0.5B [10] large language model (LLM) as the language decoder. The model retains excellent semantic comprehension and text generation capability with a lightweight architecture, which is more efficient and practical.

2.2 Pre-training Tasks

To enhance the fundamental capabilities of the multi-modal large model for document understanding, we design six pre-training tasks to drive the model to focus on fine-grained regions. Through a multi-task joint learning mechanism, the model's understanding of document structures and semantics is strengthened, laying a foundation for downstream tasks.The details are as follows:

Optical Character Recognition (OCR). For OCR task, the prompt is: "*OCR the image*", and the output adopts a structured format, see Fig. 3(a). Taking text lines as the basic unit, each line includes a bounding box composed of the top-left pixel coordinates $[x_0, y_0]$ and bottom-right pixel coordinates $[x_1, y_1]$, as well as the corresponding text content within the bounding box. As a basic task, OCR plays a key role in document digitalization, enabling the accurate conversion of unstructured images into structured text information.

Layout Analysis. The layout analysis task aims to detect various document elements and facilitate understanding of spatial relationships between them. Through this task, the model enhances both its grounding ability and capacity to perceive overall layout information,especially in complex layout scenarios (e.g., single-column, double-column, and interleaved layouts).The prompt and output example are visualized in Fig. 3(b).

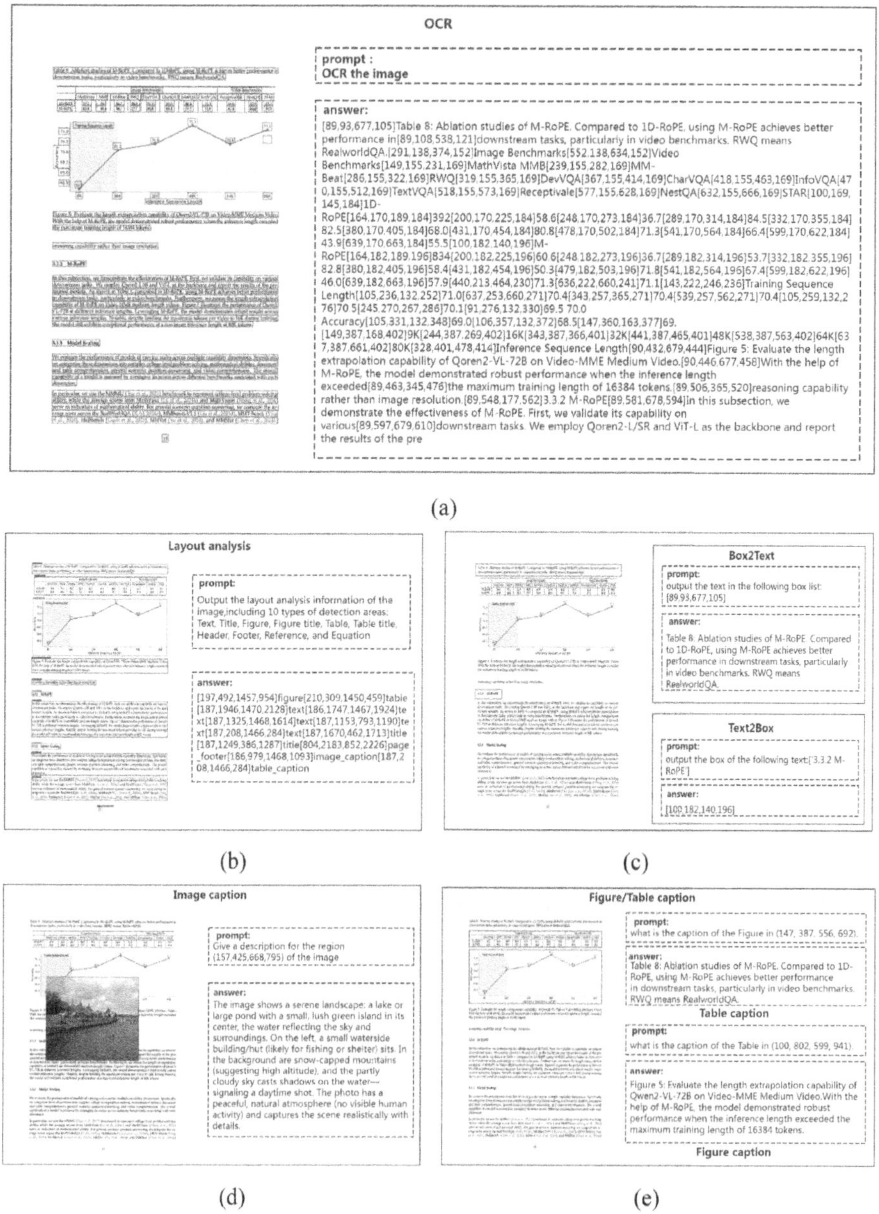

Fig. 3. Pre-training tasks. (a) OCR, (b) Layout analysis, (c) Box2Text and Text2Box, (d) Image caption, (e) Figure/Table caption.

Text2Box. The text localization task is mainly dedicated to accurately identifying the spatial coordinates of given text from document images, as shown in Fig. 3(c). The task enhances the model's perception of the spatial distribution of the document images, thus strengthening its grounding and cross-modal alignment capability.

Box2Text. As a supplement to the text localization task, the Box2Tex task focuses on recognizing text content from a given image region, as shown in Fig. 3(c). We devise fine-grained instructions based on position-aware text prompts to catalyze model to focus any fine-grained region on document images.

Image Captioning. The task aims to generate relevant descriptions for natural images within specific regions of document images, thereby enhancing the cross-modal alignment capability, as shown in Fig. 3(d). This task enables the model to not only extract features from document images which are rich in text content effectively but also extract features from natural images well. Finally, the model is capable of extracting high-quality features, thereby enhancing its overall performance.

Figure/Table Caption. For document images with figure and table elements, the figure/table caption generation task focuses on generating corresponding captions for figures and tables at specified positions. The task enhances the model's ability to learn the logical association between figure/table content and document context, as shown in Fig. 3(e).

Through collaborative optimization of those pre-training tasks, the model's document understanding capabilities are comprehensively enhanced, providing stronger foundational support for downstream applications like structured document extraction.

2.3 Fine-Tuning Task

Based on pre-trained multimodal large language model, we fine-tune the model on the downstream task of converting PDF images to markdown format, as shown in Fig. 4. Leveraging the general knowledge (e.g., semantics and layout information) accumulated during the pre-training stage, it significantly reduces data dependency and training costs in fine-tune stage. Moreover, it eliminate the need to build model from scratch and notably boost the performance of downstream tasks. The two-stage training method compensates for the limitations of downstream tasks and enhances generalization ability.

Specifically, the task aims to convert document images into markdown text that is clearly structured, editable, semantically complete, and retains the original typesetting logic. The difficulty lies in accurately identifying and converting the semantic structures in document images, such as headings, tables, code blocks, formulas. Based on the data generation strategy of the Nougat project, tens of millions of high-quality and multilingual fine-tune datasets are generated and used to train the model.

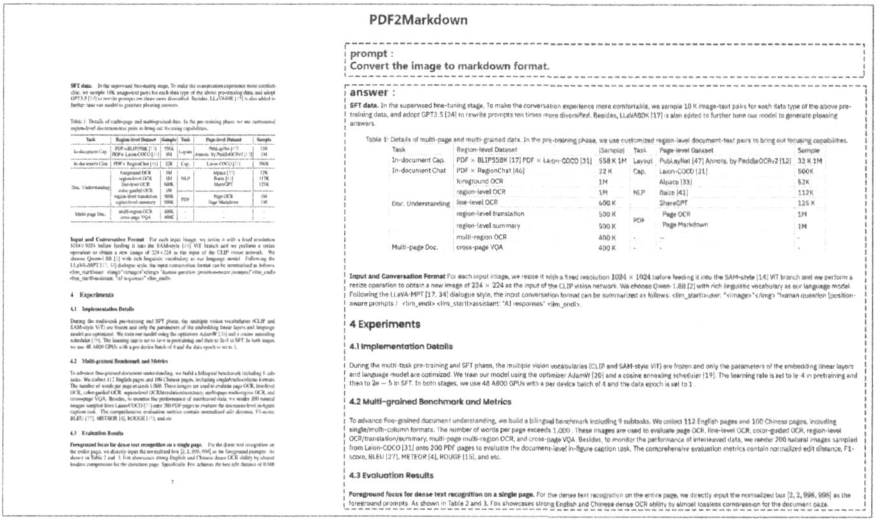

Fig. 4. Fine-tuning task. Transform PDF images to markdown format.

3 Experiments

3.1 Datasets

The data engine is a key part of the proposed method. Innovative data construction method is illustrated in this section. Numerous open-source files in PDF format are downloaded from arXiv and other open-source platforms. Different data construction methods have been designed for each pre-training and fine-tuning task. The detailed statistics of datasets are shown in Table 1.

For the layout analysis pre-training task, we download six open-source layout datasets: CDLA[1], Docgenome [11], Publaynet [12], Doclaynet [13], Docbank [14], and M6Doc [15]. And a private dataset is proposed: Layout15, which covers 15 categories including: text, page_header, document titles, image, figure captions, table, table caption, page_footer, footnote, formula, list, stamp, content, and code. The data include typical document structural elements in academic and office scenarios. The detailed information is presented in Table 1.

For OCR pre-training task, existing tools such as PaddleOCR [16] exhibit insufficient accuracy, often leading to missing detections, false detections and text recognition errors. To obtain high-quality pre-training data, we first use PaddleOCR to pre-annotate document images, thus generating numerous text boxes. These annotations are then manually corrected, then the revised data is fed into the DB [17] text detection model for training, yielding a text detection model with high accuracy. Finally, fitz[2] library is used to extract text from the detected boxes to construct high-quality OCR pre-training datasets.

[1] https://pan.baidu.com/s/1449mhds2ze5JLk-88yKVAA.

[2] https://pypi.org/project/fitz/.

Table 1. Detailed statistics of pre-training and fine-tuning datasets.

Task	Datasets	Number	Task	Datasets	Number
Layout Analysis	CDLA	5000	Box2Text	arXiv	1447011
	Layout15	51884	Text2Box	arXiv	12153616
	Docgenome	6834996	PDF2Markdown	arXiv	18438185
	Publaynet	345948	Image Caption	ReCap-CC3M	2852560
	Doclaynet	74863		ReCap-118K	117287
	Docbank	499000		ReCap-558K	556128
	M6doc	9080		Laion-coco	890883
Figure/Table Captioning	arXiv	5836612	OCR	arXiv	11842689

For image caption task, four image caption datasets are downloaded: ReCap-CC3M[3], ReCap-118K[4], ReCap-558K[5], and laion-coco[6]. Natural images are scaled and then randomly inserted into document images with their descriptive texts served as supervision labels. For Text2Box and Box2Text tasks: text blocks with bounding boxes are directly extracted using the get_text_blocks() function from fitz library. For figure/table caption task, pdffigures2[7] Java toolkit is adopted to generate bounding box and caption information of images and tables. For the fine-tuning task, we automatically generated image-markdown data pairs from the downloaded arXiv papers using the nougat project. To address the scarcity of chinese datasets, we adopted an innovative data augmentation strategy: translating the LaTeX source code of english arXiv papers into chinese, and then recompiling it to generate chinese PDFs. In the end, we follow the nougat workflow to create chinese image-markdown data pairs. The method constructs a large scale chinese fine-tuning datasets, improving language diversity and enhancing the model's cross-lingual generalization ability. The statistical information of the fine-tuning datasets are presented in Table 1.

3.2 Training Strategy

We train our model using the optimizer AdamW and a cosine annealing scheduler. The learning rate is set to 1e–4 in pre-training and then to 1e-5 in fine-tune. In both stages, we use 16 NVIDIA A800 GPUs with a per device batch of 2 and the data epoch is set to 3.In the pre-training stage, all module parameters are unlocked for end-to-end joint training. In the fine-tune stage, the model was initialized with pre-trained parameters. The visual encoder, visual language adapter, and visual token compression module are frozen, while only the large language model is optimized.

[3] https://huggingface.co/datasets/lmms-lab/LLaVA-ReCap-CC3M.

[4] https://huggingface.co/datasets/lmms-lab/LLaVA-ReCap-118K.

[5] https://huggingface.co/datasets/lmms-lab/LLaVA-ReCap-558K.

[6] https://huggingface.co/datasets/visheratin/laion-coco-nllb.

[7] https://github.com/allenai/pdffigures2.

3.3 Experiment Result

We evaluated the DSE accuracy on a custom test set, with comparative experiments involving two open-source models: Nougat and Qwen2-VL-7B [18]. Core evaluation metrics included edit distance(ED), BLEU, precision(P), recall(R), and F1 score. Since Nougat does not support Chinese PDF parsing, we compared model performance separately on chinese and english test sets. Results are presented in Table 2.

Table 2. Accuracy comparison of various models.

Model	Metric									
	English					Chinese				
	ED	BLUE	P	R	F1	ED	BLUE	P	R	F1
nougat	0.18	89.5	89.5	82.6	84.5	/	/	/	/	/
Qwen2-vl-7B	0.28	56.4	70.7	71.2	70.1	0.31	17.4	31.2	30.7	30.0
ours	0.07	88.1	92.4	91.8	91.7	0.10	67.6	83.5	79.4	80.8

The results in Table 2 show that our proposed method outperforms competitors on both Chinese and English test sets. Compared to Nougat (which lacks multi-task pre-training), our method achieves significantly higher accuracy with less visual tokens, which strongly validate the effectiveness of our multi-task pre-training strategy. Notably, although Qwen2-VL model possess basic document structure extract capabilities, their performance lags behind task-specific optimized models. This underscores the necessity of task-specific model design and pre-training optimization. In addition, the proposed method won second place in the CCKS2025 document structure extraction competition, verifying the practical application capability of the model. The evaluation metrics cover: Edit distance similarity (EDS) for text extraction (TE) and text vocabulary F1; EDS for heading concatenation (HE) and tree edit distance similarity (TEDS) for heading tree structure (HT); EDS for inline (IE) and independent formulas (OE); EDS for table concatenation (TaE) and TEDS for table structure matching (TaT); plus Kendall tau distance similarity (KTDS) for document block segmentation (SK) and token-level segmentation (WK).The results of the model on three datasets (arXiv, GitHub, Zenodo) are shown in Table 3. Experimental results demonstrate that our model achieves satisfactory performance across three types of datasets, and it particularly exhibitsstrong capabilities in title detection, text extraction, formula parsing and table parsing.

Table 3. Experiment results of document structured extraction in CCKS2025.

Datasets	Accuracy									
	TE	F1	HE	HT	IE	OE	TaE	TaT	SK	WK
arXiv	84.6	91.5	87.2	91.8	73.5	80.0	68.3	38.1	97.0	97.3
github	83.5	80.1	70.5	54.7	/	/	/	/	99.1	98.4
zenodo	92.3	91.9	72.0	52.5	/	/	/	/	96.8	97.0

4 Conclusion

The proposed document structure extraction method first pre-train the model on six designed pre-training tasks, and then fine-tune the model on the PDF-to-Markdown datasets. Since the fundamental capabilities such as document semantic understanding and layout perception are enhanced during the pre-training phase, the model demonstrates superior learning efficiency and performance in the fine-tuning stage. In addition, the lightweight architecture design and cross-attention based visual token compression technology enable the model to achieve efficient conversion while maintaining accuracy. The shape adaptive cropping module enables the model to process images of any resolution while preserving their global structure and local details. Overall, the proposed method demonstrates excellent capabilities in document structure extraction.

Acknowledgments. Thanks to team members for their valuable help for downloading the datasets. Thanks to nougat project for providing ideas on data generation.

Disclosure of Interests. The authors have no competing interests to declare that are relevant to the content of this article.

References

1. Li, Z., Abulaiti, A., Lu, Y., Chen, X., Zhang, J., Lin, H.: Readoc: a unified benchmark for realistic document structured extraction. arXiv preprint arXiv:2409.05137 (2024)
2. Paruchuri, V., Lampa, S.: Marker: convert PDF to markdown quickly with high accuracy (2024)
3. Xu , Y., Li, M., Cui, L.: Layoutlm: pre-training of text and layout for document image understanding. In: Proceedings of the 26th ACM SIGKDD International Conference on Knowledge Discovery and Data Mining, pp. 1192–1200. Association for Computing Machinery (2020)
4. Lv, T., Huang, Y., Chen, J., Zhao, Y.: Kosmos-2.5: a multimodal literate model. arXiv preprint arXiv:2309.11419 (2023)
5. Lee, K., Joshi, M., Turc, I.R.: Pix2struct: screenshot parsing as pretraining for visual language understanding. In: Neil, L. (ed.) International Conference on Machine Learning, pp. 18893–18912. International Machine Learning Society, Hawaii (2023)
6. Blecher, L., Cucurull, G., Scialom, T.: Nougat: neural optical understanding for academic documents. arXiv preprint arXiv:2308.13418 (2023)
7. Chen, Z., et al.: How far are we to Gpt-4v? closing the gap to commercial multimodal models with open-source suites. arXiv preprint arXiv:2404.16821 (2024)
8. Bai, S., Chen, K., Liu, X.: Qwen2. 5-vl technical report. arXiv preprint arXiv:2502.13923 (2025)
9. Liu, Z., Hu, H., Lin, Y.: Swin transformer V2: scaling up capacity and resolution. In: Proceedings of the IEEE/CVF Conference on Computer Vision and Pattern Recognition, pp.12009–12019. IEEE Press, Nashville (2021)
10. Team, Q.: Qwen2 technical report. arXiv preprint arXiv:2407.10671 (2024)
11. Xia, R., Mao, S., Yan, X.: Docgenome: an open large-scale scientific document benchmark for training and testing multi-modal large language models. arXiv preprint arXiv:2406.11633 (2024)

12. Zhong, X., Tang, J., Yepes, A.J.: Publaynet: largest dataset ever for document layout analysis. In: 2019 International Conference on Document Analysis and Recognition (ICDAR), pp. 1015–1022. University of Technology Sydney, Sydney (2019)
13. Pfitzmann, B., Auer, C., Dolfi, M., Nassar, A.S., Staar, P.: Doclaynet: a large human-annotated dataset for document-layout segmentation. In: Proceedings of the 28th ACM SIGKDD Conference on Knowledge Discovery and Data Mining, pp. 3743–3751. Association for Computing Machinery, Washington (2022)
14. Li, M., et al.: Docbank: a benchmark dataset for document layout analysis. arXiv preprint arXiv:2006.01038. (2020)
15. Cheng, H., et al.: M6doc: a large-scale multi-format, multi-type, multi-layout, multi-language, multi-annotation category dataset for modern document layout analysis. In: Proceedings of the IEEE/CVF Conference on Computer Vision and Pattern Recognition, pp. 15138–15147. IEEE Press, Vancouver (2023)
16. Cui, C., et al.: PaddleOCR 3.0 Technical Report. arXiv preprint arXiv:2507.05595. (2025)
17. Liao, M., Zou, Z., Wan, Z., Yao, C., Bai, X.: Real-time scene text detection with differentiable binarization and adaptive scale fusion. IEEE Trans. Pattern Anal. Mach. Intell. **45**(1), 919–931 (2022)
18. Wang, P., et al.: Qwen2-vl: enhancing vision-language model's perception of the world at any resolution. arXiv preprint arXiv:2409.12191 (2024)

Robust Detection of AI-Generated Text: Insights on Evolving LLMs and Adversarial Data

Yikai Guo[1], Bin Wang[1(✉)], Zhixiang Jiang[1], Shuo Tian[1], Kairui Wang[1], Wenjun Ke[3], and Haoran Luo[2(✉)]

[1] Beijing Institute of Computer Technology and Application, Beijing, China
wangbin1980s@126.com
[2] Nanyang Technological University, Singapore, Singapore
haoran.luo@ieee.org
[3] Southeast University, Nanjing, China

Abstract. Large language models (LLMs) can generate highly fluent text, making it increasingly difficult to distinguish AI-generated text from human-written text and raising concerns about undetected misuse. Existing detectors face two key challenges: (i) as LLMs evolve, detectors struggle to generalize to unseen models and their probability distributions, and (ii) adversaries can paraphrase AI-generated text to evade detection. To tackle these problems, we propose a twofold strategy that (a) leverages LLMs themselves as detectors and (b) employs data augmentation via back-translation to improve robustness. We systematically evaluate several LLMs on the AI-generated text detection task. Moreover, augmenting the training data with paraphrases produced by back-translation exposes the detectors to adversarial variations and significantly enhances their resilience. Our best model achieves state-of-the-art performance, winning first place in the CCKS-2025 LLM-generated Text Detection Task with a macro-F1 score of 89.59%.

Keywords: AI-generated text detection · Large language model · Data augmentation

1 Introduction

Large language models (LLMs) now generate text that rivals human authors in fluency and coherence [1]. Consequently, AI-generated text is proliferating on platforms ranging from social-media to professional content-creation pipelines. This ubiquity underscores the urgent need for reliable detectors prevent potential misuse, such as the spread of misinformation or plagiarism, and ensure the integrity of online communication [2].

The detection task is usually cast as a binary classification problem that differentiates AI-generated from human-written text. Existing detectors fall into two broad categories: statistical methods, which exploit differences in perplexity,

J. Liang et al. (Eds.): CCKS 2025, CCIS 2698, pp. 232–240, 2026.
https://doi.org/10.1007/978-981-95-8525-0_18

entropy, or word-rank distributions [3]; and fine-tuning methods, which adapt pretrained models with labeled corpora [4]. Yet two challenges remain. First, as LLMs continue to evolve, the distribution gap between AI-generated and human-written text is shrinking, causing detectors to struggle in out-of-distribution settings. Moreover, adversaries can easily paraphrase AI-generated text to bypass detection. Even subtle changes, such as small word or character adjustments, can cause detection results to flip [5].

To develop more robust detectors, we tackle these challenges from two perspectives. First, we assess the detection performance of several leading open-source LLMs to determine which model inherently offers better detection capabilities. Building on this, we investigate the potential of using LLMs themselves as detectors, evaluating whether increased model capacity leads to enhanced discrimination. Second, we propose a data-augmentation approach based on back-translation. While back-translation can be used to circumvent detectors, it also broadens the diversity of training data. Inspired by this, we generate adversarial back-translated samples during training, thereby exposing detectors to paraphrased and cross-lingual variations, significantly enhancing their robustness. Our system achieves first place in the CCKS 2025 LLM-generated Text Detection Task Competition, securing a Macro-F1 score of 89.59%.

The main contributions of this paper are threefold:

- **Comprehensive evaluation of LLMs as detectors.** We conduct systematic study of multiple open-source LLMs as AI-generated text detectors, revealing a correlation between model scale and detection capability.
- **Back-translation data augmentation.** We introduce a back-translation data augmentation method that generates paraphrased and cross-lingual variants, markedly boosting the detector's resilience to adversaries.
- **State-of-the-art performance.** Extensive experiments on the CCKS-2025 benchmark show that our method attains a Macro-F1 of 89.59%, winning first place in the CCKS-2025 LLM-Generated Text Detection Task.

2 Related Work

2.1 AI-Generated Text Detection

Research on detecting AI-generated text generally falls into two streams. **Statistical methods** judge whether a text is AI-generated by measuring distributional quirks such as token-level word-rank distributions, entropy, and perplexity [3], or by analyzing curvature of the log-probability surface, as in DetectGPT [6]. These zero-shot approaches require no extra training data, yet their reliability often declines when the generator model or domain shifts. **Fine-tuning methods** instead training supervised detectors on labeled corpora [4,7,8]. Although fine-tuned detectors excel in-domain, they struggle with unseen models or adversarial paraphrases [5,9]. Robust cross-model, cross-domain and attack-resistant detection therefore remains an open challenge.

2.2 Data Augmentation

Data augmentation broadens the training distribution and is a standard strategy for strengthening text detectors. Easy Data Augmentation (EDA) injects lexical diversity through synonym replacement, insertion, swapping and deletion [10]. An Easier Data Augmentation (AEDA) streamlines this idea by inserting random punctuation marks, adding lightweight noise without altering word identity [11]. Synonym-Replacement (SR) can also be applied in isolation for fine-grained lexical variation. A powerful complementary technique is back-translation (BT), which paraphrases a sentence via a round-trip through another language, introducing natural syntactic and phrasing changes while preserving meaning [12]. Injecting these varied yet semantically consistent examples into training helps detectors become less brittle to distribution shifts and small adversarial edits.

3 Methodology

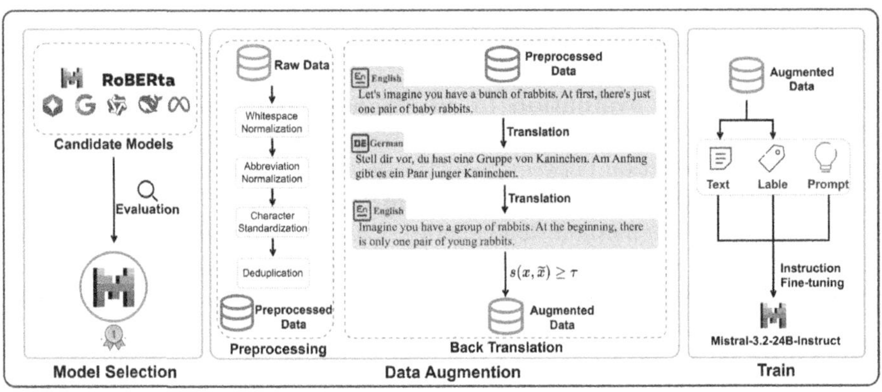

Fig. 1. Pipeline overview. **Model Selection**: multiple open-source LLM backbones are benchmarked and the best-performing model is chosen. **Preprocessing**: raw data undergo whitespace normalization, abbreviation expansion, character standardization, and deduplication. **Data Augmentation**: each preprocessed English sentence is translated to German and back; a candidate is accepted as an augmented sample if its cosine similarity with the original exceeds a threshold τ. **Training**: augmented texts, labels, and prompts are packaged into instruction format to fine-tune the selected backbone, yielding a robust AI-generated text detector.

3.1 Evaluation Dimensions

Our method is shown in Fig. 1, to address the challenges posed by rapidly advancing LLMs, we systematically evaluate the detection capabilities of seven families of open-source large models. The goal is to assess which LLM exhibits better inherent capabilities for distinguishing between AI-generated and human-written text. We apply the discriminative power of this model to AI-generated text detection.

3.2 Data Augmentation with Back-Translation

To counter the challenges posed by adversarial attacks, we propose a data augmentation technique based on back-translation to enhance the robustness of the detector. This process includes three main components: data preprocessing, data augmentation, and model training.

Data Preprocessing. We first perform thorough normalization and cleaning of the raw training corpus to improve data quality and reduce noise or redundancy. Key preprocessing steps include abbreviation normalization, character standardization, whitespace normalization, and duplicate removal.

$$\mathcal{D}_{\text{clean}} = \text{uniq}\big(\{\, (\mathcal{N}_{\text{abbr}} \circ \mathcal{N}_{\text{char}} \circ \mathcal{N}_{\text{ws}})(x) \,\big|\, x \in \mathcal{D}_0 \}\big) \tag{1}$$

where $\mathcal{D}_0$ denotes the raw training corpus, $\mathcal{D}_{\text{clean}}$ is the corpus after preprocessing, $\mathcal{N}_{\text{abbr}}$ is the abbreviation-normalization operator, $\mathcal{N}_{\text{char}}$ is the character-standardization operator, $\mathcal{N}_{\text{ws}}$ is the whitespace-normalization operator, $\circ$ denotes function composition with $(f \circ g)(x) = f(g(x))$, $\text{uniq}(\cdot)$ removes exact duplicates, and x is a single text sample.

Data Augmentation. Following data preprocessing, we augment the training data using a back-translation (BT) strategy. Back-translation generates paraphrases by translating to another language and back to the source language. By expanding the training set with semantically equivalent rephrasings, we increase data diversity and improve robustness to adversarial paraphrasing. We begin with forward translation from English to German:

$$\mathcal{D}_{\text{GE}} = \{\, \mathcal{T}_{\text{en}\to\text{ge}}(x) \,\big|\, x \in \mathcal{D}_{\text{AI}} \} \tag{2}$$

where $\mathcal{D}_{\text{AI}} \subseteq \mathcal{D}_{\text{clean}}$ is the subset of cleaned English samples labeled AI, $\mathcal{T}\text{en} \to \text{ge}$ is the forward translation operator, x is a single English sentence, and $\mathcal{D}_{\text{GE}}$ is the resulting set of German translations.

We then apply BT to obtain paraphrased English candidates:

$$\widetilde{\mathcal{D}}_{\text{EN}} = \{\, \mathcal{T}_{\text{ge}\to\text{en}}(z) \,\big|\, z \in \mathcal{D}_{\text{GE}} \} \tag{3}$$

where $\mathcal{T}_{ge\to en}$ is the reverse translation operator, z is a German sentence from $\mathcal{D}_{\text{GE}}$, and $\widetilde{\mathcal{D}}_{\text{EN}}$ is the candidate set of back-translated English sentences.

To guarantee semantic preservation, we score each original–candidate pair using cosine similarity between sentence embeddings:

$$s(x, \tilde{x}) = \frac{\phi(x) \cdot \phi(\tilde{x})}{|\phi(x)| \cdot |\phi(\tilde{x})|} \tag{4}$$

where $\phi(\cdot)$ denotes a sentence encoder, $x \in \mathcal{D}_{\text{AI}}$ is the original sentence, $\tilde{x} \in \widetilde{\mathcal{D}}_{\text{EN}}$ is its back-translated candidate, $s(\cdot, \cdot)$ represents the cosine similarity, and $|\cdot|$ stands for the Euclidean norm.

We filter candidates using a fixed similarity threshold τ:

$$\mathcal{D}_{\text{BT}} = \left\{ \tilde{x} \in \widetilde{\mathcal{D}}_{\text{EN}} \;\middle|\; \exists x \in \mathcal{D}_{\text{AI}} : \tilde{x} = \left(\mathcal{T}_{\text{ge}\to\text{en}} \circ \mathcal{T}_{\text{en}\to\text{ge}}\right)(x),\; s(x, \tilde{x}) \geq \tau \right\} \tag{5}$$

where $\mathcal{D}_{\text{BT}}$ denotes the set of accepted back-translations, $\left(\mathcal{T}_{\text{ge}\to\text{en}} \circ \mathcal{T}_{\text{en}\to\text{ge}}\right)$ represents the composition of English→German followed by German→English, and τ enforces semantic fidelity.

Finally, we assemble the augmented corpus and assign labels:

$$\mathcal{D}_{\text{aug}} = \mathcal{D}_{\text{clean}} \cup \mathcal{D}_{\text{BT}}, \qquad \ell(\tilde{x}) \equiv 1, \quad \forall \tilde{x} \in \mathcal{D}_{\text{BT}}. \tag{6}$$

where $\mathcal{D}_{\text{aug}}$ denotes the final training set for fine-tuning, $\mathcal{D}_{\text{clean}}$ is the preprocessed corpus, $\mathcal{D}_{\text{BT}}$ contains paraphrased AI variants, and $\ell(\cdot)$ is the labeling function that assigns the label AI to all accepted back-translation samples.

Model Training. After data augmentation, we fine-tune the LLM by appending a lightweight linear classification head that maps the model's hidden representation $\mathbf{h}(x)$ of an input sentence x to a scalar logit $f_\theta(x)$. The detector is trained as a binary classifier with labels using the standard cross-entropy objective over the augmented corpus $\mathcal{D}_{\text{aug}}$:

$$\mathcal{L}(\theta) = -\frac{1}{|\mathcal{D}_{\text{aug}}|} \sum_{(x,y)\in\mathcal{D}_{\text{aug}}} \left[y \cdot \log\big(\sigma(f_\theta(x))\big) + (1-y) \cdot \log\big(1 - \sigma(f_\theta(x))\big) \right] \tag{7}$$

where $\sigma(\cdot)$ denotes the sigmoid function and θ represents all trainable parameters of the backbone model and the classification head.

Model Inference. At test time, the detector outputs a probability $p(x) = \sigma\big(f_\theta(x)\big)$ that a given sentence x is AI-generated. A fixed decision threshold $\eta \in (0, 1)$ is chosen to balance precision and recall. The final predicted label $\hat{y}$ is therefore:

$$\hat{y} = \begin{cases} 1, & \text{if } p(x) \geq \eta, \\ 0, & \text{otherwise.} \end{cases} \tag{8}$$

where $\hat{y} \in \{0, 1\}$ is the final binary prediction, represents human-written or AI-generated, respectively.

4 Experiments

4.1 Experimental Setup

Models. We benchmark seven series of open-source LLMs: **RoBERTa**[1], **Mistral**[2], **Qwen**[3], **DeepSeek**[4], **GLM**[5], **Llama**[6], and **Gemma**[7]. Each model is initialized from its publicly released checkpoint and tokenizer to ensure comparability.

Back-Translation. We adopt the `opus-mt-en-de`[8] model for English→ German and the `opus-mt-de-en`[9] model for German→English. Semantic consistency between the original and back-translated sentences is assessed with **Sentence-BERT**[10], candidates with cosine similarity $s(x, \tilde{x}) \geq 0.90$ are kept.

Fine-Tuning Protocol. We adopt the parameter-efficient Low-Rank Adaptation (LoRA) [13] strategy for all backbones. Optimization relies on AdamW starting at a learning rate of 2e-6. This unified protocol isolates the effect of model capacity from training-time confounders.

Evaluation Metrics. Performance is measured by the Macro-F1 score on the official test set, which consists of Test Set A and Test Set B.

4.2 Results on Different Models

To evaluate the effectiveness of different LLMs on the AI-generated text detection task, we conducte experiments with ten representative models: Roberta-large, Mistral-7B-v0.1, Qwen2.5-7B, Qwen2.5-14B, DeepSeek-R1-14B, GLM-4-9B-0414, Llama3.2-11B, Gemma-2-9B, Magistral-small-2506-24B, and Mistral-3.2-24B-Instruct. Each model is fine-tuned under comparable hyper-parameter settings, and their Macro-F1 scores are recorded on Test Set A and Test Set B. The outcomes are summarized in Table 1 and Table 2.

The results indicate that the Mistral family of models decisively leads the field. Under the same hyper-parameter settings, Mistral-3.2-24B-Instruct attains the highest Macro-F1 score 0.9754 on Test Set A, while Mistral-3.2-24B-Instruct

1 https://huggingface.co/FacebookAI.
2 https://huggingface.co/mistralai.
3 https://huggingface.co/Qwen.
4 https://huggingface.co/deepseek-ai.
5 https://huggingface.co/zai-org.
6 https://huggingface.co/meta-llama.
7 https://huggingface.co/google.
8 https://huggingface.co/Helsinki-NLP/opus-mt-en-de.
9 https://huggingface.co/Helsinki-NLP/opus-mt-de-en.
10 https://huggingface.co/sentence-transformers/bert-base-nli-mean-tokens.

Table 1. Test Results of Different Models on Test Set A

Model	LR	Length	Batch	Macro-F1
Roberta-large	1e-5	512	8	0.8839
Mistral-7B-v0.1	2e-6	256	16	0.9411
Qwen2.5-7B	2e-6	256	16	0.9438
Qwen2.5-14B	2e-6	256	16	0.9518
DeepSeek-R1-14B	2e-6	256	16	0.9586
GLM-4-9B-0414	2e-6	256	16	0.9607
Llama3.2-11B	2e-6	256	16	0.9654
Gemma-2-9B	2e-6	256	16	0.9693
Magistral-small-2506-24B	2e-6	256	16	0.9707
Mistral-3.2-24B-Instruct	2e-6	512	8	**0.9829**

Table 2. Test Results of Different Models on Test Set B

Model	LR	Length	Batch	Macro-F1
Qwen2.5-7B	2e-6	256	16	0.8432
DeepSeek-R1-14B	2e-6	256	16	0.8461
Mistral-7B-v0.1	2e-6	256	16	0.8550
Gemma-2-9B	2e-6	256	16	0.8632
GLM-4-9B-0414	2e-6	256	16	0.8653
Qwen2.5-14B	2e-6	256	16	0.8736
Llama3.2-11B	2e-6	256	16	0.8768
Magistral-small-2506-24B	2e-6	256	16	0.8796
Mistral-3.2-24B-Instruct	2e-6	512	8	**0.8959**

attains the highest Macro-F1 score 0.8864 on Test Set B. With data augmentation and hyper-parameter fine-tuning, the Macro-F1 score further increases to 0.9829 and 0.8959. These outcomes highlight the strong aptitude of Mistral-based architectures for detecting AI-generated text. A clear pattern also emerges, models with larger parameter counts (e.g., 14B–24B parameters) consistently outperform their smaller counterparts, underscoring the advantage of scale. Taken together, and relative to conventional pre-trained language models, these findings underscore the considerable promise of leveraging large-scale LLMs for reliable AI-generated text detection.

Table 3. Test Results of Different Data Augmentation Types on Test Set A

Model	Data Augmentation Method	Macro-F1
Mistral-3.2-24B-Instruct	EDA	0.9786
Mistral-3.2-24B-Instruct	AEDA	0.9800
Mistral-3.2-24B-Instruct	SR	0.9807
Mistral-3.2-24B-Instruct	BT(English-French)	0.9789
Mistral-3.2-24B-Instruct	**BT(English-German)**	**0.9829**

4.3 Results on Different Data Augmentation

To evaluate how different data-augmentation strategies influence detection accuracy, we fine-tuned our strongest baseline model, Mistral-3.2-24B-Instruct with 5 data augmentation methods: Easy Data Augmentation (EDA), An Easier Data Augmentation (AEDA), Synonym Replacement (SR), and two back-translation (BT) variants that route English text through French and German, respectively. Macro-F1 scores for each setting are reported in Table 3, enabling a head-to-head comparison of these techniques on Test Set A.

The results reveal that back-translation is the most effective family of methods, with English→German→English achieving the top Macro-F1 of 0.9829. Synonym Replacement follows closely 0.9807, underscoring that lexical diversity alone can produce meaningful gains. Overall, these findings demonstrate the robustness of BT, particularly with linguistically distant target languages and confirm that thoughtful data augmentation broadly enhances robustness in AI-generated text detection.

5 Conclusion

This study presents a comprehensive investigation into robust detection of AI-generated text. We first benchmark seven families of open-source models and demonstrate that increased model capacity markedly improves inherent discriminative power. Building on this insight, we propose a back-translation data-augmentation method that generates adversarial paraphrases, thereby exposing detectors to cross-lingual and lexical variation during training. Combining the strongest backbone with our augmentation strategy yielded state-of-the-art performance, winning the CCKS 2025 LLM-Generated Text Detection Task with a Macro-F1 of 89.59%.

Future work will explore more lightweight detector architectures for deployment efficiency, adaptive augmentation that targets emerging evasion strategies, and broader evaluations across multilingual and multimodal data to further strengthen societal safeguards against AI-generated text misuse.

References

1. Marco, G., Rello, L., Gonzalo, J.: Small language models can outperform humans in short creative writing: a study comparing SLMs with humans and LLMs. In: Proc. of COLING 2025, pp. 6552–6570 (2025)
2. Zhang, Y., Zhou, T., Qiao, H., Li, T.: Ethical issues in AI-Generated texts: a systematic review and analysis. Int. J. Hum. Comput. Interaction, 1–28 (2025)
3. Gehrmann, S., Strobelt, H., Rush, A.M.: GLTR: statistical detection and visualization of generated text. In: Proc. of ACL 2019 (System Demonstrations), pp. 111–116 (2019)
4. Verma, V., Fleisig, E., Tomlin, N., Klein, D.: Ghostbuster: detecting text ghostwritten by large language models. In: Proc. of NAACL-HLT 2024, pp. 1702–1717 (2024)
5. Krishna, K., Song, Y., Karpinska, M., Wieting, J., Iyyer, M.: Paraphrasing evades detectors of AI-generated text, but retrieval is an effective defense. In: Proc. of NeurIPS 2023 (2023)
6. Mitchell, E., Lee, Y., Khazatsky, A., Manning, C.D., Finn, C.: DetectGPT: zero-shot machine-generated text detection using probability curvature. In: Proc. of ICML 2023, PMLR vol. 202, pp. 24950–24962 (2023)
7. Bakhtin, A., Gross, S., Ott, M., et al.: Real or fake? learning to discriminate machine from human generated text. arXiv:1906.03351 (2019)
8. Fagni, T., Falchi, F., Gambini, M., Martella, A., Tesconi, M.: TweepFake: about detecting deepfake tweets. PLoS ONE **16**(5), e0251415 (2021)
9. Huang, G., Zhang, Y., Li, Z., et al.: Are AI-Generated Text Detectors Robust to Adversarial Perturbations? In: Proc. of ACL 2024, pp. 6005–6024 (2024)
10. Wei, J., Zou, K.: EDA: easy data augmentation techniques for boosting performance on text classification tasks. In: Proc. of EMNLP-IJCNLP 2019, pp. 6382–6388 (2019)
11. Karimi, A., Rossi, L., Prati, A.: AEDA: an easier data augmentation technique for text classification. In: Findings of ACL: EMNLP 2021, pp. 2748–2754 (2021)
12. Sennrich, R., Haddow, B., Birch, A.: Improving neural machine translation models with monolingual data. In: Proc. of ACL 2016, pp. 86–96 (2016)
13. Hu, E.J., Shen, Y., Wallis, P., et al.: LoRA: low-rank adaptation of large language models. ICLR (2022)

A Fact-Aware Cascaded Framework for Dynamic-Granularity Timeline Summarization

Guanqiu Qin, Yu Jia, Yaxuan Zhang, Yi Shen(✉), and Jianjiang Liu(✉)

Shenzhen CyberAray Network Technology Co., Ltd., Shenzhen 518038, Guangdong, China
{jiayu_wlar,zhangyaxuan_wlar,shenyi_wlar,liujianjiang_wlar}@cetc.com.cn

Abstract. In this paper, we propose a Fact-Aware Cascaded Framework for Dynamic-Granularity Timeline Summarization (DTELS), designed to address the limitations of LLM-generated timelines in social media contexts, which often lack satisfactory performance in Informativeness, Granular Consistency, and Factuality. By incorporating a fact-checking mechanism and employing a decoupled, modular task design, the framework sequentially executes data preprocessing, timeline initialization, atomic event extraction, node deduplication, dynamic granularity control, and low-quality node pruning. In the CCKS2025 Event Context Generation for Social Media Evaluation, this framework demonstrated balanced performance across all metrics, achieving the highest overall score and ranking first, validating its effectiveness and practical utility.

Keywords: Cascaded Framework · Dynamic Granularity · Timeline Summarization

1 Introduction

Timeline Summarization (TLS) is a core NLP task that integrates information summarization with temporal reasoning. It aligns well with the long-text processing and generation abilities of Large Language Models (LLMs). The Dynamic Granularity Event Timeline Summarization (DTELS) task, introduced in CCKS2025, focuses on public opinion monitoring and event tracking. It evaluates a model's capacity to generate timelines that meet user-specified granularity across three criteria: Informativeness, Granular Consistency, and Factuality, thereby aiding in topic tracking and decision-making.

In social media scenarios, the DTELS task faces challenges such as high noise and semantic sparsity in text data [1]. Despite the long-text processing capabilities of LLMs (e.g., GPT-4), research by Zhang et al. [2] shows that LLMs still lack satisfactory Factuality and Granular Consistency in DTELS tasks. The

G. Qin, Y. Jia and Y. Zhang—These authors contributed equally to this work.

J. Liang et al. (Eds.): CCKS 2025, CCIS 2698, pp. 241–253, 2026.
https://doi.org/10.1007/978-981-95-8525-0_19

end-to-end generation methods based on LLMs lead to the accumulation of hallucinations, which causes events to deviate from source documents. Meanwhile, fixed output lengths fail to adapt to dynamic requirements. These shortcomings restrict the widespread and reliable application of DTELS.

Against the backdrop of these challenges, we pose a key question: Can task decomposition and modular constraints enable dynamic granularity adaptation while ensuring Factuality and Informativeness? Further, this question can be specifically decomposed into:

- Q1: How to design a subtask pipeline to ensure verifiable outputs at each stage and suppress error propagation?
- Q2: How to establish a granularity-informativeness balance mechanism to avoid the loss of key events?

In this evaluation, we propose A Fact-Aware Cascaded Framework for Dynamic-granularity Timeline Summarization. By introducing a fact-checking mechanism and adopting a task decomposition and modular design, this framework sequentially accomplishes multiple tasks, including data preprocessing, timeline initialization, event atom extraction, node deduplication, dynamic granularity control, and low-quality node pruning. Our framework demonstrated balance performance across all three metrics and achieved the first place in the overall ranking, which verifies the effectiveness of our method. Ablation studies further validate the contribution of each module to the overall system.

2 Task Definition

This evaluation utilizes a multi-domain dataset (covering 7 categories including politics and economics) that includes social media short texts and news reports. It introduces event atoms into the quality evaluation benchmark to address the deficiency that ROUGE [7,8] cannot quantify semantic-level information coverage, and assesses models' ability to generate event timelines meeting different users' granularity requirements. This task includes evaluation metrics as follows:

- **Informativeness**: Measures the amount of valid information contained in each node of the generated event timeline.

$$Info(\hat{\mathcal{S}}) = \frac{1}{|\hat{\mathcal{S}}|} \sum_{(\hat{S}_i, S_j) \in \mathcal{M}} \frac{1}{|\hat{t}_i - t_j|^2 + 1} \text{Entail}(\hat{E}_i, E_j) \tag{1}$$

  where $\mathcal{M}$ is the set of generated nodes $\hat{s}_i$ matched with reference nodes s_j via the Hungarian algorithm, and Entail$(\cdot)$ is the ROUGE-1 recall score for event atom entailment.
- **Granular Consistency**: Evaluates whether the granularity of edges in the generated event timeline is consistent with that of the reference event timeline at the corresponding granularity G.

$$Granu(\hat{\mathcal{S}}) = \frac{1}{|\hat{\mathcal{S}}| - 1} \sum_{(\hat{edge}_m, edge_n) \in \mathcal{M}_{edge}} \left[\hat{edge}_m \in EDGE^G \right] \tag{2}$$

where $\mathcal{M}_{edge}$ is the set of generated edges $\hat{edge}_m$ matched with reference edges $edge_n$, $EDGE^G$ denotes the edge set of the reference event timeline at granularity G, and $[\cdot]$ is an indicator function.

- **Factuality**: Ensures that the information in the generated event timeline is true and reliable.

$$Fact(\hat{\mathcal{S}}) = \frac{1}{|\hat{\mathcal{S}}|} \sum_{(\hat{e}_i,\hat{t}_i)\in\hat{\mathcal{S}}} \text{Entail}(\hat{e}_i, A_{\hat{t}_i}) \tag{3}$$

where $\hat{\mathcal{S}}$ represents the generated event timeline, $\hat{e}_i$ is an event atom in the generated summary, $A_{\hat{t}_i}$ is an event atom extracted from supporting documents.

- **Overall Score**: The average of the above three indicators

$$score(\hat{\mathcal{S}}) = \frac{1}{3}(Info + Granu + Fact) \tag{4}$$

3 Methodology

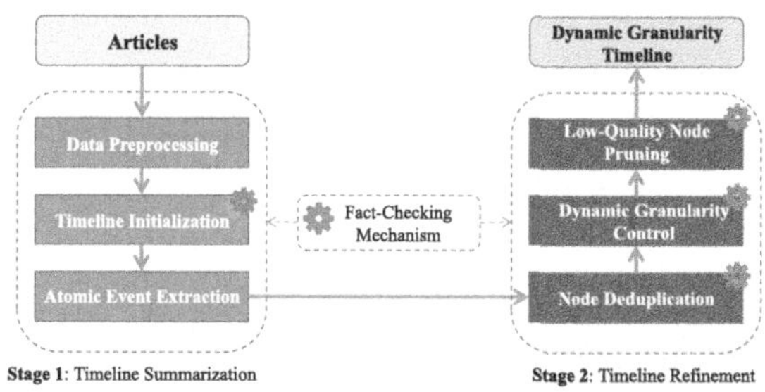

Fig. 1. The Fact-Aware Cascaded Framework for DTELS.

We propose the Fact-Aware Cascaded Framework for Dynamic-Granularity Timeline Summarization, which prioritizes factual consistency and controllable granularity through a modular pipeline. By decoupling the end-to-end process into verifiable submodules, the framework reduces error propagation and adapts flexibly to different granularity needs.

As is shown in Fig. 1, the framework comprises: (1) **Fact-Checking Mechanism**, a verification layer that uses character-level matching to ensure all generated content is traceable to source texts, minimizing hallucination; (2) **Timeline Summarization Stage**, which includes data preprocessing, timeline initialization, and atomic event extraction to build a factually-accurate timeline from multi-source documents; (3) **Timeline Refinement Stage**, where node deduplication, dynamic granularity control, and low-quality node pruning are applied to compress and polish the timeline.

3.1 Fact-Checking Mechanism

To minimize factual errors (e.g., hallucinations) in LLM output, this framework formalizes most subtasks, excluding data preprocessing and atomic event extraction, as a subset selection problem based on exact string matching. A core fact-checking mechanism is integrated as an end-to-end function to verify and constrain all steps with LLM reasoning.

The mechanism treats the original input data as a candidate set $\mathcal{H} = h_i$, from which the LLM produces a verified subset $\mathcal{L} \subseteq \mathcal{H}$. The key idea is to leverage the LLM's semantic understanding capabilities to anchor its outputs to textual evidence from the original candidate set $\mathcal{H}$. We define a fact-checking function to encapsulate this process:

$$\mathcal{L} = \text{FactVerifiedSubset}(LLM, \mathcal{H}, Prompt) \tag{5}$$

The function first uses the LLM and a task prompt to extract a subset $\hat{\mathcal{L}}$:

$$\hat{\mathcal{L}} = LLM(\mathcal{H}, Prompt) \tag{6}$$

Then we apply a character-level exact matching filter with threshold μ_s to eliminate potential hallucinations. For each $\hat{h_i} \in \hat{\mathcal{L}}$, the maximum ratio of Longest Common Subsequence (LCS) to any $h_k \in \mathcal{H}$ is computed. Only items exceeding the threshold μ_s are retained:

$$\rho(\hat{h_i}, \mathcal{H}) = \max_{h_k \in \mathcal{H}} \frac{|LCS(\hat{h_i}, h_k)|}{|\hat{h_i}|} \tag{7}$$

$$\mathcal{L} = \{\hat{h_i} \in \hat{\mathcal{L}} | \rho(\hat{h_i}, \mathcal{H}) \geq thd\} \tag{8}$$

3.2 Timeline Summarization Stage

This stage constructs an initial timeline $\mathcal{T}_0 = \{(t_i, s_i, \mathcal{E}_i)\}$, where each event is described by its date t_i, summary s_i, and a set of atomic events $\mathcal{E}_i = e_{i,j}$, all extracted from verifiable real-world events. The process involves three modules: data preprocessing, timeline initialization, and atomic event extraction.

Data Preprocessing Module. Before timeline construction, we deduplicate and filter low-quality text from raw data. Deduplication uses MinHash+LSH [13]. We identify two noise types: (1) irrelevant articles, and (2) titles summarizing broad news with only minor relevant content, already covered elsewhere.

We employ an LLM-based method to assess the relevance between the target news and the article title, avoiding threshold-based similarity metrics. The prompt is as shown in Fig. 2, to reduce LLM misjudgment, the content of the article will be included in the input as contextual knowledge based on the title information.

Title-Topic Relevance Assessment

```
## Role
你是一个时间轴生成器
## Task
我将给你[目标事件]以及[文章]两个信息，
请判断[文章]的事件信息是否能被归纳到[目标新闻]的时间轴中，
如果相关请回复：<能>， 否则请回复<不能>
### Example 1
样例说明： 文章与目标新闻无关
Input:
[目标新闻]：重庆暴雨
[文章]:
  {{
    "title": "汶川“敬礼娃娃”高考志愿公布！他有个理想",
    "content": "郎铮在接受采访前透露已决定报考北大国际关系学院……"
  }}
Output:
不能
## 注意
1. 不要输出答案以外无关的内容
2. 可能存在噪声文章，只根据文章title判断，content仅供title事件背景参考
## Input
[目标新闻]：{topic}
[文章]：{doc}
```

Fig. 2. Prompt for Judging the Relevance of Articles to Target Events.

Timeline Initialization Module. To minimize factual deviations from LLM paraphrasing, we construct initial timeline nodes by extracting original content from articles through two methods: (1) extracting relevant original sentences that describe milestone events, and (2) incorporating article titles as summaries when necessary. Method 1 uses LLM judgment to identify milestone events and extract their core descriptive sentences (Fig. 3). Method 2 leverages the journalistic "inverted pyramid" principle [14], utilizing titles as high-quality event summaries.

Timeline Initialization

```
## Role
你是一位经验丰富的记者
## Task
请判断以下[文章]是否具有关于{topic}事件发展的里程碑事件，
如果有请从文章原文中选择一条概括了事件的核心句子（包括文章标题），以便归纳到时间线中，如
果没有，回复<没有>
### 输出格式1
<sent>核心句子</sent>
### 输出格式2
<没有>
## Input
[文章]
{article}
```

Fig. 3. Prompt for Extracting Milestone Event Sentences.

Empirical support (Fig. 4) shows that titles serve as effective summaries for 30–50% of topics across datasets. Subsequent processing stages systematically address potential issues such as information redundancy and quality inconsistencies arising from direct title usage.

Atomic Event Extraction Module. This module further refines and decomposes the timeline summaries into an atomic fact timeline suitable for direct logical reasoning and visualization. Initial summaries often contain multi-event composites, subjective evaluations, or speculative content. To ensure factual

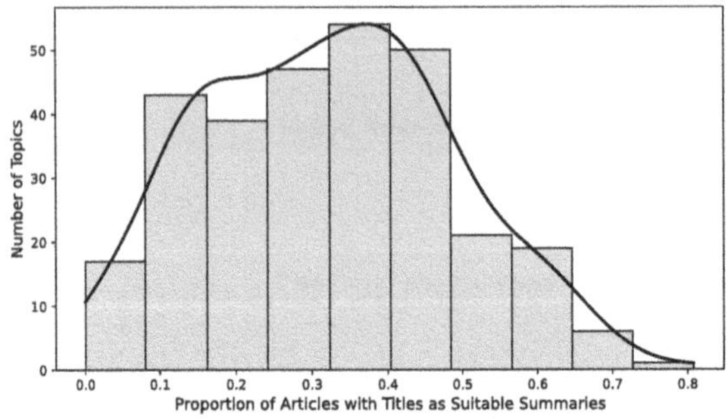

Fig. 4. Assessment of Title Effectiveness as Event Summaries Across Topics.

accuracy and structural conciseness, we designed a two-stage pipeline consisting of fact verification followed by atomic event decomposition.

Atomic Event Extraction

```
## Role
你是一个专业的原子事件分解者。
## Task
请判断给定句子是否能抽取原子事件，如果能，请进行抽取
你需要完成二阶段任务，以完成原子事件抽取：
1. 判断句子是否而非标题党、情绪化表达、推测，具有真实信息或者已发生事件，可以生成原子事件
2. 如果不可生成原子事件，直接输出空列表 []
### 输出格式
请使用以下格式输出：
["原子事件_1", "原子事件_2", ...]
## 注意
* 请保证原子事件的信息精简化，一个原子事件组成最多包含一个主语、一个谓语和一个宾语。
* 要确保原子事件符合事实，不可捏造，虚构
* 不要输出答案以外无关的内容
## Intput
"{summary}"
```

Fig. 5. Prompt for Atomic Event Extraction.

As detailed in the prompt in Fig. 5, we employ a few-shot prompting strategy to guide the LLM. The Model is first tasked to determine whether a summary describes a concrete, verifiable event. If confirmed, the summary is decomposed into atomic events.

3.3 Timeline Refinement Stage

The primary objective of this stage is to select the most representative N key nodes from the initial timeline $\mathcal{T}_0$ under the dynamic granularity constraint, resulting in a high-quality event timeline $\mathcal{T}$ that satisfies the desired criteria. This process is accomplished through three key modules: Node Deduplication, Dynamic Granularity Control, and Low-Quality Node Pruning.

Node Deduplication

```
## Role
你是一名经验丰富的记者，为目标新闻优化时间线。
## Task
从给定的时间线中选取时间线节点，减少事件冗余和时间冲突问题，得到更好的时间线
## 输出格式
1. <timestamp>yyyy-MM-ddTHH:mm:ss+HH:mm</timestamp><event>事件1</event>
2. <timestamp>yyyy-MM-ddTHH:mm:ss+HH:mm</timestamp><event>事件2</event>
...
N. <timestamp>yyyy-MM-ddTHH:mm:ss+HH:mm</timestamp><event>事件N</event>
## Example
### 不相同事件
#### 输入
1. <timestamp>2020-01-14T00:00:00+00:00</timestamp><event>王某被法庭判决监禁5年</event>
2. <timestamp>2025-01-13T00:00:00+00:00</timestamp><event>王某被判决监禁5年出狱</event>
#### 输出
1. <timestamp>2020-01-14T00:00:00+00:00</timestamp><event>王某被法庭判决监禁5年</event>
2. <timestamp>2025-01-13T00:00:00+00:00</timestamp><event>王某被判决监禁5年出狱</event>
### 相同事件去重
#### 输入
1. <timestamp>2019-08-30T00:00:00+00:00</timestamp><event>贩毒组织头目李某被拘捕</event>
2. <timestamp>2019-08-31T00:00:00+00:00</timestamp><event>警方拘捕了李某</event>
#### 输出
1. <timestamp>2019-08-30T00:00:00+00:00</timestamp><event>贩毒组织头目李某被拘捕</event>
## 注意
* 存在大量事件相似重复节点，注意判别，得到具有区分度的时间节点。
* 事件去重，应以最早的时间戳为准。
* 不允许修改原节点的任何信息
* 不要输出答案以外无关的内容
## Input
[主题]
{topic}
[待合并时间轴]
{timelines}
```

Fig. 6. Prompt for Timeline Node Deduplication.

Node Deduplication Module. Semantic redundancy among timeline nodes not only lengthens the input context but also introduces interfering information, complicating subsequent dynamic granularity control. This module removes duplicate event mentions to yield a concise timeline $\mathcal{T}_{\text{dedup}}$ that serves as a cleaner input for the Granularity Control Module.

To balance deduplication accuracy with computational efficiency, we propose a two-step strategy that first aggregates potentially redundant nodes based on semantic similarity, followed by fine-grained deduplication using LLM reasoning. Specifically, given the initial timeline node set $\mathcal{T}_0$, we encode their textual descriptions $\{s_i\}$ into dense vector representations $\{u_i\}$ using a pre-trained text embedding model. Next, we construct a semantic similarity matrix M, where each entry M_{ij} is computed as the cosine similarity between vectors u_i and u_j:

$$M_{ij} = \cos(u_i, u_j) = \frac{\mathbf{u_i} \cdot \mathbf{u_j}}{\|\mathbf{u_i}\| \cdot \|\mathbf{u_j}\|} \tag{9}$$

Based on matrix M, we group nodes with high semantic similarity into clusters. An association graph $G = (V, E)$ is constructed under the constraints of a semantic similarity threshold μ_s and a maximum allowable time span μ_t.

$$V = \mathcal{T}_{dedup}, (i, j) \in E \Leftrightarrow M_{ij} \geq \mu_s \wedge |t_i - t_j| \leq \mu_t \tag{10}$$

Nodes that form connected components in G are grouped into candidate deduplication clusters $\mathcal{T}_0^{(k)}$, where each cluster corresponds to a set of potentially redundant timeline nodes. For each connected component $\mathcal{T}_0^{(k)}$ in G, we apply fact-verified subset selection (Sect. 3.1) via few-shot prompting (Fig. 6) to merge duplicates:

$$\mathcal{T}_{\text{dedup}}^{(k)} = \text{FactVerifiedSubset}\left(LLM, \mathcal{T}_0^{(k)}, Prompt\text{dedup}\right) \tag{11}$$

The final deduplicated timeline is $\mathcal{T}_{dedup} = \bigcup_k \mathcal{T}_{dedup}^{(k)}$.

```
Dynamic Granularity Control
## Role
你是一名经验丰富的记者，为目标新闻优化时间线。
## Task
你需要从给定的时间线中选取时间线节点，得到选择与{topic}脉络发展相关的最多*{topN}*个节点。
## 输出格式
1. <timestamp>yyyy-MM-ddTHH:mm:ss+HH:mm</timestamp><event>事件1</event>
2. <timestamp>yyyy-MM-ddTHH:mm:ss+HH:mm</timestamp><event>事件2</event>
...
N. <timestamp>yyyy-MM-ddTHH:mm:ss+HH:mm</timestamp><event>事件N</event>
## 注意
* 尽量保证时间轴中事件的叙述顺序因果连贯，节点描述的事件互不重复，每个节点都提供了新信息
* 时间轴最多包含*{topN}*个最重要的事件节点。
* 选择围绕【{topic}】的关键事件节点构建时间轴，因为并非所有事件都相关或值得选择。
* 不允许修改原节点的任何信息
* 不要输出答案以外无关的内容
## Input
[主题]
{topic}
[待合并的时间轴]
{timelines}
```

Fig. 7. Prompt for Dynamic Granularity Control.

Dynamic Granularity Control Module. This module employs the LLM to dynamically filter and adjust timeline $\mathcal{T}_{dedup}$ according to a specified granularity N, producing the timeline $\mathcal{T}_{Granu=N}$. The prompt design is detailed in Fig. 7. By enforcing output format and ordinal constraints, the model generates a structured timeline of exactly N nodes:

$$\mathcal{T}_{Granu=N} = \text{FactVerifiedSubset}(LLM, \mathcal{T}_{dedup}, Prompt_{granu}, N) \tag{12}$$

During empirical evaluation, we observed that some complex cases require multiple attempts to satisfy the cardinality constraint. As shown in Algorithm 1, an iterative divide-and-conquer strategy is incorporated to reduce single-inference burden and improve accuracy.

Algorithm 1: Dynamic Granularity Control Algorithm

```
Input  : T_dedup: The deduplicated timeline
         N: Target number of events (granularity)
         max_iter: Maximum number of iterations (default = 3)
Output: T_{Granu=N}: The filtered event timeline with the desired granularity
Procedure
    T* ← T_dedup
    current_granu ← |T*|
    prev_granu ← ∞ ;                      // Initialize for iterative control
    cnt ← 0
    while |T*| > N and cnt < max_iter do
        if (current_granu == prev_granu or |T*| > 80) and |T*| > N + 5 then
            // Apply divide-and-conquer strategy
            mid ← |T*|//2
            T_a, T_b ← T*[0 : mid], T*[mid :]
            if |T*| ≤ 2 × N then
                N' ← N//2 + 3 ;            // Sub-goal for context preservation
            else
                N' ← N
            T_a, T_b ← get_granu(T_a, N'), get_granu(T_b, N')
            T* ← T_a ∪ T_b
        else
            T* ← get_granu(T*, N)
        Sort T* by the timestamp field ;   // Maintain temporal coherence
        prev_granu ← current_granu
        current_granu ← |T*|
        cnt ← cnt + 1 ;                    // Increment iteration counter
    T_{Granu=N} ← T*
    return T_{Granu=N}
```

It iteratively condenses the timeline $\mathcal{T}_{dedup}$ to a target granularity N within a set number of iterations ($max\_iter = 3$). The key mechanisms of Algorithm 1 are as follows:

- **Iterative Control**: The loop runs until the timeline is shortened to $\leq N$ events or max_iter is reached. The prev_granu variable checks for stalled progress.
- **Divide-and-Conquer Trigger**: Activated if the timeline length is unchanged, very large (>80), and exceeds N by more than 5. It splits the timeline into two halves for processing.
- **Adaptive Sub-Goal**: For a split timeline, the sub-goal N' for each half is set to $N/2 + 3$ (to preserve context) if the total length is $\leq 2N$; otherwise, the full target N is used.
- **Chronological Sorting**: The merged results are sorted by timestamp after every iteration to maintain temporal order.

Low-Quality Node Pruning Module. To ensure the final timeline $\mathcal{T}$ clearly, objectively, and accurately reflects the evolutionary logic of the target event,

Timeline Refinement

```
## Role
你是一名经验丰富的记者
## Task
请优化现有的新闻时间线的节点。
优化要求：
1. 节点推动或者揭示了[目标新闻]发展、进度、影响程度等信息，否则删除。
2. 删除 毫无实质信息的低质量节点，比如节点仅为标题党、情绪化表达、推测
3. 删除 无信息来源的评论性节点
### 可删除的事件叙述样例
a. "英雄联盟大乱斗新地图怎么样 2024大乱斗新地图介绍"
b. "爆火的《双城之战》为游戏IP改编带来什么启示?"
c. "《双城之战2》:被剧情拖后腿的顶级制作"
### 可保留的事件叙述样例
a. "《英雄联盟:双城之战》第二季今天完结:臻彩4K限时免费看" (该叙述可知 《英雄联盟:双城之战》第二季在今天完结的信息)
## 输出格式
1. <timestamp>yyyy-MM-ddTHH:mm:ss+HH:mm</timestamp><event>事件1</event>
2. <timestamp>yyyy-MM-ddTHH:mm:ss+HH:mm</timestamp><event>事件2</event>
...
N. <timestamp>yyyy-MM-ddTHH:mm:ss+HH:mm</timestamp><event>事件N</event>
## 注意
* 不允许修改原节点的任何信息
* 不要输出答案以外无关的内容
## Input:
[目标事件]
{topic}
[待优化的时间轴]
{timelines}
```

Fig. 8. Prompt for Pruning Low-Quality Nodes.

this module performs quality-based pruning on $\mathcal{T}_{Granu=N}$. As the prompt design shown in Fig. 8, we use the fact-verified subset selection method to get $\mathcal{T}$:

$$\mathcal{T} = \mathcal{T}_{prune} = \text{FactVerifiedSubset}(LLM, \mathcal{T}_{Granu=N}, Prompt_{prune}) \tag{13}$$

We retain nodes that reflect substantial developments, such as those indicating thematic progression, key turning points, or changes in impact, and remove nodes that lack informational value, including those dominated by subjective evaluations, speculative statements, or emotionally charged narratives unrelated to factual event descriptions.

4 Experiments

4.1 Implementation Details

In our experimental setup, we employed Qwen3-32B-FP8 as the primary LLM and Qwen3-Embedding-0.6B as the embedding model. The LLM was configured with the temperature of 0 and used in "no-thinking mode" to ensure reproducible and deterministic outputs. For deduplication-related modules, the semantic similarity threshold μ_s was set to 0.95, and the maximum temporal span threshold μ_t was set to 31 days.

4.2 Main Result

The main results are presented in Table 1. The Overall score variations among teams are primarily attributed to differences in the Info and Fact metrics. Our method achieves a significant lead in the Info score and attains the second-highest

Table 1. Main Result of the CCKS2025 Event Context Generation for Social Media Evaluation

Rank	Team	Overall	Info	Granu	Fact
1	CArray (Ours)	**0.6971**	**0.1444**	0.9916	0.9552
2	Team 1	0.6934	0.1049	0.9780	0.9975
3	Team 2	0.6929	0.1013	0.9793	**0.9979**
4	Team 3	0.6900	0.0783	**0.9965**	0.9954
5	Team 4	0.4580	0.0180	0.9850	0.3710

position in the Granu score. Although our Fact score is slightly lower than those of teams ranked 2nd to 4th, our overall composite score remains the highest. These results indicate that our approach effectively balances performance across all evaluation criteria, demonstrating its overall superiority.

4.3 Ablation Study

Table 2. Ablation Study

Method	Overall	Info	Granu	Fact
All-Modules	**0.6970**	**0.1440**	**0.9914**	**0.9557**
-Dedup	0.6938	0.1440	0.9847	0.9526
-IDC	0.6949	0.1413	0.9885	0.9534
-Pruning	0.6808	0.1081	0.9796	0.9548
-FactCheck	0.5102	0.1101	0.9901	0.4304

To evaluate the contribution of each module to the overall framework, we conducted a systematic ablation study as shown in Table 2. The following components were successively removed: the deduplication module (—Dedup), the iterative divide-and-conquer strategy within the dynamic granularity control (—IDC), the low-quality node pruning (—Pruning), and the entire fact verification mechanism—including the event consistency check from Sect. 3.1 and the non-factual filtering from Sect. 3.2.3 (—FactCheck).

The experimental results indicate that the removal of the first two modules (—Dedup and —IDC) leads to only minor performance fluctuations. This suggests that current LLMs remain sensitive to context length when processing long texts, and that appropriately reducing the input context can, somewhat counter-intuitively, facilitate the generation of more concise and informative timelines.

When the pruning module is ablated (—Pruning), both the Info and Granu metrics drop considerably. This implies that the timeline $\mathcal{T}_{\text{Granu}=N}$ produced by dynamic granularity control still contains redundant nodes, and that further pruning can enhance information density and granularity accuracy even with fewer nodes.

Most notably, removing all the fact-checking method (—FactCheck) causes the Fact score to drop sharply from 0.9557 to 0.4304, underscoring the critical role of event verification in maintaining factual consistency and reliability throughout the timeline.

5 Related Work

Early Timeline Summarization (TLS) methods used unsupervised similarity measures [3], submodular optimization [4], or task decomposition [5], but often suffered from poor scalability, error accumulation, or redundancy. DATEWISE [6] introduced candidate filtering yet remained prone to redundancy. Event-based approaches [7] grouped articles by event but struggled with clustering granularity and stability.

Recently, LLMs have enabled abstractive TLS [8,9] and handled knowledge-intensive tasks [10]. Strategies like divide-and-conquer [11] and event graphs [12] improved coherence and standardization. However, LLMs still lack mechanisms for factual consistency and dynamic granularity control.

6 Conclusion

Focusing on the dynamic-granularity timeline summarization task, this study proposes a fact-aware cascaded framework that effectively addresses the issues of hallucination accumulation and granularity mismatch in event timeline generation using Large Language Models (LLMs). Through a modular subtask pipeline and multi-level fact verification, this method maintains high informativeness while significantly enhancing factual consistency and granularity control capabilities.

Experimental results demonstrate that the framework exhibits strong robustness and scalability in complex social media environments, providing a reliable foundation for the construction of future event summarization systems. Future work will further optimize dynamic granularity strategies and cross-lingual generalization capabilities.

References

1. Wang, H., Koh, J.-L.: Timeline summarization for event-related discussions on a chinese social media platform. In: International Conference on Industrial, Engineering and Other Applications of Applied Intelligent Systems, LNCS, vol. 10351, pp. 579–594. Springer, Cham (2017). https://doi.org/10.1007/978-3-319-60045-1_50
2. Zhang, C., et al.: DTELS: towards dynamic granularity of timeline summarization. arXiv preprint arXiv:2411.09297 (2024). https://doi.org/10.48550/arXiv.2411.09297

3. Chieu, H.L., Lee, Y.K.: Query based event extraction along a timeline. In: Proceedings of the 27th Annual International ACM SIGIR Conference on Research and Development in Information Retrieval, pp. 425–432. ACM, Sheffield (2004). https://doi.org/10.1145/1008992.1009056
4. Martschat, S., Markert, K.: A temporally sensitive submodularity framework for timeline summarization. In: Korhonen, A., Titov, I. (eds.) Proceedings of the 22nd Conference on Computational Natural Language Learning, pp. 230–240. Association for Computational Linguistics, Brussels (2018). https://doi.org/10.18653/v1/K18-1021
5. Tran, G.B., Alrifai, M., Nguyen, D.Q.: Predicting relevant news events for timeline summaries. In: Proceedings of the 22nd International Conference on World Wide Web, pp. 91–92. ACM, Rio de Janeiro (2013). https://doi.org/10.1145/2488388.2488405
6. Ghalandari, D.G., Ifrim, G.: Examining the state-of-the-art in news timeline summarization. arXiv preprint arXiv:2005.10107 (2020). https://doi.org/10.48550/arXiv.2005.10107
7. Li, M., Ma, T., Yu, M., Wu, L., Gao, T., Ji, H., McKeown, K.: Timeline summarization based on event graph compression via time-aware optimal transport. In: Proceedings of the 2021 Conference on Empirical Methods in Natural Language Processing, pp. 6443–6456. Association for Computational Linguistics, Online (2021). https://doi.org/10.18653/v1/2021.emnlp-main.522
8. Zhang, T., Ladhak, F., Durmus, E., Liang, P., McKeown, K., Hashimoto, T.B.: Benchmarking large language models for news summarization. arXiv preprint arXiv:2301.13848 [cs.CL] (2023). https://doi.org/10.1162/tacl_a_00632
9. Shen, C., Cheng, L., Nguyen, X.-P., You, Y., Bing, L.: Large language models are not yet human-level evaluators for abstractive summarization. arXiv preprint arXiv:2305.13091 [cs.CL] (2023). https://doi.org/10.48550/arXiv.2305.13091
10. Guo, B., Zhang, X., Wang, Z., Jiang, M., Nie, J., Ding, Y., et al.: How close is chatgpt to human experts? comparison corpus, evaluation, and detection. arXiv preprint arXiv:2301.07597 (2023). https://doi.org/10.48550/arXiv.2301.07597
11. Sojitra, D., Jain, R., Saha, S., Jatowt, A., Gupta, M.: Timeline summarization in the era of LLMs. In: Proceedings of the 47th International ACM SIGIR Conference on Research and Development in Information Retrieval, pp. 2657–2661. ACM, Taipei (2024). https://doi.org/10.1145/3626772.3657845
12. Hu, Q., Moon, G., Ng, H.T.: From moments to milestones: incremental timeline summarization leveraging large language models. In: Proceedings of the 62nd Annual Meeting of the Association for Computational Linguistics (Volume 1: Long Papers), pp. 7232–7246. Association for Computational Linguistics, Bangkok (2024). https://doi.org/10.18653/v1/2024.acl-long.402
13. Guilherme, P., et al.: The RefinedWeb dataset for Falcon LLM: outperforming curated corpora with web data, and web data only. arXiv preprint arXiv:2306.01116 (2023). https://doi.org/10.48550/arXiv.2306.01116
14. Horst, P.: News and its communicative quality: the inverted pyramid—when and why did it appear?. Journalism Stud. **4**(4), 501–511 (2003). https://doi.org/10.1080/1461670032000136596

Multi-agent for Dynamic-Granularity Timeline Summarization

Jun Ma, Han Yang(✉), Xianhui Guo, Jian Li, Qishan Song, Dadong Wu, and Xinyun Jiang

Shenzhen CyberAray Network Technology Co., Ltd., Shenzhen, China
{majun_wlar,yanghan_wlar,guoxianhui_wlar,lijian_wlar,songqishan_wlar, wudadong_wlar,jiangxinyun_wlar}@cetc.com.cn

Abstract. Dynamic-granularity Timeline Event Summarization (DTELS), a specialized variant of Timeline Summarization, is pivotal for distilling coherent narratives from large text corpora under flexible granularity constraints. Despite its importance, existing methods struggle to balance narrative coherence with adaptive granularity. To address this gap, we introduce a novel multi-agent framework that revolutionizes DTELS by dividing the task into three distinct stages: article grouping, event extraction, and summary generation. Our approach leverages predefined rules and a collaborative multi-agent architecture to enhance information extraction accuracy and ensure granular consistency across diverse datasets. Empirical evaluations on the newly curated DTELS-Bench demonstrate that our framework significantly outperforms state-of-the-art methods, achieving superior narrative coherence and granularity adaptability. Furthermore, our method achieved second place in the CCKS 2025 Shared Task on Event Timeline Generation for Social Media, validating its effectiveness in real-world scenarios. Our method nearly achieved perfect scores in granularity and factuality, while achieved 0.2 informativeness score, a 20% enhancement over other top-ranking methods. These advancements establish a new benchmark for timeline summarization, offering robust tools for applications requiring dynamic event summarization.

Keywords: Timeline Summarization · Dynamic Granularity · Multi-agent · Information Extraction

1 Introduction

Timeline summarization (TLS) is a natural language processing task that involves creating a concise, chronological summary of events from a set of documents or data sources. Previous research has focused on constructing comprehensive event summaries, but fails to meet the diverse granularity requirements across different scenarios. To address this limitation, dynamic-granularity

J. Ma and H. Yang—These authors contributed equally to this work.

J. Liang et al. (Eds.): CCKS 2025, CCIS 2698, pp. 254–262, 2026.
https://doi.org/10.1007/978-981-95-8525-0_20

timeline summarization (DTELS) has been proposed. DTELS aims to generate adaptive timelines tailored to user-specified instructions or contextual requirements [1]. An example of dynamic-granularity timeline summarization is shown in Fig. 1. The study [1] proposes the Hierarchical Merging (HM) method for the limited context length of language models. This approach first generates summaries for input segments based on their timestamps, and then hierarchically merges these summaries following predefined merging prompts. The method made a significant contribution and achieved strong performance; however, improving the consistency between informativeness and granularity remains a challenge.

To address these challenges, we propose a novel multi-agent framework for DTELS with the following key contributions:

1. **Modular three-stage pipeline**: We decompose DTELS into article grouping, event extraction, and summary generation, ensuring precise control over narrative coherence and granularity adaptability
2. **Hybrid multi-agent structure**: Our multi-agent approach combines multiple large language models with rule-based mechanisms to achieve high granular consistency and factuality, effectively improving informativeness without sacrificing performance in other metrics.
3. **State-of-the-art performance**: Our method achieves superior results on the DTELS-Bench dataset [2], and ranks second in the CCKS 2025 Shared Task on Event Timeline Generation for Social Media [3], validating its real-world effectiveness.

The rest of this paper is organized as follows: Sect. 2 presents the problem definition, dataset, and evaluation metrics. Section 3 describes our proposed method. Section 4 reports the experimental results. Section 5 discusses related work, and Sect. 6 concludes the paper.

2 Preliminaries and Dataset

2.1 DTELS Definition

The input includes a news topic q, a time range $T = t_1, \ldots, t_n$, associated news articles $A = A_{t_1}, \ldots, A_{t_n}$, and a user-specified granularity G, denoting the number of nodes in the event timeline. The task is to generate an event timeline $S = S_1, \ldots, S_G$, where each node S_j includes a timestamp t_j and a summary of news events at that time.

2.2 Dataset

The DTELS-Bench dataset [2] is a comprehensive Chinese dataset designed to support research on the dynamic-granularity timeline summarization (DTELS) task. It comprises 55,432 Chinese news articles across 543 topics from 2,858 domestic and international Chinese-language sources, covering seven categories: politics, economy, society, military, technology, health, and environment.

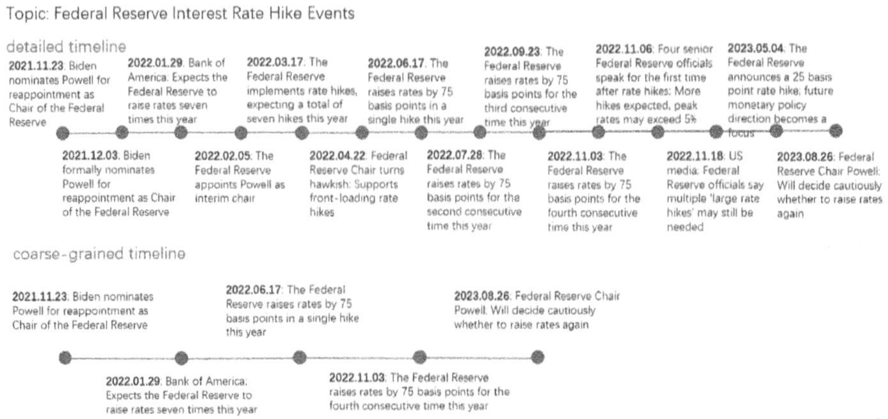

Fig. 1. Example of dynamic-granularity timeline summarization. Note: Additional information or clarification about the figure can be placed here.

The dataset features multi-granularity annotations with levels such as G_{40} (fine-grained, up to 40 nodes), G_{20}, G_{10}, G_5, and G_3 (coarse-grained, 3 nodes), indicating the number of timeline nodes and the level of event detail or omission. Each topic contains an average of 102 articles. Annotations were created using a consensus mechanism with GPT-4o to simulate agreement among journalists, followed by expert refinement. All articles were published after October 2023 to avoid overlap with the pretraining data of large language models.

2.3 Evaluation Metrics

Following Zhang et al. [1], we evaluate the generated outputs in terms of three dimensions: informativeness, granular consistency, factuality.

Before introducing the evaluation metrics, we first present the concept of event atoms and the entailment score, which underlie the computation of the numerical scores for the three criteria.

Inspired by recent advances in atom-based evaluation [4–6], the concept of event atom is introduced as fundamental units for factual assessment [1]. Event atom is defined as the smallest distinguishable unit of events in a sentence, which is achieved via LLM (detailed in [1]).

The entailment score measures the valuable event information between predicted summary and reference summary. The precision of the entailment score between a predicted node summary $\hat{s}_i$ and a reference node summary s_j is calculated as::

$$ent_p(\hat{s}_i, s_j) = \frac{1}{|\hat{\mathcal{E}}_i|} \sum_{\hat{\mathcal{E}}_{i,s} \in \hat{\mathcal{E}}_i} Entail(\mathcal{E}_j, \hat{\mathcal{E}}_{i,s})$$

$\hat{\mathcal{E}}_i$ and $\mathcal{E}_j$ are their event atoms. Similarly, we can compute the recall of entailment score, and the F1 score of entailment score by:

$$ent_{f1} = 2 * (\frac{ent_p * ent_r}{ent_p + ent_r})$$

Informativeness. Informativeness score measures how effectively a timeline's node summaries capture essential event information without redundancy or omissions, ensuring key events are included at correct timestamps. It is calculated by:

$$InfoScore(\hat{S}_i, S_j) = \delta_{\hat{t}_i, t_j} * ent_{f1}(\hat{S}_i, S_j)$$

The temporal interval penalty $\delta_{\hat{t}_i, t_j}$ is defined as:

$$\delta_{\hat{t}_i, t_j} = \frac{1}{|\hat{t}_i - t_j|^2 + 1}$$

Granular Consistency. Granular consistency score assesses whether the timeline's granularity (degree of omission between adjacent nodes) matches the required level (e.g., G10 or G5), viewing timelines as edges. It involves treating adjacent predicted nodes as edges $\hat{e}_m = (\hat{S}_m, \hat{S}_{m+1})$, computing a mapping cost based on the sum of $InfoScores$ for paired nodes by:

$$map(\hat{e}_m \rightarrow e_n) = -InfoScore(\hat{S}_m, S_n) - InfoScore(\hat{s}_{m+1}, S_{n+1})$$

then applying the Hungarian algorithm [7] to compute the optimal edge mapping M, and calculating the ratio of mapped edges aligning with the target granularity G:

$$Granu_i(\hat{S}) = \frac{1}{|E|} \sum_{(\hat{e}_m, e_n) \in M} [e_n \in E^G]$$

where $[\cdot]$ is a binary indicator function.

Factuality. Factuality score evaluates the faithfulness of summaries to source articles, checking for hallucinations [8,9] by verifying if node information traces back to references. It can be computed by:

$$Fact(\hat{S}) = \frac{1}{|\hat{S}|} \sum_{(\hat{s}_i, \hat{t}_i) \in \hat{S}} ent_p(\hat{s}_i, A_{\hat{t}_i})$$

where $\hat{t}_i$ is timestamp in the predicted node $\hat{S}_i$, and the reference articles $A_{\hat{t}_i}$ which are closest to the timestamp.

The final evaluation score is the average of the three metrics:

$$score(\hat{S}) = \frac{1}{3}(InfoScore + Granu + Fact)$$

3 Method

We first propose a rule-based method, focusing on generating summaries with high granular consistency and factuality. It involves a three-step process: (1) Articles are grouped according to granularity G based on predefined rules; (2) Event atoms are extracted and factuality is verified using an LLM; (3) Summaries are generated based on the constructed timeline.

Consider we must generate G timeline summarization to meet granularity requirement, our initial approach is to evenly partition articles into G groups. The first $G-1$ groups each contain $g = \lfloor \frac{N}{G} \rfloor$ articles, where N is the total number of input articles, with the remaining articles assigned to the last group. This rule-based grouping strategy effectively improves granular consistency and achieve decent score. However, it leads to a low informativeness score, as critical information is often unevenly distributed and may be omitted in some groups. Moreover, in groups with low informativeness, the LLM is more likely to generate inaccurate or unreliable content in an attempt to achieve higher informativeness scores. Additionally, as the input may include numerous irrelevant articles, a relevance-based filtering step is required. To generate the final summary, we identify three key stages: **cleaning and grouping**, **summarization**, and **factuality verification**.

Given the need to dynamically adjust cleaning and grouping strategies based on varying inputs, rule-based methods risk overlooking critical information or failing to preserve appropriate granularity (see Table 1). Moreover, our experiments reveal that while individual LLMs may not achieve optimal performance, they tend to capture different aspects of the input. To harness this diversity in representation, we design a multi-agent framework, inspired by [10], to collaboratively handle the cleaning and grouping stages.

Specifically, dedicated agents are employed to filter irrelevant articles and perform adaptive grouping. The query and granularity G are provided as inputs to the respective agents, ensuring that articles are not over-filtered and that all groups remain relevant to the query. The outputs from these agents, such as candidate articles for removal and preliminary groupings, are combined with the initial rule-based grouping and fed into a final coordination agent. This agent synthesizes the information to produce a refined cleaning strategy and an optimized grouping plan, ensuring both relevance to the query and balanced information distribution. Figure 2 illustrates the workflow of the multi-agent framework for the cleaning and grouping stages. The resulting cleaned and grouped articles are then used in subsequent summarization and factuality verification stages. For the summarization and factuality verification stages, we employ a single LLM to extract event atoms. A carefully designed prompt guides the extraction process, ensuring the preservation of informativeness. Each extracted event atom is then verified against the source text to confirm factual support; hallucinated or unsupported atoms are filtered out during this step.

Experimental results show that, although this multi-agent approach incurs higher computational overhead, it achieves a notable improvement in overall performance, particularly in informativeness, while maintaining high granular consistency and factuality.

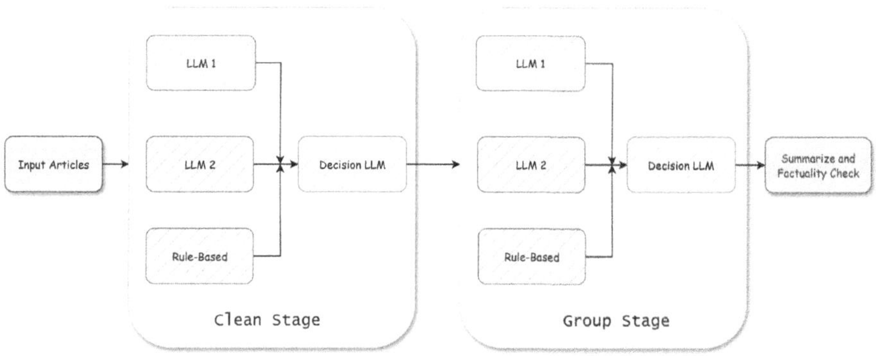

Fig. 2. Example of Multi-agent framework in clean and group stage. Note: The same LLM1, LLM2, and decision LLM are used in both the cleaning and grouping stages.

4 Experiments

4.1 Experimental Setup

To align with the linguistic nature of the DTELS-Bench dataset, our experiments are conducted using three large language models known for their strong Chinese capabilities: DeepSeek-R1-0528 [11], Qwen3-235B-A22B [12], and Kimi-K2 [13].

Rule-Based Method. In the *cleaning* stage, keywords are extracted from the query. An article is considered relevant if its topic contains any of these keywords. Additionally, to increase recall, we also examine the top-k most frequent words in each article, as they are likely to include query-related terms. Based on empirical analysis and sampling, we set $k = 300$ in our experiments. In the *grouping* stage, articles are evenly partitioned into G groups. Finally, event atoms are extracted using an LLM, and their factuality is verified against the source text.

Multi-agent Based Method. In the *cleaning* stage, two LLMs evaluate article relevance, and their judgments, combined with rule-based result, are aggregated by a decision agent to filter articles. In the *grouping* stage, two LLMs are used to assign articles into G groups based on topic coherence. We evaluate all pairwise combinations of the three Chinese LLMs. The grouping proposals from these models, along with the rule-based grouping, are integrated by the decision agent to produce the final grouping. For *summarization and factuality verification*, an LLM extracts event atoms from each group and verifies their factual consistency with the original articles; hallucinated or unsupported atoms are filtered out.

4.2 Result and Analysis

Table 1. Performance Comparison on DTELS-Bench

Method	Model	Informativeness	Granularity	Factuality	Score
Baseline [1]	/	0.02	0.99	0.37	0.46
Rule-based	DeepSeek-R1	0.08	0.99	0.97	0.68
	Qwen3-235B-A22B	0.08	0.99	0.95	0.67
	Kimi-K2	0.10	0.98	**1.00**	0.69
Multi-agent	Qwen3 + DeepSeek	0.18	0.95	0.94	0.69
	Qwen3 + Kimi	**0.20**	**0.99**	0.91	**0.70**
	DeepSeek + Kimi	0.17	0.97	0.90	0.68

Note: In the multi-agent approach, Qwen3 + DeepSeek indicates the use of Qwen3 and DeepSeek (denoted as LLM1 and LLM2 in Fig. 2) for the cleaning and grouping stages. Their outputs and rule-based results are integrated by a decision agent (Kimi-K2) to produce the final outcome for each stage. The final score is the average of informativeness, granular consistency, and factuality.

The evaluation shown in Table 1 compares the rule-based method with the multi-agent method, highlighting the effectiveness of the multi-agent structure in the DTELS task. The final scores of the different approaches are similar, with the combination of Qwen3-235B-A22B and Kimi-K2 achieving the best result: 0.20 in informativeness, 0.99 in granular consistency, and 0.91 in factuality. As shown, multi-agent methods improve informativeness by 0.10 – 0.12 points, with a minor decrease in factuality (0.03 – 0.10 points). This is because the multi-agent structure enhances information extraction capability, but as more information is generated, the likelihood of hallucination increases.

4.3 Ablation Study

To validate the necessity of both the rule-based component and the multi-agent design, we conduct ablation studies. Specifically, we compare our approach with the following variants: (1) a rule-based strategy for the cleaning and grouping stages, (2) a single LLM handling these stages, and (3) a multi-LLM setup—similar to a multi-agent framework but without rule-based components—applied to cleaning and grouping.

The results of the ablation study are presented in Table 2. As shown, the rule-based method achieves high scores in granular consistency and factuality, demonstrating strong reliability. In contrast, while the multi-LLM approach extracts more informative content, it also exhibits a higher tendency to generate hallucinated outputs. The single LLM variant performs the worst across metrics. These results highlight the complementary strengths of rule-based precision and multi-agent diversity, justifying our adoption of the multi-agent framework for the DTELS task.

Table 2. Ablation Study

Method	Informativeness	Granularity	Factuality	Score
Multi-agent	0.20	0.99	0.91	0.70
Rule-based	0.10	0.98	1.00	0.69
Single LLM	0.05	0.90	0.82	0.59
Multi-LLM	0.13	0.95	0.82	0.63

5 Conclusion

In this paper, we propose two solutions for the DTELS task, both achieving state-of-the-art performance on the DTELS-Bench dataset (Table 1). Our multi-agent approach notably improves the informativeness score by 0.10–0.12 points. Despite these advances, the DTELS task remains challenging, as existing methods often exhibit an imbalance among informativeness, granular consistency, and factuality. A high informativeness score may lead to increased hallucination, while low granularity can limit the amount of useful information extracted. In future work, we aim to refine the multi-agent framework to enhance event atom extraction, incorporating external knowledge bases to reduce hallucinations while maintaining factual accuracy and granular consistency.

References

1. Zhang, C., et al.: DTELS: towards dynamic granularity of timeline summarization (2024). arXiv preprint arXiv:2411.09297
2. https://github.com/chenlong-clock/DTELS-Bench
3. https://tianchi.aliyun.com/competition/entrance/532361/rankingList
4. Min, S., et al.:Factscore: fine-grained atomic evaluation of factual precision in long form text generation. arXiv preprint arXiv:2305.14251 (2023)
5. Setty, V.: Factcheck editor: Multilingual text editor with end-to-end fact-checking. In: Proceedings of the 47th International ACM SIGIR Conference on Research and Development in Information Retrieval, pp. 2744–2748 (2024)
6. Xu, J., et al.: Faithful logical reasoning via symbolic chain-of-thought (2024). arXiv preprint arXiv:2405.18357
7. Kuhn, H.W.: The Hungarian method for the assignment problem. Naval Res. Logistics Quarterly **2**(1–2), 83–97 (1955)
8. Chen, L., et al.: Beyond factuality: a comprehensive evaluation of large language models as knowledge generators (2023). arXiv preprint
9. Gekhman, Z., Herzig, J., Aharoni, R., Elkind, C., Szpektor, I.: Trueteacher: learning factual consistency evaluation with large language models (2023). arXiv preprint arXiv:2305.11171
10. Wang, J., Wang, J., Athiwaratkun, B., Zhang, C., Zou, J.: Mixture-of-agents enhances large language model capabilities. arXiv preprint arXiv:2406.04692 (2024)

11. Guo, D., et al.: Deepseek-r1: incentivizing reasoning capability in LLMs via reinforcement learning. arXiv preprint arXiv:2501.12948 (2025)
12. Yang, A., et al.: Qwen3 Technical report. arXiv preprint arXiv:2505.09388 (2025)
13. Team, K., et al.: Kimi k2: open agentic intelligence. arXiv preprint arXiv:2507.20534 (2025)

Advancing Grounded Multimodal NER via Self-reflective Prompt Refinement and Visual Noise Mitigation

Qiao Liang[1,2], Weixiang Zhou[2(✉)], Shijie Cao[1,2], Wenkai Zhang[2], and Jia Zheng[2]

[1] University of Chinese Academy of Sciences, Beijing, China
{liangqiao2022,caoshijie2025}@iscas.ac.cn
[2] Institute of Software, Chinese Academy of Sciences, Beijing, China
{weixiang,wenkai2019,zhengjia}@iscas.ac.cn

Abstract. Grounded Multimodal Named Entity Recognition (GMNER) aims to jointly identify named entities, their semantic types, and corresponding locations in images from text-image pairs. While Multimodal Large Language Models (MLLMs) show great potential for GMNER due to their ability to process visual and textual information simultaneously, their application faces two critical challenges: the difficulty of defining effective task-specific prompts for specialized domains and the visual noise interference that degrades recognition performance. To address these challenges, we propose Self-Reflective Prompt Refinement (SRPR) and a Multi-Model NER-VG Framework. SRPR leverages reasoning models to automatically optimize prompts through iterative self-reflection, while the multi-model framework separates textual entity recognition from visual grounding to mitigate visual noise interference. Our approach achieved first place in the CCKS 2025 evaluation with an F1 score of 65.78%, demonstrating its effectiveness for domain-specific applications.

Keywords: Grounded Multimodal Named Entity Recognition · Multimodal Large Language Models · Visual Grounding

1 Introduction

Grounded Multimodal Named Entity Recognition (GMNER) aims to jointly identify named entities, their semantic types, and their corresponding locations in images from text-image pairs. This task significantly enhances the multimodal service capability of entity recognition by not only leveraging visual information to improve NER performance but also grounding entities to specific regions in images. In military domains, where data increasingly appears in diverse multimodal forms such as satellite imagery and tactical documents, GMNER is crucial for automatically extracting key equipment entities and constructing comprehensive multimodal knowledge graphs.

J. Liang et al. (Eds.): CCKS 2025, CCIS 2698, pp. 263–273, 2026.
https://doi.org/10.1007/978-981-95-8525-0_21

Most prior GMNER work [5,6,13,15] builds upon Multimodal Named Entity Recognition (MNER) by adding visual grounding capabilities. MNER methods [7,8,12,14,16] primarily employ sequence-labeling approaches with models such as BERT and Bi-LSTM as backbone structures, focusing on fusing visual and textual modalities to improve NER performance. Some studies [4,9] further incorporate external knowledge as auxiliary information. GMNER methods typically extend these MNER approaches by integrating an additional visual grounding module to predict bounding boxes for entities in images.

Recent advances in Multimodal Large Language Models (MLLMs) have demonstrated powerful capabilities in simultaneously processing visual and textual information, while possessing rich world knowledge that makes them naturally well-suited for GMNER tasks. However, leveraging MLLMs for GMNER presents two critical challenges. First, the prompt optimization challenge: while LLMs demonstrate high sensitivity to prompt design for specific tasks [10,11,17], defining and optimizing task-specific prompts manually is extremely difficult and time-consuming, particularly in specialized domains like military applications where domain expertise is crucial. Second, the visual noise problem: images often contain substantial visual elements unrelated to the textual content, which we term visual noise [16]. Traditional approaches that fuse visual and textual features inevitably suffer from interference by these irrelevant visual elements, leading to degraded entity recognition performance.

To address the challenges of prompt optimization and visual noise interference, we propose two key innovations: Self-Reflective Prompt Refinement (SRPR) and a Multi-Model NER-VG Framework. The SRPR method leverages the reasoning capabilities of thinking models to automatically generate and iteratively optimize task-specific prompts by analyzing failure cases. The Multi-Model NER-VG Framework separates textual entity recognition from visual grounding, mitigating the negative impact of visual noise by processing pure text for NER in the first stage, then using MLLMs to verify entity presence and predict locations in the second stage.

Our method achieved first place in the CCKS 2025 evaluation with an F1 score of 65.78%, demonstrating its effectiveness and practical value. The approach is entirely training-free, making it readily applicable to specialized domains with limited annotated data.

The main contributions are:

- We propose Self-Reflective Prompt Refinement (SRPR), which leverages reasoning models to automatically optimize task-specific prompts through iterative self-analysis.
- We introduce a Multi-Model NER-VG Framework that mitigates visual noise interference by separating textual entity recognition from visual grounding.
- Our training-free approach achieves state-of-the-art performance, ranking first in CCKS 2025 with 65.78% F1 score, demonstrating practical value for specialized domains.

2 Related Works

Multimodal Named Entity Recognition (MNER) was first introduced by Moon et al. [8] to enhance NER performance by incorporating visual information. Existing MNER approaches can be broadly categorized into modality fusion methods and external knowledge integration methods. The former focuses on effectively combining textual and visual information. Moon et al. [8] fuse word embeddings, character embeddings, and visual features via modality attention with Bi-LSTM+CRF decoder. Lu et al. [7] compute correlations between image region features and text tokens to obtain weighted visual representations. Yu et al. [14] propose a Unified Multimodal Transformer that addresses visual context insensitivity and mitigates visual biases. Zhang et al. [16] develop UMGF framework for fine-grained semantic alignment while reducing visual noise, and Sun et al. [12] explicitly model text-image correlations for selective visual information incorporation. The latter category incorporates additional knowledge sources, where Ok et al. [9] retrieve Wikipedia knowledge for candidate entities, and Li et al. [4] leverage ChatGPT as an implicit knowledge base.

Grounded Multimodal Named Entity Recognition (GMNER) extends MNER by adding visual grounding capabilities. Yu et al. [15] first formalized this task, targeting the recognition of named entities and their types from text-image pairs while grounding entities to specific image regions. Their hierarchical index generation framework (H-Index) uses a pretrained BART model to hierarchically generate entity-type-region triplets. Li et al. [6] address data scarcity through data augmentation, synthesizing texts via improved InstructBLIP [2] and generating images using latent diffusion models. Li et al. [5] reformulate GMNER as a joint task integrating entity expansion, visual entailment, visual grounding, and entity grounding. Tang et al. [13] introduce learnable queries that explicitly align textual entities with visual regions, reframing GMNER as a set prediction problem through their Query-guided Fusion Network (QFNet).

Different from prior GMNER approaches that rely on modality fusion and sequence labeling, our work leverages MLLMs' in-context learning abilities, object detection capabilities, and extensive domain knowledge. This allows us to achieve accurate, training-free GMNER without relying on task-specific fine-tuning.

3 Preliminaries

In this evaluation task, the goal is to identify the *name*, *category*, and *location* of entities based on given multimodal military-domain data. Formally, we are provided with a dataset of image-text pairs:

$$D = \{(I_1, T_1), (I_2, T_2), \dots, (I_n, T_n)\},$$

where T_i denotes the i-th text sample in the military domain, I_i denotes the corresponding associated image, and n is the total number of samples.

Task Definition . For each text-image pair (T_i, I_i), the task requires extracting all entity triplets in the form of $(name, label, bndbox)$. Here, *name* refers to the entity mention appearing in the text; *label* denotes the entity category, which must be one of the predefined types: `vehicle`, `aircraft`, `vessel`, `weapon`, `location`, or `other`; *bndbox* represents the bounding box of the entity in the image. If an entity appears only in the text and not in the image, *bndbox* is set to `null`; otherwise, it must contain the coordinates $(xmin, xmax, ymin, ymax)$, indicating the minimum and maximum values along the x and y axes, respectively.

Evaluation Protocol . The evaluation consists of three aspects: **entity**, **type**, and **visual region**, as detailed in Table 1. Entity and type correctness are assessed by exact matching: a predicted entity is counted as correct only if both its *name* and *label* exactly match the ground truth. The correctness of the visual region is determined as follows: if an entity does not appear in the image, the prediction is correct only when *bndbox* is `null`; if the entity can be located in the image, the predicted bounding box is correct if its Intersection-over-Union (IoU) with the ground-truth annotation exceeds 0.5.

The final correctness of each prediction requires all three criteria to be satisfied:

$$\text{correct} = \begin{cases} 1, & \text{if } C_e \wedge C_t \wedge C_r, \\ 0, & \text{otherwise.} \end{cases}$$

where C_e denotes entity correctness, C_t denotes type correctness, and C_r denotes region correctness. This evaluation protocol ensures that both textual and visual grounding are jointly assessed.

Table 1. Evaluation criteria for the GMNER task.

Aspect	Correctness Criterion
Entity (C_e)	The predicted entity name must exactly match the ground truth entity mention.
Type (C_t)	The predicted entity category must exactly match the ground truth label (one of `vehicle`, `aircraft`, `vessel`, `weapon`, `location`, `other`).
Visual Region (C_r)	If the entity does not appear in the image, the prediction must output `null`; otherwise, the predicted bounding box is correct if its Intersection-over-Union (IoU) with the ground-truth annotation exceeds 0.5.

4 Method

To address the challenges of defining task-specific prompts and mitigating the impact of visual noise on recognition results, we propose two key components: self-reflective prompt refinement and a multi-model collaborative system. We detail both components in the following sections.

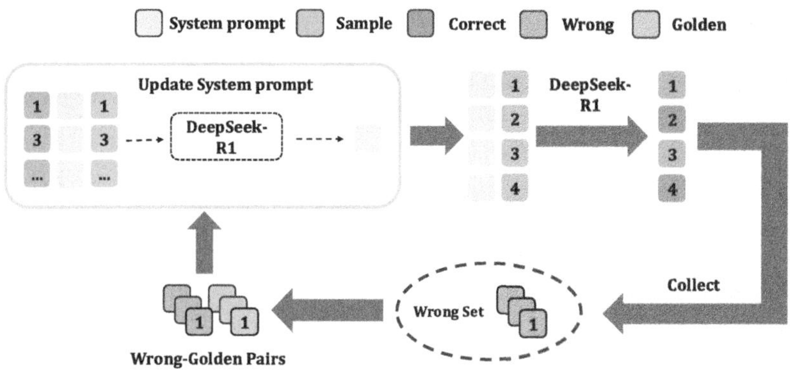

Fig. 1. Illustration of Self-Reflective Prompt Refinement (SRPR)

4.1 Self-reflective Prompt Refinement (SRPR)

LLM performance on specific tasks is highly sensitive to prompt design [10,11,17], yet task-specific prompts are difficult to optimize manually. To address this challenge, we leverage the reasoning capabilities of thinking models themselves to define and optimize prompts through a systematic iterative framework.

Our iterative prompt optimization process can be formalized as:

$$\text{System Prompt}_{i+1} = \mathcal{F}(\text{System Prompt}_i, \text{Error Samples}_i, \text{Golden Answers}_i)$$

where $\mathcal{F}$ represents the operation of instructing DeepSeek-R1 [3] to analyze the current system prompt, error samples, and their corresponding golden answers to generate an improved prompt.

Specifically, we first provide DeepSeek-R1 with the definition of the military GMNER task and instruct it to generate an initial prompt based on this task definition (round 0). We then test this initial prompt on the validation set and collect all samples where the results are incorrect. Next, we provide DeepSeek-R1 with the current prompt, the wrong samples, and their corresponding golden samples, allowing it to analyze the causes of errors and improve the prompt iteratively until the provided wrong samples can be answered correctly in testing, yielding the next iteration prompt. We repeat this iterative process, and after three rounds, we obtain the optimal NER prompt. The detailed workflow is illustrated in Fig. 1.

4.2 Multi-model NER-VG Framework

In GMNER tasks, images contain numerous visual elements unrelated to the text, known as visual noise. Previous methods typically fuse textual and visual features as the basis for NER, inevitably being affected by visual noise. To solve

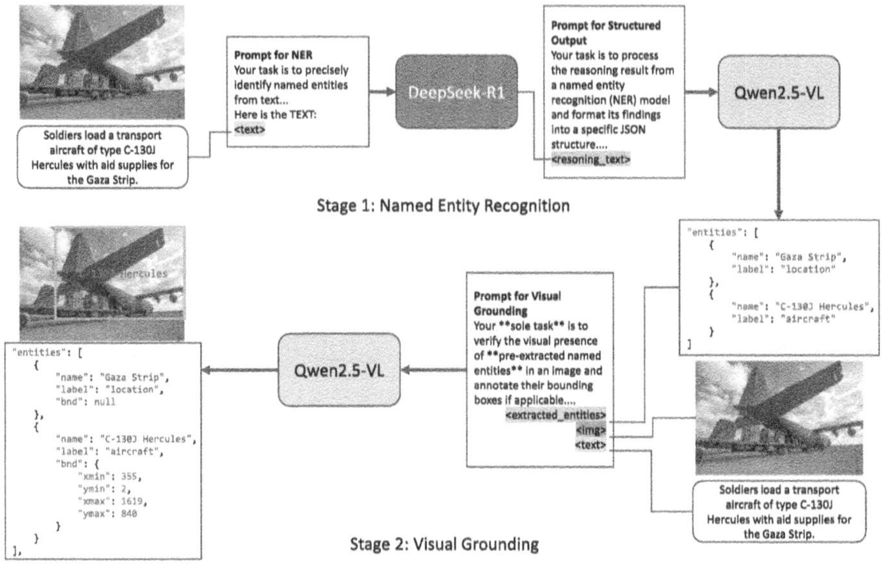

Fig. 2. Illustration of Multi-Model NER-VG Framework

this problem, we decouple the textual and visual tasks of GMNER, dividing it into two stages: NER and VG (Visual Grounding). In the first NER stage, we primarily use DeepSeek-R1 [3] to perform NER on pure text without introducing any visual information. In the second VG stage, we prompt Qwen2.5-VL [1] to verify whether the previously identified entities exist in the image, and if so, predict the location of these entities in the image. The detailed workflow is shown in Fig. 2.

5 Experiment

5.1 Experiment Setup

Baselines and Data. To evaluate the effectiveness of our method, we choose YOLOv5 and Qwen2.5-VL-72B-AWQ as our baselines to compare the visual grounding and NER ability perspectively. The YOLOv5 only used for object detection tasks, we only compare the IoU metric. The Qwen2.5-VL-72B-AWQ is choosed as a integrated MLLM for GMNER task, which demonstrate the advantages of our method. We use the validation set to update our system prompt.

Implementation Details. The Qwen2.5 series models are deployed locally by using vllm with 4 A100 80G GPUs. Other models are used by accessing the API provided by SiliconFlow. The temperature parameter of all models are setting to 0.

5.2 Main Results

Table 2 reports the performance of baselines and our method (SRPR) on both the validation and evaluation sets. Compared to YOLOv5 and Q-72B-AWQ, SRPR consistently achieves higher F1 scores across all rounds. On the validation set, SRPR reaches its best performance at round 2 with an F1 of 0.79, showing clear improvement over round 1.

However, additional updates (round 3) slightly reduce recall, indicating that too many rounds may lead to diminishing returns. On the final evaluation set, SRPR shows a different trend: performance drops at round 2, but improves again at round 3, achieving the highest F1 of 0.6578. We attribute this fluctuation to potential overfitting of the system prompt when the number of updates is not well balanced.

Table 2. Main Results. Q stands for Qwen2.5-VL [1]. AWQ means the quantization version.

Models	Round	F1	Precision	Recall
Baselines				
YOLOv5	-	0.37	0.35	0.38
Q-72B-AWQ	-	0.37	0.29	0.53
Validation Set				
SRPR+DS-R1+Q-72B-Ins	round 1	0.69	0.68	0.7
	round 2	**0.79**	0.78	**0.79**
	round 3	0.78	**0.8**	0.76
Evaluation Set				
SRPR+DS-R1+Q-72B-Ins	round 1	0.6407	0.6299	0.6518
	round 2	0.5957	0.6016	0.5899
	round 3	**0.6578**	**0.6467**	**0.6692**

5.3 Ablation Study

In this section, we study the effectiveness of SRPR using Qwen2.5-VL-72B-AWQ as the base model, and further analyze the impact of quantization and model size.

Effectiveness of SRPR. From Table 3, we observe that applying SRPR on Qwen2.5-VL-72B-AWQ leads to continuous improvements across rounds. Specifically, F1 increases from 0.37 in round 1 to 0.48 in round 2, and finally to 0.50 in round 3, accompanied by consistent gains in both precision and recall. This trend demonstrates that the proposed iterative refinement strategy effectively improves model performance. The results also indicate that SRPR is robust and can be applied on top of a strong base model with consistent benefits.

Influence Factors. To further understand the role of quantization and model size, we compare Qwen2.5-VL-72B-AWQ with its full-precision counterparts Qwen2.5-VL-32B-Instruct and Qwen2.5-VL-72B-Instruct, using the same system prompt from the SRPR round-3 experiment. As shown in Table 3, quantization has a negative impact on performance: the quantized Q-72B-AWQ achieves an F1 of 0.50, whereas its full-precision 72B-Instruct counterpart reaches the best score of 0.63. Moreover, increasing the model size also yields performance gains: Q-32B-Instruct attains 0.52 F1, while Q-72B-Instruct further improves to 0.63.

Table 3. Ablation Results

Models	Round	F1	Precision	Recall
SRPR + Q-72B-AWQ	round 1	0.37	0.29	0.53
	round 2	0.48	0.42	0.55
	round 3	0.50	0.44	0.58
Q-72B-AWQ	-	0.5	0.44	0.58
Q-32B-Ins	-	0.52	0.45	0.62
Q-72B-Ins	-	**0.63**	**0.61**	**0.66**

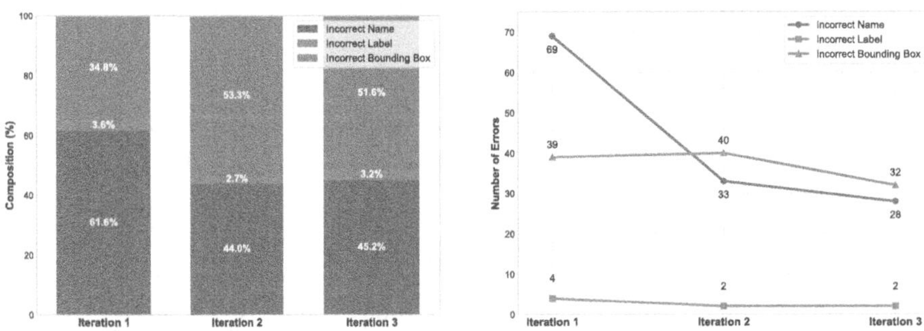

(a) Error Composition by Iteration (b) Error Trend Across Iterations

Fig. 3. A comprehensive analysis of error distribution and trends. Subfigure (a) displays the composition of errors, while subfigure (b) shows the trend of each error type over three iterations.

5.4 Error Analysis and Case Study

To conduct a more granular analysis of SRPR's efficacy on the GMNER task, an error categorization was performed. Errors were classified into three distinct types: incorrect names, labels, and bounding boxes. The findings, presented in Fig. 3, demonstrate a significant reduction in the number of incorrect names. Consequently, we identify the enhancement of the model's visual grounding capabilities as the principal remaining challenge.

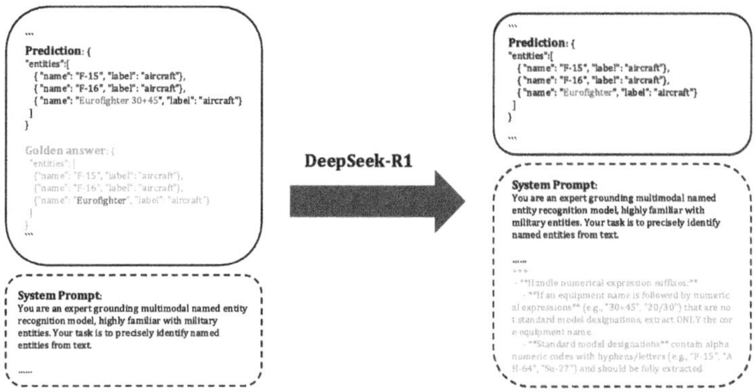

Fig. 4. Demonstration of Self-Reflective Prompt Refinement (SRPR)

We input the wrong predictions, the golden answers, and the original system prompt into DeepSeek-R1, leveraging its think mode to summarize a universal rule for correcting the wrong predictions. In the case of Fig. 4, DeepSeek-R1 initially recognized "Eurofighter 30+45" as the entity name, while SRPR corrected the answer by introducing an extra rule for handling numerical expression suffixes.

6 Conclusion

This paper presents a novel approach for Grounded Multimodal Named Entity Recognition (GMNER) that addresses two critical challenges: the difficulty of defining task-specific prompts for specialized domains and visual noise interference. We introduce Self-Reflective Prompt Refinement (SRPR), which leverages reasoning models to automatically optimize prompts through iterative self-analysis of failure cases, eliminating the need for manual prompt engineering. Additionally, our Multi-Model NER-VG Framework decouples textual entity recognition from visual grounding, effectively mitigating the negative impact of visual noise by processing pure text for NER before verifying entity presence and locations in images. Our approach achieved first place with an F1 score of 65.78% in the CCKS 2025 evaluation.

References

1. Bai, S., et al.: Qwen2.5-VL Technical report. arXiv preprint arXiv:2502.13923 (2025)
2. Dai, W., et al.: Instructblip: towards general-purpose vision-language models with instruction tuning (2023). https://arxiv.org/abs/2305.06500
3. DeepSeek-AI: Deepseek-r1: incentivizing reasoning capability in LLMs via reinforcement learning (2025). https://arxiv.org/abs/2501.12948

4. Li, J., et al.: Prompting ChatGPT in MNER: enhanced multimodal named entity recognition with auxiliary refined knowledge. In: Bouamor, H., Pino, J., Bali, K. (eds.) Findings of the Association for Computational Linguistics: EMNLP 2023, pp. 2787–2802. Association for Computational Linguistics, Singapore (Dec 2023). https://doi.org/10.18653/v1/2023.findings-emnlp.184
5. Li, J., et al.: LLMs as bridges: reformulating grounded multimodal named entity recognition. In: Ku, L.W., Martins, A., Srikumar, V. (eds.) Findings of the Association for Computational Linguistics: ACL 2024, pp. 1302–1318. Association for Computational Linguistics, Bangkok, Thailand (2024). https://doi.org/10.18653/v1/2024.findings-acl.76
6. Li, Z., Yu, J., Yang, J., Wang, W., Yang, L., Xia, R.: Generative multimodal data augmentation for low-resource multimodal named entity recognition. In: Proceedings of the 32nd ACM International Conference on Multimedia, pp. 7336–7345. MM '24, Association for Computing Machinery, New York, NY, USA (2024). https://doi.org/10.1145/3664647.3681598
7. Lu, D., Neves, L., Carvalho, V., Zhang, N., Ji, H.: Visual attention model for name tagging in multimodal social media. In: Gurevych, I., Miyao, Y. (eds.) Proceedings of the 56th Annual Meeting of the Association for Computational Linguistics (Volume 1: Long Papers), pp. 1990–1999. Association for Computational Linguistics, Melbourne, Australia (2018). https://doi.org/10.18653/v1/P18-1185
8. Moon, S., Neves, L., Carvalho, V.: Multimodal named entity recognition for short social media posts. In: Walker, M., Ji, H., Stent, A. (eds.) Proceedings of the 2018 Conference of the North American Chapter of the Association for Computational Linguistics: Human Language Technologies, Volume 1 (Long Papers), pp. 852–860. Association for Computational Linguistics, New Orleans, Louisiana (2018). https://doi.org/10.18653/v1/N18-1078
9. Ok, H., Kil, T., Seo, S., Lee, J.: SCANNER: knowledge-enhanced approach for robust multi-modal named entity recognition of unseen entities. In: Duh, K., Gomez, H., Bethard, S. (eds.) Proceedings of the 2024 Conference of the North American Chapter of the Association for Computational Linguistics: Human Language Technologies (Volume 1: Long Papers), pp. 7725–7737. Association for Computational Linguistics, Mexico City, Mexico (2024). https://doi.org/10.18653/v1/2024.naacl-long.427
10. Razavi, A., Soltangheis, M., Arabzadeh, N., Salamat, S., Zihayat, M., Bagheri, E.: Benchmarking prompt sensitivity in large language models (2025). https://arxiv.org/abs/2502.06065
11. Sclar, M., Choi, Y., Tsvetkov, Y., Suhr, A.: Quantifying language models' sensitivity to spurious features in prompt design or: how i learned to start worrying about prompt formatting (2024). https://arxiv.org/abs/2310.11324
12. Sun, L., Wang, J., Zhang, K., Su, Y., Weng, F.: Rpbert: a text-image relation propagation-based Bert model for multimodal NER. Proc. AAAI Conf. Artif. Intell. **35**(15), 13860–13868 (2021)
13. Tang, J., Wang, Z., Gong, Z., Yu, J., Zhu, X., Yin, J.: Multi-grained query-guided set prediction network for grounded multimodal named entity recognition. In: Proceedings of the Thirty-Ninth AAAI Conference on Artificial Intelligence and Thirty-Seventh Conference on Innovative Applications of Artificial Intelligence and Fifteenth Symposium on Educational Advances in Artificial Intelligence. AAAI'25/IAAI'25/EAAI'25, AAAI Press (2025). https://doi.org/10.1609/aaai.v39i24.34711

14. Yu, J., Jiang, J., Yang, L., Xia, R.: Improving multimodal named entity recognition via entity span detection with unified multimodal transformer. In: Jurafsky, D., Chai, J., Schluter, N., Tetreault, J. (eds.) Proceedings of the 58th Annual Meeting of the Association for Computational Linguistics, pp. 3342–3352. Association for Computational Linguistics, Online (2020). https://doi.org/10.18653/v1/2020.acl-main.306
15. Yu, J., Li, Z., Wang, J., Xia, R.: Grounded multimodal named entity recognition on social media. In: Rogers, A., Boyd-Graber, J., Okazaki, N. (eds.) Proceedings of the 61st Annual Meeting of the Association for Computational Linguistics (Volume 1: Long Papers), pp. 9141–9154. Association for Computational Linguistics, Toronto, Canada (2023). https://doi.org/10.18653/v1/2023.acl-long.508
16. Zhang, D., Wei, S., Li, S., Wu, H., Zhu, Q., Zhou, G.: Multi-modal graph fusion for named entity recognition with targeted visual guidance. In: Proceeding AAAI Conference Artificial Intelligence, vol .35, no. 16, pp. 14347–14355 (2021)
17. Zhuo, J., Zhang, S., Fang, X., Duan, H., Lin, D., Chen, K.: Prosa: assessing and understanding the prompt sensitivity of LLMs (2024). https://arxiv.org/abs/2410.12405

ReFineG: Synergizing Small Supervised Models and LLMs for Low-Resource Grounded Multimodal NER

Jielong Tang[1,2], Shuang Wang[3], Zhenxing Wang[4], Jianxing Yu[1,2], and Jian Yin[1,2(✉)]

[1] School of Artificial Intelligence, Sun Yat-sen University, Guangzhou, China
tangjlong3@mail2.sysu.edu.cn

[2] Key Laboratory of Sustainable Tourism Smart Assessment Technology, Ministry of Culture and Tourism, Sun Yat-sen University, Guangzhou, China
issjyin@mail.sysu.edu.cn

[3] Beijing Normal University, Beijing, China

[4] Institute of Software, Chinese Academy of Sciences, Beijing, China

Abstract. Grounded Multimodal Named Entity Recognition (GMNER) extends traditional NER by jointly detecting textual mentions and grounding them to visual regions. While existing supervised methods achieve strong performance, they rely on costly multimodal annotations and often underperform in low-resource domains. Multimodal Large Language Models (MLLMs) show strong generalization but suffer from Domain Knowledge Conflict, producing redundant or incorrect mentions for domain-specific entities. To address these challenges, we propose t**R**aining-r**EFINE**ment-**G**rounding (**ReFineG**), a three-stage collaborative framework that integrates small supervised models with frozen MLLMs for low-resource GMNER. In the Training Stage, a domain-aware NER data synthesis strategy transfers LLM knowledge to small models with supervised training while avoiding domain knowledge conflicts. In the Refinement Stage, an uncertainty-based mechanism retains confident predictions from supervised models and delegates uncertain ones to the MLLM. In the Grounding Stage, a multimodal context selection algorithm enhances visual grounding through analogical reasoning. In the CCKS2025 GMNER Shared Task, ReFineG ranked second with an F1 score of 0.6461 on the online leaderboard, demonstrating its effectiveness with limited annotations. The code and data will be available at https://github.com/tangjielong928/ReFineG.

Keywords: Multimodal Named Entity Recognition · MLLMs

1 Introduction

Grounded Multimodal Named Entity Recognition (GMNER) is an emerging information extraction task that aims to jointly identify entity mentions of predefined types and their corresponding visual regions from text–image pairs. It

J. Tang, S. Wang and Z. Wang—These authors contributed equally.

J. Liang et al. (Eds.): CCKS 2025, CCIS 2698, pp. 274–286, 2026.
https://doi.org/10.1007/978-981-95-8525-0_22

has broad applications in domains such as multimodal knowledge graph construction [17], visual question answering [9], etc. However, existing multimodal NER datasets (e.g., Twitter-15 [23], Twitter-17 [13]) lack explicit visual entity annotations, making it difficult to align textual entities with visual regions. To bridge this research gap, Yu et al. [21] extended these datasets with extensive fine-grained annotations of visual entities and proposed a new GMNER benchmark. Building upon this foundation, a variety of supervised approaches have since been introduced, including sequence generation [16,21], set matching [15], sequence labeling [10], and knowledge-enhanced models [14].

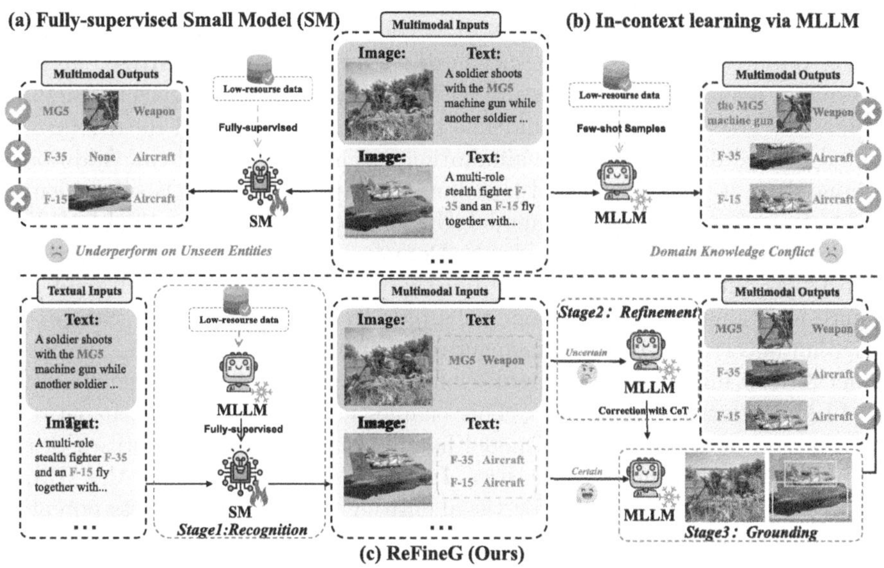

Fig. 1. The comparison of existing approaches and our **ReFineG**.

Despite their effectiveness, these methods typically rely on large-scale training data, which limits their applications to real-world scenarios. In vertical domains such as military and medical, multimodal annotations, especially for visual entities, require strong domain expertise, making large-scale labeling costly and impractical. As shown in Fig. 1 (a), fully supervised methods often underfit in low-resource military domain, failing to recognize **Unseen Entities**, such as the visual regions of F-35 and F-15. With the rapid advances in multimodal pretraining and model scaling, multimodal large language models (MLLMs) have demonstrated extensive knowledge and strong visual generalization capabilities, making them promising solutions in low-resource settings. However, directly applying MLLMs to GMNER task remains challenging, as their generic knowledge often conflicts with domain-specific knowledge—a phenomenon we term **Domain Knowledge Conflict**. This issue typically arises in textual entity recognition. As illustrated in Fig. 1 (b), in a military dataset,

MLLMs will produce redundant generic mentions for textual entity (e.g., "the MG5 machine gun"). Such intrinsic discrepancies in knowledge understanding are difficult to resolve through a simple prompt design [3]. In contrast, these domain-specific knowledge can be effectively captured by supervised models when data is sufficient. Considering that fine-tuning an MLLM still requires substantial computational resources, we pose the question: *Can small-scale supervised models be leveraged to resolve Domain Knowledge Conflict in textual entities, while MLLMs/LLMs contribute their knowledge and generalization ability to tackle unseen entities in low-resource settings?*

To this end, as shown in Fig. 1 (c), we propose a three-stage collaborative framework, t**R**aining-r**EFINE**ment-**G**rounding (**ReFineG**), where the small supervised model and the freezing MLLM complement each other's capabilities for low-resource GMNER task. Specifically, **in the Training Stage**, we first introduce a domain knowledge-aware NER data synthesis strategy. This method maintains a global annotation guideline table, allowing the LLM to traverse the limited labeled data, summarize annotation details, and store them. Additional training data are then generated based on this guideline, which is subsequently used to train a small supervised model. Unlike directly prompting the LLM with the guideline, this approach avoids the Domain Knowledge Conflict that arises when LLMs output textual entities directly, while enabling the small model to acquire additional knowledge from the LLM. **In the Refinement Stage**, we design an uncertainty-based refinement mechanism, where the small supervised model retains high-confidence predictions and passes uncertain predictions to the LLM for further refinement. This enables effective collaboration between the two models: the supervised model handles domain-informed entities, while the LLM focuses on uncertain entities. **In the Grounding Stage**, the MLLM leverages textual entity results for visual entity grounding. To address potential Domain Knowledge Conflict, we propose a multimodal in-context sample selection algorithm, which selects the most appropriate in-context examples from entity, sentence, and image levels. This enhances the MLLM's ability to perform visual analogical reasoning using similar examples, thereby improving the accuracy of visual entity grounding.

Our contributions are summarized as follows: (1) We identify the challenges of low-resource GMNER task, highlighting both the Domain Knowledge Conflict in MLLMs and the underfitting of small supervised models. (2) We propose **ReFineG**, a three-stage collaborative framework that effectively integrates small supervised models with frozen MLLMs to overcome these limitations. (3) Extensive experiments demonstrate the effectiveness of our approach, ranking second place on the CCKS2025 GMNER Shared Task.

2 Related Work

Unlike prior multimodal NER studies [13,23] that focus only on textual mentions, GMNER seeks to extract multimodal entity information, including entity mention, type, and corresponding visual region from text–image pairs. Existing methods, including sequence labeling [10], sequence generation [16,21], and set-matching [15], predict mention–type–region triplets by fine-tuning Transformer-based models [2,8] on large annotated GMNER datasets. While effective, they perform poorly in low-resource domains, where alignment between text and visual regions often suffers underfitting. Some works have explored knowledge enhancement, such as web retrieval [14,18], LLMs [10,19], and multimodal data augmentation [11]. However, retrieved and augmented data usually introduces noise, while domain-specific inconsistencies in LLMs often lead to redundant or inaccurate mentions. In contrast, our ReFineG framework combines small supervised models with frozen MLLMs to address annotation scarcity and domain knowledge conflicts in GMNER.

3 ReFineG Framework

Task Definition. Given a text sequence T and its paired image I, the GMNER task requires predicting a set of triplets $\{(e_k, c_k, r_k)\}_{k=1}^{N}$, where e_k is the k-th entity mention, c_k denotes its entity category, and r_k corresponds to the 4D bounding box of the entity in I. If the entity is absent from the image, r_k is set to `None`.

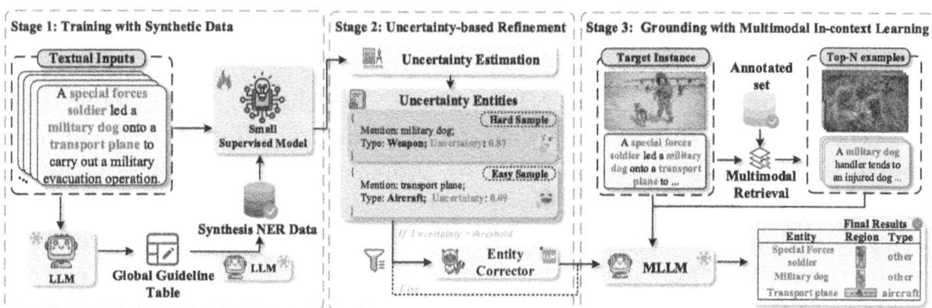

Fig. 2. The overall framework of our **ReFineG**.

Overall Workflow. As illustrated in Fig. 2, our ReFineG framework consists of three stages. (1) *Training Stage:* we first introduce a domain knowledge-aware NER data synthesis strategy, which maintains a global schema guideline. The LLM traverses the limited labeled data to summarize schema details and stores them in a guideline table. Additional training samples are then generated based on this guideline, which are used to train a supervised sequence labeling model. (2) *Refinement Stage:* the small supervised model is first applied to directly infer test samples. An uncertainty-based refinement mechanism allows the model to retain high-confidence predictions while passing uncertain cases to the LLM for further correction. The final textual NER output integrates results from both models. (3) *Grounding Stage:* the integrated textual predictions are fed into an MLLM acting as an entity region detector. To address potential domain knowledge gaps, a multimodal in-context selection algorithm selects the most relevant top-N examples, which are then combined with the multimodal input for few-shot visual entity grounding.

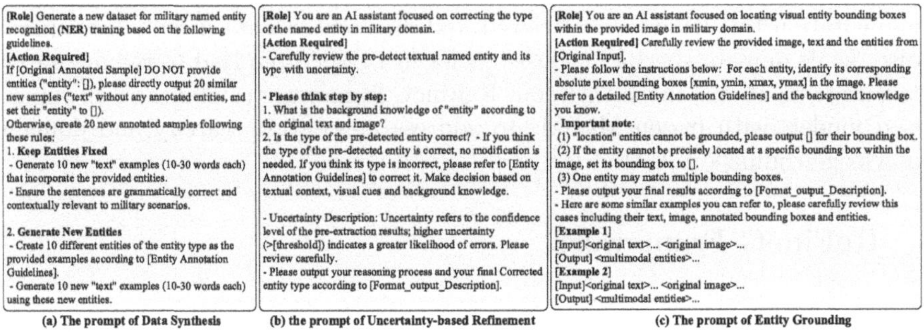

Fig. 3. The prompt details designed for data synthesis, refinement, and entity grounding.

3.1 Stage 1: Training with Synthetic Data

Domain Knowledge-aware NER Data Synthesis. Prior supervised approaches heavily rely on large-scale annotations and often degrade in low-resource settings. To mitigate this, we propose Domain Knowledge-aware NER Data Synthesis. Given a low-resource multimodal annotated set $\mathcal{D} = \{(s_i; e_i; v_i)\}_{i=1}^{|\mathcal{D}|}$, where s_i denotes a sentence, e_i is labeled entities, and v_i indicate the corresponding image with annotated bounding boxes, we construct domain-specific schema guidelines. Specifically, we maintain a global guideline table $\mathcal{G} = \{Typ.; Des.; Neg.\}$, where $Typ.$ indicates the entity schema, $Des.$ provides its schema description, and $Neg.$ includes LLM-generated negative sample descriptions to guide boundary cases. $\mathcal{G}$ is dynamically updated by prompting an LLM to traverse the limited annotations in $\mathcal{D}$. We formulate it as following:

Update $\{Neg.\}$: Given $\{\mathcal{G}\}$ and $\{s_i\}$, provide your NER results. Compare them with $\{e_i\}$, analyze error samples and update $\{Neg.\}$.
Update $\{Des.\}$: Given $\{\mathcal{G}\}$ and $\{(s_i; e_i)\}$, analyze the guideline of $\{e_i\}$ carefully. Update $\{Des.\}$ accordingly.

After constructing $\mathcal{G}$, we adopt it as the guideline for prompting the LLM (as shown in Fig. 3 (a)) and design two data synthesis strategies: (1) *Entity-level Substitution*, where new entity mentions consistent with $\mathcal{G}$ are injected while preserving the original semantics and structure; (2) *Sentence-level Paraphrasing*, where sentences are rephrased with contextual variations while keeping entity mentions unchanged. Finally, we obtain the synthesized dataset $\mathcal{D}^* = \{(s_i^*; e_i^*)\}_{i=1}^{|\mathcal{D}^*|}$

Named Entity Recognition Training. Han et al. [3] have shown that in-context learning paradigm often fails to deliver satisfactory NER results, primarily because the limited input length of LLMs restricts access to sufficient domain knowledge. To mitigate domain knowledge conflicts, we further train a small supervised model on the synthesized data. We first obtain representations of the input text sequence, $\{w_1, \ldots, w_n\}$, by feeding it into a Transformer-based encoder. A subsequent linear-chain Conditional Random Field (CRF) [7] layer is then applied to predict the target label sequence $y = \{y_1, \ldots, y_n\}$:

$$P(y|s^*) = \frac{\prod_{i=1}^{n} \psi(y_{i-1}, y_i, w_i)}{\sum_{y' \in C} \prod_{i=1}^{n} \psi(y'_{i-1}, y'_i, w_i)} \tag{1}$$

where ψ denotes the potential function, and C represents the set of all possible label sequences. The negative log-likelihood (NLL) loss is used for final training:

$$\mathcal{L}(\theta) = -\log P_\theta(\boldsymbol{e}^*|s^*) \tag{2}$$

3.2 Stage 2: Uncertainty-Based Refinement

Due to the limited generalization of the small supervised model, it inevitably produces errors, especially for entities unseen in the training set. To mitigate this, we design an uncertainty-based refinement mechanism. Given the trained small supervised model, the token-level entropy are computed as:

$$\text{Entropy}(w_i) = \sum_{c \in C} -P(y_i = c|T) \log P(y_i = c|T) \tag{3}$$

Based on the above equation, we define the entity-level uncertainty[1] as:

$$\text{Uncertainty}(e_i) = \frac{\sum_{w_i \in e_i} \text{Entropy}(w_i)}{|e_i|} \tag{4}$$

where $|e_i|$ denotes the length of the entity mention e_i. Higher uncertainty indicates lower confidence of the small supervised model in its predictions. We set a threshold β (Uncertainty(e_i) $> \beta$) to filter highly uncertain predictions, which are then passed, along with the corresponding image, to the MLLM for refinement. In this work, β is set to 0.8. Additionally, we leverage chain-of-thought (CoT) [20] reasoning to guide the MLLM through step-by-step corrections. The prompt design of MLLM refinement is shown in Fig. 3 (b).

3.3 Stage 3: Grounding with Multimodal In-Context Learning

Considering the challenges of aligning fine-grained visual regions with entities under low-resource conditions, we employ in-context learning for MLLM to perform entity grounding. In-context examples provide MLLM with direct domain

[1] Maximum entropy arises when all token labels are equally likely, indicating the model's uncertainty [24].

knowledge, and the relevance between these examples and the target instance largely determines grounding performance [12]. To this end, we propose a *multi-modal in-context examples selection algorithm* to choose the most relevant examples for in-context learning. Given the limited annotated set $\mathcal{D} = \{(s_i; e_i; v_i)\}_{i=1}^{|\mathcal{D}|}$ and the refined output $\mathcal{R} = \{(s'_j; e'_j; v'_j)\}_{j=1}^{|\mathcal{R}|}$, where s'_j,e'_j, and v'_j denote the raw sentence, refined entities, and raw image, respectively, we compute similarity matrices at the entity, text, and image levels. Let $\mathcal{M}_{text}$ and $\mathcal{M}_{image}$ represent the pre-trained encoders for the textual and visual modalities, respectively.

Entity-Level Similarity Matrix. For entities e_i from annotated set and e'_j from refined output, we define a type-aware entity similarity matrix as:

$$\mathbf{S}_{\text{entity}}(i,j) = \frac{\mathbf{H}_E^{\mathcal{D}}\left(\mathbf{H}_E^{\mathcal{R}}\right)^\top}{||\mathbf{H}_E^{\mathcal{D}}||_2||\mathbf{H}_E^{\mathcal{R}}||_2} + \delta\mathbf{M}, \quad \mathbf{H}_E^{\mathcal{D}} = \mathcal{M}_{text}(e_i),\ \mathbf{H}_E^{\mathcal{R}} = \mathcal{M}_{text}(e'_j). \quad (5)$$

where $\mathbf{M}_{i,j} = 1$ if Type(e_i) = Type(e'_j) and 0 otherwise. δ is a type-consistency margin, which is set to 0.6. Entity-level similarity is obtained by aggregating over the corresponding entity mention ranges.

Sentence-Level Similarity Matrix. For sentence s_i and s'_j, we define a sentence similarity matrix as:

$$\mathbf{S}_{\text{sentence}}(i,j) = \frac{\mathbf{H}_S^{\mathcal{D}}\left(\mathbf{H}_S^{\mathcal{R}}\right)^\top}{||\mathbf{H}_S^{\mathcal{D}}||_2||\mathbf{H}_S^{\mathcal{R}}||_2}, \quad \mathbf{H}_S^{\mathcal{D}} = \mathcal{M}_{text}(s_i),\ \mathbf{H}_S^{\mathcal{R}} = \mathcal{M}_{text}(s'_j). \quad (6)$$

Image-Level Similarity Matrix. For image v_i and v'_j, we define an image similarity matrix as:

$$\mathbf{S}_{\text{image}}(i,j) = \frac{\mathbf{H}_I^{\mathcal{D}}\left(\mathbf{H}_I^{\mathcal{R}}\right)^\top}{||\mathbf{H}_I^{\mathcal{D}}||_2||\mathbf{H}_I^{\mathcal{R}}||_2}, \quad \mathbf{H}_I^{\mathcal{D}} = \mathcal{M}_{image}(v_i),\ \mathbf{H}_I^{\mathcal{R}} = \mathcal{M}_{image}(v'_j). \quad (7)$$

where the images without entity regions are assigned $\mathbf{S}_{\text{image}}(i,j) = 0$.

Multimodal Examples Selection. The multi-level similarity matrices $\mathbf{S}_{\text{entity}}$, $\mathbf{S}_{\text{sentence}}$, and $\mathbf{S}_{\text{image}}$ are integrated to guide in-context sample selection, ensuring that retrieved examples are both semantically and visually aligned with the target instance. The overall top-K similarity matrix is calculated as:

$$\mathcal{I}_{overall} = \underset{i\in\{1,2,\ldots,K\}}{\text{argTopK}} \left\{\lambda_1\mathbf{S}_{\text{entity}}(i,j) + \lambda_2\mathbf{S}_{\text{sentence}}(i,j) + \lambda_3\mathbf{S}_{\text{image}}(i,j)\right\} \quad (8)$$

where λ_1, λ_2, and λ_3 denote the weighting hyperparameters, $\mathcal{I}_{overall}$ is the index set of top-K similar examples in $\mathcal{D}$. The multimodal in-context examples $\mathcal{C}$ are defined as follows:

$$\mathcal{C} = \{(s_j, e_j, v_j) \mid j \in \mathcal{I}_{overall}\} \quad (9)$$

Finally, the prompt designed for entity grounding is illustrated in Fig. 3 (c).

4 Experiments

4.1 Experiment Setting

Dataset. We conduct experiments on CCKS-GMNER in the military domain and Twitter-GMNER in the social media domain. Detailed statistics of the two datasets are presented in Table 1. Since CCKS-GMNER provides only 500 annotated instances, we randomly split them into 100 samples for low-resource training and 400 samples for test. To ensure a low-resource setting, we follow [11] to select the same 10% of the Twitter-GMNER data as the training data.

Table 1. The statistics of two GMNER datasets.

Dataset	Samples	Types	Entities	Regions
Twitter-GMNER	10,000	4	16,778	8,090
CCKS-GMNER	500	6	384	307

Evaluation. We adopt F1 score, Recall, and Precision as evaluation metrics. A multimodal entity is regarded as correct only when the textual entity mention, type, and visual region are all correctly predicted. For visual grounding, a region is considered correct if the Intersection-over-Union (IoU) between the predicted and ground-truth regions exceeds 0.5. For entities without visual regions, the model is required to output `None`.

Implementation Details. In Stage 1, all experiments are conducted on a single NVIDIA RTX 3090 GPU. We employ the Qwen-Max[2] API as the LLM to synthesize training data, while Bert-based[3] and XLM-Roberta-Large[4] are adopted as the small supervised models. The learning rate is set to 1e−5, with a CRF layer learning rate of 5e−2, a batch size of 32, 10 epochs, and a maximum sequence length of 128. AdamW is used as the optimizer. In Stages 2 and 3, we utilize Qwen2.5VL-72B-Instruct[5] as the MLLM, deployed on four NVIDIA A100 SXM4 80GB GPUs, with 3-shot multimodal examples for in-context learning. The pretrained models for computing text and image similarity are Sentence Transformer[6] and CLIP-ViT-L-14[7], respectively. The hyperparameters λ_1, λ_2, and λ_3 are set to 0.6, 0.4, and 0.2, respectively.

Baselines. We compare our approach against three types of baselines: (1) Fully supervised models, including **H-index** [21] and **MQSPN** [15], which

[2] https://qwenlm.github.io/blog/qwen2.5-max.
[3] https://huggingface.co/google-bert/bert-base-uncased.
[4] https://huggingface.co/FacebookAI/xlm-roberta-large.
[5] https://huggingface.co/Qwen/Qwen2.5-VL-72B-Instruct.
[6] https://huggingface.co/sentence-transformers/all-MiniLM-L6-v2.
[7] https://huggingface.co/openai/clip-vit-large-patch14.

adopt pretrained YOLOv11 [6] (for CCKS[8]) or VinVL [22] (for Twitter) as the object detector and are trained in an end-to-end manner to predict entity mention–type–region triplets; (2)MLLMs, including **Qwen2.5VL-72B** [1], and **GPT-4o** [5], where multimodal entity information is obtained via 3-shot in-context learning; and (3) Multimodal data augmentation methods, including **GMDA** [11] and **MixGen** [4], which synthesize image–text pairs to enhance the training of the H-index model.

4.2 Main Results

Comparison with Previous Baselines. Table 2 presents the performance comparison between our proposed ReFineG and various baseline methods. On the Twitter-GMNER dataset, ReFineG (Qwen2.5VL-72B+BERT-base) outperforms the supervised model H-index by 7.3% F1 and surpasses GPT-4o by 13.47% F1. On the CCKS-GMNER dataset in the military domain, ReFineG achieves superior performance over all state-of-the-art (SOTA) models. This improvement can be attributed to the collaborative framework of large and small models in ReFineG, which effectively leverages their complementary strengths. Furthermore, compared with the SOTA multimodal data augmentation method GMDA, ReFineG achieves a 5.53% F1 gain on Twitter-GMNER. These results demonstrate that ReFineG brings substantial performance improvements under low-resource settings.

Performance on the CCKS2025 GMNER Online Leaderboard. Table 3 presents the performance of different ReFineG variants on the final CCKS2025@GMNER online leaderboard. The results show that each stage consistently improves over baseline. Notably, Stage 1 plays a crucial role in the overall framework, where the main gain comes from higher precision. This improvement is primarily attributed to leveraging the global schema guideline to synthesize training data, enabling the small supervised model to effectively acquire domain knowledge and thereby cooperate with the MLLM to reduce domain conflicts. Furthermore, both the refinement stage and the multimodal in-context example selection yield additional improvements, demonstrating the effectiveness of our design.

[8] Yolov11 is pretrained as regions proposal model on open-sourced military dataset: https://www.kaggle.com/datasets/rawsi18/military-assets-dataset-12-classes-yolo8-format.

Table 2. Performance comparison of different baselines on two GMNER datasets. Bold indicates the optimal result, and underlined denotes the suboptimal result. ♣ represents that the model results on Twitter-GMNER are from [11]. Others are implemented based on our low-resource experiment setting.

Category	Methods	Twitter-GMNER			CCKS-GMNER		
		Pre.	Rec.	F1	Pre.	Rec.	F1
Supervised Models	MQSPN	46.28	43.51	44.85	52.14	46.72	49.28
	H-index ♣	47.54	47.39	47.46	49.59	43.47	46.33
MLLMs	Qwen2.5VL-72B	36.85	45.54	40.74	58.01	64.20	60.95
	GPT4o	38.01	45.19	41.29	62.17	66.67	64.34
Data Augmentation	MixGen ♣ (H-index)	45.72	50.84	48.15	-	-	-
	GMDA ♣ (H-index)	48.99	49.47	49.23	-	-	-
Ours	**ReFineG (Bert-base)**	52.49	57.23	54.76	74.57	71.19	72.84
	ReFineG (Roberta-large)	**54.13**	**60.24**	**57.02**	**76.52**	**73.09**	**74.76**

Table 3. Results of different ReFineG variants on the CCKS2025@GMNER Online Leaderboard. w/o denotes the removal of the corresponding module.

Methods	Online Test		
	Pre.	Rec.	F1
Baseline (Qwen2.5VL-72B)	49.45	60.93	54.59
ReFineG (w/o Stage 1)	56.51	60.37	58.38
ReFineG (w/o Stage 2)	60.20	63.61	61.86
ReFineG (w/o Stage 3)	60.74	64.09	62.37
ReFineG (Overall)	**62.61**	**66.73**	**64.61**

4.3 Ablation Study

To further investigate the effectiveness of each module, we conduct a series of ablation studies on the two GMNER datasets, with results shown in Fig. 4. (1) **w/o TSD** removes the supervised training of the synthesized dataset. We observe a substantial F1 drop on both datasets, with a decrease of 10.21% on Twitter-GMNER and 8.51% on CCKS-GMNER. This indicates that supervised training of the small model is essential for learning domain knowledge, while the synthetic data generated by the large model transfers its general knowledge to the small model. (2) **w/o UR** removes the MLLM refinement stage, leading to consistent performance degradation across both datasets. This demonstrates that refinement from MLLM is crucial for handling uncertain or unseen entities. (3) **w/o MES** replaces dynamic multimodal example selection with fixed 3-shot examples. The observed decline confirms that multimodal examples provide visual cues for entity grounding, enabling the MLLM to leverage analogical reasoning to improve target entity grounding.

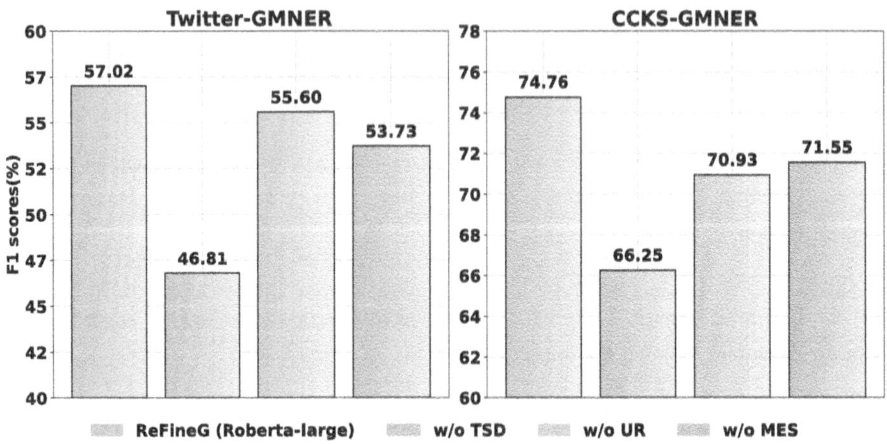

Fig. 4. Ablation study results. (a) Training with Synthetic Data (TSD) (b) Uncertainty-based Refinement (UR) (c) Multimodal Examples Selection (MES).

5 Conclusion

In this work, we presented ReFineG, a three-stage collaborative framework that integrates small supervised models with frozen MLLMs for low-resource grounded multimodal NER. By synthesizing domain knowledge-aware training data, leveraging uncertainty-based refinement, and performing multimodal in-context grounding, our method effectively addresses the challenges of annotation scarcity and domain knowledge conflict. Extensive experiments on Twitter-GMNER and CCKS-GMNER demonstrate that ReFineG achieves substantial improvements over state-of-the-art baselines, and ranks second on the CCKS2025 GMNER shared task leaderboard. Future directions include extending our framework to other multimodal information extraction tasks and exploring adaptive strategies for dynamically balancing the contributions of small models and MLLMs across domains.

Acknowledgements. This work is supported by the Research Foundation of Science and Technology Plan Project of Guangzhou City (2023B01J0001, 2024B01W0004).

References

1. Bai, S., et al.: Qwen2. 5-VL Technical report. arXiv preprint arXiv:2502.13923 (2025)
2. Devlin, J., Chang, M.W., Lee, K., Toutanova, K.: Bert: pre-training of deep bidirectional transformers for language understanding, (2019). ArXiv abs/1810.04805
3. Han, R., Peng, T., Yang, C., Wang, B., Liu, L., Wan, X.: Is information extraction solved by chatgpt? An analysis of performance, evaluation criteria, robustness and errors. arXiv preprint arXiv:2305.14450, p. 48 (2023)

4. Hao, X., Zhu, Y., Appalaraju, S., Zhang, A., Zhang, W., Li, B., Li, M.: Mixgen: a new multi-modal data augmentation. In: Proceedings of the IEEE/CVF Winter Conference on Applications of Computer Vision, pp. 379–389 (2023)
5. Hurst, A., et al.: GPT-4o system card (2024). arXiv preprint
6. Khanam, R., Hussain, M.: Yolov11: An overview of the key architectural enhancements (2024). arXiv preprint
7. Lafferty, J., McCallum, A., Pereira, F.: Conditional random fields: probabilistic models for segmenting and labeling sequence data. In: Proceedings of ICML. vol. 1, pp. 282–289 (2001)
8. Lewis, M., et al.: Denoising sequence-to-sequence pre-training for natural language generation, translation, and comprehension, Bart (2019). arXiv preprint
9. Li, F., et al.: Answering complex geographic questions by adaptive reasoning with visual context and external commonsense knowledge. In: Proceedings of the 63rd Annual Meeting of the Association for Computational Linguistics (Volume 1: Long Papers), pp. 25498–25514 (2025)
10. Li, J., et al.: LLMs as bridges: reformulating grounded multimodal named entity recognition. arXiv preprint arXiv:2402.09989 (2024)
11. Li, Z., Yu, J., Yang, J., Wang, W., Yang, L., Xia, R.: Generative multimodal data augmentation for low-resource multimodal named entity recognition. In: Proceedings of the 32nd ACM International Conference on Multimedia, pp. 7336–7345 (2024)
12. Liu, J., Shen, D., Zhang, Y., Dolan, B., Carin, L., Chen, W.: What makes good in-context examples for GPT-3? arXiv preprint, (2021). arXiv:2101.06804
13. Lu, D., Neves, L., Carvalho, V., Zhang, N., Ji, H.: Visual attention model for name tagging in multimodal social media. In: ACL, pp, pp. 1990–1999 (2018)
14. Ok, H., Kil, T., Seo, S., Lee, J.: Scanner: knowledge-enhanced approach for robust multi-modal named entity recognition of unseen entities (2024). arXiv preprint
15. Tang, J., Wang, Z., Gong, Z., Yu, J., Zhu, X., Yin, J.: Multi-grained query-guided set prediction network for grounded multimodal named entity recognition. In: Proceedings of the AAAI Conference on Artificial Intelligence, vol. 39, pp. 25246–25254 (2025)
16. Wang, J., Li, Z., Yu, J., Yang, L., Xia, R.: Fine-grained multimodal named entity recognition and grounding with a generative framework. In: Proceedings of the 31st ACM International Conference on Multimedia, pp. 3934–3943 (2023)
17. Wang, X., Meng, B., Chen, H., Meng, Y., Lv, K., Zhu, W.: Tiva-kg: a multimodal knowledge graph with text, image, video and audio. In: Proceedings of the 31st ACM International Conference on Multimedia, pp. 2391–2399. MM '2023, Association for Computing Machinery, New York, NY, USA (2023). https://doi.org/10.1145/3581783.3612266
18. Wang, X., Cai, J., Jiang, Y., Xie, P., Tu, K., Lu, W.: Named entity and relation extraction with multi-modal retrieval. In: Findings of the Association for Computational Linguistics: EMNLP 2022, pp. 5925–5936 (2022)
19. Wang, Z., et al.: Granular entity mapper: advancing fine-grained multimodal named entity recognition and grounding. In: Findings of the Association for Computational Linguistics: EMNLP 2024, pp. 3211–3226 (2024)
20. Wei, J., et al.: Chain-of-thought prompting elicits reasoning in large language models. Adv. Neural. Inf. Process. Syst. **35**, 24824–24837 (2022)
21. Yu, J., Li, Z., Wang, J., Xia, R.: Grounded multimodal named entity recognition on social media. In: Proceedings of the 61st Annual Meeting of the Association for Computational Linguistics (Volume 1: Long Papers), pp. 9141–9154 (2023)

22. Zhang, P., et al.: Vinvl: revisiting visual representations in vision-language models. In: Proceedings of the IEEE/CVF Conference on Computer Vision and Pattern Recognition, pp. 5579–5588 (2021)
23. Zhang, Q., Fu, J., Liu, X., Huang, X.: Adaptive co-attention network for named entity recognition in tweets. AAAI. vol 32 (2018)
24. Zhang, Z., Zhao, Y., Gao, H., Hu, M.: Linkner: linking local named entity recognition models to large language models using uncertainty. In: Proceedings of the ACM Web Conference 2024, pp. 4047–4058 (2024)

Author Index

J. Liang et al. (Eds.): CCKS 2025, CCIS 2698, pp. 287–288, 2026.
https://doi.org/10.1007/978-981-95-8525-0

The manufacturer's authorised representative in the EU is Springer Nature Customer Service Centre GmbH, Europaplatz 3, 69115 Heidelberg, Germany. If you have any concerns regarding our products, please contact ProductSafety@springernature.com

Printed and bound by CPI Group (UK) Ltd, Croydon, CR0 4YY

30/07/2026

02181608-0004